THE INDUSTRIOUS REVOLUTION

In the long eighteenth century, new consumer aspirations combined with a new industrious behavior to alter fundamentally the material cultures of northwestern Europe and North America. This "industrious revolution" is the context in which the economic acceleration associated with the Industrial Revolution took shape. This study explores the intellectual understanding of the new importance of consumer goods as well as the actual consumer behavior of households of all income levels.

Jan de Vries examines how the activation and evolution of consumer demand shaped the course of economic development, situating consumer behavior in the context of the household economy. He considers the changing consumption goals of households from the seventeenth century to the present and analyzes how household decisions have mediated between macro-level economic growth and actual human betterment. Ultimately, de Vries's research reveals key strengths and weaknesses of existing consumer theory, suggesting revisions that add historical realism to economic abstractions.

Jan de Vries has been a professor of history and economics at the University of California at Berkeley since 1973. At Berkeley he holds the Sidney Hellman Ehrman endowed chair in European history. De Vries has also served as chair of the History Department, dean of Social Sciences, and vice provost for Academic Affairs. He has written five books, 65 published articles and book chapters, and 45 book reviews. In addition, he is co-editor of three books. He is the recipient of the Woodrow Wilson and Guggenheim fellowships, among others; has held grants from the National Science Foundation and the National Institutes of Health; and has held visiting fellowships to the Netherlands Institute for Advanced Study, the Getty Center for the History of Art and the Humanities, and All Souls College, Oxford. He has been elected to membership in the American Academy of Arts and Sciences, the British Academy, the Royal Netherlands Academy of Sciences, and the American Philosophical Society. He is the 2000 recipient of the A. H. Heineken Prize in History.

Het Thee en Koffy-Gereedschap. Jan Luiken, *Het leerzaam huisraad* (Amsterdam, 1711)

The Industrious Revolution

Consumer Behavior and the Household Economy, 1650 to the Present

JAN DE VRIES
University of California at Berkeley

CAMBRIDGE
UNIVERSITY PRESS

CAMBRIDGE UNIVERSITY PRESS
Cambridge, New York, Melbourne, Madrid, Cape Town, Singapore, São Paulo, Delhi

Cambridge University Press
32 Avenue of the Americas, New York, NY 10013-2473, USA

www.cambridge.org
Information on this title: www.cambridge.org/9780521719254

First published 2008

Printed in the United States of America

A catalog record for this publication is available from the British Library.

Library of Congress Cataloging in Publication Data
De Vries, Jan, 1943 Nov. 14–
The Industrious revolution : consumer behavior and the household economy, 1650 to the
present / Jan de Vries.
p.   cm.
Includes bibliographical references and index.
ISBN 978-0-521-89502-6 (hardback) – ISBN 978-0-521-71925-4 (pbk.)
1. Consumption (Economics) – History.   2. Consumers – History.   I. Title.
HC79.C6D42   2008
339.4'709–dc22   2007036721

ISBN   978-0-521-89502-6 hardback
ISBN   978-0-521-71925-4 paperback

For my wife, Jeannie, and my children, Nicholas and Saskia

Contents

Figures

Preface and Acknowledgments

This study of long-term economic development differs from most that have gone before by addressing consumer aspirations rather than productive activities, and by focusing on the household unit rather than the individual. It examines a period in Western history that experienced the Industrial Revolution, but this revolution stands in the background here in order to give due consideration to the initiatives of households as their consumption goals as well as their strategies to achieve them change. This complex of household behaviors – an industrious revolution – formed the broader context in which the productive initiatives we know as the Industrial Revolution could unfold.

In the economists' world of supply and demand, an emphasis on demand as the agent of change in long-term development is uncommon; indeed, it is usually viewed as a sign of heterodoxy. Yet, in the social sciences more broadly considered, the central importance of consumption in contemporary society is treated as a commonplace. It simultaneously fuels the anxieties of solemn critics of late capitalism and excites the imaginations of postmodern self-fashioners. Between those who set consumption aside as too difficult to model and those who regard it as too self-evident to warrant further scrutiny, a large terrain has been left underexamined and undertheorized. This study seeks to contribute to a sounder understanding of an historical phenomenon that too many social scientists have neglected – purposefully neglected, one could say.

This is a study in economic history. It offers a history of the household considered as an economic unit that seeks to contribute to a new economic framework for the study of long-term consumer behavior. That is, I argue in this book that consumer aspirations have a history; they are not simply the second-order consequences of other, more fundamental forces, nor are they autonomous acts of creative individuality. To this end, I develop

ix

an economic framework in which to interpret household decision making that has usually been interpreted primarily in social, cultural, and ideological terms. I have gathered the elements of this framework under the conceptual term *industrious revolution*. In a specific historical period in a specific geographical zone, a new form of household economic behavior became increasingly influential, increasing simultaneously the supply of market-oriented production and the demand for a broad but not indiscriminate range of consumer goods.

The industrious revolution unfolded in the course of the long eighteenth century. This capacious "century" stretches across the period 1650–1850, spanning the British Industrial Revolution and the French and American political revolutions. This unconventional periodization challenges – is, indeed, intended to question – longstanding assumptions about the origins of modern industrial society in Western history. While I do not wish to substitute one simple story for another, I do hope this study will help place the familiar "revolutionary" events in the broader context of early modern markets, households, and material culture.

While the industrious revolution as developed here is largely a spent force by the mid–nineteenth century, this study does not end there but continues to trace the consumer behavior of the household economy up to the present time. The book's last two chapters have a dual purpose. The first is to sharpen our understanding of the distinctive characteristics of the "industrious household" by contrasting it with the very different household economy that took its place in the century after 1850: the breadwinner–homemaker household. The second is to understand better the present and the future. Our beliefs about our future options and prospects are shaped to a large extent by where we think we have been and how we think we got to where we are now. This study argues that the common understandings on these matters, as they pertain to the household economy and modern consumer society, are incorrect. It is this book's final task, therefore, to suggest alternative ways to think about our present and our possible futures.

This is not a study of a single country's experience, nor does it claim to offer an historical framework applicable to all of Europe or the world. The industrious revolution and the household organization linked to it had their chief impact in a restricted zone of indefinite boundaries. It is best observed in northwestern Europe: England, the Low Countries, and parts of France and Germany. The North American colonies share in these characteristics, even though the economic environment differed in important respects. Elsewhere, the larger cities exhibit some of its features, but neither eastern Europe nor the Mediterranean zones participate fully in its main developments. Consequently, this study moves from country to country, assembling historical evidence. It is not a comparative study but a composite history of the common experience of a zone that is not defined primarily by political boundaries.

I have been thinking about the theme of this book, off and on, for quite a while. Indeed, some of the ideas I develop here first came to me as I was preparing my doctoral dissertation in 1968–9. After a few early articles, I set aside my interest in households and consumer behavior for many years, returning to it only in 1990, when the British historian John Brewer invited me to participate in one of a series of seminars he organized around the theme of material culture and consumption. I might not have accepted his invitation had it not been for a brief discussion I had had in 1986 with the Japanese demographic historian Akira Hayami. His argument that Japanese economic development took the form of an "industrious revolution" – a highly labor-intensive form of economic growth – had set me to thinking anew about pre-industrial development in the West. Brewer's invitation led to my first articles introducing a Western "industrious revolution."

Other commitments led me, once again, to set this interest aside for several years, until a sabbatical year as a visiting Fellow at All Souls College, Oxford, in 1997–8 allowed me to read more broadly and deeply in the economics of consumption and the political economy of consumer behavior. I discovered that the stories told about Oxford and the even richer stories told about All Souls College are all true. If the reasons for all their practices are not apparent at first, or even after long reflection, their net effect is highly successful in stimulating the intellect and broadening one's academic perspectives. Looking back, there are years in which I have worked harder, but probably none in which I learned more or took greater pleasure in the daily pursuit of the academic life. The many British economists and historians who assisted me form a very long list, but I must acknowledge here the late Charles Feinstein, Paul David, Avner Offer, Jane Humphries, Maxine Berg, John Robertson, and the late Rees Davies.

My year at Oxford allowed me to develop the industrious revolution concept more fully, and to extend the argument to the nineteenth and twentieth centuries. Thanks once again to the generosity of British colleagues, I had the opportunity to present my findings at the McArthur Lectures at Cambridge University in 2000. The invitation to give these lectures was extended by Sir Tony Wrigley, whose work has set a standard I have striven to attain throughout my career. Exposure to a learned and critical audience is a great gift, and I left Cambridge with a clearer idea of how to transform the lectures into the book that is now before you.

For this I wish to thank especially Martin Daunton, Richard Smith, John Hatcher, Alan Macfarlane, Paul and Margaret Spufford, Emma Rothschild, and Sheilagh Ogilvie.

Events then intervened that slowed my development of the four McArthur Lectures into the six chapters of this book. Fortunately, I was rescued from the tasks of academic administration that have occupied most of my time since presenting the McArthur Lectures by an opportunity to spend a sabbatical semester in the fall of 2005 at the Netherlands Institute for Advanced Study (NIAS). This was not my first stay at NIAS; indeed, it was my fourth. NIAS has been instrumental in bringing to completion nearly every major academic project in which I have been engaged, for which I will forever be in its debt. The hospitality of its rector, Wim Blockmans, the efficient support of its staff, and the stimulation of the international gathering of visiting Fellows gathered there combined to create at once a welcoming sanctuary, a focused research environment, and a forum for fruitful academic exchange. Wassenaar, the town in which NIAS is located, also deserves mention here, for its subtle pleasures are, I think, best appreciated by those deeply immersed in their work. It was serendipitous that my NIAS stay overlapped with those of Eric Jones, Tony Atkinson, Barbara Hanawalt, and Ruth Mohrmann, and it was an added benefit that I was able to meet with many Dutch colleagues, including Peer Vries, Henk Wesseling, Ad van der Woude, Jan Luiten van Zanden, and, in Belgium, Bruno Blondé, Erik Thoen, Walter Prevenier, and Herman van der Wee.

The transformation of a set of ideas and questions into the present book was the product of a series of opportunities made available to me and of suggestions and questions from many people in several countries. I am grateful to them all and absolve them, with the customary disclaimer, of any responsibility for the errors and shortcomings of this book.

I am grateful in a different way, but one not less important for this study, to my family. I developed my ideas over a span of years in which my children left home and formed their own households. Observing this at close range has been instructive and gratifying. It has made it impossible for me to be pessimistic about the future of the family, my natural pessimism notwithstanding.

Berkeley and Wassenaar

I

The Transformation of Consumer Desire
in the Long Eighteenth Century

On April 20, 1697, an advertisement appeared in the *Amsterdamsche Courant* for a new product: the *zak-aardebol*, or pocket globe. This globe was no more than two inches (five cm.) in diameter and was encased in a leather cover on the inside of which was presented the heavens with constellations – one of the earliest geocentric representations of celestial space. The producers of this pocket globe, the mapmakers Abraham van Ceulen and Gerrit Drogenham, recommended their new product as "Very appropriate for all devotees of astronomy and other sciences, as well as [all those] who would customarily carry a pocket watch with them."[1]

The pocket watch was then a recent development of the clockmaking industry, which had extended its markets from church towers and other public structures to private homes with the invention by Christiaan Huygens of the pendulum clock in 1657. Its diffusion through bourgeois and even middling and farm families was remarkably rapid,[2] and the new

---

[1] The advertisement reads: "Seer bequam voor alle Liefhebbers der Astronomie en andere Konsteyn, gelyk een sak-horlogie alom by sig te dragen." *Amsterdamsche Courant*, 20 April 1697.

[2] Clocks, as opposed to watches, may have diffused faster in commercialized rural areas than in the towns. In Friesland, no farmers (relatively large farmers, with at least ten milk cows) left clocks at their deaths as late as 1677–86. But by 1711–50, 86 percent of the probate inventories for such farmers recorded the presence of a clock in the house. In the village of Weesperkarspel, near Amsterdam, 80 percent of all late–eighteenth-century farmers' inventories included clocks. Likewise, in the English county of Kent, few inventories listed clocks in the seventeenth century, but by 1720–49, 54 percent did so. In distant Cornwall, on the other hand, clocks remained a rarity. In 1720–49, only 9 percent of inventoried households possessed a clock. Jan de Vries, "Peasant Demand Patterns and Economic Development. Friesland, 1550–1750," in W. N. Parker and E. L. Jones, eds., *European Peasants and Their Markets. Essays in Agrarian Economic History* (Princeton, N.J.: Princeton University Press, 1975), pp. 205–66; H. van Koolbergen, "De materiële cultuur van Weesp en Weesperkarspel in de zeventiende en achttiende

---

I

pocket watches, adding mobility to the science of time keeping, met with a very positive reception among those who could afford the steep price. Van Ceulen and Drogenham presented their pocket globe as the logical companion to the pocket watch – something that the well-equipped modern man would find essential. The owner of both instruments would always know where he or she was – both in time and in space. The appeal will not be lost on those who move about today with mobile phones and BlackBerrys always on their person.[3]

As it happens, the pocket globe did not catch on. Peter the Great, who was in Holland at the time of its introduction, picked one up,[4] but most cutting-edge consumers passed it by. The pocket watch, on the other hand, quickly became a coveted possession of every social class. European watch production rose from the tens of thousands per year at the time of the pocket globe's introduction to nearly 400,000 per year in the last quarter of the eighteenth century.[5] In a ten-year span enough timepieces of all types and qualities were then produced to supply one-quarter of the adult males of western and central Europe (the putative customers in the geographical zone where nearly all watches were produced and sold).[6]

eeuw," *Volkskundig Bulletin* 9 (1983): 3–52; Mark Overton, Jane Whittle, Darron Dean, and Andrew Hann, *Production and Consumption in English Households, 1600–1750* (London: Routledge, 2004), p. 111.

[3] Nor was it lost on Adam Smith. "How many people ruin themselves," he mused, "by laying out money on trinkets of frivolous utility? What pleases these lovers of toys is not so much the utility, as the aptness of the machines which are fitted to promote it. All their pockets are stuffed with little conveniences. They contrive new pockets, unknown in the clothes of other people, in order to carry a greater number. They walk about loaded with a multitude of baubles, in weight and sometimes in value not inferior to an ordinary Jew's-box, some of which may sometimes be of some little use, but all of which might at all times be very well spared, and of which the whole utility is certainly not worth the fatigue of bearing the burden." Adam Smith, *The Theory of Moral Sentiments* [1759, rev. 1790], D. D. Raphael and A. L. Macfie, eds. (Oxford: Oxford University Press, 1976), p. 180.

[4] Renee Kistemaker, et al., eds., *Peter de Grote en Holland* (Bussem: Amsterdam Historisch Museum, 1996), p. 163.

[5] David Landes, *Revolution in Time. Clocks and the Making of the Modern World* (Cambridge, Mass.: Harvard University Press, 1983), p. 231, fn 19; p. 442.

[6] A similar calculation was made by Hans-Joachim Voth for England, where at least 40 percent of all European watches were produced in the 1775–1800 period. If watches had a useful life of between five and twelve years (his upper and lower estimates), the stock of watches in 1800 would have been between 1.4 and 3.1 million. This compares to an adult population (men and women) of 5.5 million. Hans-Joachim Voth, *Time and Work in England, 1750–1830* (Oxford: Oxford University Press, 2001), p. 51. In 1700, an independent estimate puts the English stock of watches and clocks at 200,000. Paul Glennie and Nigel Thrift, "The Spaces of Time" (University of Bristol, unpublished ms, 1999).

Timepieces of all kinds, mentioned in less than 10 percent of English probate inventories around 1675, were recorded in over a third of all inventories by the 1720s, and by no less than 38 percent of pauper inventories in 1770–1812.[7] Parisian inventories reveal that as early as 1700, 13 percent of servants and 5 percent of wage earners owned a watch. Later in the century more than half of the owners of stolen watches who brought prosecutions for watch theft in northern English courts were working-class men.[8] By the 1780s, 70 percent of the inventories of Parisian servants mention watches, as do 32 percent of those for wage earners.[9] The pocket watch long remained a costly item – even cheap watches cost several weeks' pay – but became common because it was one of the chief objects of expenditure for extraordinary and windfall earnings. The sailor returning from years in the East Indies, or from a successful fishing or whaling trip, the farm laborer at the end of the harvest, the recipient of a small inheritance, the successful thief – these and others had a high propensity in the eighteenth century to spend on a narrow range of articles, including pocket watches, that had come to symbolize working men's status.[10] Many eighteenth-century families that periodically found basic subsistence to be beyond their financial reach nonetheless possessed clocks and pocket watches – but probably not pocket globes.[11]

---

[7] Lorna Weatherill, "The Meaning of Consumer Behavior in Late Seventeenth and Early Eighteenth Century England," in John Brewer and Roy Porter, eds., *Consumption and the World of Goods* (London: Routledge, 1993), p. 220. The pauper inventories are for Essex. Peter King, "Pauper Inventories and the Material Lives of the Poor in the Eighteenth and Early Nineteenth Centuries," in Tim Hitchcock, Peter King, and Pamela Sharpe, eds., *Chronicling Poverty, The Voices and Strategies of the English Poor, 1640–1840* (New York: St. Martin's Press, 1997), pp. 155–91. Further English evidence is provided by Estabrook, whose study of Bristol and environs found timepieces in only 3 percent of inventories drawn up in 1660–99, but in 22 percent of those dating from 1700–39. He went on to distinguish a category of "early adopters" (those more likely, given their socioeconomic status, to acquire new luxury items). Among these households, 22 percent already owned timepieces in 1660–99, and 72 percent by 1700–39. Carl B. Estabrook, *Urbane and Rustic England. Cultural Ties and Social Spheres in the Provinces, 1660–1780* (Manchester: Manchester University Press, 1998), p. 141.

[8] John Styles, "Manufacturing, Consumption and Design in Eighteenth-Century England," in Brewer and Porter, eds., *Consumption and the World of Goods*, p. 538.

[9] Daniel Roche, *Le Peuple de Paris. Essai sur la culture populaire au XVIIIe siècle* (Paris: Aubier Montaigne, 1981), p. 226.

[10] E. P. Thompson, "Time, Work-Discipline and Industrial Capitalism," *Past and Present* 38 (1967): 56–97; Paul Glennie, "Consumption within Historical Studies," in Daniel Miller, ed., *Acknowledging Consumption. A Review of New Studies* (London: Routledge, 1995), p. 174.

[11] Anne McCants, "Petty Debts and Family Networks. The Credit Markets of Widows and Wives in Eighteenth-Century Amsterdam," in Beverly Lemire, et al., eds., *Women and Credit. Researching the Past, Refiguring the Future* (Oxford: Berg Publishers, 2001),

This episode in the history of product innovation and consumer demand is evocative of current preoccupations at the same time that it calls attention to the early development of historical man and woman as consumers. Given the mixture of anxiety and fascination that colors our efforts to understand the consumer society in which we live, it is natural to inquire into the history of consumption. Does consumer behavior have a history? That is, is there some structured progression to consumer wants? Have there been turning points or points of divergence in the evolution of consumption and consumer society?

Standing behind this seemingly innocent question is a basic problem of the social sciences, the agency–structure problem. Are individuals active, creative agents in consumption, or are their choices in fact highly structured, if not wholly determined, by external forces? Should we focus our attention primarily on the putative agent, the consumer, or on the social, economic, cultural, and political forces (producers, merchants, laws, cultural traditions, religious beliefs, etc.) that constrain and direct the consumer? Investigations of historical consumer behavior, whether written by historians or economists, are usually approached from one or another of these positions, leaving little conceptual space for a history of consumer behavior located between the chaos of arbitrary individual impulses on one side and the remorseless push of overarching structural and institutional forces on the other.

Historians are prone to labor under the misapprehension that one can answer fundamental questions about a phenomenon by seeking its origins. There one hopes to observe naked, innocent acts that reveal the true character of what is later shrouded in mystery and forced into deeply grooved paths by encrusted habit. It does not help our task that historians have claimed repeatedly to discover the origins of modern consumerism, proclaimed as "consumer revolutions," in at least five distinct eras stretching from the Renaissance to the post–World War II decades.[12] Over and again, historians have ushered Western man, or a large subset thereof, out

pp. 33–50. The attraction of timepieces to the plebian consumer extended beyond their status connotations. Watches, especially those in gold or silver cases, were eminently pawnable, and pawn shops and pawn banks were major institutions in the economic life of working people in Europe's large cities. See Laurence Fontaine, "The Circulation of Luxury Goods in Eighteenth-Century Paris. Social Redistribution and an alternative Currency," in Maxine Berg and Elizabeth Eger, eds., *Luxury in the Eighteenth Century. Debtes, Desires and Delectable Goods* (Basingstoke: Palgrave Macmillan, 2003), pp. 89–102.

[12] See the appendix to this chapter for a historiographical overview of the five "consumer revolutions."

of an Edenic world of customary and traditional consumption patterns, well integrated with all aspects of life, and have chronicled with a mixture of fascination and horror the entry of the objects of their concern into the brave new world of "consumerism."[13] The consumer revolutions detected before the nineteenth century tend to meet with fascination. For better or worse, these consumers are regarded as pioneers in the construction of modernity; something heroic attaches to even their most ordinary acts of consumption. Thereafter, historians' accounts tend to darken. The new consumers are more often seen as victims, or as the bitter, alienated fruit of modern society; something tawdry cleaves to even the most beneficial of their new consumer practices.

The interpretation long favored by most historians relied on maintaining a sharp distinction between true and false needs and emphasized the powerful forces – the needs of capitalist producers, the influence of fashion elites, the directives of the state – that prevented individuals from recognizing the difference. The implosion of the worldview underpinning this social interpretation of consumption has left a void that in recent times has come to be filled by a cultural interpretation of consumption. There are certainly many scholars who remain locked in embrace with the lifeless forms of old ideologies, but the now-prevailing academic climate is inclined to celebrate the triumph of the will of the self-fashioning individual. Consumer behavior is viewed as a cultural phenomenon enjoying a broad, if not complete, autonomy, detached from constraining economic and social forces. Consumption is not primarily an economic event; instead, it is thought to serve communicative and demonstrative functions in which consumers play with market signs to "construct their own

---

[13] *Consumerism* is a term I will seek to avoid wherever possible in this study. Often invoked, it is rarely defined. Stearns ventures to offers a definition remarkable chiefly for its shortcomings: "Consumerism describes a society in which many people formulate their goals in life partly through acquiring goods that they clearly do not need for subsistence or for traditional display." Peter N. Stearns, *Consumerism in World History. The Global Transformation of Desire* (London: Routledge, 2001), p. ix. Steven Miles does not get us much further when he proposes that "the study of consumerism should actually attempt to come to terms with the complexities that lie behind the act of consumption. In effect, while consumption is an act, consumerism is a way of life." This distinction depends on an uncomplicated definition of *consumption* that, as we shall see, fails to take seriously the important distinction economists make between the acquisition of goods and ultimate consumption. Once one accepts that an act of consumption gives utility in a variety of dimensions, including cultural dimensions, Miles's distinction collapses. Steven Miles, *Consumerism as a Way of Life* (London: Sage, 1998), p. 4. For an overview, see Peter N. Stearns, "Stages in Consumerism. Recent Work on the Issues of Periodization," *Journal of Modern History* 69 (1997): 102–17.

meaning for every single product and activity."[14] In short, under post-modernism, "the politics of class, based on production, everywhere gives way to the politics of cultural identity, built around consumption."[15]

Economists are always ready to acknowledge supply and demand – production and consumption – as paired forces in the shaping of market economies, but they do not commonly accord to demand a causative role in the process of economic growth. Studies of modern economic growth are inevitably founded on a decisive "supply-side" advance, which economic historians have variously located in technological change, enlarged supplies of capital, energy and raw materials, and new institutions that allowed these factors of production to be deployed more effectively. The locus of decision making in these accounts is almost always the firm and the entrepreneur. In all of this it remains true, as Adam Smith put it, that "consumption is the sole end and purpose of all production."[16] But Smith's language did not leave his readers in doubt as to the direction of the causal arrow connecting supply and demand: The consumer responds to the developing productive forces, not the other way around.[17]

This is where my interest in consumer behavior began: in trying to disentangle the relations between demand and supply. The Industrial Revolution, with its technology-driven, hence supply-driven, economic growth, long stood as a formidable barrier to any effort to search for economic growth based on any other factors or in any earlier period. Yet the accumulating evidence for an earlier increase of per capita income in northwestern Europe paired with a major refinement of material life casts serious doubt on the orthodoxy that the Industrial Revolution was the actual

---

[14] Liisa Uusitalo, "Consumption in Postmodernity. Social Structuration and the Construction of Self," in Marina Bianchi, ed., *The Active Consumer* (London: Routledge, 1998), p. 227. Particularly influential in this line of thought is the semiotics-inspired neo-Marxism of Jean Baudrillard, who argues that, "in capitalist societies, consumption should be understood as a process in which only the signs attached to goods are actually consumed." Colin Campbell, "Consumption. The New Wave of Research in the Humanities and Social Sciences," *Journal of Social Behavior and Personality* 6 (1991): 61.

[15] Jonathan Clark, *Our Shadowed Present. Modernism, Postmodernism, and History* (Stanford, Calif.: Stanford University Press, 2004), p. 4.

[16] Adam Smith, *An Inquiry into the Nature and Causes of the Wealth of Nations* ([1776] Cannon edition, London: Methuen, 1904; republished, Chicago: University of Chicago Press, 1976), Vol. II, Book IV, Ch. VIII, p. 179.

[17] Joel Mokyr, "Demand vs. Supply in the Industrial Revolution," *Journal of Economic History* 37 (1977): 981–1008. "The determination of 'when,' 'where,' and 'how fast' are to be sought first and foremost in supply, not demand-related processes" (p. 1005).

starting point for long-term economic growth. Consequently, I turned my attention increasingly toward a reconsideration of the place of consumer demand in economic development.[18]

What began as an effort to restore demand as one of the cutting blades of Marshall's supply and demand scissors led me to an even larger – and even less tractable – problem.[19] Standard consumer theory posits a "sovereign" individual consumer standing face to face with the market and behaving in a manner calculated to maximize his or her individual utility independently of the decisions of others. However inadequate this focus on the decontextualized individual might be in our own time, its silence concerning the individual's family ties and obligations in the historical past is too conspicuous to be ignored. Consequently, as demand led me to the consumer, the consumer led me to the family and its household economy.

My project quickly became not simply to add demand to supply but also to relate the behavior of the household to that of the market. Several modern developments in history and economics have guided my thinking about the household economy and consumer demand as historical phenomena. Briefly stated, they are:

1. *The Revolt of the Early Modernists.* Three decades of work on early modern European agriculture, urbanization, proto-industry, and demographic and family history have fundamentally challenged the conventional belief in a growthless, traditional economy. It is now sometimes conceded that substantial economic growth occurred before the technological breakthroughs of the Industrial Revolution, but the dynamics of this process of pre-industrial economic growth remain unclear.[20]

2. *The Revisionist Macroeconomics of the British Industrial Revolution.* The currently accepted view of overall British economic performance in the classic Industrial Revolution era, 1760–1830, reduces the earlier

---

[18] For a full discussion of the problems that adhere to the concept of modern economic growth, see Jan de Vries, "Economic Growth Before and After the Industrial Revolution. A Modest Proposal," in Maarten Prak, ed., *Early Modern Capitalism* (London: Routledge, 2001), pp. 177–94; Jan de Vries and Ad van der Woude, *The First Modern Economy. Success, Failure, and Perseverance of the Dutch Economy, 1500–1815* (Cambridge: Cambridge University Press, 1997), pp. 711–22.

[19] Alfred Marshall, in his *Principles of Economics* of 1890, put the matter as follows: "We might as reasonably dispute whether it is the upper or the under blade of a pair of scissors that cuts a piece of paper, as whether value is governed by utility [demand] or cost of productions [supply]." Book 5, Ch. 3.

[20] For a fuller account of this concept, see Jan de Vries, "The Industrial Revolution and the Industrious Revolution," *Journal of Economic History* 54 (1994): 251–3.

growth estimates by more than half.[21] This slow macroeconomic growth bathes in a rather less luminous light the traditional arguments about the relative importance of technology and augmented supply factors in "initiating" modern economic growth in this era. It also reduces the contrast with earlier decades and makes pre-industrial Britain as well as several neighboring regions/countries "richer," more industrial societies than long had been supposed.

3. *The Western European Marriage Pattern.* The pioneering work of "The Cambridge Group for the History of Population and Social Structure" established the view that the nuclear family structures of modern western European countries and their offshoots are not a product of industrialization but have much earlier origins. In addition, the seminal articles of John Hajnal called attention to specific characteristics of these conjugal families, which also long predate industrialization, that appear to be unique to western Europe and had far-reaching and not yet fully understood influences on society and economy.[22] While the demographic behavior of this household type has been explored in some detail, its distinctive economic behavior remains an open question.

4. *The New Household Economics.* Developments in consumer theory and new approaches to the behavior of family members pioneered by Gary Becker and others have illuminated some corners of that notorious "black box": the family, or household, as an economic unit. Through a focus on the allocation of time, this literature relates production and consumption decisions to each other in a fruitful way. Although some of these theoretical writings date from the 1960s, they have yet to be applied historically, or extended to accommodate historical change in household behavior.[23]

---

[21] N.F.R. Crafts and C. K. Harley, "Output Growth and the British Industrial Revolution. A Restatement of the Crafts-Harley View," *Economic History Review* 45 (1992): 703–30. Joel Mokyr, "Accounting for the Industrial Revolution," in Roderick Floud and Paul Johnson, eds., *The Cambridge Economic History of Modern Britain* Vol. I., *Industrialisation, 1700–1860* (Cambridge: Cambridge University Press, 2004), pp. 4–10. The earlier accepted wisdom had been established by Phyllis Deane and W. A. Cole, *British Economic Growth, 1688–1959* (Cambridge: Cambridge University Press, 1967).

[22] John Hajnal, "European Marriage Patterns in Perspective," in D. V. Glass and D. E. C. Eversley, eds., *Population in History. Essays in Historical Demography* (London: Edward Arnold, 1965), pp. 101–43; John Hajnal, "Two Kinds of Preindustrial Household Formation System," *Population and Development Review* 8 (1982): 449–94.

[23] Gary S. Becker, "A Theory of the Allocation of Time," *The Economic Journal* 75 (1965): 493–517; K. Lancaster, *Modern Consumer Theory* (Aldershot: Edward Elgar, 1991); Staffan B. Linder, *The Harried Leisure Class* (New York: Columbia University Press, 1970).

Together, these discrete literatures offer the raw materials with which to fashion a new way of approaching the economic history of the early modern period – and, indeed, of more than that. This new approach is intended more as a supplement to, rather than a replacement of, earlier interpretations. However, it *does* aspire to question the claims of the twin revolutions – the British Industrial and the French political – to function as gatekeepers to modern history.[24] In so doing, this study seeks to add to the macrohistorical processes of modern economic growth and state formation that dominate most theorizing about long-term structural change a third, anterior process: the structure and behavior of the household.[25]

The Household and the Market

I recognize that an historian proposing to introduce a new metahistorical concept with an accompanying master narrative in this day and age has a lot of explaining to do.[26] And even more explanation is needed when the name given to this concept is borrowed, imprecise, and, perhaps, just a bit too clever.[27] Thus, my task is a formidable one, and I must begin by

[24] For more on the notion that the stark difference between economic life before and after the Industrial Revolution is overdrawn, see de Vries, "Economic Growth Before and After the Industrial Revolution," pp. 177–94. However much historians have been open to epistemological and philosophical challenges in the past three decades, we have jealously protected a periodization that, because it determines how new generations of historians will be trained, stands as a formidable obstacle to progress in the discipline – to use a figure of speech.

[25] Although directed to other ends, a similar claim has recently been made in Mary S. Hartman, *The Household and the Making of History. A Subversive View of the Western Past* (Cambridge: Cambridge University Press, 2004), pp. 1–5.

[26] A leading exponent of postmodernism, Jean-François Lyotard, defined this elusive term in 1979 with admirable precision and concision: It is "incredulity towards meta narratives." Jonathan Clark offers a similar definition: "Postmodernism is the most theoretically expressed version of a rejection of the historical. This rejection is a consequence of the way in which postmodernism has set itself against what it takes to be 'modernist' ideas of truth and objectivity, replacing what it sees as a set of grand narratives claiming objective authority with a diverse pattern of localized narratives and fluid identities." Clark, *Our Shadowed Present*, p. 3. This study focuses on a major object of postmodern interest, consumption, but seeks to supply it with a history.

[27] The term was coined by Akira Hayami to contrast the labor-intensive path of industrial development of Japan with the capital-intensive industrialization of the West. I first encountered the term in conversation with Professor Hayami. The "East Asian" and the "Western" industrious revolutions are compared and analyzed in Chapter 3.

On the "East Asian Industrious Revolution" and its relationship to the concept introduced here, see Akira Hayami, "A Great Transformation. Social and Economic Change in Sixteenth and Seventeenth Century Japan," *Bonner Zeitschrift für Japanologie* 8 (1986): 3–13; Osamu Saito, "Population and the Peasant Family Economy in Proto-Industrial

trying the reader's patience with a discussion of the "nuts and bolts" of the analytical framework of this study.

The key propositions of my argument concern the *household* (usually a family, or with a family at its core) and the *terms of interaction between households and the market economy*.[28] The family-based household is an entity that performs functions of reproduction, production, consumption, and resource redistribution among its members, as well as wealth transmission across generations. These functions are all interrelated and involve the interests of individuals with unequal standing, which makes household decision making highly complex. In this book the focus rests primarily on decisions affecting production and consumption. At the household level, as I will attempt to make clear, these decisions are directly related to each other. Consequently, in studying the household economy one can sidestep the chicken-and-egg question of the primacy of supply or demand by focusing on a single set of decisions that simultaneously determines both. Specifically, my historical claim is that northwestern Europe and British North America experienced an "industrious revolution" during a long eighteenth century, roughly 1650–1850, in which a growing number of households acted to reallocate their productive resources (which are chiefly the time of their members) in ways that increased *both* the supply of market-oriented, money-earning activities *and* the demand for goods offered in the marketplace. Increased production specialization in the household gives access to augmented consumption choices in the marketplace.

Japan," *Journal of Family History* 8 (1983): 30–54; Eiji Takemura, *The Perception of Work in Tokugawa Japan* (New York: University Press of America, 1997).

[28] The family, a biological/social unit, is based on kinship. In this study the family is normally the nuclear family of conjugal couple plus children. The household, an economic unit, is commonly defined by co-residence with a decision-making process that leads to a degree of coordination in production and of internal redistribution of resources. Ordinarily it refers to a family plus, in the early modern context, possible resident servants and apprentices. However, it also incorporates the economic relations (via earnings remittances and other transactions) between the family and nonresident members such as those engaged in migrant labor, in service in the households of others, or payments made to nonresident grandparents or other relatives. The household defined as a long-term income pooling arrangement is broader than the household defined by co-residence, and this is of particular importance to the themes of this study, because the broader the network of claimants of the household's pooled income, the more constrained is consumer decision making. Michiel Baud, "Huishouden, gezin en familienetwerk," in Baud and Engelen, eds., *Samen wonen, samen werken?* (Hilversum: Verloren, 1994), pp. 13–20; Peter Laslett, "Family and Household as Work Group and Kin Group. Areas of Traditional Europe Compared," in Richard Wall, J. Robin, and Peter Laslett, eds., *Family Forms in Historic Europe* (Cambridge: Cambridge University Press, 1983), pp. 513–63.

This study is concerned with the *interaction* of the market economy and the family-based household. My first task is therefore to defend as correct the use of the word *interaction*. To an economist, the first question would be whether the household behavior with which we are concerned can be accounted for satisfactorily by conventional commercial incentives, such as changes in relative prices and real wages (i.e., by income and substitution effects). If so, we should be speaking simply of the "influence" of the market *upon* the household. A social–historical approach would grant more economic autonomy to the household in some far-distant past. But the dominant social scientific models trace a progressive emptying of the household's economic substance as the market expands to rob it first of its self-sufficiency and then of its productive role, as the "family economy" evolves into the "family-wage economy" before achieving its modern form: the "family consumer economy." This is the influential typology of linear development proposed by Louise Tilly and Joan Scott, which is similar to many efforts to relate family forms to economic development.[29]

Their typology (to which we will have occasion to return in Chapter 2) is inspired by Parsonian structural-functionalism, which is based on the proposition that family structure changes over time to fit the functional role required of it by societal change. The most important social changes associated with industrialization are assumed to be the emergence of nonkinship structures such as the state, schools, business organizations, insurance programs, and labor unions. All these institutions remove functions from the family. Ultimately, industrial society leaves the family with only two functions: the socialization of children (perhaps) and the establishment of a private sphere of affective relations, a "haven in a heartless world." The structural change associated with this radical simplification of family functions is assumed to be the transformation of complex, extended family forms into the eviscerated nuclear families of urban, industrial society.

Historians' acceptance of this theoretical framework has not been without consequences. Richard J. Evans puts it succinctly: "[The family's] incorporation into a private sphere removed from society has been

---

[29] Louise Tilly and Joan Scott, *Women, Work and Family* (New York: Holt, Rinehart & Winston, 1978; revised ed., London: Methuen, 1987). See also Talcot Parsons, "The American Family. Its Relations to Personality and the Social Structure," in Talcot Parsons and Robert F. Bales, *Family, Socialization and Interaction Process* (Glencoe, Ill.: The Free Press, 1955), p. 9; Niel Smelser, *Social Change in the Industrial Revolution. An Application of Theory to the Lancashire Cotton Industry, 1740–1840* (London: Routledge & Kegan Paul, 1959).

followed by its removal from history in a wider sense and its incorporation in a de-politicized history of private life."[30]

This study does not engage structural functionalism, per se, in extended critique, but it holds that households have a substantially greater autonomy (because they are more functional?) than is provided for by these theories. It emphasizes the degrees of freedom that households possess in negotiating the options opened by the evolving society and economy, rather than the absence of such choices. This, of course, is how economics is often distinguished, whether fairly or not, from sociology.[31]

Another common view with which this study takes exception, one closely related to the functional model of family structure, holds that families are the repository of obsolete values – indeed, are the last refuge of atavisms of all sorts. They resist the imperious functional requirements laid upon them by an industrializing society; they even try to make use of the changing economy to defend their increasingly anachronistic values. But this is ultimately a hopeless cause in which the family members, more often than not the women of the family, seek to reconcile the irreconcilable. In the fullness of time, functionalism triumphs, as it must, and the defensive actions of families appear as "cultural lag." They are caught in what German scholars call *gleichzeitige Ungleichzeitigkeit* (synchronous anachronism).[32] This concept of lag is most uncongenial to the concept of an industrious consumerism: The family is looking backward rather than forward, using its economic resources to defend old ways of living rather

---

[30] Richard J. Evans, "Politics and the Family. Social Democracy and the Working-Class Family in Theory and Practice Before 1914," in Richard J. Evans and W. Robert Lee, eds., *The German Family. Essays on the Social History of the Family in Nineteenth- and Twentieth-Century Germany* (London: Croom Helm, 1981), p. 256.

[31] The familiar quip that "economics is all about how people make choices; sociology is about how they don't have any choices to make" appears to have originated with the economist James Duesenberry. While the current study seeks to correct the "undersocialized" conception economists have advanced of the individual, optimizing consumer, it objects as well to the "oversocialized" position found in sociology, which questions the notion that households can be said to engage in strategic behavior, caught as they are assumed to be in the embrace of norms and structures. For a discussion of this problem, see Michael Anderson, Frank Berchhofer, and Jonathan Gershuny, "Introduction," in Anderson, Berchhofer, and Gershuny, eds., *The Social and Political Economy of the Household* (Oxford: Oxford University Press, 1994), pp. 1–16.

[32] The clearest application of this concept to family history is Hans Medick's theory of the proto-industrial family economy. Such households, seeking to preserve the forms of peasant society in a market economy, formed "part of the long post-history of peasant society to the same extent that it formed a part of the pre-history of industrial capitalism." Hans Medick, "The Proto-industrial Family Economy. The Structural Function of Household and Family During the Transition from Peasant Society to Industrial Capitalism," *Social History* 1 (1976): 293, 310.

than to achieve new goals. In any society, some number of households will define and defend a "lifestyle" that involves a self-conscious resistance to change, but this study does not define these choices as "cultural lag," nor does it assume such behavior to be typical.

A final question is whether the process of historical change ends with any family at all, for a body of social scientific theory oddly attractive to both right and left regards capitalist-market rationality as a force that corrodes the essentially extra-capitalist institution of the family, loosening the ties that bind its members in its last remaining functions.[33] Joseph Schumpeter, in his influential *Capitalism, Socialism and Democracy*, introduced the concept of "family decomposition," arguing that the same capitalist rationality which undermines the authority of popes and kings does not stop there but continues on to question the domestic roles of wives and the subordination of children. The decomposition of the family is part of a more general tendency within the dynamic of capitalism: "In

---

[33] For a sociological analysis, see David Popenoe, *Disturbing the Nest. Family Change and Decline in Modern Societies* (New York: A. de Gruyter, 1988); see also the work of the political scientist James Q. Wilson, *The Marriage Problem. How Our Culture Has Weakened Families* (New York: HarperCollins, 2002); for an economic perspective, see Shirley P. Burggraf, *The Feminine Economy and Economic Man. Reviving the Role of Family in the Post-Industrial Age* (Reading, Mass.: Addison-Wesley, 1997). Burggraf's central claim (p. 2) is that "Disinvestment in our most basic social institution [the family] is rapidly bringing our culture to a critical point in social evolution and creating unprecedented problems for social and economic policy."

For a Marxist interpretation, see Claude Meillassoux, *Maidens, Meal and Money. Capitalism and the Domestic Economy* (Cambridge: Cambridge University Press, 1981). Meillassoux argues that it is in the interest of the capitalist to preserve the nonmarket household sector as a zone in which the reproduction of labor power can take place cheaply, thus allowing for the "super-exploitation" of the labor force: "Thus, to reproduce itself, the capitalist mode of production depends upon an institution which is alien to it, but which it has until now maintained as that most adapted to this function, and also the most economical, on account of its capacity for utilising unpaid – particularly female – labour, and by exploiting the emotional attachment which still dominates parent-child relations" (p. 142). But Meillassoux goes on to describe an inexorable logic of capitalism's historical development that speeds the emancipation of youth (the better to exploit them as workers) and liberates women from the family (to recover the cost of educating them via labor force participation). "But capitalism's logical advance here contains its own contradiction, for, by removing all vestiges of freedom, it modifies the very nature of productive relations. Ties of personal subjugation may disappear with the family, but so will the 'free labourer' who is freed from one set of bonds (the family), only to be reduced to a condition of *total* alienation *vis à vis* his employer." Here the tone of his discussion of the family suddenly shifts: "Thus threatened, the family is coming to be regarded, by reason of the few affectionate relationships it preserves, as one of the last bastions of individual liberty. It is, however, a very fragile bastion, for nothing any longer predestines it to withstand the corrosive influence of money-relations; and in this we have the measure of the totalitarian menace with which capitalism is heavy" (p. 144).

breaking down the pre-capitalist framework of society, capitalism broke not only barriers that impeded its progress but also flying buttresses that prevented its collapse."[34]

Viewed from this perspective, modern feminism, with its insistence on the removal of all remaining laws, social obligations, and customs that limit the participation of women as unencumbered individuals in society and economy, appears to press for the decanting of the last remaining substance of the family into the market economy. As it removes the last significant pre-capitalist institution from the historical stage, feminism takes the place Lenin had reserved for imperialism as the "highest stage of capitalism." These considerations lead us well beyond the eighteenth century, but if the character of the family-based household is determined entirely by forces emanating from outside – the market, capitalist rationality, and the state – then the value of the approach I wish to develop here is diminished considerably.

My position in these debates is that the Western family is a sufficiently enduring and autonomous entity, but simultaneously a sufficiently weak entity, to justify use of the term *interaction* to describe its relations with the market economy. Instead of a "substantialist" notion of the household that sees it as a total unity – *das ganze Haus* of the German tradition – I prefer the view that it is the site of alliances between husband and wife and of implicit contracts between parents and children.[35] The market casts its shadow – literally, shadow prices[36] – upon this entity, affecting the behavior of its members. But the family alliances are generally sufficiently resilient to endow the family with the capacity to develop adaptive strategies and chart common consumption objectives.

Moreover, the relatively fragile nuclear family structures of northwestern Europe should not be interpreted as the functionalist products of

---

[34] Joseph Schumpeter, *Capitalism, Socialism and Democracy* (New York: Harper & Row, 1941), Ch. 14, p. 139. The general theme – that capitalism depends on a moral world it is destined to erode – is explored in detail in Krishan Kumar, "Pre-capitalist and Non-capitalist Factors in the Development of Capitalism. Fred Kirsch and Joseph Schumpeter," in Adrian Ellis and Krishan Kumar, eds., *Dilemmas of Liberal Democracies* (London: Tavistock Publications, 1983), pp. 148–73.

[35] David Sabean, *Property, Production, and Family in Neckerhausen, 1700–1870* (Cambridge: Cambridge University Press, 1990), pp. 97–8.

[36] A "shadow price" is the imputed price or value of a good or service in the absence of an ordinary price-determined market. To impute a price is to make the best estimate possible of what the price would be if a normal market existed. Such an estimate is typically guided by the opportunity cost of the factors of production that enter into the production of the good or service at issue – that is, the alternative use forgone.

nineteenth- and twentieth-century urbanization and industrialization. A generation of historical demographers and family historians has "demonstrated the untenability of the close association between the extended family household and pre-industrial Europe."[37] Nuclear family structures had existed for centuries before industrialization in most of western Europe. Indeed, I will argue here that it was precisely these weak nuclear families that had a greater capacity to respond strategically to market opportunities than did the hardier, more complex family structures found in most other parts of the world.

The household in most of western Europe was small, being confined largely to the members of the nuclear family. Such a social unit was vulnerable to disruption or dissolution; even in the absence of catastrophic events it faced considerable stress on its internal cohesion at several points in the family life cycle. Whereas more extended family structures appealed to kin for assistance in time of stress, the Western family from medieval times tended to have recourse to external institutions, especially the church and the civil community.[38] The Christian church, as Max Weber argued, asserted the superiority of the individual soul to the claims of biological bonds, thus helping to demystify the sacrality of family and lineage. A practical consequence of this teaching was the nurturing, particularly in western European towns and cities, of a popular Christianity "based on community models and institutionalized sub-communities that challenged the hegemony of ties of blood and descent in western society...."[39]

The nuclear family of western Europe was formed by the marriage of a husband and wife, who thereby established a separate residence and, hence, an independent household. That is, young married couples did not join the existing households of a parent or sibling but formed new economic units. They did so at a high average age, especially for brides (ages twenty-four to thirty); and partly because of the economic difficulty of forming a new, viable household, a significant percentage of both men and women (10–20 percent) never married. Notwithstanding the late age

---

[37] Angélique Janssens, *Family and Social Change. The Household as a Process in an Industrializing Community* (Cambridge: Cambridge University Press, 1993), p. 18. This position is associated most closely with the influential publications of "the Cambridge Group": Peter Laslett and Richard Wall, eds., *Household and Family in Past Time* (Cambridge: Cambridge University Press, 1972); Richard Wall, ed., *Family Form in Historic Europe* (Cambridge: Cambridge University Press, 1983).

[38] Katherine A. Lynch, *Individuals, Families, and Communities in Western Europe* (Cambridge: Cambridge University Press, 2003), pp. 66, 103–35.

[39] Ibid., p. 22.

of marriage, most children left their parental homes in their teens (ages fifteen to eighteen), working and residing until marriage as servants and apprentices in the households of others. These characteristics define the "European Marriage Pattern," are evident from at least the late Middle Ages onward, and appear to be unique to western Europe.[40] In most world civilizations marriage was, and remains, nearly universal, young, and arranged. Women leave their parental homes only to enter those of their husbands or, more commonly, the homes of the husbands' parents. Men often never leave their parental homes.

The importance of this European Marriage Pattern (EMP) has been explored and debated ever since it was explicitly recognized in the 1960s. The demographic consequences were the first to be developed: Late and non-universal marriage could limit fertility, while the need to form independent households could make nuptiality sensitive to economic conditions. The nuclear family appeared to be an entity engaged in planning and economic calculation.[41] The EMP seemed also to place a special, more individualistic stamp on personality formation, given the context provided for the socialization of children and the relative freedom offered by lifecycle servanthood and courtship.[42] The implications of EMP for gender relations have also been explored, especially in relation to the similarity of the life courses of men and women and the opportunities for women to assume family headship (because of the fragility of the nuclear family).[43] Finally, we come to the economic importance of EMP. The chief claim made to date is that late marriage and servanthood gave young people, especially women, the opportunity to save and bring resources to a new household. Did this endow non-elite European households with more capital or a richer material culture than households elsewhere? Hajnal felt confident that it did:

In the European pattern, a person would usually have some years of adult life before marriage; for women especially this period would be much larger than outside Europe. It is a period of maximum productive capacity without responsibility for children; a period during which saving would be easy. These savings (e.g. by means of the accumulation of household goods in preparation of marriage)

[40] Hajnal, "European Marriage Pattern."
[41] A claim made most fully and convincingly in E. A. Wrigley and R. S. Schofield, *The Population History of England, 1541–1871. A Reconstruction* (London: Edward Arnold, 1981), pp. 454–84.
[42] Peter Laslett, *Family Life and Illicit Love in Earlier Generations* (Cambridge: Cambridge University Press, 1977).
[43] Hartman, *The Household and the Making of History*, pp. 34–69.

might add substantially to the demand for goods other than the food, etc. required for immediate survival. ... [W]hen later marriage is the norm the total volume of demand generated might be much larger than that which can be caused by a small class of wealthy families in a population at subsistence level. Could this effect, which was uniquely European, help to explain how the groundwork was laid for the uniquely European "take-off" into modern economic growth?[44]

The "entry costs" of marriage under the EMP were uniquely high, because the aspirants faced the obligation to assemble the capital for a viable, independent household. No studies have yet pursued Hajnal's speculations on the economic effect of induced savings during lifecycle servant-hood, although, as we shall see in Chapter 4, the *spending* of servants has attracted the attention of historians interested in fashion and emulative behavior.

Most economic arguments based on EMP rely on the notion that nuclear families breed individualism, and that individualism breeds capitalism and economic development.[45] In this study, the focus will be not on the individual but on the household in which the individual makes decisions. Did the nuclear household – small, flexible, and autonomous – offer a uniquely propitious context for innovations in consumer behavior? Did the elements of planning and calculation that characterized its demographic behavior extend to its economic decision making as well? Complex family structures greatly limit and complicate decisions about consumption. There are numerous claimants to available resources, both within the household and in larger kin networks. Such complex households are "strong" in the sense that they have a greater self-insurance capacity than nuclear households. But this capacity to absorb risk comes at a price: more rigid rules and conventions governing the allocation of economic resources.[46] In addition, many married men and women in complex

---

[44] Hajnal, "European Marriage Patterns in Perspective," p. 132.

[45] This argument is made with style and a certain Anglocentric assertiveness in Alan Mac-farlane, *The Origins of English Individualism* (Cambridge: Cambridge University Press, 1978); and *The Culture of Capitalism* (Oxford: Basil Blackwell, 1987).

[46] In the West, where households were less tied to larger lineage groups, "Extended kinship solidarity and cushioning of risks within broad kinship groups is to some extent replaced by particular forms of communal risk devolution. Greater reliance on neighbors, on organizations like guilds and corporations (especially in cities), or on community charity funds is a fundamental characteristic of the Western European system." Ronald Lesthaeghe, "On the Social Control of Human Reproduction," *Population and Development Review* 6 (1980): 531.

Within western Europe, a further distinction can be made between northwestern and southern Europe. David Reher notes that children in Mediterranean societies were retained within the household until marriage, while in northern Europe, they left to enter

household structures are not in charge of their households, deferring for many years, if not forever, to the decisions of more senior figures.[47] The claustrophobic bonds of extended kinship must act to restrict and inhibit new consumer behavior, given the complexity of decision making and the potential claims made by even distant family members on whatever surpluses a given household may acquire. This contrast with the nuclear family household would appear to be important to our project. While the historical development of the European Marriage Pattern cannot shed much light on the *timing* of the industrious revolution, it may well have been influential in determining its *geographical range*.

The geographical limits of the industrious revolution cannot be drawn with precision. This is partly attributable to the limitations of the historical evidence and partly a reflection of the tendency of highly urban areas, even when distant from the core region, to exhibit at least some of the consumer behavior that is of concern here. The basic elements of the European Marriage Pattern can be found reaching east to a line that Hajnal described as extending from St. Petersburg to Trieste, but much of this vast zone was beyond the reach of the consumer

---

service typically in their mid-teens. Likewise, "in Mediterranean societies much of the aid given to vulnerable members of society came from the family or from individual charity, while in northern societies this was largely accomplished through public and private institutions." David Sven Reher, "Family Ties in Western Europe. Persistent Contrasts," *Population and Development Review* 24 (1998): 209. What concerns us here is how the claims of kin will affect the family as consumer, and how those claims affect the redistribution of income among nuclear family members. The northern nuclear family appears better suited than the families described by Reher to focus its resources on consumer goods.

47 Consider this evidence from a survey of the consumer decision making of 800 recently married women in northern Italy between 1880 and 1910. Asked who had made the decisions about the purchase of their own clothing in the first two years of their marriages, the wives of white-collar workers either made these decisions on their own (30 percent) or after discussion with their husbands (59 percent). Among the wives of sharecroppers, only 6 percent reported that they had made these decisions on their own, while an additional 22 percent made them together with their husbands. However, another 50 percent of sharecroppers' wives reported that the decisions had been made by one or both of their parents-in-law. This finding reflects a household structure inimical to the emergence of the industrious revolution. Raffaella Sarti, *Europe at Home. Family and Material Culture, 1500–1800* (New Haven, Conn.: Yale University Press, 2002), p. 218.

Even ostensibly nuclear families had important obligations to (nonresident) kin. Hagen describes the peasant households of eighteenth-century Brandenburg as focused on the obligation of the head to support the retired family members and endow, with marriage portions, the non-inheriting siblings. The household's strategy was reproduction rather than accumulation. William Hagen, "Peasant Fortunes. Standards of Living in the Eighteenth-Century Brandenburg Countryside" (unpublished, University of California at Davis, 1987).

behaviors of interest to us because of the restrictive influence of corporate and institutional controls on household decision making and/or the absence of sufficiently developed urban networks for the emergence and diffusion of new consumer practices. Where the relevant elements – nuclear families, urban networks, and market institutions – were most fully present, in northwestern Europe, the industrious revolution could take shape.[48]

In summary, the Western family has long been a "weak" family. It had – and has – a public as well as a private aspect; its members participated as individuals in the public sphere, and it had the autonomy to respond to altered market conditions and act on the consumer aspirations of its members.[49] It was, and remains, an active agent in history. One will not find here a household model that moves in a linear progression from the autarchic patriarchy of legend, via the sentimentalized, privatized family nurtured by the past generation of social historians, to the vestigial and eviscerated family that fuels so many modern anxieties.[50]

---

[48] Corporate controls on household behavior in central Europe are described in detail in Sheilagh C. Ogilvie, *A Bitter Living. Women, Markets, and Social Capital in Early Modern Germany* (Oxford: Oxford University Press, 2003). For further discussion of the "boundaries" of new consumer practices, see Sandgruber's pioneering study of consumer behavior in the Austrian lands: He placed this region within a south German–Austrian cultural zone "which in the eighteenth and nineteenth centuries tended to be hostile to innovation." Consumer innovations "such as coffee, potatoes, sugar, white bread [*butterbrot*] brandywine, or new mealtimes were here, in peasant circles, unknown or only sporadically known – with the exception of the Wiener Umland [zone around Vienna] and perhaps also Vorarlberg." He goes on to note that rural and urban lifestyles [*lebenformen*] tended gradually to merge in northern German lands but remained clearly distinguishable and slow to change in the south. Sandgruber, *Die Anfänge der Konsumgesellschaft*, p. 242.

[49] Lynch, *Individuals, Families and Communities in Europe*, pp. 12–14; Peter Laslett, "Family, Kinship and Collectivity as Systems of Support in Pre-Industrial Europe. A Consideration of the Nuclear-hardship Hypothesis," *Continuity and Change* 3 (1988): 153–75; Michael Anderson, *Family Structure in Nineteenth-Century Lancashire* (Cambridge: Cambridge University Press, 1971), pp. 170–9.

[50] For another affirmation of these claims, see Pat Hudson and W. R. Lee, eds., *Women's Work and the Family Economy in Historical Perspective* (Manchester: Manchester University Press, 1990). In the introductory chapter, the editors critique "both pessimist and optimist interpretations … which tend to be very influenced by a functionalist and economic determinist perspective which sees the family economy and intra-family relationships as passive and dependent variables in the process of change" (p. 20). They go on to state that "women's work, the family economy and family strategies are not merely reactive in the process of economic change but function in a pro-active manner which itself contributes to the material and ideological outcome of economic development" (p. 34). Their approach to this subject differs substantially from mine, emphasizing disaggregation to observe regional, occupational, lifecycle, and gender-specific behaviors, but the break with linear and functionalist accounts of family behavior is decisive.

Consumption Theory

Thus far I have argued that the household possesses sufficient cohesion to form an economic unit that interacts with, rather than simply reflects and yields to, the market. What forms does this interaction take over the course of time, as the market economy develops and changes? In particular, how does the household chart a course as a consumer?

We can begin with standard consumer theory, although this is based on a set of assumptions that seems unpromisingly designed to confine the study of consumption to limited, short-term questions. To begin with, consumer theory focuses on the individual, not the household, and assumes the individual to be utterly autonomous, with unchanging preferences. That is, the individual knows what he or she wants independent of the economic system. In this sense the consumer is said to be "sovereign." The sovereign consumer, with a given income, is assumed to possess perfect knowledge of all available goods and their prices, and to be capable of effortless and costless maximization. A popular textbook puts it this way: "The economic theory of the consumer is very simple. Economists assume that consumers choose the best bundle of goods they can afford." Or, restated more formally, "consumers choose the most preferred bundle from their budget sets."[51]

"Best" and "most preferred" in these citations refer to the consumer's goal of maximizing "utility." *Utility* can be a misleading term. It appears to suggest a narrow concept of consumer satisfaction focused on the objective qualities of goods – their usefulness. But the term also embraces the subjective attributes, including the anticipated happiness that attaches to the contemplation of a purchase. It is a measure of the intensity of desire. Faced with such a metaphysical and empirically unobservable concept, economists beginning with Vilfredo Pareto and culminating with Paul Samuelson set about replacing it with something more tractable.[52] Pareto chose to focus on "the pure and naked fact of choice." What Samuelson later called the "revealed preference" of consumers is an ordering of these "naked facts of choice" into indifference curves that mark an "imaginary divide between what is preferred and what is not." In this way, what

51 Hal R. Varian, *Intermediate Microeconomics. A Modern Approach* (New York: W. W. Norton, sixth ed., 2003), pp. 20, 73.

52 Vilfredo Pareto, *Manuel d' économie politique*, second ed. (Paris: Giard, 1927); Paul Samuelson, "A Note on the Pure Theory of Consumer's Preference," *Economica* 5 (1938): 61–71; Fabio Ranchetti, "Choice Without Utility?" in Bianchi, ed., *The Active Consumer*, pp. 28–30.

continues to be called utility is simply what consumers show they prefer by their actions, and it is transformed from an originally *cardinal* to a purely *ordinal* notion. The price of this move, as noted by Bianchi, is that "consumer motivation or the incentive to action is unknown, unknowable. Since preferences, as revealed by market choices, are the ultimate, indecomposable, and given elements of action, what is maximized is no longer known, knowable, or even relevant."[53]

It is no accident, one might observe here, that the application of such a theory, by reducing the concept of demand to the logic of isolated choices, has been unable to find any but a passive role for consumer choice in dynamic economic processes. There are, however, new approaches to the study of consumer behavior that have, without wholly abandoning the foundations of conventional theory, extended the range of human activities over which economic reasoning can fruitfully be applied.

When faced with a difficult concept such as "utility," it is understandable that one would simply concede that whatever individual action shows to be "most preferred" must maximize utility, and to leave it at that: *de gustibus non est disputandum*. Yet, there *are* a few things that can be observed about utility as a dynamic process that remove it, at least partially, from its black box and shed light on the historical evolution of consumer demand. A useful starting point is Tibor Scitovsky's division of utility into two parts: the search for comfort and the search for pleasure.[54] By *comfort*, Scitovsky refers to consumption that reduces pain or discomfort. It includes, of course, providing for basic necessities but does not stop there, for there are a multitude of ways in which one can be made (even more) comfortable. The consumption of pleasure is related to arousal and stimulation. Pleasure and comfort can be experienced together in a single act of consumption. Scitovsky observed that while the desire for comfort could be satiated, that for pleasure could not, and is inherently an open-ended process. Going further, he argued that the closer one came to perfect comfort and, hence, lack of stimulation, the more one sought forms of consumption that provided excitement and that increased the level of arousal. The modern condition, a product of the comforts of consumer society, is boredom; yet, ironically, boredom itself is a driving force of consumption, because the alleviation of boredom activates the unending pursuit of novelty and excitement.

[53] Maria Bianchi, "Introduction," in Bianchi, ed., *The Active Consumer*, p. 8.
[54] Tibor Scitovsky, *The Joyless Economy* (Oxford: Oxford University Press, 1976, rev. ed., 1992).

A further decomposition of these categories of utility is possible. The consumption of comfort may itself be divided between those goods that act, as Scitovsky supposed, to increase personal comfort, and those that provide what I will call social comfort. Veblen and many since him have called attention to the fact that much consumption is intended not only, or even primarily, for personal use, but for use as a social signal, or sign. This "conspicuous consumption" distinguishes individuals from others and strengthens claims to status.[55] Positional goods (inherently scarce goods, the consumption of which necessarily denies them to others) are a variant of this aggressive signaling. But social comfort is also achieved via "defensive consumption" (consuming goods to defend against the consequences of the consumption practices of others). This is an important part of the striving for "respectability," which, in the view of Woodruff Smith, emerged in the course of the seventeenth and eighteenth centuries as a concept that contextualized a broad range of consumption practices.[56] All these sources of social comfort, whereby individuals distinguish themselves from others and assert or protect status claims, are open ended. Because they respond to the consumption acts of others, no equilibrium exists and no point of satiation is ever reached.[57] Indeed, economic growth only intensifies the demand for the positional goods that supply social comfort.[58]

---

[55] Thorstein Veblen, *The Theory of the Leisure Class. An Economic Study of Institutions* ([1899] New York: New American Library, 1953); Pierre Bourdieu, *Distinction. A Sociological Critique of the Judgment of Taste*, trans. Richard Nice (London: Routledge & Kegan Paul, 1984). Both Veblen and Bourdieu interpret consumption as a competitive "other-regarding" behavior (activities done for their effects on others more than for their intrinsic utility) that reinforces the hierarchies of society through the continual re-creation of relationships of domination and submission. While Veblen saw conspicuous consumption as performing this function directly, through displays of wealth, Bourdieu emphasizes the indirect power of cultural capital as it is manifested in displays of taste.

[56] Woodruff D. Smith, *Consumption and the Making of Respectability, 1600–1800* (London: Routledge, 2002). Smith sees the bourgeoisie as having "formed itself as a self-conscious class around a culture of respectability..." (p. 27), but, ultimately, by the nineteenth century it is not only a middle-class characteristic: "It seems as though the formulation of respectability was connected with the formation of *all* modern classes" (p. 244, emphasis in original).

[57] The basic point was made long ago by James S. Duesenberry. He argued, in effect, that that "sovereign consumer" is not sovereign because of the "demonstration effect" of the consumption practices of others. One's contact with the superior consumption goods and higher standards of living of others leads to a desire to increase one's own consumption. Thus, consumption depends not only on one's own income but on the income of others. *Income, Saving, and the Theory of Consumer Behavior* (Cambridge, Mass.: Harvard University Press, 1949).

[58] Fred Hirsch, *Social Limits to Growth* (Cambridge, Mass.: Harvard University Press, 1976).

The consumption of pleasure also may be decomposed with the aid of allied terms: *hedonism* and *novelty*. Colin Campbell, in an inventive inversion of Max Weber's "Protestant Ethic," proposed that a "Romantic Ethic" shaped the "Spirit of Modern Consumerism."[59] In its traditional form hedonism was the pursuit of sensual pleasure through direct experience. The pleasure was in the act of consumption, be it wine, women, or song. The romantic ethic transformed hedonism into its modern form, where the image of consumption, its anticipation – the yearning for fulfillment of one's "daydreams of desire" – is at the core, while the actual act of consumption is often something of an anticlimax. In fact, Campbell argues, in modern society the illusions people are capable of nurturing are always better than the reality they can experience, causing the consumer always to be vaguely dissatisfied with reality, longing for something more, something better.[60] This longing eventually attaches to specific objects of desire, thereby restarting the cycle of consumption, over and again.

Thus, traditional hedonism is dependent on anticipatory images that are socially generated and static, and finds pleasure in "goods" that gratify the appetites; modern hedonism depends on individual, volatile "daydreams of desire" and can find pleasure only in novelty. Novelty – new fashions and styles, new goods and services – comes from the initiatives of producers, but in the marketplace they meet the *actively searching consumer*. The desire for novelty engages the "modern hedonist" in exploratory behaviors and learning processes.[61]

Such a consumer is far removed from the passive maximizer, scanning the prices of a fixed and known array of goods and matching them against a stable preference schedule in order to select with the greatest possible efficiency his or her consumption set. We now have a consumer actively engaged in a process of discovery. One might wonder why consumers would reject old goods, with their known satisfactions, for new ones with their as yet uncertain benefits. Of course, many consumers do not take this risk, and nearly all consumers reject that which is wholly unfamiliar.

[59] Campbell, *The Romantic Ethic and the Spirit of Modern Consumerism.*
[60] Campbell's "modern man" whose illusory world is inevitably richer than any available reality is not very different from the "human nature" described by Adam Smith, which features an inherent capacity "by which we convince ourselves that the possession of goods will make us happy." Under the spell of this deception we work to acquire luxuries, "baubles," that when "viewed in an abstract and philosophical light ... will always appear in the highest degree contemptible and trifling." This results in the "comic irony" on which economic prosperity depends: Our exertions do not bring the happiness and satisfaction we seek, but they do make us better off. Adam Smith, *Theory of Moral Sentiments*, p. 183.
[61] Bianchi, "Introduction," pp. 4, 8.

Scitovsky notes that "[a] new activity, as well as a novel good...can be enjoyable only if recognizable, if some of its potentiality is understood, if tastes have develop[ed] and adapted in order to appreciate it." In order to be a source of pleasure, the new good must encounter the skilled consumer, one whose knowledge and experience allow him or her to recognize its potential.[62]

To the need for recognizability we must add the need for combinability. The potential utility of new goods is rarely evident from the qualities of the goods in isolation. "They are," as Bianchi observes,

part of a complex and changeable network of interrelations with other goods and characteristics. It is this combinable potential of goods which allows for variations and change in consumption. New goods, in order to become "goods," have to play on recognizability, exploiting known similarities and rivalries among goods. But to be new they have to introduce characteristics and functions which alter the existing order and timings in the consumption set. Often in this process small changes activate large ones.[63]

The structure of utility as we have delineated it thus far appears to have two variants each of a demand for comfort and a demand for pleasure. The search for comfort leads to a demand for specific goods and services to relieve specific discomforts, and the search for pleasure governed by traditional hedonism leads to a demand for specific experiences. In both cases demand is at least theoretically limited as discomforts are addressed and the desire for pleasure is satiated. In contrast to this, the search for social comfort, with its concern for status, distinction, and identity, is limitless and tends to be intensified by the very process of economic growth. Finally we have the search for pleasure driven by modern hedonism. The relief of discomfort produces genuine utility, but through the removal of stimulation it also creates and intensifies the modern condition of boredom. Boredom has no simple antidote. More consumption of existing goods does not relieve boredom; instead, escape is offered by a potentially wide variety of goods and services incorporating novelty. The escape is inevitably partial and temporary – lasting as long as novelty adheres to the new objects of consumption, but the now-active and imaginative consumers have been launched on their never-ending quests for novel sources of pleasure.

[62] Scitovsky, *The Joyless Economy*, pp. 74, 225. Amartya Sen, "Economics and the Family," *Asian Development Review* 1 (1985): 14–26, speaks of the "capabilities" of consumers that determine what can be accomplished with goods.
[63] Bianchi, "Introduction," p. 10.

This exercise in the decomposition of consumer behavior into its basic parts offers no more than a brief sketch of the dynamic structure of demand. It suggests the existence of an historical process in which demand patterns develop *within* the economic system in a coherent, sequential manner. This, in turn, requires that we set aside the passive consumer of conventional theory, with his stable, exogenously determined (i.e., external to the economy) preferences, who maximizes utility through a sequence of isolated choices. I propose that we replace this stock figure with an active, searching consumer whose acts of discovery interact with the array of goods supplied by producers to form tastes, and whose selection of goods, in a trial-and-error process, exploits complementarities to achieve new "consumption clusters" and new ways of signaling meaning to others. Her utility is not simply dependent on the intrinsic qualities of the goods consumed but depends on knowledge and experience (consumer capital) and the exploitation of the combinatory possibilities of available goods.

Household Economics

Thus far we have focused on individuals and their demand for goods, yet this study's stated concerns are households and a concept of consumption that embraces more than the physical utility of goods. That is, without denying Adam Smith's dictum that "consumption is the sole end and purpose of all *production*," one can affirm that consumption is not the sole end of *human activity* but is better understood as the means to some further end. Here, too, new approaches to the economics of consumer behavior can come to our assistance.

An important development in the study of consumer behavior is the distinction introduced by Kelvin Lancaster between "goods," which are purchased, and their "characteristics," which give rise to utility and are consumed. This allows one to distinguish goods, their prices, and the budget constraints that govern consumer behavior in conventional theory from the characteristics of goods (they typically possess multiple characteristics) that give utility and are the qualities for which individuals possess preferences. Just as goods have multiple characteristics, so characteristics can be shared by more than one good. Indeed, "goods in combination may possess characteristics different from those pertaining to the goods separately."[64] This invites the economist to inquire into the complex processes

---

[64] Lancaster, *Modern Consumer Theory*, p. 13.

by which households convert goods into the consumed characteristics, a process Lancaster called the "consumption technology."

These insights were developed further by Gary Becker, leading to a body of theory called the "new household economics." Instead of focusing on the individual as an autonomous decision maker, Becker took the household as his unit of study. He treated the household as an entity dedicated to consumption, just as a firm is dedicated to production, and posited that, just as the process whereby firms convert inputs into their output of goods is described by a production function, so the process by which households convert their purchased goods into ultimate consumption could be summarized by a "consumption technology" (the term *consumption function* having already been appropriated for other purposes by John Maynard Keynes).

The household purchases goods (purchased goods $= x_i$) on the market until it has exhausted its money income and combines these goods with the labor (T_i) and other resources of the household to produce that which is ultimately consumed. Becker called this ultimate consumption "Z," or Z-commodities.[65] The household (typically, but not exclusively, a family) is seen here as an entity that allocates its resources, chiefly the time of its members, in such a way as to maximize the utilities of its individual members.[66] This allocation is a complex one, involving labor to acquire the money income to purchase goods (T_w), labor retained within

---

[65] Becker, "A Theory of the Allocation of Time," p. 495. Z-commodities: "the more basic commodities that directly enter utility functions."

[66] The discussion will be clarified for some readers by recourse to formal notation. The household's production of Z-commodities takes place via a consumption technology that combines purchased goods and household labor:

$$Z_i = f(x_i, T_i) \qquad (1)$$

The household allocates the time of its members among three major categories: labor to acquire the money income to purchase goods (T_w), labor retained within the household to transform purchased goods into Z-commodities (T_c), and leisure, which includes the time to actually consume the commodities (T_r).

$$T = T_c + T_w + T_r \qquad (2)$$

The time constraint (2) defines the amount of labor devoted to money earning activity, which in the simple case of wage labor yields a goods constraint:

$$\Sigma\, p_i\, x_i = I = T_w w \qquad (3)$$

where (w) equals the wage rate, and (I) is total money income.

The presence of T_w in both equations (2) and (3), the time and goods constraints, respectively, highlights the importance of the degree of "substitutability" between goods and time in the consumption technologies available to secure the desired Z-commodities.

the household to transform purchased goods into Z-commodities (T_c), and leisure, which includes the time to actually consume the commodities (T_r).[67] When the available time of household members is divided into these categories, it becomes apparent that the household's allocation of the time of its members is of fundamental importance. The more time devoted to market work, the more goods (x) the household can buy, but the less time is left for the transformation of these goods into the ultimately consumed commodities (Z) and for the consumption time to enjoy them.

What choices are available to households in making these allocations of time? This depends on alternative consumption technologies available to secure the desired Z-commodities and the degrees of "substitutability" between goods and time that they offer. That is, in a given technological and commercial regime, are the ways available to combine goods and time to achieve a given Z numerous, or are there only one or two? Over time, technical and commercial developments can increase the range of choices faced by households to achieve their Z-commodities. As households change their consumption technologies, they generate changes in the demand for individual goods (x_i). This does not necessarily reflect a change in tastes, because they may well continue to seek the same Z-commodities, the actual source of utility. In this context one can readily see how, say, a reduction in the price of a good could induce the selection of a different consumption technology, one that uses goods (x_i) more intensively. Similarly, an increase in the wage, by increasing the opportunity cost of household work and leisure, would encourage a shift toward more goods-intensive consumption technologies.

In this Beckerian framework, the industrious revolution refers to household decisions that go beyond these adjustments to prices and wages. Examples would include allocations of household time to market labor that exceed those suggested by the changes in wages and prices; an exploitation of a greater substitutability in consumption technologies to pursue specialization and, hence, productivity gains in both production and consumption; and, ultimately, revisions in the mix of desired Z-commodities (which implies a change in preferences in Becker's terms) toward those with more goods-intensive consumption technologies.

---

[67] This last claim on time, consumption time, is not considered by Becker but is explored in Linder, *The Harried Leisure Class*, pp. 13–15. Linder takes in earnest the quip of Arthur Schopenhauer in 1851 that "Buying books would be a good thing if one could also buy the time in which to read them." See also Ian Steedman, *Consumption Takes Time. Implications for Economic Theory* (London: Routledge, 2001).

Several observations with implications for an historical analysis of the household flow from these extensions of consumer theory.

Full income and household efficiency. The household members derive utility, shaped by their preferences (or tastes) from the consumption of Z-commodities. Hence, a full measure of well-being would be the summation of the "value" of all consumed Z-commodities. (Because Z-commodities are inherently nontraded, this is no simple exercise, requiring the invocation of what economists call "shadow prices.") Yet the conventional study of standards of living limits its attention exclusively to money income, which defines the household's budget constraint and hence its command over goods (x). The gap between these two definitions of living standards – of the purchase of goods (x) times their prices versus the consumption of Z-commodities times their shadow prices – is a measure of the "value added" of household production.[68]

The two measures are analogous to the narrow definition of gross domestic product and the broader definitions, or "extended accounts," often advocated by feminist and other critics of conventional national income accounting, which include the value of nonmarket production.[69] The gap will grow or contract depending on the household's choice of consumption technologies – that is, depending on how "goods intensive" is the production of Z-commodities.

This gap will also vary at the micro level of the household itself according to the household's "consumer efficiency." Maximization of the complex decisions discussed above is far from effortless and costless, and households vary considerably in the efficiency with which they are capable

---

[68] The household members derive utility, shaped by their preferences (or tastes) from the consumption of Z-commodities. Hence, a comprehensive measure of well-being – the "full income" of the household – is:

$$\Sigma Z_i \Pi_I \qquad (4)$$

where Π_i = the shadow price of the inherently non-traded Z-commodities. This can be compared to the conventional measure of the household's standard of living, which limits itself to total money income and the household's command over goods (as in equation 3 of note 66). The gap between these two definitions of living standards is a measure of the "value added" (VA) of household production:

$$VA = \Sigma Z_i \Pi_I - \Sigma p_i x_i \qquad (5)$$

This gap will grow or contract depending on the household's choice of consumption technologies.

[69] Extended accounts add nonmarket production but often go on to subtract outputs that are viewed as "regrettable necessities": disamenities of modern life. See William Nordhaus and James Tobin, "Is Growth Obsolete?" in James Tobin, *Essays in Economics*, Vol. III, *Theory and Policy* (Cambridge, Mass.: MIT University Press, 1982), pp. 360–450; Robert Eisner, *The Total Incomes System of Accounts* (Chicago: University of Chicago Press, 1989).

and willing to transform their resources into Z-commodities.[70] The degree of calculation in decision making chosen by consumers will be related to the knowledge and experience (social capital, consumption capital) they bring to the enterprise. Thus, the retained nutrients of consumed food depend on the cook's human capital; detecting the combinatory possibilities of available goods requires consumption capital; fully exploiting the symbolic values of goods requires social capital. Moreover, while production inefficiency in firms is signaled and punished by market competition, no such external forces discipline families and push them toward greater consumer efficiency.[71] Even when households efficiently produce individual Z-commodities, the problem of the mix of commodities and their distribution among household members remains.

The main point of the "full income" concept can readily be grasped by considering the most common measure of income: Historians of preindustrial societies typically define the economic resources available to a household by the wage rate deflated by the price level. This real-wage measure commonly stands as a first approximation of household purchasing power.[72] The allocation-of-time model discussed above alerts us to the possibility that reallocations of time use by the members of the household – changes in leisure, redeployment of labor between the household and the market – can cause household money income to follow a different course from that suggested by the wage rate alone. But even

---

[70] Jeffrey James, *Consumption and Development* (New York: St. Martin's Press, 1993), pp. 186–8.

[71] No *external* forces discipline families, but *within* the household, dissatisfaction and criticism can be intense and induce in the person held most responsible – in most cases the wife and mother – a great anxiety. Daniel Miller calls attention to the considerable power that accrues to the modern housewife as she exercises consumer choice on behalf of the family, but he hastens to add that "[this power] is not experienced as empowerment in the daily life of those who wield it." The housewife is in the unenviable position of simultaneously negotiating the household economy (find the right position, somewhere between Martha Stewart and sloven) and the political economy (somewhere between acting as the manipulated tool of international capitalism's advertising and the savvy beneficiary of the international market economy). Because most academic writers on this subject appear to view their own consumption practices as elevated above the mundane concerns of the housewife, analyses of these issues untouched by condescension are not common. Daniel Miller, "Consumption as the Vanguard of History. A Polemic by Way of an Introduction," in Daniel Miller, ed., *Acknowledging Consumption. A Review of New Studies* (London: Routledge, 1995), pp. 34–5.

[72] For example, see the recent study of Robert Allen, "The Great Divergence in European Wages and Prices from the Middle Ages to the First World War," *Explorations in Economic History* 38 (2001): 411–47. For a critical discussion of this venerable tradition, see Jan de Vries, "Between Purchasing Power and the World of Goods. Understanding the Household Economy in Early Modern Europe," in John Brewer and Roy Porter, eds., *Consumption and the World of Goods* (London: Routledge, 1993), pp. 95–8.

this more comprehensive measure of income does not comprehend "full income," which includes nonmarketed labor and the efficiency of consumption. The extent to which full income is greater than the others measures of income depends on the consumption technologies used to produce Z-commodities and the consumer efficiency of the household's labor.

Utility and income redistribution. It is individuals who consume, and derive utility, but most Z-commodities are either consumed jointly or are allocated to individuals by some household decision-making process.[73] The character of that process – whether it is grounded in altruism or reflects the unequal power of family members – is as important a topic as it is obscure. The opacity of family life – most people are less forthcoming about their monetary practices than their sexual practices – has caused normative pronouncements, ideological claims, and convenient assumptions to substitute for direct knowledge of income distribution within the household. (I will examine this in more detail in Chapter 5.) Here it will suffice to recall that the household economy necessarily involves decisions about production (who will work, and at which tasks?) and consumption (what will be consumed – invested, saved – and how will it be distributed among the members?).

Most income is earned by individuals, most goods are purchased by individuals, and all utility is "registered" by individuals. Yet, the consumption resources eligible for redistribution within the household are a large fraction of total societal resources. Becker claims that "families in all societies, including modern market-oriented societies, have been responsible for ... – half or more [of all economic activity] – for they have produced much of the consumption, education, health, and other human capital of the members."[74] Other, more formal, estimates of household production (for the United States, the United Kingdom, and Australia) place it at 40–25 percent of national income.[75] The quality of these

---

[73] For an influential effort to sidestep this problem, see Paul A. Samuelson, "Social Indifference Curves," *Quarterly Journal of Economics* 70 (1956): 1–22. Samuelson considered the family to constitute "a realm of altruism." His definition of paternalism was that an individual's utility depended on others' conforming to his/her preferences. In contrast, the altruist includes the utility of other members (as *they* define it) in his or her own. Gary Becker explores this topic in "A Theory of Social Interactions," *Journal of Political Economy* 82 (1974): 1063–93.

[74] Gary Becker, *A Treatise on the Family* (Cambridge, Mass.: Harvard University Press, 1981), p. 303.

[75] Eisner, *Total Incomes System of Accounts*, p. 73; Avner Offer, *The Challenge of Affluence. Self-Control and Well-Being in the United States and Britain Since 1950* (Oxford: Oxford University Press, 2006), p. 85.

redistribution decisions also determines the extent to which total utility (full income), as defined by each member, exceeds the monetary cost of the inputs – that is, the quality of these decisions determines the value of the household as a common economic enterprise in the eyes of its members. If individual preferences are similar, as Becker assumes, redistributive decisions are not the most important determinant of the household's success. Rather, the efficiency in transforming goods into Z-commodities, which Becker regards to be highly heterogeneous across households, is more important. But the more individual family member tastes differ, the more challenging is the decision-making process within the household, and the more those decisions will affect total utility.

Consumption bundles. At the heart of both Lancaster's and Becker's models is the distinction between the goods we buy and the Z-commodities that we consume and that give utility. There is no longer a stable, one-to-one relationship between the purchase of a good and the derivation of utility. Goods in combination may possess characteristics different from those pertaining to the same goods consumed separately. These "indivisibilities" in consumption can be obvious, if not trivial. Tea and teacups, for example, is a "consumption bundle" that readily comes to mind. But these bundles can also be much more complex and much more powerful. To stay with tea for a moment, its combination with sugar is anything but obvious. This is not how tea was consumed in China, nor was coffee drunk with sugar in its Arabian places of origin. The contemplation of this bundling innovation filled Sidney Mintz, the anthropologist of sugar, with awe:

The first sweetened cup of hot tea to be drunk by an English worker was a significant historical event, because it prefigured the transformation of an entire society, a total remaking of its economic and social basis. We must struggle to understand fully the consequences of that and kindred events, for upon them was erected an entirely different conception of the relationship between producers and consumers, of the meaning of work, of the definition of self, of the nature of things.[76]

Mintz believes that this act, if we could observe it, would place us at the point of origin of modern life, something akin to observing Adam's eating of the apple. He asks his reader to believe that all the things that flowed from this act (a mass change of consumer behavior, consumerism, slave-based plantation economies, colonialism, capitalism) were truly *consequences* of a fatal, inherent taste of "an" – more likely he means

---

[76] Sidney W. Mintz, *Sweetness and Power. The Place of Sugar in Modern History* (New York: Viking Press, 1985), p. 214.

the – "English worker."[77] The approach to consumer tastes I have presented here seeks to contextualize and thereby endogenize the process of consumer capital formation – to treat consumption innovations as flowing from accumulated experience and knowledge rather than appearing as an exogenously determined event. Nonetheless, Mintz is surely correct to call attention to the far-reaching ramifications of consumer clusters.

The custom of taking tea and coffee with sugar appears to have taken form in northwestern Europe between 1685 and 1700, but the development of consumption clusters did not stop there.[78] Tea and coffee were combined with wheat bread to form a breakfast economical of household labor that, in the early–eighteenth-century Netherlands, not only replaced morning meals of porridge or pancakes and beer but reorganized the daily meal system as a whole from a two-meal to a three-meal regime. Across the North Sea, Woodruff Smith describes how "The British ritual called 'tea' was one of two major meals invented or radically revised in the late seventeenth and early eighteenth centuries that centered around the consumption of overseas imports and that possessed important social and cultural meanings for its participants. The other was breakfast, in the form in which it came down to the twentieth century."[79]

Consumer clusters can also emerge when goods are linked in more subtle ways, by the consumer's sense of fitness, itself the product of an

---

[77] Before concluding that the appeal of sugar is natural and irresistible, consider Sandgruber's account of its diffusion in Austria: "One must conclude that before 1800 the great majority of Austrian inhabitants made no use of it [sugar] at all. The growth of consumption is overwhelmingly accounted for by the kitchens of the highest classes (*der Oberschichtenküche*), where in the eighteenth century sugar was much appreciated and profoundly influenced dishes and recipes." Sandgruber, *Die Ängange der Konsumgesellschaft*, p. 208. Here, in central Europe, sugar's appeal appears to have originated at court and long remained associated with refined dishes rather than the workingman's refreshment. Sangruber again: "Court society [*höfische Gesellschaft*] created the new hot drinks, coffee, tea, and cacao, which, in contrast to their places of origin, were sweetened, and which now seems so obvious to us." Sandgruber, "Leben und Lebensstandard im Zeitalter des Barock," p. 179.

[78] Woodruff Smith describes Mintz's moment of creation rather more matter-of-factly: "Although tea and coffee were undoubtedly taken with sugar in the Netherlands and England by some of the more gastronomically adventurous before about 1685, there is no sign of a general fashion for doing so. By 1710 at the latest, however, there are clear indications of the prevalence of the practice in Britain, and by the 1720s and 1730s, it had become quite general in other countries as well. The years between about 1685 and just after 1700, therefore, appear to be the key period. Probably not coincidentally, the period immediately after 1700 also saw immense increases in the importance of tea, coffee, and sugar in Europe." Smith, *Consumption*, pp. 122–3.

[79] Ibid., p. 172.

accumulating "consumer capital." This is sometimes called the "Diderot Effect" after Dennis Diderot's account of his experience as a consumer in his essay "Regrets on Parting with my Old Dressing Gown."[80] Soon after the *philosophe* had replaced his old dressing gown with a splendid new one, he looked about his study and found it somehow deficient. His desk appeared shabby as he sat before it in his new gown, and after he replaced it with a grand new one, the wall tapestry appeared rather threadbare. New draperies were ordered, and, in this way, soon everything in the study was replaced with new things. The cluttered space that had satisfied Diderot a week before had been transformed into an elegant but rather sterile chamber. Diderot had not set out to remodel his study, but a sense of style and coherence had led him to this result nonetheless.

Diderot expressed regret over his new ensemble, but the larger point is that new commodities by themselves do not possess the utility that they come to acquire once they are bundled with others. Moreover, when bundled, consumer goods can acquire nontangible qualities that affect their utility to the consumer. Goods embedded within "worlds of goods" acquire, or acquire more strongly, the marking functions that supply social distinction, and they provide a means of communicating meaning and cementing reciprocal relations with others. These staples of the anthropological approach to consumption connect directly with the economic model introduced here. The economists Lancaster and Becker could readily subscribe to the celebrated dictum of the anthropologists Douglas and Isherwood that "all goods carry meaning, but none by itself."[81]

As noted earlier, the processes of discovery whereby consumers seek comfort and pleasure should not be thought of simply as a matter of acquiring new goods. Rather, novelty consists in the discovery of new

[80] Dennis Diderot, "Regrets on Parting with my Old Dressing Gown," in *Rameau's Nephew and Other Works by Dennis Diderot*, trans. Jacques Barzun (New York: Bobbs-Merrill, 1964), pp. 309–17.

[81] Mary Douglas and Baron Isherwood, *The World of Goods* (New York: W. W. Norton, 1979), p. 72. Despite this affinity, anthropologists appear to regard Douglas and Isherwood's claims as a direct challenge to the "ludicrous assumptions" of economic. The quote is from Daniel Miller, "Consumption Studies in Anthropology," in Miller, ed., *Acknowledging Consumption*, pp. 266–7. Douglas and Isherwood, for their part, discuss economists, including Lancaster, with an unbecoming condescension. "Lancaster," they conclude dismissively, "is no more able than anyone else to explain which properties of today's luxuries will make some of them, but not others, become tomorrow's necessities" (p. 111). They then proceed confidently to predict from their own anthropological theory "that a rise in real income will tend to be accompanied by an increase in the frequency of large-scale private social events" (p. 112). Predicted in 1979, it did not take long before it could be proved wrong.

complementarities. "New complementarities and the definition of use systems determine the success of new items of consumption and their diffusion paths."[82] The complementarities, or consumption bundles, can range from simple technical indivisibilities to complex lifestyles.[83] It follows that the more consequential changes in consumer demand do not simply involve smooth, continuous marginal changes in response to relative prices and incomes but require discontinuous moves to achieve new consumption complexes.

Figures 1.1a, b, and c are sketches that illustrate this point. Figure 1.1a represents continuous, marginal change: Consumption rises (measured in consumption bundles of increasing quantity and quality; hence the vertical axis is labeled "lifestyle") monotonically with household income (measured on the horizontal axis). Material culture is strongly correlated with income level. It evolves marginally and continuously, following some predictable hierarchy of utility. Figure 1.1b preserves continuous, marginal change but introduces the notion that consumer choice increases as incomes rise and that consumers will differentiate themselves – that they will purchase social distinction.[84] With a given income, some will become "modernizers" while other consciously "traditionalize" their consumption patterns. Others will differentiate themselves along urban – rural or cosmopolitan – provincial continua. This process of distinction seeking together with the variable consumer efficiency of households will cause consumers with the same income to distribute themselves among a range of "tastes" while consumers with differing incomes may seek to mimic a specific style of life. If income alone determines one's material culture in Figure 1.1a, income and taste combine to determine one's position in Figure 1.1b.

Finally, Figure 1.1c illustrates a material world where consumption does not change only marginally and continuously but often takes a discontinuous form, requiring leaps to new consumption clusters. Each cluster

---

[82] Davide Gualerzi, "Economic Change, Choice and Innovation in Consumption," in Bianchi, ed., *The Active Consumer*, p. 56.

[83] *Lifestyle* is not a clearly defined term, but it is used here to signify the material embodiment of a sense of identity. "Lifestyle is both a result and a guiding star of the pursuit of identity and of the invention of consumption practices within an evolving system of commodities." Gualerzi, "Economic Change, Choice, and Innovation in Consumption," p. 55. See also Peter E. Earl, *Lifestyle Economics* (New York: St. Martin's Press, 1986).

[84] Thera Wijsenbeek-Olthuis describes the process of taste differentiation in eighteenth-century Delft. *Achter de gevels van Delft. Bezit en bestaan van rijk en arm in een periode van achteruitgang (1700–1800)* (Hilversum: Verloren, 1987). See also Anton Schuurman, *Materiele cultuur en levensstijl* (Wageningen: A. A. G. Bijdragen 30, 1989).

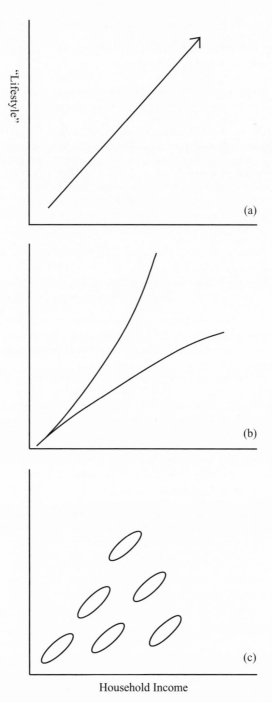

FIGURE 1.1a, b, c. Three models of the relationship between household income and consumer choice.

constitutes a kind of equilibrium: a pool of local attraction, in which consumption elements reinforce one another and coexist with the productive activities of the household. Movement *within* the cluster is continuous, as in Figures 1.1a and 1.1b, but movement *between* clusters is a different matter. One does not drift into a new cluster by inadvertence; the change requires an element of strategy, typically effected at the household level.

Ordinarily, consumer preferences are stable, in the sense that the tastes of individuals do not vary randomly, impulsively, or wantonly. Consumption remains within a cluster according to household incomes and relative prices. Of course, individuals can differ in their tastes in inexplicable ways. That is, they can differ in ways that may not be worth explaining, hence the economists' affection for the Latin aphorism *de gustibus non est disputandum*.[85] There is no point arguing about tastes. This, as we have noted, is what led Pareto and economists in general to divert their gaze from anything standing behind the "naked fact" of consumption. But there *are* changes in preferences that, as Albert Hirschman put it, are "non-wanton." These are changes about which we *do* argue – with others and with ourselves. These are tastes that turn into values that express our identity.[86] And it is values (when one asks "How should we live?") that are at stake when the discrete moves illustrated in Figure 1.1c are contemplated.

To summarize the argument thus far, individuals consume primarily in the context of households, and households, much like firms that combine inputs to produce goods according to a production function, combine purchased goods and household labor to produce the ultimately consumed Z-commodities according to available consumption technologies. How do households decide what their members will consume? Unlike firms, no profit motive guides and evaluates this process, but this does not mean that consumer behavior is unfathomable and arbitrary. Nor does it mean it is wholly determined by forces external to the household or to the economy as a whole. Consumer experience creates "consumption capital," and this, in turn, is influenced by household decisions, for household specialization in production gives access to enhanced choice in consumption. Decisions to alter household productive activities can be responses to new market

[85] Gary Becker and George Stigler, "De Gustibus non est Disputandum," *American Economic Review* 67 (1977): 76–90.

[86] Albert Hirschman, *Rival Views of Market Society and Other Recent Essays* (New York: Viking, 1986), p. 145; James, *Consumption and Development*, p. 1.

opportunities, but they can also respond to the new aspirations of the "active searching consumer" introduced above, whose acts of discovery become consequential when discrete elements of consumption, which, taken individually, may be no more than foolish mimicry or a routine response to transitory market phenomena, are codified into consumption clusters to achieve a reformulation of lifestyle.

Appendix: Five Consumer Revolutions

For Renaissance origins, see Lisa Jardine, *Worldly Goods. A New History of the Renaissance* (London: Macmillan, 1996); Evelyn Welsh, *Shopping in the Renaissance* (New Haven, Conn.: Yale University Press, 2005); Chandra Mukerji, *From Graven Images. Patterns of Modern Materialism* (New York: Columbia University Press, 1983). Mukerji locates the beginning of "hedonistic consumerism" in the fifteenth and sixteenth centuries. "[It] developed as an artifact of expanding trade when the meaning and value of goods became problematic with the arrival of new goods in European markets" (p. 256). She also emphasizes the role of print culture in shaping a broad, international pattern of taste that could support large-scale production (pp. 77–8).

The "era of the Baroque" (sixteenth to eighteenth centuries) is the preferred point of origin for consumer society in the work of Roman Sandgruber: *Die Anfänge der Konsumgesellschaft* (Vienna: Verlag für Geschichte und Politik, 1982); "Leben und Lebensstandard im Zeitalter des Barock – Quellen und Ergebnisse," in Othmar Pickl and Helmuth Feigl, eds., *Methoden und Probleme der Alltagsforschung im Zeitalter des Barock* (Vienna, Österriechischen Akademie der Wissenschaften, 1992), pp. 171–89. Sandgruber concludes: "Die Konsumgessellschaft beginnt im Barockzeitalter. Dass die Konsumgewohnheiten wie die gesamte Alltagskultur und Zivilsation vom 16. bis zum 18. Jahrhundert so sehr in Bewegung geraten waren, ist insgesamt auf eine Gesellschaftsordnung zurückzuführen, in der consumptive Schichten wie nie zuvor und nach her den Ton angaben und im dauernden Drang der höflischen Gesellschaft nach ständischer Abgrenzung immer neue Zivilisationsnormen und formen des demonstrativen Konsums kreieren mussten. Die Technik der Konsumption hat sich seit dem Barock nicht mehr wesentlich geändert: Was sich in der Industrialiserung änderte, war vornehmlich die Technik der Produktion" (p. 187).

For eighteenth-century origins, see Neil McKendrick, John Brewer, and J. H. Plumb, *The Birth of a Consumer Society. The Commercialization of Eighteenth-Century England* (Bloomington: Indiana University Press, 1982); Colin Campbell, *The Romantic Ethic and the Spirit of Modern Consumerism* (Oxford: Basil Blackwell, 1987); Carole Shammas, *The Pre-Industrial Consumer in England and America* (Oxford: Oxford University Press, 1990); T. H. Breen, *The Marketplace of Revolution. How Consumer Politics Shaped American Independence* (Oxford: Oxford University Press, 2004); Daniel Roche, *A History of Everyday Things. The Birth of Consumption in France, 1600–1800* (Cambridge: Cambridge University Press, 2000); Maxine Berg, *Luxury and Pleasure in Eighteenth-Century Britain* (Oxford: Oxford University Press, 2005).

For late–nineteenth and early–twentieth-century origins, see Michael Miller, *The Bon Marché. Bourgeois Culture and the Department Store, 1869–1920* (Princeton, N.J.: Princeton University Press, 1981); Rosalind Williams, *Dream Worlds. Mass Consumption in Late Nineteenth Century France* (Berkeley and Los Angeles: University of California Press, 1982); John Benson, *The Rise of Consumer Society in Britain, 1880–1980* (New York: Longman, 1994); Richard Wightman Fox and Jackson Lears, eds., *The Culture of Consumption. Critical Essays in American History, 1880–1980* (New York: Pantheon Books, 1983); Daniel Horowitz, *The Morality of Spending. Attitudes Toward the Consumer Society in America, 1875–1940* (Baltimore: The Johns Hopkins University Press, 1985). Fox states that "the 1920s and 1930s were the critical decades in the consolidation of modern American consumer society" (p. 103), while Lears views consumerism as a force released by the evolution of Protestantism into a secularized "flaccid creed, without force or bite or moral weight." Horowitz asserts that consumer society emerged as the religious, ethical and communal values and institutions (of traditional society) that restrained individualism and materialism eroded at the end of the nineteenth century, and "a shift started from self-control to self-realization, from the work of the producer, based on the values of self-denial and achievement, to a consumer culture that emphasized immediate satisfaction and the fulfillment of the self through gratification and indulgence" (pp. xxi, xxvii).

For twentieth-century origins, see S. Strasser, C. McGovern, and M. Judt, eds., *Getting and Spending. European and American Consumer Societies in the Twentieth Century* (Cambridge: Cambridge University Press, 1998); Lizbeth Cohen, "Citizens and Consumers in the United States in the Century of Mass Consumption," in Martin Daunton and Matthew Hilton, eds., *The Politics of Consumption* (Oxford and New York: Berg, 2001), pp. 203–21; Gary Cross, *Time and Money. The Making of Consumer Culture* (London: Routledge, 1993); Roland Marchand,

Advertising the American Dream. Making Way for Modernity, 1920–1940 (Berkeley: University of California Press, 1985).

Of particular importance to twentieth-century studies of consumer society are works of the Frankfurt School of critical theory. See Jurgen Habermas, "Konsumkritik," *Frankfurter Hefte* 12 (1957): 641–5; Max Horkheimer and Theodor Adorno, *Dialectic of Enlightenment* ([1944] London: Allen Lane, 1973), esp. "The Culture Industry. Enlightenment as Mass Deception," pp. 120–67; Herbert Marcuse, *One-Dimensional Man* (Boston: Beacon Press, 1964); Herbert Marcuse, *Eros and Civilization. A Philosophical Inquiry into Freud* ([1955] New York: Vintage Books, 1962). For an introduction to this literature, see Martin Jay, *The Dialectical Imagination. A History of the Frankfurt School and the Institute of Social Research, 1923–1950* (Boston: Little, Brown and Co., 1973). These thinkers saw consumer society as the product of alienation, a condition rendering individuals incapable of distinguishing use-value from exchange-value, objective needs from subjective wants.

2

The Origins of the Industrious Revolution

I move now from a theoretical account of how consumer demand can change to a brief and schematic historical account of how an industrious revolution could emerge from a society in which most manifestations of consumer demand had long been socially restricted and morally suspect.

From Prodigality and Profusion to a Consumer Society

The leisure-rich society. The ideal of most Western societies from Greek republican ideology to the aristocratic cultures of the early modern era was to have abundant leisure. Leisure is itself a tricky concept with at least three distinct dimensions: (1) "consumption time" – the time needed to actually use the goods and services we have acquired; (2) "cultural time" – the time devoted to the cultivation of mind and spirit, and to governance and charity; (3) "free time" – passive idleness, which, to the extent that it achieves the physical recuperation necessary for active labor, is not properly leisure at all.[1] Modern leisure is very much focused on the first dimension, "consumption time," but this was not the case in the leisure-rich societies of the past. In the terms of the household consumption model (introduced in Chapter 1), the desired Z-commodities of a leisure-rich society were achieved with relatively few goods (x) and much time, the time being chiefly "cultural time." The ideal was to be freed from manual work, a prerequisite for the autonomy of action that allowed one to pursue the cultivation of virtue. The problem with this ideal was that it always required the subordination of large classes of people – slaves, serfs, and nearly all women (categories of persons deemed incapable of benefiting from cultural time) – in order to support the leisure of the

[1] Linder, *The Harried Leisure Class.*

40

few.[2] These subordinated groups may also have had substantial leisure, but this was a product not of prosperity but of the absence of incentive in a coercive economy. Adam Smith's observation that "It is better, says the proverb, to play for nothing, than work for nothing" captures well the dilemma faced by workers in such societies, as did the *bon mot* of Europe's former socialist societies that "they pretend to pay us, and we pretend to work."[3]

Could the leisure-rich but oppressive societies of the past have been modernized in such a way that, as workers became more productive, society could have transformed itself from one supporting an elite leisure class to one capable of creating the conditions in which everyone could become at least a part-time Greek philosopher – or a worker-citizen rather than a worker-consumer? This, in a nutshell, is the question that haunts the cultural critics of the consumer societies that developed in the twentieth century. How is it that workers appear to prefer more money (and, hence, more labor) to more free time, and more consumption time to more cultural time?

The Frankfurt School of social critics, viewing with jaundiced eyes a triumphant post–World War II American capitalism and the materialist frenzy of western Europe's reconstruction, theorized that the meaningless work of industrial capitalism led to alienation, a condition that rendered the masses incapable of distinguishing use value from exchange value, objective needs from subjective wants. The corporate mass-production economy exploited this weakness to satisfy its own need for a mass-consumption society. In this environment, advertising sped the creation of what Max Weber had feared, the *Genussmensch ohne Herz* (heartless hedonist) – what Herbert Marcuse, a member of the Frankfurt School, famously labeled the "one-dimensional man." The alienated worker, once wrenched by capitalism from a traditional culture, loses all self-control and develops a voracious appetite for goods and an insatiable need for fantasy, distraction, and ostentatious display.

Perhaps even more broadly influential than the critical theory of the Frankfurt School was the political economy of John Kenneth Galbraith, whose *Affluent Society* of 1958 diagnosed American society as one that overemphasized the production of private consumption, thereby leading

---

[2] J. G. A. Pocock, "The Mobility of Property and the Rise of Eighteenth-Century Sociology," in Ibid., *Virtue, Commerce and Society* (Cambridge: Cambridge University Press, 1985), pp. 103–25.

[3] Adam Smith, *The Wealth of Nations*, Book II, Ch. III, p. 356.

to too little spending on public goods and services and too little leisure.[4] Increased affluence, Galbraith reasoned, should be reducing the appeal of ever more private consumption (assuming a declining marginal utility of consumption). Galbraith, in effect, proclaimed the United States of 1958 to have reached the point predicted for twenty-first-century Britain by John Maynard Keynes in his 1930 essay "Economic Possibilities for Our Grandchildren." In that essay Keynes looked a century into the future, when, he reasoned, an average rate of growth of 2.0 percent per annum will have generated an eight-fold increase in real per capita income. Such a fabulous increase in material prosperity would lead people to refocus their efforts to non-economic pursuits, to more leisure, less stress, and less competitiveness.[5] Yet, in Galbraith's United States there was no sign of this trend; to the contrary, consumer wants seemed to be growing at least as fast as the means to satisfy them. Galbraith – as many others before and after him – was confident he knew the identity of the culprit responsible for subverting the natural tendency toward satiation: advertising in the service of capitalist producers.

Whether the appeal is to the alienated *Genussmench*, or to the manipulative powers of advertising, these critiques see modern consumer behavior as historically aberrant and destructive of personality and culture alike. Only a century ago, according to Juliet Schor, a healthy demand for leisure time sustained a vibrant public culture; today too much work has atrophied our "leisure skills" and all we can imagine is more work and more consumption. Schor calls for government intervention to change the direction of society – to achieve a breakout from "capitalism's squirrel cage" – by providing "affordable, non-commodity-related leisure activities."[6] Even in 1930, Keynes worried that few of his contemporaries had sufficiently cultivated the art of life to know how to make effective use of the coming abundance of leisure. Today the problem of chronic consumption – unsustainable, unedifying, unsatisfying consumption – appears hopeless.

---

[4] John Kenneth Galbraith, *The Affluent Society* (Boston: Houghton Mifflin, 1958).

[5] John Maynard Keynes, "Economic Possibilities for Our Grandchildren," in *Essays in Persuasion* ([1931] New York: W. W. Norton, 1961), pp. 358–73. With the economic problem (scarcity) no longer a dominant force in society, Keynes predicted, economists would cease to be particularly important. Their work "should be a matter for specialists – like dentistry" (p. 373).

[6] Juliet Schor, *The Overworked American* (New York: Basic Books, 1992). Another call to action is found in Gary Cross, *Time and Money. The Making of Consumer Culture* (London: Routledge, 1993).

The industrious revolution concept holds that the basic premises of these jeremiads are flawed. First, the fatal turn away from a leisure-based society (leisure in the classical sense) began earlier, in the seventeenth century. By the time the Frankfurt School and the disillusioned intellectuals of the late twentieth century fixed their horrified gazes on the consumer choices of ordinary people, the die had long since been cast. Man as a "desiring subject" whose subjectivity is shaped by "'desire' as a fundamental aspect of the self" is not a product of modern industrial capitalism; his origins are to be found earlier, as I shall seek to demonstrate.[7] Second, there is a basic contradiction between the goal of universal cultural leisure and a highly productive economy. The leisure-rich society, what Plato described as the "simple society," was founded upon the autonomy of the human personality, and the achievement of this condition required substantial economic autarky.[8] The price of autarky is low productivity, and, hence, a subordinate population to provide the few with the leisure to cultivate a reasoning, autonomous intellect. The alternative is to secure a higher level of economic well-being via specialization and the division of labor. But any such move – essential to greater human productivity – simultaneously undermines the autonomous, unalienated personality in favor of something new. This concession, or tradeoff, is not a trivial one – it goes to the heart of the classical republican concept of the free man of virtue.[9] So, a big question looms: Could this "something new," this replacement of the unalienated free man of virtue, possibly be something better? Was the turn to consumer society lamented by cultural critics not only a much earlier achievement than they realize, but not even a lamentable one?

---

[7] For a sociological critique of the "desiring subject" as a product of the "needs" of modern capitalism, see John Levi Martin, "The Myth of the Consumption-Oriented Economy and the Rise of the Desiring Subject," *Theory and Society* 28 (1999): 425.

[8] Ronald Fletcher, *The Shaking of the Foundations. Family and Society* (London: Routledge, 1988), pp. 204–5.

[9] I write "free *man* of virtue" because republican thought located the weakness of human beings in their desires – the envy, vanity, and lust that led to irrational actions. It associated these weaknesses especially with women, youth, slaves, and servants. Restricting the freedoms of such people in the support of autonomous males simultaneously solved the economic problem of securing republican autonomy for those possessing reason and the moral problem of checking the desires of weak humanity for goods they do not need. Discussion of Aristotelian republican thought as they apply to luxury are available in John Sekora, *Luxury. The Concept in Western Thought, Eden to Smollet* (Baltimore: Johns Hopkins University Press, 1977); J. G. A. Pocock, *The Machiavellian Moment. Florentine Political Thought and the Atlantic Republican Tradition* (Princeton, N.J.: Princeton University Press, 1975).

Old luxury and new luxury. To be sure, the leisure-rich society had known consumerism; they called it "luxury." When desires brushed aside ideals and appetites displaced sentiments, the "simple society" of Plato was transformed into the "inflamed society."[10] The resulting consumption, extravagant and unrestrained, was associated in Christian culture with nearly all of the seven deadly sins. The material goods that embodied high culture and refinement and signified the right to rule in aristocratic societies could easily be diverted to personal excess, not only submerging a healthy personality in debauchery but also undermining the stability of society as a whole. Thomas Mun expressed his concern for the fate of a luxury-prone Restoration England as follows:[11]

The general leprosie of our piping, potting, feasting, fashion, and the mis-spending of our time in idleness and pleasure...hath made us effeminate in our bodies, weak in our knowledge, poor in our treasure, declined in our valour, unfortunate in our enterprises, and condemned by our enemies.

This critique of luxury, drawing upon both the Christian and Classical traditions, was as durable as it was venerable, and it continued to dominate Western thought into the eighteenth century. Indeed, in a secularized form, it continues to influence us to the present day. Simply put, luxury is the enemy of virtue.

In the course of the seventeenth century a New Luxury emerged in a sufficiently developed form to present an alternative to the Old Luxury that had lived in symbiotic tension with the leisure-rich society for many centuries. Rather than being defined by royal courts, the New Luxury was generated by urban society. Rather than presenting a coherent style and hegemonic cultural message, it consisted of heterogeneous elements. The Old Luxury, striving for grandeur or exquisite refinement, could be emulated only by distinctly inferior adaptations. The New Luxury, striving more for comfort and pleasure, lent itself to multiplication and diffusion. Sensuality and the indulgence of one's natural instincts characterized the Old Luxury, making it the prerogative of elites sufficiently privileged to claim exemption from the moral strictures to which others remained subject.

In contrast to all this, the concept of "taste" adhered to the New Luxury, and "taste represented a refinement of sensibility...[which] was

---

[10] Fletcher, *Shaking of the Foundations*, pp. 204–5.
[11] Thomas Mun, *England's Treasure by Forraign Trade or the Balance of Our Forraign Trade in the Rule of our Treasure* (London: n.p., 1664), pp. 180–1.

something for which essentially everyone had the capacity. . . . It was the-oretically possible for anyone, regardless of social standing, to display taste." Taste does not eschew luxury but tames it, requiring that luxury be aesthetically restrained. "The rules of taste," as Woodruff Smith puts it, "provide a set of limits to exuberance and sensuality."[12]

Where the Old Luxury served primarily as a marker, a means of discrim-inating among people, times, and places, the New Luxury served more to communicate cultural meaning, permitting reciprocal relations – a kind of sociability – among participants in consumption. A consumer soci-ety characterized by the breeding and practice that shapes taste (Becker's accumulation of consumption capital) supplied the basis for a sociable society, which, in turn, allowed for open, civilized communication among citizens. Far from being the enemy of virtue, such consumption – the New Luxury – could claim to establish the very foundation of virtue in society.

Finally, while the Old Luxury could be viewed only as a drain on the economy and a threat to the economic well-being of those who indulged in it, the New Luxury paired what David Hume called a "refinement in the gratification of the senses" with incentives to the expansion of commerce:

> If we consult history, we shall find that in most nations foreign trade has preceded any refinement in home manufactures, and given birth to domestic luxury. . . . Thus men become acquainted with the *pleasures* of luxury, and the *profits* of commerce; and their *delicacy* and *industry* being once awakened, carry them on to further improvements in every branch of domestic as well as foreign trade; and this per-haps is the chief advantage which arises from a commerce with strangers.[13]

Luxury consumption and economic development could now be paired rather than set against each other. Thus, within two or three generations beginning in the late seventeenth century, luxury was transformed, first in material reality and then in theory, as its new forms came to be understood as the very foundation of virtue rather than as virtue's mortal enemy.[14]

---

[12] Smith, *Consumption*, pp. 81–2.

[13] David Hume, *Essays, Moral, Political and Literary* ([1752] London: Longmans, 1989), Part II. "Of Commerce," pp. 259–75; "Of Refinement in the Arts," pp. 275–89; quota-tion, p. 270.

[14] Perhaps the final stage of the diffusion of this insight is found in the second edition of T. R. Malthus's *Essay on the Principles of Population* (London, 1803). Only then, in an extensive revision of his "First Essay" of 1798, does he come to link "moral restraint" explicitly with the beneficent influences of the desire to consume. "[D]esires for comfort and convenience were crucial to the 'moral restraint' that allowed sufficient control over the principle of population to maintain happiness in a society: 'throughout a very large class of people [in Britain], a decided taste for the conveniences and comforts of life, a strong desire of bettering their condition, that master-spring of public prosperity, and, in

Emulation versus innovation. Luxury is sometimes called "timeless," calling to mind the stable social and political hierarchies at whose pinnacles rarified elites were the exclusive practitioners of luxury consumption. When luxury is given motion, it comes to be governed by fashion. This motion is widely held to be the product of emulative behavior. Georg Simmel's theory of fashion starts by assuming humanity's universally imitative character. The combination of inequality and social mobility introduced by capitalist society provokes groups excluded from the elite to aspire to appropriate a part of their status by emulating elite material culture. This emulation forces the elites to continuous innovation in order to rejuvenate the capacity of their material goods to serve as public symbols of status and to maintain social distinctions. Thus does fashion become an integral part of modern society: "once set in motion the windmill of fashion rolls as if it were self-activating."[15]

There are defenses against emulative behavior. It can be outlawed – and was, repeatedly – by sumptuary legislation, and it can be made difficult and costly by embracing designs and materials that do not lend themselves to cheap imitation. Indeed, the Old Luxury sought these protections assiduously.[16] But the New Luxury, as we have noted, possessed the intrinsic capacity to be adapted to the circumstances of progressively larger, and lower, social circles. By establishing more broadly shared material cultures (homogenization), and by developing markets for the distribution of fashions (commercialization), the New Luxury aided the diffusion of new goods. But, whether luxury is old or new, a fundamental problem remains: Where do new consumer aspirations come from? Do they originate with the elites – the only creative consumers – and diffuse via emulation to lower social strata, or do consumption practices emerge from

---

consequence, a most laudable spirit of industry and foresight, are observed to prevail.'" This has ever since been a foundation of theories of the fertility transition. Quoted in John Crowley, "From Luxury to Comfort and Back Again. Landscape Architecture and the Cottage in Britain and America," in Berg and Eger, eds., *Luxury of the Eighteenth Century,* p. 146.

[15] Georg Simmel, "Fashion," *International Quarterly* 10 (1904): 130–55. Simmel's and other theories of emulation and fashion are discussed in Alan Hunt, *Governance of the Consuming Passions. A History of Sumptuary Law* (New York: St. Martin's Press, 1996). Quotation from Hunt, p. 49.

[16] Hunt, *Governance of the Consuming Passions.* Hunt surveys the enactment of sumptuary laws throughout Europe, noting a sixteenth-century peak in legislation. By 1604, England repeals its sumptuary laws, while the Netherlands had never had them. Other countries continue, or even intensify, their efforts to control the inappropriate diffusion of fashion until the eighteenth century when such laws everywhere fell into abeyance.

the self-motivated initiatives of multiple social groups, each with its own objectives?

The concept of emulation is fundamental to most historical writings on consumer revolutions. At its heart is the belief that creative consumers are confined to an elite stratum. For society at large the issue is how and why the lower strata emulate elite example.

The emulation argument has several variants. One focuses on the influence of royal and princely courts, whose development in the early modern era gave them the prestige to lead a "civilizing offensive." Within court circles a new courteous, self-governing behavior sought to channel the energies of courtiers toward cultivating the arts and sciences, thereby redirecting consumption from people (that is, an ongoing supply of services providing sensuous luxury and offering immediate gratification) toward things (that is, cultural artifacts promising durable, continuing satisfaction). Norbert Elias described this civilizing offensive as a phenomenon far broader in its reach than material culture alone, but among the functions of court society he emphasized was its role as an instructor of the "wants of the mind" – as the instructor of tastes.[17]

While Elias leaves the specific agents of instruction unclear, the earlier writings of Werner Sombart, in *Luxury and Capitalism*, identified the "rule of women" in elite environments as the active agents of luxury consumption.[18] Sombart, of course, was not the first to think along these lines. Edward Hundert has observed that:

The association of luxury with women's inconstancy and the social power of female desire was ancient. It served most potently as a standard resource in classical republican as well as Augustinian-inspired accounts of political decline, where "effeminacy" and the luxury it entailed were standardly considered integral features of moral and political corruption.[19]

---

[17] Norbert Elias, *The Civilizing Process* (Oxford: Basil Blackwell, 1978); Elias, *The Court Society* (Oxford: Basil Blackwell, 1983).

[18] Werner Sombart, *Luxury and Capitalism* ([1913] Ann Arbor: University of Michigan Press, 1967). Sombart's argument may have been misogynist, but it was not without subtlety. Capitalism, he argued, found its driving force not among the women of Europe's urban bourgeois circles but among the mistresses tempting aristocratic men into the reckless pursuit of sensuous pleasure. What brought ruin to an old class brought new opportunities to the capitalist strata.

[19] Edward Hundert, *The Enlightenment's Fable. Bernard Mandeville and the Discovery of Society* (Cambridge: Cambridge University Press, 1994). This theme is elaborated in Hanna Pitkin, *Fortune Is a Woman. Gender and Politics in the Thought of Niccolo Machiavelli* (Berkeley: University of California Press, 1984).

By the eighteenth century, however, commentators came to place women's prideful desire to consume in a different, somewhat more positive light. Bernard Mandeville, ever eager to shock his readers, asserted that British prosperity itself, or, as he put it, "all the worldly Interest of the Nation" hinged on "the Deceit and vile Strategems of Women. . . . The number of hands employ'd to gratify the Fickleness and Luxury of Women," is nothing short of "prodigious." Moreover, women "could never have come at [their capacity to purchase luxury goods] by any other means, than pinching their families, Marketting, and other ways of cheating and pilfering from their Husbands."[20] The compliment to women embedded in these rather sour comments is, perhaps, not evident to all modern readers. But, Mandeville's intention in all this is to illustrate his thesis that societal felicity finds its foundation in individual vice.

Later in the century, Montesquieu, in the *Persian Letters*, elaborated on the key role of women as intermediaries between the old nobility and new commercial elites. As arbiters of polite society they advanced the civilizing process, the chief mechanism being the competition among men for their favors. Satisfying their "frivolous and refined taste... [in Montesquieu's view] incited a general passion to work, invention and industry."[21] These speculations are of interest primarily for their effort to find a *primum mobile* to account for what contemporaries sensed to be a major expansion of luxury consumption. They do not pretend to account for changes below a rarified sector of society, so that one need not reject them out of hand to still regard them as inadequate to the task of accounting for the larger phenomenon of consumer demand as a whole.

Another explanation for the new power of emulation in society focuses on urban life in the early modern era, when cities, especially capital cities, grew to very large sizes. The contemplation of social life in the metropolis moved Montesquieu to propose a law: "Luxury is... proportionate to the size of towns and above all of the capital...." Emulating one's

---

[20] Bernard Mandeville, *The Fable of the Bees* ([1723] London: Wishart & Company, 1934), I, 356; Remark T, pp. 175–6. Mandeville went on, as though anticipating an opportunity to debate Max Weber's Protestant Ethic thesis, to declare "that the Reformation has scarce been more Instrumental in rend'ring the Kingdoms and States that have embraced it, flourishing beyond other Nations, than the silly and capricious Invention of Hoop'd and Quilted Petticoats" (pp. 219–20). Mandeville insisted on seeing society as it is rather than as theorists and theologians imagined it should be. However, he felt compelled to preface this deflation of the Reformation's beneficent influences by first proclaiming: "I protest against Popery as much as ever Luther and Calvin did, or Queen Elizabeth herself."

[21] Tjitske Akkerman, *Women's Vices, Public Benefits. Women and Commerce in the French Enlightenment* (Amsterdam: Het Spinhuis, 1992), p. 48.

social superiors and cultivating a culture of appearances more generally, he argued, is encouraged in populous cities, because "If their number is so great that most are unknown to one another, the desire to distinguish oneself redoubles because there is more expectation of succeeding." This led Montesquieu, ever the law giver, to declare another social regularity: "The more men there are together, the more vain they are, and the more they feel arise within them the desire to call attention to themselves by small things."[22]

Obviously no advantage can be exploited by anonymity in a society that is highly segmented, nor would a culture of appearances be expected to succeed in a society in which information is openly available and nearly costless, and advancement is meritocratic. In this context, an interesting feature of many early modern European societies is that they held something of an intermediate position in these two respects. Social segmentation was not so complete as to preclude the possibility of social mobility. On the other hand, society was far from meritocratic, or market based. Many of the most desirable goods were "socially-provided private goods" – honors, marriage alliances, offices, and the like. It is precisely such "goods" that are allocated not through the market but rather through social interaction where information is incomplete.

Societies with an influential court life that were also in the process of becoming more heavily urbanized offered powerful incentives to engage in demonstrative consumption, driven by emulation, in order to signal information (false information in many cases) designed to secure these private goods.[23] Their enlarged public spheres invited the cultivation of what came to be known as *politesse*: refined and elegant behavior, a stylish presentation of self that was pleasing to others and that, indeed, could seem to define civilized behavior itself. To its critics, *politesse* was at heart a cynical emulation that theatricized the public sphere via an exaggerated attention to outward appearance, a dependence on the whims of fashion, and hypocrisy in human communications.[24]

---

[22] Montesquieu, Baron du, *The Spirit of the Laws* ([1748] New York: Hafner Publishing, 1949), Vol. I, pp. 95, 97.

[23] Giacoma Corneo and Oliver Jeanne, "Segmented Communication and Fashionable Behavior," *Journal of Economic Behavior and Organization* 39 (1999): 371–85; "Conformism, Snobbism, and Conspicuous Consumption," *Journal of Public Economics* 66 (1997): 55–71; "Demonstrative Consumption, Rivalry and Development" (unpublished paper, Jena University Workshop on "Escaping Satiation," 11–13 Dec. 1997).

[24] This characterization of *politesse* is drawn from Wyger R. E. Velgema, "Ancient and Modern Virtue Compared. De Beaufort and Van Effen on Republican Citizenship," *Eighteenth-Century Studies* 30 (1997): 437–8.

Was emulation something peculiar to monarchical societies, or to "half-modernized" social settings? The Dutch "spectatorial" writer Justus van Effen offered an implicitly affirmative answer to this question when, in a series of essays written in the 1730s, he condemned French *politesse* for all the reasons just mentioned and contrasted it with Dutch *beschaafdheid* (politeness). Commercial societies, and especially the Dutch Republic, did not force consumers to focus obsessively on outward impressions and to engage in emulative behavior. Rather, they encouraged an interior process of taste development leading to a politeness that was reasonable, virtuous, and sociable. The republican consumer "had to distrust both the authority of tradition and the whims of fashion. He could learn to do so by constantly sharpening his reason through sociability."[25]

Van Effen's portrait of the commercial/republican consumer as cultivating preferences through a learning process rather than following the cues of elite practice is of particular interest because it not only distinguishes Dutch politeness from French *politesse* but also sets the Republic (as van Effen saw it) apart from England as it has been interpreted by many modern historians. Margaret Hunt asserts that emulation is "the central explanatory concept employed by eighteenth-century social historians in the post-war period, at least where commercial people are concerned."[26] Perhaps the most influential exponent of the centrality of emulation in British social history is Harold Perkins, who argues that this commercializing society did not yet possess an authentic commercial culture. Consequently, its "trading people" could formulate no other goal than to leave their origins behind and enter the aristocracy. It follows, according to Perkins, that emulation should be the "prime mover" in eighteenth-century English social and economic life.[27]

Not everyone follows Perkins in his assertion of the dominance of aristocracy in English life, but this does not necessarily diminish the emphasis placed on emulation, for there are yet other features of English society that are thought to have turned emulation into a powerful force for a consumer-led economic development. The argument is made most fully and most forcefully by Neil McKendrick. In his view, "the market for mass

---

[25] Ibid., pp. 437–48.

[26] Margaret Hunt, *The Middling Sort. Commerce, Gender, and the Family in England, 1680–1780* (Berkeley: University of California Press, 1996), p. 2.

[27] Harold Perkins, *The Origins of Modern English Society* (London: Routledge & Kegan Paul, 1969). Perkins did not mince words: "Consumer demand was the ultimate economic key to the Industrial Revolution..." (p. 91). "If consumer demand, then, was the key to the Industrial Revolution, social emulation was the key to consumer demand" (p. 96).

consumer goods reached lower than [the middling groups], it reached as far as the skilled factory worker and the domestic servant class...," and this could occur because "English society provided an ideal breeding ground for those commercially intent on exploiting new consumer wants." What made England ideal in this respect? McKendrick identifies three things: the structure of English society, by which is meant "the social competition bred by its closely packed [status] layers"; the large size and the character of its capital city, which projected desirable lifestyles to the entire country; and, finally, setting these propitious conditions for emulative consumption in motion, as it were, the domestic servant class, a vast army of women who "acted as a very important channel of communication for transmitting the latest styles and spreading a desire for new commodities" from their employers to their own social milieux.[28] McKendrick acknowledges that these ingredients were not new to the eighteenth century, but he argues that they formed the combustible material of consumerism that became more plentiful and was set alight in the eighteenth century with the arrival of entrepreneurs who possessed the marketing talents to activate and enlarge emulative consumption.

McKendrick's emulation-based interpretation of consumer behavior brings together many of the set pieces of English social history to argue that the consumer revolution was a very English event. Yet, as we have seen, historians have fashioned emulation to suit the historiographical needs of central Europe (court culture) and France (*politesse*), as well as England (social mobility). Less national exclusivity may be needed to establish the proper place of emulative behavior in consumer behavior.

Another weakness of the concept resides in the assumption that consumer culture is a unitary phenomenon that spreads through society from top to bottom. In general, emulation-based arguments depend on the positing of a pre-existing society in which a refined consumer culture is restricted to a small, stable circle and is then let loose, like an accidentally released virus in a laboratory, to spread to new environments populated by urban parvenus and female servants, who transmit the virus by stages to the nether reaches of society, forever changing its behavior. Such a model denies agency to most of society and is almost wholly abstracted from the economic sphere. It has the earmarks of a *deus ex machina*. Even where it offers accurate descriptions of consumer behavior, it tends to beg the question of *why* people (appear to) emulate their betters.

[28] Neil McKendrick, "The Consumer Revolution in Eighteenth-Century England," in McKendrick, Brewer, and Plumb, eds., *Birth of a Consumer Society* (Bloomington: Indiana University Press, 1982), pp. 20–2.

The industrious revolution had more profound origins than emulation alone. The new consumer behavior required important changes in daily life – in how people lived and worked within their families – and this suggests that innovation rather than emulation will have been the more important agent. Innovation in this context can best be understood by linking fashion and taste not to a higher social order but to, for lack of a better word, modernity. The desire for new goods and new fashions is part of what Herbert Blumer called "a collective groping for the proximate future."[29] In short, social groups are not so much looking above as they are looking ahead.

The first innovative consumers? Can we turn to contemporary observers for clues about the form that consumer innovation could have taken in this period? It is a commonplace among economic historians that even perceptive contemporary observers did not have a very clear view of the productive changes of the Industrial Revolution as it unfolded before their very eyes.[30] The same cannot be said of the consumer changes of the industrious revolution. On the contrary, consumption was the object of a vast body of moral debate, philosophical speculation, and political–economic theorizing.

Where can we first observe this innovative consumer behavior? It would be foolish to suppose that this question has a precise and unique answer. But the seventeenth-century Dutch Republic certainly deserves consideration as a society in which new forms of material culture spread broadly through society and transformed the practice and experience of consumption. Here, for the first time on such a scale and on so enduring a basis, we find a society in which the potential to purchase luxuries and novelties extended well beyond a small, traditional elite and where the acquired goods served to fashion material cultures that cannot be understood simply in terms of emulation.

A substantial tranche of society was now in a position to exercise *choice*. Choice gives freedom, and freedom exposes one to moral dilemmas. In the Dutch Republic these dilemmas were faced by large numbers who

---

[29] Herbert Blumer, "Fashion. From Class Differentiation to Social Selection," *Sociological Quarterly* 10 (1969): 281.

[30] Douglass North, *Structure and Change in Economic History* (New York: W. W. Norton, 1981), pp. 160–2; Joel Mokyr, "Editor's Introduction," in Joel Mokyr, ed., *The British Industrial Revolution. An Economic Perspective* (Boulder, Colo.: Westview Press, 1998), pp. 1–127. There are also those who hold that the unfolding industrial progress of the time does not deserve the label "Industrial Revolution." To Rondo Cameron, it is a misnomer: Rondo Cameron, *A Concise Economic History of the World* (Oxford: Oxford University Press, 1989), pp. 163–5.

earlier, and in other societies still, had their consumer choices constrained by the heavy hands of scarcity and custom, and whose extravagances were channeled narrowly into well-choreographed displays of excessive eating and drinking.

Simon Schama, in his celebrated book *Embarrassment of Riches*, draws with evident relish on the venerable arguments about the moral pitfalls that surround luxury consumption in order to conjure a society caught on the horns of a dilemma: Its own singular virtues, producing economic prosperity, lead inexorably to the vices of luxury. In making his argument, Schama appeals repeatedly to the exhortations of Calvinist preachers[31] and relies heavily on paintings and other visual images evoking the ancient themes of the dangers of luxury.[32]

An ally in Schama's project is the view held by many historians of earlier generations that the Republic's decline after the 1670s was closely associated with, if not caused by, the onset of a cultural overripeness which

---

[31] Schama writes of the "hellfire" of opposition to luxury of the Calvinist clergy and asks, "For all its rant and cant, [did] the strictures of the Calvinist church against the corruption of money [go] unheeded, except for the occasional propitiatory gesture of philanthropy?" Simon Schama, *The Embarrassment of Riches* (New York: Knopf, 1985), p. 335.

[32] In view of the popular understanding that Calvinism imposes on its adherents an unusual austerity – a Puritanical abstemiousness – it may appear that any society shaped by Calvinist teachings would be an unlikely candidate for cutting-edge consumer behavior. Calvinists, just as the adherents of other Christian traditions, have, over the centuries, responded variously to specific innovations in material life. But the teachings of John Calvin himself offer little support for the common association of his teachings with self-denial. Calvin's views on the material world, which he did not address *in extenso*, did not really differ from those found more generally among sixteenth-century humanists. With Erasmus, and following Aristotle, he recommended the *via media* – moderation in the use of God's gifts – rather than abstinence. In his explication of the Lord's Prayer, where Christians petition God to "Give us this day our daily bread," Calvin wrote that the petition concerns not only "all things in general that our bodies have need to use" – that is, the basic necessities of food and clothing – "but also everything God foresees to be beneficial to us...." Later, in his discourse on Christian freedom, Calvin gives evidence that the range of goods "God foresees to be beneficial to us" might be quite broad: "Let every man live in his station, whether slenderly, or moderately, or plentifully, so that all may remember God nourishes them to live, not to luxuriate." Calvin did not counsel otherworldliness; rather, his concept of Christian freedom led him to recommend something requiring rather more in the way of individual decisions: station- or income-specific moderation in appropriating "everything God foresees to be beneficial to us." John Calvin, *Institutes of the Christian Religion* (Atlanta, 1973; 1536 edition), pp. 109–10, 246.

On this same theme, the Swiss reformer Zwingli preached against the Church's traditional bans on certain foods. He appealed to Scripture to pronounce such restrictions to be inconsistent with Christian freedom. Huldreich Zwingli, "Von Erkeisen und Freiheit der Speisen. 16 April 1522," in Emil Egli and Georg Finsler, eds., *Huldrich Zwinglis sämtliche Werke*, Vol 1. *Corpus reformatorum* (Berlin, 1904), pp. 74–136.

befell a decadent generation of Dutchmen accustomed to luxury and, therefore, lacking the noble character and fortitude of their forefathers. On their watch, French fashion overwhelms Calvinist simplicity, classicism pollutes the fresh spring of Dutch artistic genius, and prosperous burgher families succumb to the blandishments of aristocratic lifestyles.

These arguments, owing far more to the contemplation of the fall of Rome than to the reality of seventeenth-century Dutch society, were once uncritically embraced by historians eager for simple explanations of a difficult subject. The weakness of these explanations is their reliance on an old discourse that no longer applies to the reality of the new practice. Rather than succumb to the seductive vision of republican society in the grips of the Old Luxury, we should set this venerable but derivative imagery aside and attempt to see the new consumer culture actually being constructed by the innumerable choices of an enlarged population newly endowed with discretionary income. In discussing their choices, the old discourse remained influential for the simple reason that it long remained the only available vocabulary, but the reality of their behavior brought into being a distinctive material culture in which the luxuries were directed toward the home more than the body, and adorned the interior – of both home and body – more than the exterior. They tended to achieve comfort more than refinement.[33]

This is what most struck foreign visitors to the Republic. The world-traveling Englishman Peter Mundy, after making his oft-cited remarks about the abundant presence of paintings in even the houses of butchers and bakers, blacksmiths and cobblers, went on to observe in 1640:

Such is the generall Notion, enclination and delight that these Countrie Native[s] have to Paintings Allsoe their other Furniture and Ornaments off their dwellings very Costly and Curious, Full of pleasure and home contentment, as Ritche Cupboards, Cabinetts, etts., Imagery, porcelaine, Costly Fine cages with birds etts., all these commonly in any house off indifferent quality; wonderfull Nett and cleane, as well in their houses and Furniture, service, etts., within doores, as in their streetes.[34]

A broadly diffused domestic comfort also impressed the Papal Nuncio to Cologne, Pallavicino. His 1676 visit to Amsterdam came as the system of radial canals around the old medieval city was nearing completion. He noted that "only a nation that does not squander its wealth on clothes

---

[33] For a stimulating discussion of the origins of domesticity, see Witold Rybczynski, *Home. A Short History of an Idea* (New York: Viking Press, 1986), p. 77.

[34] R. C. Temple, ed., *The Travels of Peter Mundy in Europe and Asia, 1608–1667*, Vol. IV (1639–47) (Cambridge: Hakluyt Society, 1925), pp. 70–1.

or servants could have succeeded in doing all this with so little fuss."[35] "All this," of course, was the erection of many thousands of comfortable burgher homes, restrained by a 30- to 40-foot exterior frontage from blatantly advertising the occupants' wealth but endowed by a 190-foot depth with ample opportunity to achieve a new form of private domestic comfort.

Exotic luxuries from the four corners of the world found their way into these homes. They also contained costly products of high craftsmanship such as tapestries and furniture. These often came from the Southern Netherlands, where craft traditions of long standing were sustained by the patronage of local and Spanish courts.

What the cities of Holland themselves offered were New Luxuries. These products required real craft skills, to be sure, but the objective was not to fabricate something unique. New Luxuries were products capable of multiplication, or capable of being offered in a gradated range of qualities and prices. The canal houses, just as more humble abodes, were lined with Delft tiles of varying qualities, just as their kitchens and tables made use of the orientally inspired Delft faience.[36] Similarly, the canal houses were filled with the work of cabinetmakers' wardrobes and linen chests – and much else. Here again, the great pieces were the highest expression of a furniture tradition that came up from below, for even farmers had – more modest – versions of these same items.

Then we come to the paintings. Netherlandic art, as is well known, was reconstructed after the Reformation from an Old Luxury to a New Luxury as elite patronage gave way to a broad-based art market. By developing both product innovations (new themes in paintings) and process innovations (new techniques of painting), Dutch artists opened new markets, allowing by midcentury some 700 to 800 masters to be active simultaneously, producing over the course of the century many millions of paintings ranging in price from hundreds of guilders to the *dozijnwerk* – work by the dozen – that fetched a guilder or two at the fair. Indeed, if the possession of paintings in Delft can be generalized to all of Holland – the province – something like three million paintings must have hung on the walls of

---

[35] Cited in Johan Huizinga, *Dutch Civilization in the Seventeenth Century* ([1941] London: Collins, 1968), p. 62.

[36] In view of the great success of Dutch ceramics, it is instructive to contemplate the Dutch failure in developing a porcelain industry. No porcelain industry arose comparable to those of Meissen, Vienna, Copenhagen, Sèvres, or Worcester. The technical skills were not missing; rather, the missing element was the court associations essential to design and market what was, in essence, a new "Old Luxury."

Holland's houses by the 1660s, nearly all of them produced within that century.[37]

One could go on to discuss clock and instrument making, book publishing, popular luxuries like tobacco pipes, and decorative and utilitarian silverware. In contrast to the exotic extra-European objects, or the most refined material possessions from Brabant or farther afield in Europe, the new luxuries were usually produced in the Dutch cities. Some were imitations and adaptations of foreign luxuries, such as Delftware, responding to Chinese porcelain; some were cheaper versions of European luxuries, such as Delft and Gouda's tapestries, or Amsterdam and Utrecht's silk.

Craft production everywhere in Europe depended on specific skills that could be transferred successfully only by the migration of artisans. Thus, the Republic's new crafts and industries inevitably find their origin in diffusion from abroad. Still, in their new home they developed a particular form, shaped by the nature of Dutch demand – urban, *burgerlijk*, broad-based – and by the prevailing cultural imperatives.

These imperatives could be stamped with the label Calvinist, but it might be better to invoke the concept of "Confessionalization."[38] Calvinists, Lutherans, Catholics – all Christian denominations – were concerned in the era of the Dutch Golden Age to consolidate their projects of religious revitalization, to penetrate to the broad base of society with programs of education, institutionalization, and, of course, conversion of souls. While an awakened desire for God's grace should not be made one with a new desire for a more refined manner of living, or genteel grace, the *practice* by which the construction of both types of desire was cultivated interacted with each other. The inward religious project assumed material forms (church architecture, bibles, books, and, in Counter-Reformation

[37] Jan de Vries, "Art History," in de Vries and Freedberg, eds., *Art in History, History in Art*, pp. 249–82; Ad van der Woude, "The Volume and Value of Paintings in Holland at the Time of the Dutch Republic," in de Vries and Freedberg, eds., *Art in History, History in Art*, pp. 285–330. Seventeenth-century Dutch paintings were not only qualitatively excellent, they were also quantitatively overwhelming. The number of active, professional painters per capita was strikingly high both in comparison to earlier and later times in the Netherlands, but also in comparison to other European countries in any time period. Van der Woude estimated that the annual value of Dutch paintings in the seventeenth century equaled half the value of all cheese marketed annually in North Holland, the center of commercial cheese production (p. 302).

[38] On this concept, see Heinz Schilling, "Confessionalization in the Empire," in Heinz Schilling, ed., *Religion, Political Culture, and the Emergence of Early Modern Society* (Leiden: E. J. Brill, 1992), pp. 205–46; Philip S. Gorski, *The Disciplinary Revolution. Calvinism and the Rise of the State in Early Modern Europe* (Chicago: University of Chicago Press, 2003).

Catholicism, objects of veneration for the home) while the outward projection of more elevated or refined daily life depended on the development of a suitable material culture.[39]

The Confessionalizing projects left deep marks on the design of everyday articles, on accessible luxuries, on interior decoration, and on clothing. This movement was European and North American in scope rather than specifically Dutch, but it resonated with Holland's social and economic structures more fully and more creatively than elsewhere, which caused the output of Dutch ceramics, paintings, prints, maps, books, furniture, silver, glass, and the dyeing and printing of textiles to be seen as particularly well suited to the temper and purpose of the Confessional era.[40] The integrating rather than differentiating impact of these New Luxuries – their socializing rather than status-differentiating function – is revealed in the broader study of material culture. By the late seventeenth century the striking feature of Dutch material culture is its uniformity. The basic forms of expressing status and achieving comfort were remarkably similar between city and country, and between rich and poor. It was the cost and specific quality rather than the types of objects and their general form that differed.[41]

From the perspective of the outsider, Dutch society seemed to eschew luxury altogether, for the Old Luxury was thin on the ground and hidden from view. A New Luxury, one we might call modern, or proto-modern, was in fact taking shape, but it could not easily be "read" by the cultural

---

[39] These arguments are developed, with application to Puritan New England, in Mark A. Peterson, "Puritanism and Refinement in Early New England. Reflections on Communion Silver," *William and Mary Quarterly* 58 (2001): 307–46. In his discussion of the growing Puritan demand for silver communion vessels, Peterson takes pains to avoid conflating Puritanism and gentility, but concludes: "[I]f we understand Puritanism as a culture that replicated itself by cultivating in believers a demand for certain experiences, a demand that could only be satisfied (and then only partially and temporarily) through access to sophisticated cultural products, of which communion silver was one, then we can begin to see how Puritanism created patterns of thought and feeling that flowed as easily into the genteel forms of a culture of consumption as they did into the frugal and disciplined norms of the 'spirit of capitalism'" (pp. 343–4).

[40] For an argument that a new economy of accessible quality and comfort in the seventeenth and eighteenth centuries helped create the conditions for modern technological progress, see John U. Nef, *Cultural Foundations of Industrial Civilization* (Cambridge: Cambridge University Press, 1958). "With the help of a new artistic craftsmanship, a style of living spread through Europe that led all Europeans to want to share, at least to some extent, in that *douceur de vivre*, accompanied by high *standards* of virtue in actual living, which a very considerable few were coming to possess for the first time in history" (p. 138).

[41] Van Koolbergen, "De materiële cultuur van Weesp en Weesperkarspel," pp. 45–50; Jan de Vries, "Peasant demand patterns and economic development," pp. 234–6.

outsider. Nor did the Dutch themselves offer much interpretive assistance. Late–seventeenth-century Dutch Republican theory, about which more will be said below, initiated what would become important arguments in the rethinking of consumer behavior, but this did not lead immediately to a broad debate that sharpened self-understanding of the new reality. Perhaps the new commercial society was simply too self-evident, and the opponents with whom battle had to be waged were too weak: There was no landed political elite to rail against imported luxuries; no influential court from which to wrest the power to define fashion; no Episcopal hierarchy with the power to add bite to the Reformed Church's anti-luxury bark.

I have argued here that a New Luxury, and a new pattern of consumer behavior, first emerged in seventeenth-century Holland, although even there the practice of a new consumerism was more often than not misunderstood by contemporary observers, and by later historians, who could interpret it only as a Calvinist frugality standing in tension with the Old Luxury traditions.[42] Only in later decades, beginning in England after 1688, would the New Luxury be adequately theorized, and would moral philosophers gradually come to accept a society of consumers as a suitable basis on which to build a stable social order. But in this as in so many things, theory followed practice. "Commercial moderns had, largely unknowingly, traversed an unbridgeable gulf, separating themselves irrevocably from an antique or Christian ethic of private restraint."[43] The task of explaining what had taken place still remained. And, one might add, *remains* still today, for much of contemporary social criticism continues to be influenced by secularized versions of the Old Luxury discourse already obsolete at the time of the Glorious Revolution.

Desire Tempered by Commerce: Theorizing the New Luxury

The achievement of a new and more positive interpretation of consumer demand, and of its place in a stable and moral society, turned around a new understanding of how the human personality is shaped in its social context. The intellectual origins of this new understanding must be sought in an unlikely quarter, the theologies of Calvinists and, especially, of their Augustinian cousins the Jansenists. Both shared the view that man is

---

[42] Jan de Vries, "Luxury in the Dutch Republic in Theory and Practice," in Berg and Eger, eds., *Luxury in the Eighteenth Century*, pp. 41–56.

[43] Edward Hundert, "Mandeville, Rousseau and the Political Economy of Fantasy," in Berg and Egar, eds., *Luxury in the Eighteenth Century*, p. 33. Hundert does not suggest, as I do here, that these "commercial moderns" were Dutch.

driven by passions (such as avarice, pride, envy, and lust) reflecting a deep sinfulness, the legacy of the Fall. Jansenists of the seventeenth-century "Port-Royal" school (such as Blaise Pascal and Pierre Nicole, but also the Huguenot Pierre Bayle) went on to assert that these passions notwithstanding, God's providence made it possible for fruitful social relations to emerge from the patently anti-social passions of self-interest and self-love, or *amour-propre*. This was possible because *amour-propre* incorporated the desire for the recognition (*regard*) of others. Persons acutely sensitive to *regard* learn to "mirror [their] needs through the eyes of others, the effect being the release of an endless spiral of needs."[44] Moreover, it was precisely in commercial societies where this providential aspect of *amour-propre* was most emphasized, because there *regard* was especially instrumental in the pursuit of one's self-interest. As a consequence of this line of thought, self-love was no longer despised "as a pre-social passion of natural man" that needed to be suppressed by moral instruction. It could now be seen for the first time in an historical and social context, as incorporating a useful, constructive passion "which emerged at a certain stage in the development of society."[45]

Perhaps the earliest application of this moral reasoning is found in seventeenth-century Dutch Republican theory, especially as developed by Johan and Pieter de la Court. The de la Courts distinguished what they called Monarchical from Republican luxury.[46] All persons, they reasoned, seek their own interest, motivated by the passion of *amour-propre*. But, in monarchies this passion is unbridled, uninspected, and unresisted, leading inevitably to the excesses and decadence of the Old Luxury. In republics (and, they insisted, *only* in republics) the human passions are subject to self-examination and social examination, and therefore they are governed and directed toward virtuous, moderate consumption and frugality.[47] Thus, in a republican commercial society the passion of self-love

---

[44] Akkerman, *Women's Vices, Public Benefits*, p. 23.

[45] Akkerman, *Women's Vices, Public Benefits*, pp. 15–16. On the influence of the Port Royal School, see also Hundert, *The Enlightenment's Fable*.

[46] Johan and Pieter de la Court, *Politieke Discoursen*, 2 vols. (Amsterdam, 1662); Anonymous, but attributed to the de la Courts, *Zinryken Fabulen* (Amsterdam, 1685), translated as *Fables Moral and Political, With Large Explications*, 2 vols. (London: 1703). This last work is discussed in Hundert, *The Englightenment's Fable*, pp. 24–7.

[47] H. W. Blom, "Political Science in the Golden Age. Criticism, History and Theory in Dutch Seventeenth-Century Political Thought," *The Netherlands Journal of Sociology* 15 (1979): 47–71. Pieter de la Court held that the passions are much stronger than reason; he concluded from this that the best government is not one that seeks to impose its "reason" on the passions of the people but one "in which the well-being and ill of government goes hand in hand with the well-being and ill of the subjects. Such a government is a republic,

encounters countervailing forces that channel it toward the achievement of the societal good.

Had the Dutch Republic and northwestern Europe more generally entered that "developmental stage" foreseen by the de la Courts, Pierre Bayle, and the Port Royal thinkers in the second half of the seventeenth century? Beginning in the 1690s a long list of observers and philosophers struggled to explain a social and economic transformation occurring before their eyes, one that had as yet no theoretical underpinnings or even settled vocabulary. Despite these disabilities, a new literature of economic commentary emerged making numerous references to the curious power of the force of desire. An early example is provided by Nicholas Barbon, who in his *Discourse of Trade* of 1690 distinguished two categories of human wants: those of the body (by which he meant basic needs) and those of the mind.

Wares that have their value from supplying the Wants of the Mind are all such things that can satisfy Desire; Desire implies Want: it is the Appetite of the Soul.... The Wants of the Mind are infinite, Man naturally Aspires and as his Mind is elevated, his Wants increase with his Wishes....[48]

Barbon recognized man to be naturally desirous, but he also suggested that the direction in which this desirousness is channeled depended on a training of the mind – which calls to mind the role of "consumption capital" in the theory of Gary Becker. That is, when Barbon asserts that "the wants of the mind are infinite" he does not intend to endorse gargantuan appetites and an endless indulgence in sensual pleasure. He pairs desire with the "elevation of the mind." This leads us, as it led Europeans of the late seventeenth century, to the concept of taste. We have already considered the importance of this concept, which establishes consumption on a foundation of knowledge and information rather than on one of wealth and power.[49]

---

where each looks after himself, everybody is looked after and nobody is neglected. This is the natural freedom of which the rulers should never rob their subjects" (*Welfare of the City of Leiden*, p. 44).

[48] Nicholas Barbon, *Discourse on Trade* (London, 1690), p. 14.

[49] An example of what is intended here is provided in Jennifer M. Jones, "Repackaging Rousseau. Femininity, and Fashion in Old Regime France," *French Historical Studies* 18 (1994), p. 947. Jones "shows how Parisian merchants, with the help of the press, promoted commerce by abandoning luxury and adopting taste as the fundamental criterion of fashion. They made fashion a function of knowledge rather than wealth, and gave power to those who carried the authority of taste." See also Dena Goodman, "Furnishing Discourses. Readings of a Writing Desk in Eighteenth-Century France," in Berg and Eger, eds., *Luxury in the Eighteenth Century*, p. 77.

By drawing upon the Jansenist development of the concept of self-love, and adding the tempering powers of a commercial society to restrain *amour-propre* with *regard*, the intellectual means were at hand to fashion a moral justification of a commercial society in general, and a consumer culture in particular. This comforting, if not complacent, line of thought was consolidated by Montesquieu when, in the 1750s, he defended the pursuit of wealth by insisting that it led not to *la dolce vita* – the corrupting, unstable indulgence of vice – but to *doux commerce*, a powerful civilizing agent that polished and softened manners because of the heightened importance of reputation in a commercial society.[50]

Well before then, this line of continental thought was introduced to England (in a secularized and sensational form) by Bernard Mandeville, a Dutchman who had become familiar with this tradition before moving to England in his early twenties.[51] But in his hands, the comforting assurances that consumer desire and morality may yet be reconciled are brusquely cast aside. In the preface to his scandalous success *The Fable of the Bees* he states his purpose plainly:

The main design of the Fable ... is to show the impossibility of enjoying all the most elegant comforts of life that are to be met with in an industrious, wealthy and powerful nation, and at the same time be blessed with all the virtue and innocence that can be wished for in a Golden Age.[52]

---

[50] Montesquieu, *The Spirit of the Laws*. "Commerce is a cure for the most destructive prejudices; for it is almost a general rule that wherever we find agreeable manners, there commerce flourishes; and that wherever there is commerce, there we meet with agreeable manners" (I: 316). For a spirited treatment of the pre-Smithian economic literature, see Albert Hirschman, *The Passions and the Interests* (Princeton, N.J.: Princeton University Press, 1977).

[51] Bernard Mandeville was born Barend de Mandeville in Rotterdam. His time as a student at the city's Illustrious School coincided with that of Pierre Bayle as a teacher. John Robertson surmises that "In view of the radically Baylean character of Mandeville's essays, it is likely that Bayle had been his teacher at Rotterdam." John Robertson, *The Case for Enlightenment* (Cambridge: Cambridge University Press, 2005), p. 261.

Mandeville left the Netherlands soon after earning his doctorate in medicine at Leiden in 1691. He and his family had been implicated in the "Costerman Riot" of 1690, an anti-tax riot in Rotterdam. The Mandevilles appear to have authored and distributed a satirical poem directed at Rotterdam's *schout*, or bailiff, a figure in bad popular odor because of his insistence on applying the death penalty to Cornelis Costerman, a town militia member, who stood accused of fatally stabbing a tax collector for detaining a group in possession of a cask of wine on which no excise had been paid. Bernard Mandeville's career, even his liberty, was under a cloud, and he decided to leave the country, eventually settling in England. For more on this interesting pre-history of the author of *Fable of the Bees*, see Rudolf Dekker, "'Private Vices, Public Virtues' Revisited. The Dutch Background of Bernard Mandeville," *History of European Ideas* 14 (1992): 481–98.

[52] Mandeville, *The Fable of the Bees*, p. 24.

Societies had to choose between temporal happiness and virtue, and for Mandeville there was no doubt that the "civilized societies" with which he was familiar had already, and decisively, made their choice. His task was to strip away the veil of moralizing that hid the reality of these societies from the view of his contemporaries.

The starting point of Mandeville's *Fable of the Bees* appears to be the *Fables, Moral and Political* of the de la Courts. First published in Dutch in 1685, the English version appeared in 1703, two years before Mandeville composed and published the doggerel poem, which first appeared as *The Grumbling Hive*, and formed the basis of *The Fable of the Bees*.[53] The de la Courts had used various creatures – ants, flies, bees – to advance their argument that in "well constituted and free republics" men will acquire a "well-grounded self love."[54] They criticized bees for their fatal lack of self-control. Mandeville saw no merit in this argument[55] and appropriated the beehive as a metaphor to describe human society as it is rather than as the fog of moralizing philosophers and theologians would have it be. The beehive, long a symbol of the orderliness of absolute monarchies, became in Mandeville's hands "a symbol of morally unbridled economic activity."[56] In the *Fable*, the bees are driven by every vice known to man. Yet their avarice, prodigality, luxury, envy, vanity, and gluttony lead not to social decay and disorder but to prosperity. As Mandeville famously and scandalously summarized in his poem:

> Thus every part was full of vice,
> Yet the whole mass a paradise;

Activated individually by pride and greed, people collectively nonetheless serve the public good. Their social usefulness is not enhanced by forces of reform, restraint, and moderation. Up to a point, there is a similarity with the de la Courts' argument, but where the earlier use of *amour-proper* saw personal behavior being tempered by social interaction, Mandeville saw untempered, self-interested behavior nonetheless leading to a

---

[53] Mandeville's famous poem appeared in 1705 as *The Grumbling Hive*. It was republished, but now with the addition of remarks on the text and extended essays, as *The Fable of the Bees* in 1714. The *Fable* did not attract broad attention until it was published in a second, enlarged edition in 1723.

[54] *Fables, Moral and Political*, quoted in Hundert, *Enlightenment's Fable*, p. 24.

[55] Mandeville's flight from the Dutch Republic certainly gave him reason to view with skepticism the complacent assumptions of republican virtue asserted by the de la Courts.

[56] Hundert, *Enlightenment Fable*, pp. 28–9. One wonders if the founders of Holland's leading department store, and a formidable temple of consumption, had Mandeville in mind when they named their concern *De Bijenkorf* (The Beehive).

beneficial outcome. Economic prosperity depended upon emulation and a continual striving to out-do one another. Mandeville insisted that no valid distinction could be made between good and bad, moderate or excessive consumption: "The prodigal is a blessing to the whole society, and injures nobody but himself."[57] Or, as the poem puts it:

> Such were the blessings of that state;
> Their crimes conspir'd to make them great:

To his readers, still imagining naïvely that their identities were defined primarily by their moral and political personalities rather than by their corporal desires, his message could only shock and scandalize. After generations of Protestant efforts to sacralize everyday life, Mandeville's poem asserted that profane commercial life is, in effect, all there is. He might as well have said: "we are all [just] consumers now."[58]

While Mandeville introduced *amour-propre* to the British luxury discourse, he reduced it to a selfishness ready to countenance any vice, which he accepted as a naked fact of commercial society and the basis of economic prosperity. As John Robertson notes, "Mandeville did not believe that sociability came naturally to man." Rather, he shared with Bayle the conviction that men live their lives in defiance of their moral principles, and he shares with the Jansenists a "keen sense of man's capacity for hypocrisy in pursuit of the satisfaction of the ends of self love, and of the manifold, unintended ways in which hypocrisy none the less enables men to live together in society."[59]

The tempering influence of *regard*, the opinion of others, was to Mandeville nothing more than another vice: the cynical use of social relations to advance one's self-interest through deceit.[60] Sociability, in sum, was

---

[57] *Fable*, I, p. 116.

[58] Echoing President Richard Nixon's remark (made as Keynesian economics was about to go into eclipse) that "We are all Keynesians now," as well as Edward Hundert's conclusion that, Mandeville's scandalous phrasing notwithstanding, "we are all Mandevillians now." Hundert, "Mandeville, Rousseau and the Political Economy of Fantasy," p. 37.

[59] Robertson, p. 270.

[60] It is interesting to compare two divergent interpretations of how *regard* acts to temper the passion of self-interest. The strand we have followed from the de la Court's through Montesquieu emphasizes the politeness (reasonable, sociable behavior) that had room to grow precisely in the public sphere created by a commercial, consumer-oriented society. The strand that begins with Mandeville and extends to Rousseau interprets the self-interest of individuals as turning sociability into another weapon in the arsenal of self-interest. Instead of politeness, one finds *politesse* (a stylish presentation of self that is pleasing to others). This distinction was developed by Justus van Effen to contrast the reasonable republican consumer and citizen from the devious consumers of monarchical

simply "a process of learning over time, in which man reasons by experience, *a posteriori*.... Such learning advances by slow degrees and is slowest among those who live in remote parts, nearer the state of nature; it is most extensive among those who live in or near 'great cities or considerable towns.'"[61]

Later in the century, Jean Jacques Rousseau accepted Mandeville's stripped-down definition of *amour-propre*, but he used it to condemn commercial society and its attendant consumerism. He objected to Mandeville's message, seeing it as "The unembarrassed expression of modernity's immoral voice, proclaiming that luxury is the 'paradox so worthy of our time', in which 'a man is worth no more to the state than the value of his domestic consumption.'"[62]

Rousseau's physiocratic understanding of economic life denied any possibility of growth: The prosperity of the rich only deepened the poverty of the poor; the consumer demand that enlivened manufactures only depressed agriculture, and so on. More profoundly, he saw that the use of consumer luxuries to craft one's outward, public identity was not the end of the matter; consumer luxuries also had "the symbolic power to shape the self-understanding of the private man behind the public mask."[63] Thus, unlike Mandeville, he saw no public benefits arising from the pursuit of private vice; he himself took to wearing the rustic garb of the Corsican peasant (which quickly became the fashion in Paris) and advocated government regulation of consumer behavior where voluntary rejection of the world of luxury goods did not suffice.[64]

Defenses of consumption more intellectually coherent than Mandeville's came after him – and in direct response to his challenge – especially from David Hume, who offered a more nuanced concept of *amour-propre*, presenting human beings as complex entities seeking to satisfy contradictory impulses, or passions. A commercial society driven by the pursuit of wealth and consumption offered, in Hume's view, the best environment in which to direct these passions away from war, violence, and wretched excess by harnessing them via competition (requiring interdependence

---

and aristocratic societies. Velgema, "Ancient and Modern Virtue Compared," pp. 437–48.

[61] Robertson, pp. 272–3. The interior quotation is from *Fable*, part II, pp. 189–90.

[62] Hundert, "Mandeville, Rousseau and the Political Economy of Fantasy," p. 34. The internal quotations are from Rousseau's *Discourse on the Arts and Sciences*.

[63] Ibid., p. 37.

[64] Donald Winch, *Riches and Poverty. An Intellectual History of Political Economy in Britain, 1750–1834* (Cambridge: Cambridge University Press, 1996), pp. 62–77.

and sociability) and material desire. He acknowledged the shortcomings of such a society but did not flinch from recommending it as, on balance, preferable to the characteristic failings of alternative social orders. Thus, "luxury, when excessive, is the source of many ills; but is in general preferable to sloth and idleness, which would commonly succeed in its place."[65] He contrasts an industrious society, activated by natural appetites that spur industry, with societies of idleness and ease, in which unnatural appetites flourish. Here, again, our distinction between Old and New Luxury comes into view. Hume's sensibility to this distinction allowed him to move beyond Mandeville's simple linkage of all virtue with self-denial and all vice with indulgence of the passions via a more complex understanding of the passions. Instead, "Luxury did not undermine, it refined manners, improved knowledge, and increased sociability."[66] In sum, while Hume agreed with Mandeville that luxury was a beneficial feature of a commercial society, he denied that this benefit was founded on vice. For Hume, the desires arising from active, industrious persons not only serve their passions but, more important, shape future output through the refinement in production techniques and designs, which, in turn, go on to stimulate the arts and sciences more generally. "Industry, knowledge and humanity," he concludes, "are linked together by an indissoluble chain."[67]

Running through all this literature is the language of arousal, of an inner awakening of desire that emerges as a distinctive "consumption capital" is assembled in the context of a commercial society. These accumulating experiences, the exposure to urban life and access to imported goods, cause men to "feel arise within them the desire to call attention to themselves by small things" (Montesquieu); cause "his desires [to be] enlarged" (Barbon); "[arouse] in them a desire of a more splendid way of life" (Hume). The refinement and elevation of tastes that these authors speak of is often interpreted by intellectual historians in aesthetic terms, but I believe the primary intention is to refer to something more basic that was shaping consumer behavior – the New versus the Old Luxuries – that had been developing since at least the mid–seventeenth century.

By the third quarter of the eighteenth century, a fully developed theoretical understanding had emerged to account for the new consumer behavior. Sir James Steuart described the new place of consumption in society by

---

[65] Hume, "On Commerce," *Essays*, pp. 287–99.
[66] Robertson, p. 294.
[67] Hume, "On Refinement in the Arts," *Essays*, pp. 299–309.

distinguishing between "ancient luxury," which was quite arbitrary, and "modern luxury," which is "systematical." The former is unlimited, based on plunder and oppression, and is negligent of production. "Drunkenness and a multitude of useless servants were the luxury of former times." The new luxury, on the other hand, can exist only in an orderly, well-governed society, where it advances economic prosperity.[68] Montesquieu in the *Persian Letters* had distinguished the arbitrary, depleting luxury consumption of Persia from what we ironically must call "Parisian luxury": a luxury that furthers a work ethic as it stimulates innovation among producers.

Montesquieu's remarks alert us to the fact that many participants in the "luxury debate" of the eighteenth century also made a connection between consumption and production. Luxury consumption took a novel and more beneficial direction, as we have just seen, and in so doing it also activated the motivation to increase one's income and, hence, to increase production. Sir Dudley North, writing in 1691, followed Barbon in distinguishing between necessities and those goods satisfying "the exorbitant appetites of men." However, he placed his emphasis on how the nonessentials that satisfied these appetites were "the main spur to trade, or rather to industry and ingenuity." The prospect of acquiring such goods "disposes [people] to work, when nothing else will incline them to it; for did men content themselves with bare necessities, we should have a poor world."[69]

Mandeville, who scandalously sang the praises of a vice-fueled consumerism as the underwriter of societal well-being, doubted that manual workers possessed the requisite "exorbitant appetites" to participate in the new social order. His moral iconoclasm notwithstanding, he was unable to free himself from the conventional economic wisdom that low wages are the surest spur to industry among the common people, who lack a sufficiently developed sense of pride and avarice. In this he soon was contradicted by Daniel Defoe and a long list of "high wage" advocates who supposed the passions at issue to be universal.[70]

---

[68] Sir James Steuart, *An Inquiry into the Principles of Political Economy* (London, 1767), Ch. 22, p. 325; Ch. 17, p. 281.

[69] Sir Dudley North, *Discourses upon Trade* (1691), p. 27.

[70] Daniel Defoe, in his *Compleat English Tradesman*, 2 vols. (London, 1726–7), echoed Mandeville in his appreciation of the beneficial effects of vice: "If a due calculation were made of all the several trades besides labouring, manufacturing, and handicraft business, which are supported in this nation merely by the sins of the people, as I may call them, I mean the sumptuary trades, the ribbons, the perfumes, the silks, the cambricks, the muslins, and all the numberless gayeties of dress; as also by the gluttony, the drunkenness, and other exhorbitances of life, it might remain a question, whether the necessary or the

The high-wage advocates could refute Mandeville (and nearly all his contemporaries) on this point because they distinguished more clearly than Mandeville ever did between, on the one hand, the Old Luxury of the rich and the debauchery of the poor, and, on the other, the beneficial arousal to industrious behavior that could be expected from all classes when the trained, or awakened, consumer possessed the means to aspire to a broadened range of goods. David Hume shared Defoe's position when he proclaimed that "Everything in the world is purchased by labour; and our passions are the only causes of labour." Which is to say that the motivation for productive labor is the satisfaction of the passions – that is, desired consumer goods. In the absence of a "desiring subject," employers must resort to force. But, Hume continued, "it is a violent method and in most cases impracticable, to oblige the labourer to toil in order to raise from the land more than what subsists himself and his family. Furnish him with manufactures and commodities and he will do it himself."[71] Thus did Hume contrast an old, pre-commercial world governed by pain and aversion with a new one shaped by pleasure and desire and, hence, the self-initiated exertions to satisfy them.[72] Steuart, who was also impressed by the great power of the "little objects of ambition" to motivate ordinary persons,[73] presented this same contrast in less positive terms: In former times "men were ... forced to labour because they were slaves to others; men are now forced to labour because they are slaves to their own wants."[74]

They were slaves to a particular set of wants, however, which did not bring personal and societal ruin but instead secured a higher good. Bishop

---

unnecessary were the greatest blessing to trade; and whether reforming our vices wou'd not ruin the nation" (Vol. II, p. 101). The appraisals of Mandeville and Defoe differ chiefly in this: Mandeville focused his attention on the exorbitances of the well to do, while Defoe was precocious in his capacity to celebrate the exorbitances of the poor and middling sort.

[71] Hume, "On Commerce," *Essays*, p. 294.

[72] An anonymous author expressed this same sentiment succinctly in 1771: "It is ... more a *turn of mind* than multiplied necessities that induce men to become industrious, which will be better excited by encouragement than compulsion" (my emphasis). Anon., *Considerations on Policy, Commerce and Circumstances of the Kingdom* (London, 1771).

[73] Steuart, *Inquiry* Book II, Ch. 21, p. 315. "The difference between the highest class and the lowest, I do not apprehend to be very great. A small quantity added to what is barely sufficient, makes enough: but this small quantity is the most difficult to acquire, and this is the most powerful spur to industry. The moment a person begins to live by his industry, let his livelihood be ever so poor, he immediately forms little objects of ambition [and] compares his situation with that of his fellows who are a degree above him. ... "

[74] Steuart, *Inquiry*, Book I, Ch. 7, p. 40.

George Berkeley gave evidence of understanding this point as he pondered the poverty of Ireland from his Episcopal seat at Cloyne. In his *Querist* of 1735 he asked "Whether the Irish landowners might not be more useful to society if they spent more of their income on grander houses rather than more splendid clothing?"[75] The New Luxury would be more beneficial to society as a whole than expenditure on the old. With reference to the Irish peasant, he asked "Whether the creation of wants be the likeliest way to produce industry in a people, and whether if our peasants were accustomed to eat beef and wear shoes, they would not be more industrious?"

Berkeley's concern was not with equipping the peasants with the food and clothing necessary for sustained work but with the role of consumer goods as the agent of an arousal that would motivate a greater work effort.[76]

The century-long debate on luxury traced out thus far can be said to culminate in the work of Adam Smith. Until then, efforts to inject the active consumer into the prevailing static models of economic life led only to partial accounts of "the recirculation of wealth through consumption and employment."[77] Could an economy fueled by consumer demand truly be stable and just? Until Smith, no one had decisively answered Mandeville's charge that commercial society rested on a foundation of vice – of self-interest, vanity, and pride. What was to prevent such a society from meeting the same unhappy fate that had befallen all earlier societies that had given themselves over to luxury?

Smith's efforts to "detoxify the pursuit of wealth" focused, for our purposes, on two issues: the proper understanding of human motivation (the passions) and the proper understanding of the social consequences of consumption. The first brings us back to *amour-propre*, where Smith agrees with Mandeville that social benefits do, indeed, flow from the human passion to advance one's individual interests. But, building on Hume, Smith goes on to advance an *amour-propre* that includes a capacity for mutual sympathy, the interests one has in advancing the fortunes of others. Smith's *Theory of Moral Sentiments* begins with an anti-Mandevillian claim:

---

[75] George Berkeley, *The Querest*, 3 vols. (Dublin, 1735), I: 20.

[76] The frequent eighteenth-century references to desire and arousal reveal the close association in this era between what are today the disciplines of psychology and economics. They diverged thereafter, although today a new "behavioral economics" is exploring this terrain anew.

[77] Winch, *Riches and Poverty*, p. 89.

How selfish soever man may be supposed, there are evidently some principles in his nature, which interest him in the fortunes of others, and render their happiness necessary to him, though he derives nothing from it except the pleasure of seeing it.[78]

The mutual sympathy Smith invokes is stronger than, and goes beyond, the passion to receive the recognition of others that had long served the arguments of commercial society's defenders. Ever since, the incorporation of the utility of others as part of the utility of an individual (for example, the utility of family members as contributing to the utility of the father or mother) has been acknowledged as a necessary dimension of individual utility, even when it has been set aside as difficult to model.

Smith's second task was to tackle a critical – but in the eighteenth century usually neglected – problem in the study of individual behavior, that of "intertemporality." This refers to the fact that economic actors not only face the question of how to distribute their resources to achieve the highest utility *now* but must also consider how to distribute their resources *over time* to maximize utility over a longer time period – their lifetime and those of their posterity. This more complicated calculus influences not only *when* one consumes, but *what* one consumes, because delayed gratification can lead to the purchase of different – often costlier and more durable – goods. And, obviously, it affects the division of income between consumption and saving, which, as investment, affects the capacity for future consumption.[79]

When Mandeville pronounced "the prodigal" to be "a public benefactor" and "a blessing to the whole society [who] injures no body but himself," he implicitly denied any importance to intertemporal substitution.[80] He saw the economy as existing, self-contained, in a moment of

---

[78] Smith, *Theory of Moral Sentiments*, p. 9. Smith follows Hume in insisting that sympathy for others, and not merely a self-interested *regard*, is a natural instinct. Although, Hume conceded, it is "rare to meet with one, who loves any single person better than himself," it is equally "rare to meet with one, in whom all the kind affections, taken together, do not over-balance all the selfish." *A Treatise of Human Nature*, ed. L. A. Selby-Bigge; second ed., revised by P. H. Nidditch (Oxford: Oxford Univeristy Press, 1978), p. 487.

[79] "Modern consumption theory assumes that rational consumers...make choices that are well informed, far-sighted, and prudent.... Consumers reveal their preferences by means of market choices, and market choices correspond to their well-being.... Taking account of the expected value of lifetime wealth, they maximize welfare by smoothing consumption over the life cycle." Offer, *The Challenge of Affluence*, p. 40. But, Offer asks, what becomes of these assumptions if individuals' decisions tend, systematically, to be time-inconsistent, or "myopic" – persistently undervaluing future relative to present desires? Offer's book investigates this dilemma of contemporary society.

[80] Mandeville, *Fable*, I, p. 116.

time. Later commentators, if they considered this problem at all, shared Hume's view that people are naturally disposed to sacrifice their long-term to their short-term objectives and need to be restrained to achieve the proper balance.[81] The pursuit of the Old Luxury was clearly oblivious to arguments for deferred gratification, but the passions associated with *amour-propre* do not necessarily weaken this inclination. Consequently, Mandeville could see frugality as nothing more than "a mean starving virtue," what Winch characterizes as "a conditioned response to necessity."[82]

Smith takes Mandeville head on, proclaiming "every frugal man a publick benefactor."[83] His reasoning is motivated not by a desire to suppress consumption and frustrate the infinite wants of the mind. Rather, with Smith the passion of self-interest becomes the desire for self-betterment, in which "abstention from present enjoyment rather than extravagance" played a strategic part in the long-term pursuit of consumer desire. In other words, the foundation of a well-ordered society is "prudence," which in his *Theory of Moral Sentiments* Smith defined as the union of reason, "by which we are capable of discerning the remote consequences of all our actions," and self-command, the ability "to abstain from present pleasure or to endure present pain in order to obtain a greater pleasure or to avoid a greater pain in some future time."[84] Prudence simultaneously sustains savings and investment, the source of future economic growth, and secures an optimal consumption across the lifespan and the generations. Thus, measured self-denial today is entirely consistent with Smith's assertion in *The Wealth of Nations* that "consumption is the sole end and purpose of all production."[85] In this way Smith demonstrates, as Winch puts it, "that contrary to Mandeville's vision, commercial society was constructed on more than mere whimsy and vanity," that a commercial society driven by consumer demand could escape the cycle of luxury and decay and offer a stable future based on moral choice.[86]

---

[81] Hume, *Treatise*, Book III, Part ii, section vii. "There is no quality in human nature, which causes more fatal errors in our conduct, than that which leads us to prefer whatever is present to the distant and remote."

[82] Mandeville, *Fable*, I, p. 104. Winch, *Riches and Poverty*, p. 78. On Dutch frugality (i.e., high savings rate), Mandeville wrote: "The Dutch generally endeavor to promote as much frugality among their subjects as it is possible, not because it is a virtue, but because it is, generally speaking, their interest." *Fable*, Remark Q, p. 96.

[83] Smith, *Wealth of Nations*, Vol. 1, Book II, Ch. iii, pp. 351–71.

[84] Smith, *Theory of Moral Sentiments*, Part IV, Chapter ii, p. 189.

[85] Smith, *Wealth of Nations*, Vol. II, Book IV, Chapter viii, p. 179.

[86] Winch, *Riches and Poverty*, pp. 89, 126.

Summary: The Industrious Revolution,
the Division of Labor, and Economic Growth

My historical argument in a nutshell is this: In the "long eighteenth century," both consumer demand and the supply of market-oriented labor grew by means of reallocations of the productive resources of households. This reallocation of resources stands at the heart of the division of labor that Adam Smith held to be the driving force in economic improvement. In this era the division of labor cannot be understood simply, or even primarily, as a matter of the organization of work at the firm level (i.e., Adam Smith's pin factory), or as a macroeconomic phenomenon that increased the range of intermediate inputs. Rather, it was achieved primarily at the level of the household, where it can be identified as a *simultaneous* rise in the percentage of household production sold to others and a rise in the percentage of household consumption purchased from others.

The available paths open to households seeking to become more market dependent in this period included (1) agricultural specialization, (2) proto-industrial production, (3) wage labor, and (4) commercial service, all of which are the subject of the following chapter. As some or all family members engaged in such market-oriented activities, the household economy became more specialized, drawing its total economic support from a narrowed range of activities. Via specialization and learning-by-doing, it could expect to achieve higher levels of productivity in these activities. At the same time, it became more dependent on the market for goods and services necessary to achieve its consumption goals. That is, its consumption technologies had to depend more on purchased goods and less on household labor. The household could hope to benefit from the greater productivity with which these goods could be supplied by other specialists, but against these future and hoped-for benefits the household-as-consumer faced *immediately* the high transaction costs that attached to securing a diverse consumption packet via the market.[87]

Described in this way, the economy's ability to secure "increasing returns from a progressive division of labor"[88] depends on the solution of a major coordination problem. A multitude of households must choose a level of specialization in production the outcome of which will help determine the speed with which the transaction costs of market consumption

---

[87] Xiaokai Yang and Jeff Borland, "A Microeconomic Mechanism for Economic Growth," *Journal of Political Economy* 99 (1991): 460–82.

[88] Allyn Young, "Increasing Returns and Economic Progress," *The Economic Journal* 38 (1928): 527–42.

will decline. Thus, as Allyn Young famously remarked, not only does "the division of labor depend on the extent of the market, but the extent of the market also depends on the division of labor."[89]

The advantages of specialization surely were well known long before being put to words so memorably by Adam Smith. Yet, the coordination problem standing between the "universal poverty" where "every man provides everything for himself" and the "opulence" where "the joint labour of a great multitude of workmen" comes together to produce "the woolen coat... which covers the day-labourer" was rarely solved satisfactorily.[90] Most households remained only marginally involved in market production, and as consumers they faced markets that were both limited and costly.

It is the argument of this study that significant parts of western Europe (and colonial North America) substantially overcame this coordination problem in the course of the long eighteenth century. We observe the process as simultaneous household-level decisions about production and consumption. But it was consumption – via the creation of a common experience shared by ever-larger circles of the population – that offered the visible signals to enable the requisite coordination to take place. Consumer demand could play this economic role because of the transformation of its social and cultural roles. Contemporaries invoked providential restraints on natural passions, urban life and trade, and the social power of women to account for the emergence of new patterns of consumer behavior, which will be investigated in more detail in Chapter 4. This complex of changes in household behavior constituted an "industrious revolution," a consumption-driven commercial phenomenon that preceded and prepared the way for the Industrial Revolution, which was driven by technology and changes in organization.

---

[89] The problem at issue here is akin to that faced by eastern European economies as they began the "transition" from socialism to capitalism. A Polish economist described the problem this way: "We are about to jump from the diving board in the full confidence that by the time we enter the pool it will have filled up with water."

[90] Smith, *The Wealth of Nations*, Vol. 1, Book I, Ch. i, p. 15. Smith describes with these words the difference between the first and fourth (and final) stages of economic life: hunting, herding, farming, and commerce.

3

The Industrious Revolution

The Supply of Labor

Is it possible to marshal sufficient historical evidence to render plausible the proposition that households worked more and worked harder in the course of the long eighteenth century? And further, can it be shown empirically that these household members – on their pilgrimage from a leisure-rich society to one inured to constant labor – were motivated in their industrious behavior more by new consumption aspirations than by bitter necessity? That is, can it be shown that households worked more in order to consume more, and consume differently? These are the questions that will concern us in this chapter.

Pre-history of the Industrious Revolution

How the peasant lost his leisure time. In the study of predominantly agrarian societies, production is generally seen as the result of the interaction of labor, land, and technology. If technology is slow to change and available land is fixed in quantity, the addition of progressively more labor quickly faces diminishing returns. At the societal level this raises the specter of inadequate food supply as population grows. Thomas Robert Malthus expressed this as an inherent propensity for population to grow faster than food supply. Population, he reasoned, had the capacity to grow exponentially while food supply could grow, at best, arithmetically, a situation that would lead inexorably to recurring subsistence crises unless population growth could be held in check by other means. The Malthusian model proved highly attractive to many historians of medieval and early modern Europe, who described agrarian societies as condemned by an obstinately unyielding ceiling of production to endure repeated cycles of demographic rise and fall punctuated by crises of subsistence.[1]

Such a vision of the pre-industrial world invites one to suppose that decisive change could come only from some external force endowing the economy with new technological possibilities. It follows that economic historians generally approached the challenge of accounting for the Industrial Revolution and modern economic growth by focusing on inventiveness (technology) and augmented supplies of capital (embodying the new technologies) rather than on the growth of the supply of labor, which could only retard a growth process that depended on an increase of the capital/labor ratio.

In these economic models based on the teachings of Malthus (the positive check) and Ricardo (the stationary state), technological change is an exogenous factor relative to the interplay of land and labor. It was the contribution of Ester Boserup, in the 1960s, to integrate into a single model the interrelationships of technology, population, and land. She stood Malthus and, especially, Ricardo on their heads, so to speak: Instead of population growth's leading, via diminishing returns, to the positive check of famine or to a stationary state, Boserup described long-term population growth as the catalyst for the introduction of new agrarian techniques leading to intensified land use.[2]

Empirical observation of mid–twentieth-century Asian farming led Boserup, a development economist, to the conclusion that peasants generally have access to a considerable range of techniques. The suitability of a given set of agricultural techniques depended largely on the prevailing factor proportions, and, in her view, it is this, rather than knowledge, or invention, or culture, or tradition that tended to govern the specific choices made by cultivators. That is, cultivators did not ordinarily face a hard "knowledge frontier" but had available a shelf stocked with techniques from which they chose those most appropriate to the circumstances they faced.

The upper panel of Figure 3.1 seeks to capture the basic features of Boserup's model. The model posits a society with a fixed supply of land (T)

---

[1] For a particularly evocative invocation of the Malthusian model, see Emmanuel Le Roy Ladurie, "L'histoire immobile," *Annales. Economies, Sociétés, Civilisations.* 29 (1974): 673–92 (English trans. "Motionless History," *Social Science History* 1 (1977): 115–36. Classics of this tradition include Wilhelm Abel, *Agricultural Fluctuations in Europe* ([1935, 1966] London: Methuen, 1980); B. H. Slicher van Bath, *The Agrarian History of Western Europe, 500–1850* (London: Edward Arnold, 1963).

[2] Ester Boserup, *The Conditions of Agricultural Growth* (Chicago: University of Chicago Press, 1965).

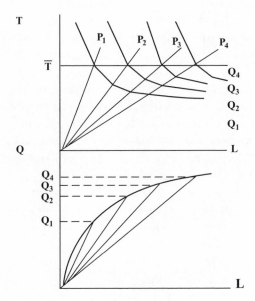

FIGURE 3.1. The Boserup model of agricultural production and population growth.

experiencing long-term population growth. As numbers increase, farmers seek to increase output to prevent per capita output from falling. Using a given set of techniques (P_1, P_2,...), output growth requires a proportionate increase in the factors of production (labor and land). Once all available land is in use ($\overline{T}$), further movement toward higher total output levels is blocked. However, in Boserup's model, this constraint creates a population-induced occasion to shift to a new set of farming techniques (moving from, say, P_1 to P_2). Over time, several such technical transformations can occur, leading a society with a fixed amount of land toward successively higher levels of total output, measured by the output isoquants Q_1, Q_2,... [3]

The lower panel of Figure 3.1 reveals a second feature of these technical changes: The growth of land productivity (agricultural output per unit of land) described in the top panel requires greater labor intensity, which

[3] For example, the population may move from a forest-fallow system of shifting agriculture to a settled two-field rotation, and later to a three-field rotation system. Each of these shifts requires new tools (plows instead of hoes) and the maintenance of more livestock for draft power and manure supplies. Because the land is cropped more intensively (from once every ten years, say, to every other year, to twice in every three years, in this example), total output rises.

leads to a declining marginal productivity of labor, which is measured by the slope of the total output curve. As total output (Q) increases, the marginal productivity declines. Labor productivity declines steeply when a growing population remains wedded to a given farming technology; shifting to more labor-intensive production functions moderates this decline. It moderates, but it does not stop, the decline, let alone establish the conditions for a rise in labor productivity per hour of work.[4]

In Boserup's view it is this "price" of increased agricultural output – drudgery and longer hours of work – that explains the slow historical pace of intensification in agriculture. Only the necessity brought about by rising population densities could induce peasants to devote more of their time – the sacrifice of their leisure – to agricultural production. This reduction of leisure time imposed upon societies experiencing population growth did not lead directly to modern economic growth (rising per capita income), but it *did* lead to a kind of economic development. The growth of output per unit of land generated a growing *total* surplus available for the support of political and religious elites, urban centers, cultural facilities, and physical infrastructure. In addition, the longer hours and increased days of labor acted, inadvertently, as a training ground for a more disciplined and a more technically skilled labor force. In Boserup's view, the combination of a more complex civilization and a population inured to continual labor formed the essential pre-conditions for modern economic development.

This vision of a pre-industrial world in which peasant societies, driven by population growth, depart a life of easy living to enter a realm of grim industriousness might be called the Genesis 3:19 model of economic development.[5] Readers disinclined to embrace "theological economics" can consider economic anthropology, which points to hunter-gatherer societies as "the original affluent society" – affluent in leisure – and sees

---

[4] "Organic agriculture" can be defined as any farming system in which (nearly) all inputs are produced on the farm, rather than purchased from non-agricultural sources (energy, artificial fertilizers). Under such a system, any rise in land productivity is very likely to be paired with declining labor productivity. The reason is that increased intensity is usually gained at the expense of the fallow period. A reduced fallow period requires the introduction of some other method of preserving soil fertility. This, in turn, almost inevitably increases the labor input per unit of crop area as well as per unit of output.

[5] When Adam and Eve are driven by God from the Garden of Eden, God curses the ground, saying to Adam: "In sorrow shalt thou eat of it all the days of thy life. Thorns also and thistles shall it bring forth to thee; and thou salt eat the herb of the field. In the sweat of thy face shalt thou eat bread. . . ." Genesis 3: 17–19.

settled agrarian societies as coursing toward ever greater labor exertions –
self-exploitation – in order to preserve the "peasant way of life."[6]

Viewed from a broad historical perspective, the world's several populous, complex, peasant-based civilizations appear to have been engaged
in a perverse race. The further "behind" they were (the lower their density of population), the higher was their labor productivity in agriculture,
but this meant only that they would be delayed in preparing the foundations upon which some breakthrough – an industrial revolution – might
be launched to liberate them from the inexorable logic of the "organic
economy."[7] The classic interpretation of the British Industrial Revolution,
the event that first brings this millennia-long process to an end, posits a
sudden efflorescence of technological change – "a wave of gadgets" –
as constituting the decisive breakthrough. Another influential approach
emphasizes contingent events – the fortuitous historical combination of
British access to coal and colonies – as the key to ushering in the modern world. Neither interpretation specifies a link between the long-term
intensification of labor in peasant agriculture and these decisive events.
Boserup's model may "set the stage" for modern growth, but it stops short
of accounting for the actual occurrence of such a novel departure.

Critique. Before either embracing or rejecting Boserup's vision, we
should take a closer look at the model, for it has two obvious limitations.
While it adds a level of complexity (and realism) to the classical Malthusian approach, it has no place for markets. The impulse to intensify land
use comes from population pressure that makes itself felt *directly* upon
presumably self-sufficient cultivators. Nothing mediates between land and
labor except technology. What difference would it make if cultivators not
only chose among agricultural technologies but also entered into market
relations and become specialized?

A second feature of the Boserup model is its insistence that the supply
of economic labor is not synonymous with the size of the population;
it recognizes a labor–leisure tradeoff. But, just as there are no markets

[6] Marshall Sahlins, *Stone Age Economics* (Chicago: University of Chicago Press, 1972),
especially the chapter "The Original Affluent Society," pp. 1–39; Eric Wolf, *Peasants*
(Englewood Cliffs, N.J.: Prentice-Hall, 1966).

[7] The Organic Economy is discussed in detail in E. A. Wrigley, *Continuity, Chance and
Change. The Character of the Industrial Revolution in England* (Cambridge: Cambridge
University Press, 1988). The notion of a common ecological fate evaded in western Europe
by "chance" is advanced most provocatively in Kenneth Pomeranz, *The Great Diver-
gence. China, Europe and the Making of the Modern World Economy* (Princeton, N.J.:
Princeton University Press, 2000).

in the model, there is only one economic sector: agriculture. The only alternative to leisure is work in agriculture. What difference would it make if cultivators faced a more complex choice than this in the allocation of their time through the availability of non-agricultural work?[8]

An exploration of these two extensions to the model has led me to the thesis that an escape from the iron logic of agricultural intensification (as summarized in Figure 3.1) was achieved by households' interacting with markets rather than, as Boserup has it, labor's simply interacting with land. Through a fuller absorption of household labor, often by pursuit of non-agricultural activities, through greater efficiencies of productive labor via specialization, and through market incentives to labor intensification, a significant increase in per capita output could be achieved in the absence of an industrial revolution.

Labor-intensive, household-based production was, of course, not unique to northwestern Europe or to the long eighteenth century. The concept of the industrious revolution advanced in this study involves something more than simply more intensive labor. Greater clarity about the concept can be achieved by comparing it to the way in which the same expression is used with respect to East Asian economic development.

The Industrious Revolution in East and West

The term *industrious revolution* was first coined by Akira Hayami, who used it (in a Japanese-language work of 1967) to contrast the labor-intensive technologies of Tokugawa Japan (1603–1868) with the capital-intensive technologies of Britain's Industrial Revolution. In Hayami's view, these represented two paths toward ultimate industrialization.[9] In his first English-language use of the term, Hayami invoked it to account for a growth of agricultural output in the last decades of the Tokugawa era that was achieved as peasants adapted their farming methods to substitute increased human exertion for the tractive power of livestock: "There must have been a conversion from 'horsepower' to 'manpower' in rural Japan. The term *industrious revolution* can be applied to this change...."[10]

[8] Jan de Vries, "Boserup as Economics and History," *Peasant Studies Newsletter* 1 (1972): 45–50.

[9] Akira Hayami, "Keizai Shakai no Seiritsu to sono Tokushitsu (The Emergence of the Economic Society and Its Characteristics)," in Shakai Keizaishi Gakkai, ed., *Atarashii Edo Jidaizo o Motomete* (Tokyo: Toyo Keizai Shinposha, 1967), as discussed in Kaoru Sugihara, "Labour-intensive Industrialisation in Global History," 13th International Economic History Congress, Buenos Aires, 2002.

[10] Akira Hayami, "A Great Transformation. Social and Economic Change in Sixteenth and Seventeenth Century Japan," *Bonner Zeitschrift für Japanologie* 8 (1986), p. 6.

Since then, Kaoru Sugihara, Osamu Saito, and others have used the term to refer more generally to a process of labor-intensive industrialization, which they see as an alternative to the capital- and resource-intensive path followed by Western countries to achieve modern economic growth.[11]

The macroeconomic context in which the term is applied in Japan (and East Asia more generally) is broadly consistent with the Boserup model introduced above. Population growth is accommodated by the adoption of labor-intensive technologies. Rice cultivation and irrigated agriculture permitted far greater intensification than the mixed farming systems of Europe, so that rural societies in Asia achieved considerably denser populations and correspondingly greater output per unit of land than was common in Europe.[12]

The microeconomic aspect of "labor-intensive industrialization" emphasizes the household as a labor-absorbing institution assiduously developing labor-intensive technologies to maintain its economic viability. However, the Asian industrious revolution concept does not see the peasant household merely as engaging in "self-exploitation" to secure a meager subsistence. Rather, industrious behavior prepares the peasant household for the tasks of modern economic growth by improving labor quality. Saito describes the Japanese peasant household as one that exerts discipline over its members and carefully plans not simply the deployment of family labor but also the composition of the family (the number of children, the intervals between their births, and the sex-order of the sibset)

---

[11] Kaoru Sugihara, "The East Asian Path of Economic Development. A Long-Term Perspective," in Giovanni Arrighi, Takeshi Hamashita, and Amark Selden, eds., *The Resurgence of East Asia. 500, 150, and 50 Year Perspectives* (London: Routledge, 2003), pp. 78–123; Kaoru Sugihara, "The State and the Industrious Revolution in Tokugawa Japan," London School of Economics, Working paper No. 02/04 (February 2004); see also Osamu Saito, "Work, Leisure and the Concept of Planning in the Japanese Past" (unpublished, 1996); Osamu Saito, "Gender, Workload and Agricultural Progress. Japan's Historical Experience in Perspective," in René Leboutte, ed., *Protoindustrialisation. Recherches récentes et nouvelles perspectives. Mélanges en souvenir de Franklin Mendels* (Geneva: Librairie Droz, 1996), pp. 129–51.

[12] The causal mechanisms behind this process are hotly debated. They can lead either to the positions established by Marc Elvin and Eric Jones – that Asia drifted toward a ecological position in which it sustained very large populations at very low living standards (a "high-level equilibrium trap") – or to the position developed more recently by James Lee and Wang Feng, and Kenneth Pomeranz, that China, up to 1800 at any rate, was a demographic success story, supporting large numbers at living standards comparable to those in Europe. James Z. Lee and Wang Feng, *One Quarter of Humanity. Malthusian Mythology and Chinese Realities* (Cambridge, Mass.: Harvard University Press, 1999); Pomeranz, *The Great Divergence*; Eric L. Jones, *The European Miracle. Environments, Economies and Geopolitics in the History of Europe and Asia* (Cambridge: Cambridge University Press, 1981); Mark Elvin, *The Pattern of the Chinese Past* (Stanford, Calif.: Stanford University Press, 1973).

in order to coordinate consumption, production, and reproduction in such a way as to ensure intergenerational continuity, protect against short-term uncertainties, and smooth consumption over a life cycle of changing individual productive power. Through generations of such complex, "rational" planning, the peasant family acquired the human capital to respond to the new threats and opportunities of modern industrialization.

Sugihara emphasizes the tendency for Japanese peasant households to absorb family labor by combining agriculture and by-employments. He contrasts this with England, where agriculture and rural industry tended to be pursued in separate, specialized households. These Japanese households were less specialized, but, by combining many activities in a single enterprise, they became a training ground for forms of managerial behavior that would prove useful in supporting numerous small-scale, labor-intensive industrial activities appropriate to a labor-rich, resource-poor economy. Similarly, the high percentage of self-employed persons would, in Sugihara's view, establish the basis for the many small- and medium-sized firms that characterized industrializing Japan. He summarizes by noting that:

In so far as labour-intensive industrialization embraced the gradual improvement of the quality of labour, this was the main route by which mankind escaped the Malthusian trap of overpopulation and the Ricardian trap of rising food prices. It was this virtuous circle, not the sudden availability of vast resources in the New World or labour-saving technology, that sustained the global diffusion of industrialization during the last two centuries.[13]

The East Asian industrious revolution emphasizes the role played by limited resources in developing resourceful, diligent, disciplined peasant households that would, in the fullness of time, transfer these painfully acquired attributes to a new industrial world. It does not place much emphasis on specialization and market relations. Indeed, much of the careful planning and the long workdays of disciplined labor *substituted* for the absence of markets. For example, family planning could be less stringent if there were labor markets for farm servants, while agricultural specialization could proceed further if taxes were paid in money rather than in rice.

Finally, the East Asian industrious revolution is very much a supply-side phenomenon. Industrious activity trained people to become more productive workers, but it did not make them more active or innovative consumers. Total output grew at the expense of labor productivity, which

[13] Sugihara, "Labour-intensive Industrialisation in Global History," p. 15.

limited rural purchasing power. Later, as this low-productivity agrarian labor entered the industrial sector, it kept wages low there as well, further limiting the expansion of the domestic market.[14]

Seen from an East Asian perspective, labor-intensive industrialization distinguishes the East from the West, where economic growth proceeded on a capital- and resource-intensive basis. Industrious, flexible family businesses with peasant roots were prominent in early industrialization in the East, while large-scale firms and factories led this process in the West. This characterization, while not without a kernel of truth, exaggerates the difference between East and West in the early stages of industrialization by mistaking the celebrated growth of certain "leading sectors" of the British Industrial Revolution for the larger process of Western economic growth, which, much as in the East, long depended on industrious, household-based production.

There are, however, important differences between the industrious revolutions of East and West. They are not the same thing, and the chief difference is located in the greater role of markets and specialization in western Europe. This is the context in which consumer aspirations could begin to play an autonomous role in motivating a further growth in market-oriented labor supply. In short, the determinants of labor intensification differed fundamentally in these two variants of the industrious revolution.

The productivity of European labor in agriculture faced the same inherent downward pressures as in Asia but remained significantly higher. Explanations for this usually focus on a combination of demographic control and agrarian technology. European populations were adjusted, in a rough way, to the available resources via indirect controls on fertility shaped by rules governing marriage, the so-called "European Marriage Pattern" introduced in Chapter 1. Markets figure prominently in this demographic interpretation, for it argues that access to marriage (whether one could marry at all, and, if so, at what age) was governed by economic conditions that were signaled by wages, land rents, and commodity prices.[15]

Also, the mixed farming systems that predominated in most of Europe (especially, north of the Mediterranean basin) were capable of supplementing human labor with agronomic forces in the struggle to maintain

---

[14] Kaoru Sugihara, "The East Asian Path of Economic Development. A Long-term Perspective," in Giovanni Arrighi, Takeshi Hamashita, and Amark Selden, eds., *The Resurgence of East Asia. 500, 150, and 50 Year Perspectives* (London: Routledge, 2003), pp. 90, 102.

[15] The most fully elaborated application of this theory is found in E. A. Wrigley and Roger Schofield, *The Population History of England, 1541–1871. A Reconstruction* (London: Edward Arnold, 1981), esp. Chapters 11–12.

soil fertility in the face of more intensive cropping. The use of live-stock, legumes, and root crops in rotation systems known as alternate and convertible husbandry had the effect of increasing livestock output (by increasing pasture and fodder supplies), eliminating fallow years, and improving soil fertility.[16] To increase physical output these systems needed to add labor per unit of land, to be sure, but under favorable relative prices they could increase the value of output even more. Again, it was mar-ket opportunities more than demographic pressure that determined the timing and location of the introduction of these more intensive farming systems.[17]

The key to achieving total productivity growth before the nineteenth century was found not in demography or technology but in the organi-zation of the household as an economic entity. In the European context the redeployment of the productive resources of households occurred in response to market opportunities. Households shifted from market *con-tact* (sale of goods to supplement household production) to market *ori-entation* (sale of goods and labor as the basis of the household economy). This shift occurred not primarily because of demographic pressure or institutional coercion (although these played important roles at times) but in response to market conditions. The full embrace of market orien-tation, or dependence, required, in turn, changes in household consumer behavior.

Household Earnings

Household earnings from market activity take several forms, but even in the seventeenth century wage labor was the single most important source of money income in much of northwestern Europe. A large and growing number of workers without land or other productive resources depended on wages, and the record of real wages in the long eighteenth century does not, on the face of it, offer much scope for innovative consumer behavior

---

[16] Alternate husbandry is a rotation system without years of fallow where grains alternate with legumes and root crops; convertible husbandry is a regime of annual cropping for five to nine years followed by the sowing of artificial grasses, thereby "converting" the arable to pasture for several years. See Bruce Campbell and Mark Overton, "Produc-tivity Change in European Agricultural Development," in Bruce Campbell and Mark Overton, eds., *Land, Labour and Livestock. Historical Studies in European Agricultural Productivity* (Manchester: Manchester University Press, 1991), pp. 1–50.

[17] On this complex topic, see Eric Jones, *Agriculture and Economic Growth in England, 1650–1815* (London: Methuen, 1967); Slicher van Bath, *Agrarian History of Western Europe*; Campbell and Overton, eds., *Land, Labour and Livestock*.

TABLE 3.1. *Real consumption wages of unskilled building laborers: Western, Southern, Central, and Eastern Europe, 1500–1849 (Index: London 1500–49 = 100)*

	1500–49	1650–99	1700–49	1750–99	1800–49
Western Europe					
London	100	96	110	99	98
Amsterdam	97	98	107	98	79
Antwerp	98	88	92	88	82
Paris	62	60	56	51	65
Southern Europe	71	[52]	61	42	[30]
Central and Eastern Europe	74	66	58	55	48

In brackets: small number of observations.

Robert Allen, "The Great Divergence in European Wages and Prices from the Middle Ages to the First World War," *Explorations in Economic History* 38 (2001): 428; Steven Broadberry and Bishupriya Gupta, "The Early Modern Great Divergence: Wages, Prices and Economic Development in Europe and Asia, 1500–1800," *Journal of Economic History* 59 (2006): 7.

or an expansive material culture. Measuring the purchasing power of wages is far from a straightforward undertaking under the best of conditions, and data limitations in the pre-industrial era are formidable, but recent studies are unanimous in finding little if any long-term growth in real wages over the early modern centuries except in a few exceptional times and places.

Table 3.1 offers a global overview of urban real wages in northwestern, southern, central, and eastern Europe. The cost-of-living indexes for each city were linked to one another, permitting not only comparisons across time but also across the cities of Europe. By indexing the London real wage in 1500–49 at 100, it immediately becomes apparent that: (1) the major cities of northwestern Europe then enjoyed substantially higher real wages than those in southern, central, and eastern Europe, (2) the gap between northwestern Europe and the other regions grew over the course of the long eighteenth century, and (3) the growing relative superiority of northwestern Europe did not take the form of an absolute rise in the real wage. The achievement of northwestern Europe was a limited one: to resist the very substantial deterioration of purchasing power experienced everywhere else.

This hardly appears to be a propitious foundation for a consumer revolution. Perhaps we should confine our attention to the most economically dynamic country in its most expansive phase. Real wages in Britain at the

TABLE 3.2. *Real wage index: Great Britain:*
1770–1879

Decade	Index
1770–9	100
1780–9	105.5
1790–9	113.1
1800–9	112.2
1810–19	107.8
1820–9	117.9
1830–9	124.2
1840–9	130.3
1850–9	140.4
1860–9	147.0
1870–9	170.4

Charles Feinstein, "Pessimism Perpetuated: Real Wages and the Standard of Living in Britain during and after the Industrial Revolution," *Journal of Economic History* 58 (1998): 652–3.

time of the Industrial Revolution have, of course, long been the object of intense scrutiny. "Optimists" felt sure that so great an achievement in production and productivity could not have failed to improve the living standards of contemporaries; "pessimists" were equally convinced that exploitation so intense as to generate the Industrial Revolution must have left workers worse off.[18]

The resulting "standard-of-living debate" continues into the twenty-first century, albeit now with less political passion and more methodological finesse. The most comprehensive recent estimates of British purchasing power, calculated by Charles Feinstein and summarized in Table 3.2, perpetuate the pessimist position:

From the 1780s to the end of the Napoleonic Wars average nominal earnings kept roughly in step with the cost of living, and there was almost no increase in average real earnings. After 1815 there was slow progress, but by the mid 1850s

[18] The original debate was launched by Hobsbawm and Hartwell: Eric J. Hobsbawm, "The British Standard of Living, 1790–1850," *Economic History Review* 10 (1957): 46–68; Robert M. Hartwell, "The Rising Standard of Living in England, 1800–1850," *Economic History Review* 13 (1961): 397–416; Eric J. Hobsbawm, "The Standard of Living During the Industrial Revolution. A Discussion," *Economic History Review* 16 (1963): 119–34; Robert M. Hartwell, "The Standard of Living. An Answer to the Pessimists," *Economic History Review* 16 (1963): 135–46. While these articles defined the debate, other important contributors include T. S. Ashton (optimist) and E. P. Thompson (pessimist).

the new index was still less than 30 percent ahead of the level of the early 1780s. On this new evidence it was only from the late 1850s that the average British worker enjoyed substantial *and sustained* advances in real wages.[19]

Outside industrializing Britain, matters were only worse. The broad collection of urban real wage data assembled by Söderberg, Jonsson, and Persson paint a somber picture of deterioration from 1730 to 1789. Over this period the grain/bread purchasing power of wages fell almost everywhere, sometimes at a rate of more than 1 percent per annum over more than half a century. And the worst was yet to come, for sharp spikes in food prices during the Revolutionary and Napoleonic era depressed real wages to historic low points almost everywhere.[20]

The "pessimists" appear to have won the debate, although not for the reasons they had originally advanced. The accumulating evidence of long-stagnant, if not declining, real wages has been paired with a fundamental reassessment of the rate of macroeconomic growth of the British economy during the early decades of the Industrial Revolution. The revisionist position does not deny the long-term importance of the new technological and organizational achievements of this era, but it significantly reduces their weight in the overall economy until later in the nineteenth century. Table 3.3 reveals the extent of the diminution of growth in the 1700–1830 period, with the estimates of Deane and Cole standing for the "traditional view" and those of Crafts and Harley representing the "revisionist" position.

The revisionist position leaves little room for a substantial rise in overall labor productivity, even as a "wave of gadgets" swept over England.[21] It removes from the real wage estimates of the pessimists much of their counterintuitive nature. On the other hand, it leaves "pre-industrial" England as a rather richer economy than had earlier been assumed, for the simple reason that less growth in the 1760–1830 period means the pre-1760

---

[19] Charles Feinstein, "Pessimism Perpetuated. Real Wages and the Standard of Living in Britain During and After the Industrial Revolution," *Journal of Economic History* 58 (1998): 642. See also Gregory Clark, "Farm Wages and Living Standards in England, 1670–1869," *Economic History Review* 54 (2001): 477–505.

[20] Johan Söderberg, Ulf Jonsson, and Christer Persson, *A Stagnating Metropolis. The Economy and Demography of Stockholm, 1750–1850* (Cambridge: Cambridge University Press, 1991), pp. 65–86. The authors compare the real wages (usually bread purchasing power) of eighteen European cities over the period 1730–89. In fourteen of the cities the trend line of real wages over this period is at least -0.50. In only one city is it positive (+0.05, in Copenhagen). In most cities, there is no lasting upward trend until after 1850.

[21] N. F. R. Crafts and C. K. Harley, "Output Growth and the Industrial Revolution. A Restatement of the Crafts-Harley View," *Economic History Review* 45 (1992): 703–30.

TABLE 3.3. *Estimates of British Per Capita National Income Growth (Average Annual Rates of Increase)*

Period	Deane & Cole	Crafts & Harley
1700–60	0.44	0.30
1760–1800	0.52	0.17
1800–30	1.61	0.52
1830–70	1.98	1.98

As summarized in Joel Mokyr, "Accounting for the Industrial Revolution," in Roderick Floud and Paul Johnson, eds., *The Cambridge Economic History of Modern Britain* Vol. 1, *Industrialisation, 1700–1860* (Cambridge: Cambridge University Press, 2004), pp. 4–10.

economy must have possessed a per capita income closer to that found in the post-1830 period.[22] The less evidence we have for productivity growth through technological change in this period, the more reason we have to focus on production growth through industrious behavior.

The industrious revolution concept argues for a shift of attention from the *daily wages of individuals* to the *annual earnings of households*. In so doing, the key variables shift from the wage rate to (1) the number of days of paid employment per year, (2) the participation of wives and children in market-oriented labor, and (3) the intensity of work effort. Various combinations of more regular work, more intense work, and greater paid labor force participation – a more elastic supply of market-oriented labor – could have overcome the impotence of the wage rate to endow households with the means to act on new consumer aspirations.

There is considerable evidence, direct and indirect, in support of changes in all three dimensions of industrious behavior. Indeed, many of the most ferocious "pessimists" in the standard-of-living debate themselves offered evidence of prolonged work hours, expanded child labor, and the suppression of holidays and irregular work attendance in support of the proposition that industrialization under capitalism brought with it an oppressive, unsought, and unnatural intensification of labor. Any resulting increase in real income, they argued, was paid for dearly by a

---

[22] Economists can hope that their accumulated knowledge will make posterity better off than it otherwise would be, but only economic historians can make our ancestors better off than they ever knew they were.

massive erosion of leisure time. I will return to these arguments toward the end of this chapter.

The Working Year

In medieval and early modern Europe, the days of labor were set by the Christian calendar, which exempted from work all Sundays and a list of holy days that could vary regionally according to the local reputations of saints.[23] Some of the saints' days also marked the annual occurrence of festivals and carnivals, when most work might stop for several consecutive days. In the early modern period, secular/political holidays were added to the holy days in some countries, to mark royal birthdays or to commemorate important events. The number of days set aside from work varied regionally as well as over time. It appears that the number of observed saints' days rose after the Black Death and in the fifteenth century, such that customary practices long taken for granted came to be seen as a problem. Christopher Dyer summarizes conditions in this period by noting:

The disapproval of journeymen "disporting themselves in the streets," the attempt to enforce annual contracts, the move to reduce the number of religious holidays and the growing disapproval of time-consuming sports and games serve to reinforce the impression of the anxiety of employers to combat workers' strong preference for leisure.[24]

Most estimates of the number of days officially available for work at the end of the fifteenth century are in the 250–60 range.[25] Beginning in the sixteenth century this high-water mark of pre-industrial leisure (in modern times, the annual days of work were brought back to this level in most Western countries only after 1950–60, with the introduction of the five-day work week) came under attack, and first and most powerfully by the Protestant Reformation. Reformed theology sought to introduce a

---

[23] Indeed, some local observances were unsanctioned, being based on popular local cults.

[24] Christopher Dyer, *Standards of Living in the Later Middle Ages. Social Change in England c. 1200–1520* (Cambridge: Cambridge University Press, 1989), p. 224.

[25] K. G. Persson, "Consumption, Labour and Leisure in the Late Middle Ages," in D. Menjot, ed., *Manger et boire au Moyen Age* (Nice: Centre d Études Médiévales de Nice, 1984), pp. 219–20; Abel, *Agricultural Fluctuations in Europe*, p. 59. Micheline Baulant finds Paris building laborers working about 250 days per year but notes that only 190 of these were full days of labor. The others were partial holidays. Micheline Baulant, "Le salaire des ouvriers du bâtiment à Paris de 1400 à 1726," *Annales: Economies, Sociètès, Civilisations* 26 (1971): 470.

fundamentally rationalized liturgical calendar, in which there was no place for saints' days and, in the Calvinist variant, little room for Lent and Advent, or even Christmas. In England the king and his church effected this reformation of time – in theory – by a ruling of 1536 to abolish approximately 49 holy days.[26] In the Netherlands, a synod of the Reformed Church abolished *all* holy days in 1574, stating that the Sabbath alone should be exempt from labor. Almost immediately popular resistance caused the synod to relent, but only by restoring Christmas and the day following, New Year's day, Easter Monday, Ascension day, and Pentecost Monday – six days altogether.[27] In lands that remained loyal to the Roman Catholic Church, there was no such sudden purification, but saints' days were removed in stages over a very long period of time. Thus, in Paris, the first substantial change affecting building laborers came in 1666, when 15 to 20 saints' days disappeared, leaving only 30 in place.[28] As one moves farther east and south, the changes come yet later. In Austria, the first steps were taken under Maria Theresa, who abolished 24 holidays by edict – a bitterly resisted edict – in 1754.[29]

The edicts of synods, archbishops, and monarchs were prescriptive, and their effects on the labor market (as opposed to religious observance) were permissive rather than compulsory. They *enabled* an expansion of the work year by more than 20 percent, from 250–60 to a maximum of 307 days per year but could not thereby mandate more industrious behavior. Indeed, customary practice may have effectively limited the work year to even fewer days than those set by the churches. In agriculture, a reduction in the number of saints' days may have permitted farmers

[26] Hans-Joachim Voth, "Seasonality of Baptisms as a Source for Historical Time-Budget Analysis. Tracing the Disappearance of Holy Days in Early Modern England," *Historical Methods* 27 (1994): 127–8.

[27] Leo Noordegraaf, *Hollands welvaren? Levensstandaard in Holland 1450–1650* (Bergen: Octavo, 1985), pp. 58–60.

[28] Baulant, "Les salaires des ouvriers du bâtiment," pp. 470–1. From 1549 through the first third of the seventeenth century, the work year numbered approximately 272 to 277 potential days. After 1666, it rose to 286 to 287 days, although by 1673 it appears to have fallen to 280 to 282 days. For France as a whole, Muchembled confirms that the number of holy days were "strictly reduced" from 60 to fewer than 30 in the course of the seventeenth century. Robert Muchembled, *Société et mentalités dans la France XVIe-XVIIIe siècles* (Paris: A. Colin, 1990), p. 89.

[29] Hans-Joachim Voth, *Time and Work in England, 1750–1830* (Oxford: Oxford University Press, 2001), p. 274n. Voth emphasizes the importance attached by the government to this reform by relating that, after clerical protests and mob violence in Vienna, the government sent mounted police to patrol the streets and force shopkeepers to open at 11:00 A.M. on the formerly sanctified days. However, it took until 1771 before compulsory Mass attendance was abolished for these former feast days. Sandgruber, *Die Anfänge der Konsumgesellschaft*, pp. 377–8.

to work in a more timely manner (to respond to threatening weather, for example) but it did not necessarily increase the total work effort. Only a decision to intensify farming and/or engage in other forms of productive activity could "activate" the newly available time. Correspondingly, only empirical evidence can reveal the true length of the work year and when, and the extent to which, the new work capacity was actually utilized.

In the Netherlands the payroll records of public employers (polder administrations, admiralty wharves and rope works, municipal agencies) show that the newly augmented "labor potential" offered by the stroke of a clergyman's pen in 1574 was being made use of regularly by the second half of the seventeenth century at the latest. Manual workers whose annual time at work (including meal breaks totaling approximately two hours per day) could not have exceeded 3,100 hours in the sixteenth century spent 3,700 hours per year at work (again, including meal breaks totaling two hours per day) after 1650. A further increase in the potential work year took place in the early nineteenth century, as (indoor) work in the hours of darkness gradually became more common.[30]

For England, matters are more complex, with scholarly opinion divided about the speed of the elimination of saints' day observances. Hans-Joachim Voth shed light on this issue by exploiting data on the week-to-week incidence of baptisms in the Shropshire village of Ludlow to detect delayed evidence of certain leisure activities nine months earlier. His regression analysis, done for twenty-year periods from 1558 through 1700, revealed that "the old Catholic holy days exercised a strong, but slowly declining influence on the timing of conceptions before the outbreak of the Civil War. After the Restoration [there is a break in the available data between 1646 and 1668], no connection between the seasonality

---

[30] Jan de Vries, "The Labour Market," in Karel Davids and Leo Noordegraaf, eds., *Economic and Social History in the Netherlands* (Amsterdam: NEHA, 1993), p. 62. Data on work day and work year in Jan de Vries, "An Employer's Guide to Wages and Working Conditions in the Netherlands, 1450–1850," in Carol Leonard and Boris Mironov, eds., *Hours of Work and Means of Payment. The Evolution of Conventions in Pre-industrial Europe* (Milan: XI International Economic History Congress, 1994), pp. 47–63. Between 1600 and 1850 the work day for manual workers varied between a maximum of 14 hours (including 2 hours of pauses = 12 hours of labor) and 13 hours (including 2.5 hours of pauses = 10.5 hours of labor). Working hours were reduced in the winter months, as the hours of daylight declined. Before 1574, the maximum annual hours of work stood at approximately 2,600 hours (plus 550 hours of pauses = 3,100 hours); thereafter the maximum rose to approximately 3,100 hours (plus 600 hours of pauses = 3,700 hours). The total annual hours of sunlight (for all days except Sundays) at 50 degrees north latitude is 4,270 hours, leaving very few nonworking daylight hours, and these only in the high summer months.

of conceptions and old feast days can be discerned."[31] While Voth's measurement technique has definite limits, and one Shropshire village is not all of England, other evidence suggests some extension of the work year in rural England in the course of the seventeenth century.

A second approach to detecting long-run change in work effort exploits the evidence of long-term trends in real wages. The often-invoked Phelps-Brown and Hopkins time series of builders' wages over seven centuries reveals a fifteenth-century real-wage level far higher than was achieved in the following centuries – indeed, until after the mid–nineteenth century.[32] While there are sound reasons to reject a literal reading of these findings, the overall patterns are durable, having been replicated in neighboring countries and by more refined local studies. Gregory Clark and Ysbrand van der Werf exploited this real-wage pattern to yield a measure of industriousness. They invoke Engel's Law as revealed by nineteenth-century budget studies and amply confirmed by modern investigations. This familiar behavioral regularity states that as incomes rise, the proportion of income spent on food declines. Because late–nineteenth-century wage levels were consistent with an average expenditure of approximately 30 percent of income on food, and because the agricultural labor force required to produce that food did not exceed 25 percent of the total labor force, Clark and van der Werf reason that, because fifteenth-century real wages were similar, consumption patterns should then have been similar as well. The labor force needed to produce the food will then have been somewhat larger because labor productivity in agriculture rose over this long interval. The precise extent of the productivity increase in this period is debated, but even the more generous claims result in estimates of the labor force in agriculture needed in the fifteenth century to be less than 40 percent of the total.

The fifteenth century should have been broadly similar in occupational structure to the mid-nineteenth, but, of course, it was not. To judge by the low level of urbanization and other evidence, agriculture then absorbed a large majority of the labor force: at least 60 percent. "How," Clark and van der Werf ask, "could medieval English society spend only one-third of its income for food products, yet need to employ most of the population in agriculture?" The resolution to this conundrum can only be that fifteenth-century *annual household incomes* actually were much lower than implied

---

[31] Voth, "Seasonality of Conceptions," p. 131.
[32] E. H. Phelps Brown and Sheila V. Hopkins, "Seven Centuries of Builders' Wage-rates," *Economica* 22 (1955): 195–206; "Seven Centuries of the Price of Consumables, Compared with Builders' Wage-rates," *Economica* 23 (1956): 296–314.

by the high *individual day wages*, and that this was so because most people then "consumed" their high income in leisure: They worked fewer and shorter days. By consuming large amounts of leisure, fifteenth-century annual household money incomes were small, and most of this was spent on foodstuffs. This brings the level and structure of consumer demand back into conformity with the occupational structure.[33] In the language of the time allocation model, introduced in Chapter 1, fifteenth-century Z-commodities were leisure-intensive.

A third and more direct approach to the issue of the length of the work year is again offered by Hans-Joachim Voth, who deployed an ingenious methodology to reconstruct detailed time use information from the testimony of witnesses in London's criminal court, the Old Bailey. His source (witnesses describing what they were doing at the time of a crime) compares favorably with modern time use studies, which usually rely on self-reported information in questionnaires.[34] This impressive body of data reveals that Londoners increased their hours of annual labor by at least 40 percent in the period 1750–1830, mostly during the second half of the eighteenth century. His separate calculations for non-agricultural labor in the north of England revealed a smaller but still noteworthy 18 percent increase in annual working hours. Once the more stable work patterns of agriculture (where long hours go further back in time) are factored in, Voth concludes that the annual working hours for the English labor force as a whole increased between 20 and 23 percent – from approximately 2,700 hours to 3,300 hours. (In London alone, annual hours of labor increased from 2,300/2,400 to 3,300/3,400.)[35]

---

[33] Gregory Clark and Ysbrand van der Werf, "The Industrious Revolution or Calvinist Middle Ages?" *Journal of Economic History* 58 (1998): 830–43. Clark and van der Werf go on to reject this conclusion, because they believe that medieval agricultural productivity – per worker as well as per task – was nearly as high as in the nineteenth century. They conclude with the implausible assertion that medieval England must have been consistent with their interpretations and, hence, must have been nearly as industrial as in the mid–nineteenth century. John Hatcher reviews the evidence concerning abundant leisure in post-plague England and concludes that people worked less after the Black Death than they had before. "After they might well have worked less than they could, but before the surfeit of labour meant many could not work as much as they wished to." He does not address in these remarks how the level of work in either period relates to the eighteenth or nineteenth centuries. John Hatcher, "England in the Aftermath of the Black Death," *Past and Present* 144 (1994): 27–8.

[34] Modern time-use studies are discussed in Chapter 6. The methodology is discussed in F. Thomas Juster, "The Validity and Quality of Time Use Estimates Obtained from Recall Diaries," in F. Thomas Juster and Frank Stafford, eds., *Time, Goods, and Well-Being* (Ann Arbor: University of Michigan Press, 1985), pp. 63–91.

[35] Voth, *Time and Work in England, 1750–1830*, p. 130.

This growth came not through an increase in hours of labor per day but through the reduced observance of holy days and of "Saint Mondays."[36] Thus, the evidence provided by the court testimony of Londoners in the 1750s showed the old pre-Reformation leisure patterns to be alive and well; the artisans, shopkeepers, and day laborers who testified in the Old Bailey continued to observe numerous saints' days in the 1750s and often took Monday – Saint Monday – off as well.[37] But by 1800 the same type of evidence reveals Londoners to be at work on the former saints' days and, mostly, on Mondays as well. Finally, the sober regime prescribed by the Protestant reformers centuries earlier had reached London – or, perhaps more correctly, London's guild craftsmen and commercial class. The "Bank Holidays" observed by the Bank of England conform to this pattern: In 1761 the Bank closed for 47 holidays; by 1834 only 4 remained. The transition to an industrious work year of some 3,300–3,400 hours that took place in London in a 50-year period began earlier outside the Great Wen (where Voth found many holy days observed but few Saint Mondays in the 1750s) and earlier still among workers in agriculture where, ironically, tradition seems to have had less of a hold than in the metropolis.

Voth's study focuses on the labor time of the (adult, male) individual in paid employment. But a large portion of the population continued to participate in market activities not entirely via labor for wages, but, in whole or in part, via the production of agricultural commodities, manufactured goods, and services for sale on the market. Here, industrious behavior takes the form not simply of a reduction of leisure time but also, and primarily, of redirected household production time from activities for home use to market sale. Such a reordering of household time, in turn, normally involves increased specialization.

Agricultural Specialization

Specialization in agriculture and related productivity gains during the long eighteenth century is a large topic, but it can be summarized here by reference to recent studies of agriculture in northern France (by Philip

---

[36] Hans-Joachim Voth, "Time and Work in Eighteenth-Century London," *Journal of Economic History* 58 (1998): 29–58. Voth, *Time and Work in England*.

[37] The practice was not unique to England. In the German lands, observance of "blauwe Montag" was a common practice among craft workers. There is no comparable expression in the Netherlands, nor does the avoidance of Monday work appear in payroll records.

Hoffman and George Grantham), England (by Mark Overton, Gregory Clark and Robert Allan), and the Low Countries (Flanders: G. Dejongh and Erik Thoen; Netherlands: Bas van Bavel and Jan-Luiten van Zanden). All have measured substantial productivity growth without anything like a corresponding improvement of technology. Grantham concluded that:

Technical innovation was not a central feature of the growth of agricultural output through the 1840s, when the appearance of commercial fertilizers and the elaboration of mechanical harvesting equipment began significantly to affect methods of production. Rather, up to that time, the growth of output depended more on intensive use of known technology than on novel methods.[38]

What Grantham found in northern France in the century before 1840, Gregory Clark found to be true in England in the two centuries before 1840: Per worker output rose by 50 percent, only 15 percent of which could be accounted for by technical progress. The rest he attributed to reduced leisure and more intense work.[39] In the Low Countries, regional variations in experience complicate the story, but nearly everywhere output growth (land productivity) was substantial and usually paired with significant labor intensification.[40] In general terms, by 1800 broad areas of northern Europe had succeeded in reducing the labor needed per hectoliter of grain produced from six to eight man-days (prevailing in the sixteenth century) to four to five, while the yields per hectare rose from eight to ten hectoliters to twelve to fifteen.[41]

It is still a widely held view that the urbanization rate is a fair general indicator of agricultural productivity: The higher the productivity of agricultural labor, the larger the share of total population that can be

---

[38] George Grantham, "Agricultural Supply during the Industrial Revolution. French Evidence and European Implications," *Journal of Economic History* 49 (1989): 44–5.

[39] Gregory Clark, "Productivity Growth without Technological Change in European Agriculture before 1850," *Journal of Economic History* 47 (1987): 432. Clark's later writings have not always been consistent with this finding.

[40] In Flanders, labor productivity appears to have been stationary over the early modern period, while land productivity rose substantially. G. Dejongh and E. Thoen, "Arable Productivity in Flanders and the Former Territory of Belgium in a Long Term Perspective," in Van Bavel and Thoen, eds., *Land Productivity and Agro-Systems in the North Sea Area* (Turnhout: Brepols, 1999), pp. 30–65. In Holland, a process of productivity growth supported by capital investment up to 1660 gave way to a process of crop diversification and labor intensification in the eighteenth century. De Vries and van der Woude, *The First Modern Economy*, pp. 229–34; B. J. P. van Bavel, "Arable Yields and Total Arable Output in the Netherlands from the late Middle Ages to the end of the Ancien Regime," in Van Bavel and Thoen, *Land Productivity and Agro-Systems*, pp. 85–113.

[41] George Grantham, "Division of Labour. Agricultural Productivity and Occupational Specialization in Pre-industrial France," *Economic History Review* 46 (1993), table 4.

released to the cities.[42] By this standard, Europe should have experienced a forceful urbanization, yet in fact not a great deal had changed in the early modern era: Urban populations, in towns of at least 5,000 inhabitants, rose modestly from 10 to 13 percent of the total between 1500 and 1800.[43] The 1800 figure appears to be nearly three times the comparable Chinese urban percentage, although it is roughly equal to that of Japan in 1800.[44]

The European population remained overwhelmingly rural until the nineteenth century, it is true, but it did not remain overwhelmingly agricultural, at least not if employment is defined by the actual allocation of days of labor rather than by the persistence of a minimal attachment to the land.

In Europe, the urban percentage is simply a poor indicator of occupational diversification. As the rural population came to be organized in more effective market networks, it acquired a more complex occupational character. Again, in broad terms, the 75 percent of the labor time devoted to agriculture in the early sixteenth century (50 percent growing grain) fell to approximately 50 percent (30 percent growing grain) by 1800, as a population of craftsmen, industrial workers, transporters, and the like grew and emerged to fill, as it were, the interstices of rural economic life, exploiting opportunities signaled by a maturing market system and establishing the basis for the Industrial Revolution, an event that *continued* rather than *initiated* northwestern Europe's economic growth process.[45] See Figure 3.2.

Increased agricultural output in the long eighteenth century was an endogenous response to market opportunities that Hoffman showed to be strongly correlated with urban developments. The response took the

---

[42] Paul Bairoch makes this claim a centerpiece of his sweeping analysis of world urbanization. Paul Bairoch, *Cities and Economic Development* (Chicago: University of Chicago Press, 1988).

[43] Jan de Vries, *European Urbanization, 1500–1800* (London: Methuen, 1984).

[44] These estimates are based on Gilbert Rozman, *Urban Networks in Ch'ing China and Tokugawa Japan* (Princeton, N. J.: Princeton University Press, 1973).

[45] The four population categories of Figure 3.2 represent a stylized account of long-term change in western and central Europe. The "large city" (above 10,000) and "small city" (5,000–10,000) categories are from de Vries, *European Urbanization*. The agricultural and non-agricultural divisions are obviously more difficult to measure accurately. The patterns shown here are derived from E. A. Wrigley, "Urban Growth and Agricultural Change. England and the Continent in the Early Modern Period," *Journal of Interdisciplinary History* 15 (1985): 683–728; Robert Allen, "Economic Structure and Agricultural Productivity in Europe, 1300–1800," *European Review of Economic History* 3 (2000): 1–25.

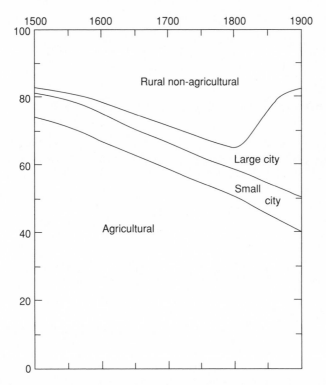

FIGURE 3.2. Shares of European population in four categories, 1500–1800.

form of more work and harder work, and shifting the output-mix toward greater market production. As Grantham put it, "[I]t is the history of markets rather than the history of technology which explains the growth of agricultural labor productivity in the 'late organic economy.'"[46]

Across the Atlantic in North America, philosophers could imagine that an Arcadian society of self-sufficient yeomen was emerging, determined to plant the classical republican virtues in a land-abundant paradise. This is an illusion – the Jeffersonian myth – to which American historians even now remain astonishingly loyal, supposing, as many of them still do, that colonial Americans condemned the modern commercial mentality and that a "market revolution," like the serpent in the garden, expelled Americans from their paradise only in the Jacksonian era, circa 1830.[47] But

[46] George Grantham, "Division of Labour," pp. 2–3.
[47] On the long-regnant "high republican" interpretation of the colonial period, see T. H. Breen, "Narrative of Commercial Life. Consumption, Ideology, and Community on the Eve of the American Revolution," *William and Mary Quarterly* 50 (1993), pp. 478–80,

eighteenth-century contemporaries knew better, remarking often on the
surprising penetration of British material culture and, hence, its commercial regime, to even the most remote North American outposts. As a New
York pamphleteer of 1768 put it, colonists ransacked "the seas and the
wilds of America . . . to make payment for [imported consumer goods],
and the improved lands are cultivated chiefly for the same purpose."[48]
From an early date colonists in British North America came to view their
land-abundant environment not as a platform for self-sufficiency but as a
resource with which to participate – through a flood of marketed tobacco,
rice, indigo, wheat, fish, timber, and tar – in the Atlantic economy's consumer offerings.

Proto-industry

Agricultural specialization was not the only path toward an intensified
commitment of rural household labor time to the market. Whether as an
alternative to agricultural specialization (where poor soils, small farms,
or remote location closed this option) or as a supplement to it (as part
of the internal division of labor), rural households turned increasingly to
what has come to be called "proto-industry."

Proto-industry refers to (usually) rural, household-based production of
manufactures that are sold in nonlocal markets rather than used within the
home or sold locally. It emerged to a position of importance in many European regions but became especially important in northwestern Europe,
where dense concentrations of rural industrial activity grew throughout
northern France, Flanders, the eastern Netherlands, and several parts of
Britain. Although proto-industrial production was commonly organized
and financed by urban merchants, the production processes themselves
relied on small-scale, household-based technologies. It focused primarily
on textiles (the spinning and weaving of flax, wool, and cotton) but also
included the fabrication of a wide variety of products based on metallurgy,
leather, wood, and ceramics.[49]

---

and references cited there. On the so-called "market revolution," see Charles Sellers, *The
    Market Revolution. Jacksonian America, 1815–1846* (Oxford: Oxford University Press,
    1991).
[48] Cited in T. H. Breen, "Narrative of Commercial Life," p. 474.
[49] For surveys of the proto-industrial literature, see Sheilagh Ogilvie and Markus Cerman,
    eds., *European Proto-Industrialization* (Cambridge: Cambridge University Press, 1996);
    René Leboutte, ed., *Protoindustrialisation. Recherches récentes et nouvelles perspectives.
    Mélanges en souvenir de Franklin Mendels* (Geneva: Librairie Droz, 1996).

Proto-industry was of particular importance in redirecting the labor of women and children toward the market and in making effective market use of labor trapped in idleness and underemployment by the seasonal constraints of agriculture. Joan Thirsk's pioneering work on this subject placed a particular emphasis on this decisive activation of household labor in seventeenth-century England. She placed no less emphasis on the simultaneous rise of consumer demand for the myriad petty goods that came to be produced in this way. Initially, poverty may have pushed many rural people in this direction, but Thirsk alerts us to the simultaneous growth of demand:

We can point to numerous communities in the kingdom, especially in towns and in the pastoral-industrial areas, where the labouring classes found cash to spare for consumer goods in 1700 that had no place in their budgets in 1550 – brass cooking pots, iron frying pans, earthenware dishes, knitted stockings, even a lace frill for a cap or apron.[50]

In short: "Purchasing power and productive capacity were thus mutually sustaining."[51] Which is to say, the "coordination problem" (described in Chapter 1) was being overcome, and Thirsk has taken particular pains to draw attention to the role that women played both as proto-industrial producers and as eager consumers of goods whose prosaic character caused them to be ignored (by male historians) for the simple reason that they were purchased primarily by women.[52]

I must dwell on the topic of proto-industry for a moment longer in order to clarify its place in the domestic arrangements of the industrious household. What had been referred to variously as putting-out, Verlag system, or simply as rural industry became a notable feature in numerous European regions over the course of the long eighteenth century, before contracting sharply under the impact of factory-based industry in the nineteenth century. Beginning in the 1970s, historians and economists applied to this phenomenon the term *proto-industry* and sought to theorize its relationship to, among other things, capitalism, modern industry, proletarianization, gender relations, family formation and structure, and

---

[50] Joan Thirsk, *Economic Policies ande Projects. The Development of a Consumer Society in Early Modern England* (Oxford: Oxford University Press, 1978), p. 175.

[51] Ibid., p. 174.

[52] "Starch needles, pins, cooking pots, kettles, frying pans, lace, soap, vinegar, stocking do not appear on [our menfolks'] shopping lists, but they regularly appear on mine. They may ignore them, but could their families manage without them?" Ibid., pp. 22–3.

demographic growth.[53] Certainly it has been overtheorized,[54] but conspic-
uously absent from this large literature (apart from the early observations
of Thirsk just cited) is a focus on proto-industry as an adaptation to an
expanding mercantile economy and its new consumer options.[55]

Fundamental to much of the theorizing, and highly influential in family
history and feminist history more generally, is the concept of the "family economy," which posits the unity of the family as a co-residential
entity and a work unit. In the "family economy," family members participated cooperatively, side by side in a single enterprise that was governed
by economic objectives that were *satisficing* rather than *maximizing*.[56]
Households of the family economy type are a pre-capitalist social formation that seek first and foremost the preservation and perpetuation of
their autonomy and integrity, or, if you will, their self-sufficiency. Peasant
and artisanal households stand as "ideal types" of the family economy.[57]
Finally, the family economy has been seen by historians of women's work
as sustaining something of a "golden age" of women's work: As part of a
family-focused laboring community, women participated equitably in the
world of work.[58]

[53] Major contributions to the concept include Franklin Mendels, "Proto-Industrialization,
the First Phase of the Industrialization Process," *Journal of Economic History* 32 (1972):
241–61; Leboutte, ed., *Protoindustrialisation; Recherches récentes*; Peter Kriedte, Hans
Medick, and Jürgen Schumbohm, *Industrialization Before Industrialization* (Cambridge:
Cambridge University Press, 1981).

[54] Donald C. Coleman, "Proto-industrialization. A Concept Too Many?" *Economic History
Review* 36 (1983): 435–48.

[55] Consider Gloria Main's explanation of the emergence of rural industrial activity where
one would least expect it, in the land-abundant setting of New England, where rural
families beginning in the first half of the eighteenth century "reorganized household
production," so that by the 1770s female weaving, among other activities, "was no
artifact of rural poverty, nor a response to frontier exigency. It was a colonial adaptation to
an expanding mercantile economy, a gendered variant of the intensification of labor...."
Gloria Main, "Gender, Work and Wages in Colonial New England," *William and Mary
Quarterly* 51 (1994): 66.

[56] Tilly and Scott, *Women, Work and the Family*, pp. 15, 21; Bridget Hill, *Women, Work and
Sexual Politics in Eighteenth Century England* (Montreal and Kingston: McGill–Queen's
University Press, 1989), p. 24.

[57] The family economy concept finds its inspiration in the influential work of A. V.
Chayanov, *The Theory of Peasant Economy* (Homewood, Ill.: R. D. Irwin, 1966). He
analyzes the Russian peasant family economy as governed not by profit or maximization
but by the maintenance of a "labor-consumer balance" over the course of the family life
cycle. It is also indebted to the central European concept of "Das ganze Haus" introduced by Otto Brunner: "Das 'Ganze Haus' und die alt-europäische Ökonomik" (1958),
in *Neue Wege der Verfassungs- und Sozialgeschichte* (2nd ed., Gottingen: Vandenhoeck
und Ruprecht, 1968), pp. 103–27.

[58] Highlights from a vast literature include Alice Clark, *Working Life of Women in the Seventeenth Century* ([1919] New York: A. M. Kelly, 1968); Ivy Pinchbeck, *Women Workers*

What happens to this family economy when capitalist market forces grow in strength, threatening the autonomy of peasant and artisanal households? Through what process is the family economy of yore transformed into the "family consumer economy" of modern industrial society, where the household's productive functions are stripped away, leaving for it only the organization of consumption? Social stratification puts pressure on the family economy, which is most obviously manifested by the growth throughout western Europe of sub-peasant social strata. To Hans Medick, and others concerned to detect the mechanisms by which a traditional agrarian society achieved the transition to capitalism, these *unterbäuerliche Schichten* – families without land, or enough land – turned to proto-industrial pursuits as part of a strategy to preserve as much as possible their old way of life and, specifically, the norms of the family economy. In the face of a decomposing traditional peasant society, families turned to industrious handicraft labor, where, as bearers of old mentalities in a new economic setting, they exhibited what Max Weber has noted as "the immensely stubborn resistance of this leading trait of pre-capitalist labor" to full proletarianization.[59] This anachronistically motivated innovation (or, *gleichzeitige Ungleichzeitigkeit*) drove these families toward the "self-exploitation" of their labor because of "the inertia of the [idea of the] traditional family economy as a self-regulating unit of labour, consumption and reproduction...."[60] Yet, ultimately, this strategy could not succeed. In the work of Franklin Mendels and David Levine the proto-industrial family was motivated by the goals of the family economy but tended, inadvertently but inexorably, to undermine itself and speed the process of full proletarianization because of a lack of demographic self-restraint.[61]

---

and the Industrial Revolution (London: George Routledge & Sons, 1930); Lawrence Stone, *The Family, Sex and Marriage in England 1500–1800* (New York: Harper & Row, 1977); Hill, *Women, Work and Sexual Politics*; Martha Howell, *Women, Production and Patriarchy in late Medieval Cities* (Chicago: University of Chicago Press, 1987); Claudia Goldin, "The U-Shaped Female Labor Force Function in Economic Development and Economic History," in T. Paul Schultz, ed., *Investment in Women's Human Capital* (Chicago: University of Chicago Press, 1995), pp. 61–90.

[59] Max Weber, *The Protestant Ethic and the Spirit of Capitalism* ([1903/04] New York: Harper & Row, 1930), p. 60.

[60] Medick, "The Proto-Industrial Family Economy," p. 297–8. The "synchronous anachronism" might best be thought of as a sort of time lag, causing the family to harbor antique ideals and forms of behavior in a new, inhospitable setting. Medick thought this hybrid constituted a distinct "mode of production" intermediary between Marx's feudal and capitalist modes of production.

[61] Franklin Mendels, "Niveau des salaires et âge au marriage en Flandre, XVIIe-XVIIIe siècles," *Annales: Economies, Sociétés, Civilisations* 39 (1984): 939–56; David Levine, *Family Formation in an Age of Nascent Capitalism* (New York: Academic Publishers, 1977).

Proto-industry endowed the Industrial Revolution with its workers, not its consumers.

Medick, pushing the argument a step further, viewed the proto-industrial family as evolving a discrete "mode of production" as its interests diverged from those of the peasantry from which it came and among whom it lived. This mode of production featured a rather egalitarian pooling of family labor in a common enterprise. Proto-industry "brought the man back into the household," according to Medick. In support of this view he quotes a Northampton shoemaker:

No single-handed man can live; he must have a whole family at work, because a single-handed man is so badly paid he can scarce provide the necessaries of life.... As soon as they [the children] are big enough to handle an awl, they are obliged to come downstairs and work.[62]

This whole family at work lived in material circumstances that led to the development of a distinctive culture. "Coffee, tea, and alcohol became necessary stimulants as the conditions of production deteriorated and work became more degrading," while "sensuality and sexuality could develop much more freely in the peer group socialization of rural artisans than was possible in a community of peasant proprietors."[63] Such families, in time, were stripped of any material sanction (inheritance) to bind the allegiance of grown children who could freely leave the house, marry, and found new nuclear family units.[64] Step by step, these rude, industrious families – with husband and wife working side by side, exploiting their children, "the capital of the poor man" – drifted away from the norms of the traditional society of peasants and artisans to form its proletariat. Here, again, proto-industry produces capitalism's workers, not its consumers.[65]

The conclusions historians have drawn from this literature, especially through the influential work of Tilly and Scott, are: (1) proto-industry was a response to poverty, usually a response that reinforced and intensified

---

[62] Quoted in Medick, "The Proto-Industrial Family Economy," p. 305.

[63] Hans Medick, "The Proto-industrial Family Economy," in Peter Kriedte, Hans Medick, and Jürgen Schlumbohm, *Industrialization Before Industrialization* (Cambridge: Cambridge University Press, 1981), pp. 69, 70.

[64] Medick, "Proto-Industrial Family Economy," p. 303.

[65] What is worse, these workers, harboring the atavistic culture and ideals of the family economy, could not readily become modern consumers. Seeking to preserve a traditional way of life, they mistook high prices as a signal for "feasting, playing and drinking in exactly those situations of potential growth in which the capitalist putter-out could have obtained maximum profits." Ibid., p. 301.

pauperization in the long run (it smoothed the path toward proletarianization, a precondition for modern industrialization); (2) the protoindustrial family was a unit of pooled family labor seeking to preserve a traditional family economy against all odds (its hybrid culture made it an intermediate mode of production); and (3) husband and wife, indeed the whole family, worked cooperatively, without a pronounced or oppressive division of labor. Proto-industry was the last vestige of a pre-capitalist world hospitable to women's labor, preceding the construction of "separate spheres."

The weight of the evidence concerning proto-industry in northwestern Europe requires us to question all three of these general statements. The key problem with each of them is found in the assumption that the protoindustrial household, true to the family economy ideal, functioned as a cooperative unit of production and labor. In fact, it was usually individuals rather than entire family units who participated in proto-industrial labor. The sub-peasant social strata pieced together livelihoods out of highly diverse market activities; these rarely featured the joint labor of husbands and wives, and in many cases the adaptive strategies of these households led them away from – rather than propelled them toward – proletarianization.[66] Pamela Sharpe showed that most female worsted hand spinners in Yorkshire and lace makers in Devon were in no sense complementing their husbands' trades; Peter Earle's study of female workers in London, based on court depositions, found that only one woman in ten worked in the same trade as her husband in the period 1695–1725.[67] Liana Vardi's study of proto-industry in eighteenth-century northern France emphasizes the entrepreneurialism of the villagers.[68] Ulrich Pfister's study of

[66] Ad Knotter, "Problemen van de 'family economy.' Gezinsarbeid en arbeidsmarkt in preindustrieël Europa," in Michiel Baud and Theo Engelen, eds., *Samen wonen, samen werken? Vijf essays over de geschiedenis van arbeid en gezin* (Hilversum: Verloren, 1994), pp. 35–71. On the adaptive family economy, see Richard Wall, "Some Implications of the Earnings, Income and Expenditure Patterns of Married Women in Populations in the Past," in Henderson and Wall, eds., *Poor Women and Children in the European Past* (London: Routledge, 1994), pp. 312–35. On the diversity of economic activities, see Michael Mitterauer, "Geschlechtsspezifischische Arbeitsteilung und Geschecterrollen in ländlichen Gesellschaften Mitteleuropas," in *Familie und Arbeitsteilung. Historischvergleichende Studien* (Wien/Koln: Böhlau, 1992), pp. 58–148.

[67] Pam Sharpe, "Literally Spinsters. A New Interpretation of Local Economy and Demography in Colyton in the Seventeenth and Eighteenth Centuries," *Economic History Review*, 44 (1991): 46–65; Peter Earle, "The Female Labour Market in London in the Late Seventeenth and Early Eighteenth Centuries," *Economic History Review* 42 (1989): 328–53.

[68] Liana Vardi, *The Land and the Loom. Peasants and Profit in Northern France, 1680–1800* (Durham, N. C.: Duke University Press, 1993).

the Canton of Zürich stressed the highly varied forms of rural industry, of which cooperative family labor was only one, and by no means the most important.[69] Focusing specifically on peasant households, Martine Segalen distinguished 69 distinct tasks performed by nineteenth-century French peasant families. The vast majority were not performed by wife and husband together, even when their work contributed to the joint enterprise of the family economy.[70] Similarly, Frederic Le Play's pioneering mid–nineteenth-century budget study found that in 80 percent of the 36 families investigated the wives were employed for at least part of the year by individuals who were not members of the family.[71] More generally, Michael Anderson's review of British family history led him to conclude "that in much of England it has been a very long time since the majority of parents and children worked together in a unitary household economy, based in or immediately around their own home."[72]

These family units did not ordinarily form a single working unit and did not carry with them the complement of mentalities ascribed to them, without much evidence, by those who constructed the family economy concept. The Achilles heel of this concept is the ahistorical assertion that social differentiation and wage labor in the countryside were novelties that spread with proto-industrial activity, thereby forcing a sudden and painful break with a traditional way of life. Wage labor, landless families, and multiple employments had been characteristic of most of western Europe for a much longer period, and in this context individual labor rather than the collective labor of the family was the prevailing pattern. Finally, one cannot find a "golden age" for women's work within this

---

[69] Ulrich Pfister, "The Proto-Industrial Household Economy. Toward a Formal Analysis," *Journal of Family History* 17 (1992): 201–32; Ulrich Pfister, *Die Züricher Fariques. Protoindustrielles Wachstum vom 16. zum 18. Jahrhundert* (Zürich: Chronos, 1992), pp. 264–80.

[70] Martine Segalen, *Love and Power in the Peasant Family. Rural France in the Nineteenth Century* (Chicago: University of Chicago Press, 1983).

[71] Frederic Le Play, *Les ouvriers Européens* (Tours: Alfred Mame et fils, 1877–89), cited in Wall, "Some Implications," pp. 312–25. Le Play determined that the wives of his 36 households worked, on average, 311 days per year: 83 in paid labor outside the household, 87 in unpaid labor as part of the productive activities of the family enterprise, and 141 in household work and child rearing.

[72] Michael Anderson, "New Insights into the History of the Family in Britain," in Anne Digby, Charles Feinstein, and David Jenkins, eds., *New Directions in Economic and Social History*, Vol. 2 (London: Macmillan, 1992), p. 131. See also Peter Laslett, "Family and Household as Work Group and Kin Group. Areas of Traditional Europe Compared," in Richard Wall, Jean Robin, and Peter Laslett, eds., *Family Forms in Historic Europe* (Cambridge: Cambridge University Press, 1983), pp. 513–63.

imagined mode of production. As Ad Knotter puts it in his comprehensive review and critique of the family economy concept: "Women's work was as confined to low-skilled occupations, with little status and low pay, in the middle ages as in the early modern, as in the modern, industrial period."[73] What Knotter concludes for western Europe as a whole has also been confirmed for the English case, where it had long been thought that a precocious capitalism and the Industrial Revolution undermined the place of women in the labor markets, confining them earlier than their sisters elsewhere to the "separate sphere" of the home.[74]

I have dwelt on this topic at some length, clearing away a thick underbrush of proto-industrial and feminist theorizing, in order to reveal a clearer view of the household as an adaptive, strategizing entity capable of responding to the opportunities and threats of the market instead of being fatally encumbered by time lags and cultural atavisms. The long eighteenth century of the industrious household exhibited a substantial continuity, despite the undeniably major changes occurring in Europe's economic, political, and cultural life. The conventions of periodization to which historians of Europe are so accustomed are not necessarily applicable to all dimensions of historical experience.[75] Here, it is important to confirm that neither an "emerging capitalism" in general nor the British Industrial Revolution in particular altered the basic patterns of women's engagement with market-oriented labor. Over time, new opportunities arose in some sectors and were closed off in others, but the efforts to measure women's rates of labor force participation in the first half of the nineteenth century, tentative though they must be, show them to be higher than they would ever be again until recent decades and higher than observed in developing economies of the twentieth century.[76]

---

73 Ad Knotter, "Problemen van de 'Family Economy,'" p. 69 (my translation).

74 Amanda Vickery, "Golden Age to Separate Spheres? A Review of the Categories and Chronology of English Women's History," *Historical Journal* 36 (1993): 383–414; Judith Bennett, "History That Stands Still. Women's Work in the European Past, *Feminist Studies* 14 (1988): 269–83.

75 Robert B. Shoemaker, *Gender in English Society, 1650–1850. The Emergence of Separate Spheres?* (London: Longman, 1998), pp. 308–18.

76 Horrell and Humphries's exhaustive survey of available data on women's labor force participation led them to conclude that early industrialization brought with it an intensification of married women's participation: By 1787–1815, they estimate, two-thirds of married women contributed monetarily to household income. This level fell off to just under half of married women by midcentury. Sheilagh Ogilvie, in a study of south German women's labor, observes that "Even the most conservative assumptions [used by her to interpret the available data] yield a female labour force participation rate that nearly equals the rate recorded for Germany in 1999 (42 per cent) and significantly exceeds

Proto-industry, whatever else it might have been, was first and foremost a form of labor intensification, a strategy of the industrious household. It drew into the market economy "marginal" labor, often in marginal seasons, residing in marginal districts. Typically, proto-industrial workers had no direct contact with consumers, depending on merchant intermediaries to organize production and find markets for their output. But other forms of industrious labor emerged in the long eighteenth century that depended on close and direct contact with consumers. Many specialties of the garment-making sector offered new opportunities for industrious labor, especially for women.

Clothing and Shopkeeping

Beginning in the mid–seventeenth century an important transformation took place in the structure of the clothing-production industry. Men had always controlled tailoring, regardless of the sex for which the garment was intended. But the newly fashionable mantua, a draped, loose-hanging female garment made of light linen and cotton fabrics, represented a shift away from heavy woolen molded garments. The mantua maker was, from the outset, a woman. After withstanding guild prosecution in London and Paris (where they became recognized in 1675), mantua makers linked to millinery and dressmaking shops established a genteel female fashion industry in major cities. By the eighteenth century the continued downward penetration of these fashions also placed plebian outer-garment fabrication in female hands.[77] The same process was at work in the Netherlands. From the late seventeenth century, nonguild female seamstresses (*naaisters*) gained ground in competition with the (male) tailors' guilds as new fashion, fabric, and production techniques increased the demand for women's garments. In the eighteenth century, the seamstresses became part of the guild system in many towns and dominated the production of female outerwear.[78]

Beverly Lemire pushes this story further downward, to the workshops that emerge to produce military uniforms (slopsellers) and many other

---

those for Latin American and the Caribbean (35 per cent), South Asia (33 per cent), or the Middle east and North Africa (27 per cent) [in 2000–1]." Sheilagh Ogilvie, "Women and Labour Markets in Early Modern Germany," *Jahrbuch für Wirtschaftsgeschichte* 2004/2 (2004): 36.

[77] John Styles, "Clothing the North. The Supply of Non-Elite Clothing in the Eighteenth-Century North of England," *Textile History* 25 (1994): 152.

[78] Bibi Panhuysen, *Maatwerk. Kleermakers, naaisters, oudkleerkopers en de gilden (1500–1800)* (Amsterdam: IISG, 2000), pp. 326–7.

routine items of clothing. While mantua making, even in the countryside, was a genteel occupation "for the daughters of the middling ranks,"
Lemire goes on to note that

women of the lower classes plied their needles stitching ready-made goods in large
workshops, back rooms of shops, garret and lodging-house rooms. These were
the sites of a vast and largely unrecorded female manufacturing infrastructure.[79]

This "vast infrastructure" constituted a ready-made clothing industry,
something historians had earlier regarded to have emerged only in the
nineteenth century. Now, "there is no doubt that ready-made cloths
appeared, and possibly became widespread, in the seventeenth century."[80]
Simultaneous with these developments the sewing and stitching of
clothes within the household shriveled into insignificance. Sir Frederic
Morton Eden complained in 1797 of the laboring families of southern
England: "Their wives seldom make up any article of dress, except making and mending clothes for the children."[81]
When the secondhand trade in garments – stolen or otherwise – is
added to the story of informal production and distribution of ready-made
clothing, one can appreciate Lemire's evocation of industrious English
womanhood:

Up and down the streets of towns and villages and throughout England's labouring
districts were shops, stalls and front rooms, where women with scant capital
bargained and sold clothing and all manner of household wares.[82]

But the larger story of the textiles and clothing sector is that a vast enlargement of demand (discussed in Chapter 4) led to the supercession and

---

[79] Beverly Lemire, *Dress, Culture, and Commerce. The English Clothing Trade Before the
Factory, 1660–1800* (New York: St. Martin's Press, 1997), p. 4.

[80] Margaret Spufford, "The Cost of Apparel in Seventeenth-Century England, and the Accuracy of Gregory King," *Economic History Review* 53 (2000): 701.

[81] Sir Frederick Morton Eden, *The State of the Poor. A History of the Labouring Classes
in England, with Parochial Reports*, abridged ed. (London: George Routledge and Sons,
1928), pp. 108–9.

[82] Lemire, *Dress, Culture, and Commerce*, p. 115. Elsewhere, Lemire affirms that the new,
textile-focused opportunities for women to participate *as individuals* in the market economy constituted a "reshaping of work patterns" that "contributed substantially to the
health of family economies and so to the demand for consumer goods." But she sees the
essential difference in this: Previously, women and children had also worked, but without regular cash payment for their efforts. "Their dependent economic position barred
them from really making personal choices as consumers. ..." Thus it was the individual
earnings, leading to a stronger voice in support of one's consumer aspirations within
the household, that she identifies as the critical innovation of the long eighteenth century. Beverly Lemire, *Fashion's Favorite. The Cotton Trade and the Consumer in Britain,
1660–1800* (Oxford: Oxford University Press, 1991), p. 51.

evasion of old, usually guild-controlled, crafts by new production methods and distribution systems. In many parts of northwestern Europe, tailors, dressmakers, mercers, seamstresses, and secondhand-clothes dealers were encroaching on one another's terrains to achieve a new flexibility in supplying a newly dynamic and varied market for clothing.

The emphasis Lamire places on the informal, irregular nature of these industrious activities in the production and distribution of clothing can be extended to the larger world of eighteenth- and early–nineteenth-century retailing. The developing retailing networks (discussed in more detail in Chapter 4) were augmented in this period by the peddling, hawking, shop keeping, and tavern keeping of working-class entrepreneurs. The historian of these "penny capitalists" in early–nineteenth-century England confesses:

It is as difficult to discover the number of aspiring publicans and shopkeepers who managed to transform their dreams into reality as it [is] to estimate the number of penny capitalists selling in the streets. Many – perhaps most – working-class owned shops and beerhouses were run by women on a part-time basis, with the result that they rarely appear in the census returns.[83]

Similarly, the director of Belgium's celebrated 1846 census, Adolphe-Lambert Quetelet, claimed that independent evidence revealed a massive undercount of the *caberets*, informal drinking establishments that had multiplied in both France and Belgium over the previous century, such that, in his view, there was then one for every fifteen to twenty households.[84]

This proliferation of retailing alerts us to the specific form that the division of labor took in the long eighteenth century. E. A. Wrigley noted that "the majority of those living in the countryside but no longer able to find work on the land went, not into industry, but to the traditional trades and services. . . . [As late as 1831] adult employment in manufacturing was only 10 percent of adult male employment, whereas retail trade and handicrafts comprised 32 percent."[85] Female employment, difficult though it is to track quantitatively, will have grown even faster: Women operated beer and gin shops, the numerous clothing shops documented

[83] John Benson, *The Penny Capitalists. A Study of Nineteenth-Century Working-Class Entrepreneurs* (New Brunswick, N. J.: Rutgers University Press, 1983), pp. 118–19.

[84] Cited in George Alter, "Work and Income in the Family Economy. Belgium, 1853 and 1891," *Journal of Interdisciplinary History* 15 (1984): 268.

[85] E. A. Wrigley, "Men on the Land and Men in the Countryside," in L. Bonfield et al., eds., *The World We Have Gained* (Oxford: Basil Blackwell, 1986), pp. 296, 297.

by Lamire, and many high-fashion boutiques as well. One can speak of a gradual feminization of retailing.[86]

Budget Studies of Industrious Households

Once the concept of proto-industrial activity is understood in its proper household context, we are prepared to see the rising supply of market-oriented labor, especially that of women and children, in a light more favorable to the industrious revolution. One can hardly ask for a better contemporary guide to this behavior than Daniel Defoe, who may fairly be called the chronicler of the industrious revolution. He described the phenomenon this way:

A poor labouring Man that goes abroad to his Day Work, and Husbandry, Hedging, Ditching, Threshing, Carting, etc. and brings home his Week's Wages, suppose at eight pence to twelve pence a Day ...; if he has a Wife and three or four children to feed, and who get little or nothing for themselves, must fare hard, and live poorly. ...

But if this Man's Wife and Children can at the same time get Employment, if at next door, or at the next Village there lives a clothier, or a Bay Maker, or a Stuff or Drugget Weaver; the Manufacturer sends the poor Woman combed Wool, or carded Wool every week to spin, and she gets eight pence or nine pence a day at home; the Weaver sends for her two little children, and they work by the loom, winding, filling Quills, etc. and the two bigger Girls spin at home with their Mother, and these earn three pence or four pence a day each: So that put it together, the family at home gets as much as the Father gets Abroad, and generally more.... The Father gets them food, and the Mother gets them Clothes....[87]

The earliest budget studies of English agricultural laborers' families confirm that women and children commonly contributed significantly to household money income, but they do not show these contributions to have been as large as Defoe suggested: Instead of contributing half of total household earnings, their earnings tended to hover nearer to 25 percent.[88] In a comprehensive analysis of available household budget studies

---

[86] Female membership of the Antwerp mercers guild (required for all retailers in the city) stood at only 7 percent of the total in 1515–85 but rose, gradually, to 25 percent (always excluding women working in the name of their husbands) by the second half of the eighteenth century. Laura Van Aert, "To Thrive or Survive? Retailers in Antwerp (ca. 1648–ca. 1748)," (Unpublished paper, University of Antwerpen, 2005).

[87] Daniel Defoe, *A Plan of the English Commerce*, 2 vols. (London, 1726–7) pp. 89–91.

[88] Thomas Sokoll, "Early Attempts at Accounting the Unaccountable. Davies and Eden's Budgets of Agricultural Labouring Families in Late-Eighteenth-Century England," in Pierenkemper, ed., *Zür Ökonomik des Privaten Haushalts*, pp. 34–60.

of English manual workers in the period 1787–1865, Sara Horrell and Jane Humphries show that Defoe was rather exuberant in his estimates, but he may not have been far from the mark for the specific stage of the family life cycle used in his illustration. In their study of 1,190 household budgets (for intact, husband–wife families), they detected a pattern of gradually rising monetary contributions by wives and children to total household income up to the 1830s (from about 25 to more than 40 percent), followed by a decline in the difficult 1840s, and a further decline in the 1860s, when rising adult male earnings begin to dominate the picture (discussed in more detail in Chapter 5).[89]

Horrell and Humphries's data, when pooled for the entire period, also allow for an analysis of the composition of total household money earnings across the family life cycle. This reveals that the subordinate role of wives and children's earnings is nothing of the sort as the (male) household head ages. While such earnings contribute little when the family is young, and the head is in his twenties or thirties, they rise steadily toward Defoe's 50 percent level when the husband is over forty-five and at least some of his children are capable of contributing substantially. In these working-class households, the earnings capacity of children was very much a substitute for that of their mothers and dominated the trend toward higher non-breadwinner contributions as the household head aged. But these earnings – whether of the mother or the children – were not substitutes for the father's earnings until his earning capacity began to falter with advancing age. Until then, the industrious market-oriented labor of the family members served substantially to raise total household earnings.[90]

Horrell and Humphries also examined another form of potential substitution. Did the earnings of wives and children play a strategic role primarily in households headed by the poorest, least-skilled male workers? That is, did these "supplementary" earnings compensate for the inadequate earnings of the economically weakest adult males, causing total household earnings to be more equally distributed than adult male earnings

---

[89] Sara Horrell and Jane Humphries, "Women's Labour Force Participation and the Transition to the Male-Breadwinner Family, 1790–1865," *Economic History Review* 48 (1995): 89–117; Sara Horrell and Jane Humphries, "The Origins and Expansion of the Male Breadwinner Family. The Case of Nineteenth-Century Britain," in Janssens, ed., *Rise and Decline*, pp. 25–65.

[90] The interpretation of Horrell and Humphries is decidedly less "optimistic" than that given here. This difference is accounted for in part by their focus on the course of events in the decades before 1830, the classic era of the Industrial Revolution. The patterns I report here are most clearly evident when the entire data set, extending to the 1860s, is taken into account.

alone? Their budget data did not support this supposition. In all subperiods of their analysis, the cross-sectional pattern of male earnings by occupation and the cross-sectional pattern of family incomes were the same: In general, the higher the earnings of the father, the higher the earnings of the rest of the family members, and this pattern became more pronounced over the period of early English industrialization.[91] The net effect of this industrious activity among manual workers was an increase in household earnings inequality.

The period examined by Horrell and Humphries is simultaneously the "culmination" of the industrious revolution and the classic period of the British Industrial Revolution. Clearly, many forces were at work on household structure, the sexual division of labor, and the position of children in the family and in the economy. Moreover, occupational groups fared differently, and the ups and downs of the business cycle had their effects as well. While generalization is risky, a few observations appear warranted:

1. Married women were heavily engaged in market work. Early industrialization appears to have intensified this engagement, although women's work remained highly concentrated within the occupational structure, and after the mid–nineteenth century women's money earnings entered a decline that would continue into the twentieth century.

2. Children and women were substitutes from the perspective of the family economy and would remain so until compulsory schooling began to remove children from the paid labor force later in the nineteenth century.

3. The lifecycle earnings of working-class households peaked as grown children became numerous and so long as they remained in the household. Consequently, the well-being of the family as a whole depended on the expenditure patterns and internal redistributions

---

[91] Horrell and Humphries note one exception to this general pattern: Male stocking knitters and handloom weavers had very low average incomes, while their family members' earnings ranked relatively highly, thus mitigating the impact of the declining earnings of these men and, perhaps, helping account for the persistence of the handloom weaver in the face of factory competition. John Lyons's study of the handloom weavers demonstrates that in the 1820s, as the factory earnings of children and youths rose above what they could earn at the loom, families chose to send their children to the factory while adults remained at the loom, even when securing such work for the children required the family's physical relocation to a factory towns. John Lyons, "Family Response to Economic Decline. Handloom Weavers in Early Nineteenth Century Lancashire," *Research in Economic History* 12 (1989): 45–91.

supported by earnings from multiple individuals. The consumer behavior of the industrious household – how it satisfied the needs and wants of its members, or allowed individual members to do so – therefore becomes of particular importance to any assessment of the household as an economic unit.

Work Intensity

The intensity of work effort is the most difficult dimension of the industrious revolution to measure. Indeed, it is a topic that even economists working with contemporary data usually prefer to sidestep. Most historical work on this topic concerns agriculture, where piece rate payments for agricultural tasks offer opportunities to observe work intensification and output changes under conditions of constant technology. Under assumptions about the competitive character of the markets that generate such data, one can make inferences about changes in work intensity. We have already alluded to some of this literature. The evidence is clear that labor intensification had reached high levels in both agriculture and industry by the late eighteenth century. What is less clear is just when this level had been attained.[92] Much remains obscure on this topic.

The same might be said of studies that seek to relate labor intensity to trends in attained height – specifically, to the unexpected deterioration of attained height observed in the early stages of industrialization. Could the declines in average height attained by the generations who grew to adulthood in the 1780–1840 period be accounted for by increased energy expenditure rather than by diminished nutritional intake?[93] The only generalizations that appear secure at present are that: (1) In the early nineteenth century the pace of agricultural work in northwestern Europe was

---

[92] Gregory Clark sometimes argues that the largest shift toward more intensive labor in English agriculture had occurred already in the fourteenth century. Gregory Clark, "Labour Productivity in English Agriculture, 1300–1800," in Campbell and Overton, eds., *Land, Labour and Livestock*, pp. 211–35. See also Gregory Clark, "Too Much Revolution. Agriculture and the Industrial Revolution, 1700–1860," in Mokyr, *The British Industrial Revolution*, pp. 226–9.

[93] For a spirited discussion of these rival explanations of the decline in stature, see the debate between Voth and Komlos: Hans-Joachim Voth, "Height, Nutrition, and Labor. Recasting the 'Austrian Model,'" *Journal of Interdisciplinary History* 25 (1995): 627–36; "Physical Exertion and Stature in the Habsburg Monarchy, 1730–1800," *Journal of Interdisciplinary History* 27 (1996): 263–75; John Komlos and Albert Ritschl, "Holy Days, Work Days, and the Standard of Living in the Habsburg Monarchy," *Journal of Interdisciplinary History* 26 (1995): 57–66; John Komlos, "Shrinking in a Growing Economy? The Mystery of Physical Stature During the Industrial Revolution," *Journal of Economic History* 58 (1998): 779–802.

greater than elsewhere in similar activities, and (2) the pace of agricultural work then exceeded that in less developed countries at much later dates, when they had attained comparable levels in their standard of living. The timing of this intensification remains a topic of debate, but the available evidence is consistent with the view that industriousness rather than immiseration led to the stature diminution of this age.

There were many margins at which the time of the household could be redeployed toward market-oriented labor. The tradeoffs were not simply between labor and leisure. They were also, and crucially, between household labor and marketed labor and between work and education. The scope for increasing marketed labor came from reducing the daily, weekly, and season irregularities in the rhythm of work; filling the time of the young, old, and housebound; and intensifying the pace of work itself. Not all of these margins were worked by all types of households, but over the course of the long eighteenth century the "per household work effort" rose considerably, and in so doing, the course of annual household money earnings diverged from the daily adult male wage. The scope of this increase in work effort cannot now be measured with any claim to accuracy. But, as a mental exercise, one might consider the following: If, over the long eighteenth century, the average days of annual labor rose by 20 percent, the number of household workers engaged in market-oriented labor rose by 20 percent, and the intensification of labor rose by 10 percent, the overall augmentation of market-oriented labor per household would have reached 58 percent. Standing against this we should find a diminution in household labor and, hence, altered consumption technologies. In Gary Becker's vocabulary, money earnings toward the end of the industrious revolution came closer than before to approximating the "full income" position of the household.[94]

The industrious revolution is not a concept that aspires to "explain" the Industrial Revolution. Our goal is rather to provide for a fuller account of the context in which the new technologies and organizational changes that characterize the Industrial Revolution took place. The industrious context of the era was not by itself sufficient to trigger the Industrial Revolution, because it can be observed in places well removed from the British regions of rapid industrial growth; and, as will be discussed in the following chapter, the new consumption patterns of industrious

---

[94] This was an era in which the adult male wage, the usual focus of studies of purchasing power, ceased to be a reliable guide. In recent decades, as the real earnings of individuals have come to follow a course distinct from the real earnings of families, the same phenomenon is in evidence.

working-class households could not by themselves account for a major share of the new industrial output. What is argued instead is that the industrious context gave early industrialization in Britain special characteristics that later industrialization processes elsewhere, occurring in different labor supply contexts, would not possess.

What I have in mind can be illustrated by calling to mind D. N. McClosky's elegant dictum on the essence of the Industrial Revolution: "Ingenuity rather than abstinence governed the industrial revolution." Written when the Industrial Revolution still appeared to mark an acceleration of production fueled by new technologies and forms of industrial organization, McCloskey's phrase held that invention, by increasing productivity, was far more important than the abstention from current consumption required to secure higher savings and capital investment. The current understanding of the macroeconomic patterns of British industrialization has greatly reduced the measured rate of productivity growth (i.e., "ingenuity"), and the evidence reviewed here of a substantial growth of factor inputs pushes these measurements down yet further. The slow growth of GDP per capita leads to an even slower growth of GDP per work hour. Voth, who detected a veritable flood of additional labor in late–eighteenth-century London, turns McCloskey's dictum on its head: "Abstinence was more important than ingenuity in . . . the industrial revolution." But now it was abstention from leisure, and this in order to secure greater consumption.[95] Indeed, Voth continues, to the extent that per capita incomes rose, it "was a result of extra toil, and not of rising productivity: perspiration, not inspiration . . . [governed the] first industrial revolution."[96]

Economists tend to dismiss input-driven growth as something other, and less, than real growth. Voth's conclusion that perspiration rather than inspiration accounted for much of Britain's eighteenth-century growth led him to associate Britain's experience with that of the Asian "Tiger" economies of the late twentieth century, whose growth Paul Krugman dismissively characterized as "Stalinist Growth": driven by additional factor inputs more than by productivity improvements.[97] My argument is different: Growth usually *begins* as factor-driven, whether in early modern Europe, nineteenth-century Japan, or twentieth-century East and

---

[95] Voth, "Time and Work," p. 56. See also M. A. Bienefeld, *Working Hours in British Industry. An Economic History* (London: Weidenfeld and Nicolson, 1972), pp. 15–19.
[96] Voth, *Time and Work*, pp. 271–2.
[97] Paul Krugman, "The Myth of Asia's Miracle," *Foreign Affairs* 73 (1994): 62–78.

Southeast Asia. Its *continuation* requires a shift toward rising productivity, and the success of this shift is related not only to the investment decisions of firms and entrepreneurs but also to the consumption and investment decisions of households.

Alternative Explanations

Before proceeding with the development of the industrious revolution model, I must pause to consider interpretations of the same general phenomena that come to very different conclusions. The industrious revolution is an "optimistic" approach in the sense that it interprets the behavior of ordinary working people in the context of their aspirations and of their choices. This is not to deny that these choices are often highly constrained, but it does reject the view that they do not exist.

Oppressed workers. The most widely held and fundamental objection to my approach argues that what I call aspiring consumers were simply oppressed workers. The argument is familiar, because it is the standard story of how a working class was forged – *had* to come into being, much against the will of the human raw material – in order to create an industrial capitalist order. The creation of this order, the construction of the iron cage that confines us all, required the destruction of an old way of life governed by the tenets of a moral economy. Men accustomed to mixing work and play according to their own lights, to seasonal work rhythms and alternative bouts of intense labor and idleness, had to be subjected to systematic work discipline[98] and:

Men who were non-accumulative, non-acquisitive, accustomed to work for subsistence, not for maximization of income, had to be made obedient to the cash stimulus. . . . [99]

The inherently collectivist, anti-individualist English worker of the eighteenth century, in E. P. Thompson's view, actively resisted consumption innovations as a threat to his way of life: "Capitalist process and non-economic customary behavior are in active and conscious conflict, as is

[98] The classic statement of work intensification under early industrialization is E. P. Thompson, "Time, Work-Discipline, and Industrial Capitalism," *Past and Present* 38 (1967): 56–97; see also Keith Hopkins, "Work and Leisure in Pre-Industrial Society," *Past and Present* 29 (1964): 50–62; Asa Briggs, "Work and Leisure in Industrial Society," *Past and Present* 30 (1965): 96–102.

[99] Sidney Pollard, *The Genesis of Modern Management* ([1965] Harmondsworth: Penguin, 1969), p. 106.

resistance to new patterns of consumption."[100] In short, emergent capitalism confronted the dual task of creating its labor force of industrious workers *and* creating its consumers.

The "needs of capital" seemed to explain this inexorable push to regularize work and lengthen the workday and the work year, and this explanation found support among Marxist and classical economists alike. Industrial capitalism, so it was argued, advances with the rise of the capital/labor ratio. As the number and cost of machines per worker increases, profits come to depend on keeping these capital assets continuously in operation. Thus, the habits of labor must be altered to conform to the insistent demands of the machine.[101] This was an insight into the workings of the capitalist economy that much impressed Karl Marx. Technology embodied in capital, which under socialism could liberate workers from drudgery, imposed under capitalism only longer hours of labor, because labor is the source of surplus value – the capitalist's profit.[102]

With such pedigrees, it is little wonder that a belief that industrialization imposed – and imposes still – additional hours of work has long been accepted as a stylized fact. Studies of the Industrial Revolution are generally in agreement that the annual working year lengthened by 20–25 percent across the classic 1760–1830 period.[103] What *is* in dispute is the motivation. Did people who valued leisure and autonomy find themselves forced to work harder and longer and forced to abandon an ancient material culture with regret? Or did they actively participate – in their own messy, inefficient ways – in the pursuit of goals of their own that helped bring about something not fully foreseen, a new sort of economy and society? In pondering this question, we must leave open the possibility that one might need assistance in pursuing "one's own" goals. The

---

[100] E. P. Thompson, *Custom in Common* (New York: New Press, 1993), pp. 12, 14. Thompson does acknowledge that later, well into the nineteenth century, working peoples' needs "were remodeled, the threshold of their material expectations raised, traditional cultural satisfactions devalued, and the authority of customary expectations destroyed." John Styles, "Custom or Consumption? Plebian Fashion in Eighteenth-Century England," in Berg and Eger, eds., *Luxury in the Eighteenth Century*, p. 103.

[101] John Rule, *The Experience of Labour in Eighteenth-Century Industry* (London: Croom Helm, 1981), p. 59.

[102] Karl Marx, *Capital* (Moscow: International Publishers, 1961), Vol. I, Part III, "The Production of Absolute Surplus Value," pp. 177–311.

[103] Nick Tranter, "The Labour Supply, 1780–1860," in Roderick Floud and Donald McCloskey, eds., *The Economic History of Britain Since 1700*, first edition (Cambridge: Cambridge University Press, 1981), pp. 204–26; Sidney Pollard, "Labour in Great Britain," in Peter Mathias and M. M. Poston, eds., *Cambridge Economic History of Europe*, vol. 7 (Cambridge: Cambridge University Press, 1978), pp. 55–9.

achievement of more regular and more intensive labor through the discipline of the factory system may have been acceded to by workers, their complaints notwithstanding, in order to achieve the higher incomes that (they sensed) would have been unrealizable if it depended on personal self-discipline. After the manner of Ulysses requesting to be tied to the mast of his ship as it sailed past the sirens, factory discipline forced workers to do what they wanted to do but could not do unaided.[104]

Two observations may be made at this point. First, it is entirely possible – indeed, likely – that necessity and opportunity both acted to intensify market labor, even in the experience of the same people over a span of time. When "opportunity" leads toward more market-oriented labor and higher incomes, a decline in wages or prices may lead not to a withdrawal from the market but to a perceived "necessity" to intensify work effort in the defense of a recently attained living standard. In discussing the backward-bending labor supply curve thought to characterize many pre-industrial workers, Persson noted that "A movement along the curve as wages rise might include learning processes and habit formation which will ascribe a certain downward rigidity to a consumption level once it has been reached." Thus, workers experiencing declining incomes may, instead of retracing the labor supply curve downward, "break out" of its trajectory by offering significantly more labor than before at any given wage. Thus, an accumulation of consumption capital – a type of "learning-by-doing" in the consumption sphere – can lead the economy, via a ratchet effect, toward an industrious revolution.[105]

---

[104] Gary Cross, in his study of work time, expresses disappointment with E. P. Thompson for giving the impression that workers, instead of guarding the autonomy of their culture, in the matter of working hours and the pace of work, voluntarily relinquished their pre-industrial proclivities toward irregular work and a backward-bending supply curve of labor in order to secure higher incomes. Gary Cross, "Worktime and Industrialization. An Introduction," in his *Worktime and Industrialization. An International History* (Philadelphia: Temple University Press, 1988), pp. 3–20. On the problem of individual self-control, see also Gregory Clark, "Factory Discipline," *Journal of Economic History* 54 (1994): 128–63. Clark argues that factory discipline is not a solution to a technical problem (the "logic" of the machine) but a solution to the problem of self-control, analogous to forced measures to induce saving or dieting. Factory discipline artificially raises the short-term cost of shirking.

[105] Persson, "Consumption, Labour and Leisure." Shammas implicitly invokes the "ratchet" model when, after decrying the abysmal nutritional practices of late–eighteenth-century plebian families, she observes that these practices – dependence on retailers, strong preferences for bakery-fresh wheat bread – had been sensible enough when they became entrenched in the early eighteenth century, but "late in the eighteenth century, with high prices and irregular supplies of dairy products... *they were trapped.*" Carole Shammas, "The Eighteenth-Century. English Diet and Economic Change,"

Second, a conspicuous weakness in the pessimist account of worker motivation is its reliance on contemporary observers who offered no end of colorful, highly charged denunciations of the sloth, fecklessness, and irresponsibility of working people. These commentaries were almost never based on disinterested observations of actual behavior. Rather, they functioned as part of an ideology that defined the otherness of the working population and its incapacity for self-governance.[106] The cultivation of this trope had the practical benefit, as a buttress to the "utility of poverty doctrine," of excusing the payment of low wages.[107] It is ironic that historians who regard themselves as champions of the common man happily appropriate these claims. What had served the original tellers to justify the subordination of the lesser orders because of their lack of self-control and weak spirit of improvement came to be used by "moral economy" advocates as evidence of the pre-capitalist natural innocence of common folk. Both do the working people of pre-industrial Europe a disservice.

Malnourished Workers

A second objection to the industrious revolution does not address whether workers preferred more goods to more leisure. It regards such questions as moot so long as many workers found themselves too malnourished to contemplate such choices.

Explorations in Economic History 21 (1984): 267 (emphasis added). Much the same thing was suggested earlier by D. E. C. Eversley, who accounted for the growth of the home market after 1750 (as food prices began to rise) thus: " ... as a result of the experiences of the previous decades [of low food prices], a large part of the population would seek to maintain in the face of increased difficulties the standards they had achieved, by combinations, by greater exertions, and if necessary by restricting fertility. And beyond that, it is still possible that they would go without some things we might consider essentials to keep the 'decencies.'" D. E. C. Eversley, "The Home Market and Economic Growth in England, 1750–1780," in E. L. Jones and G. E. Mingay, eds., *Land, Labour, and Population in the Industrial Revolution* (London: Edward Arnold, 1967), p. 218. See also Eric L. Jones, *Agriculture and the Industrial Revolution* (Oxford: Blackwell, 1974).

[106] Joseph Townsend, an English clergyman, put it this way in *Dissertation on the Poor Laws* (London, 1786): "The poor know little of the motives which stimulate the higher ranks to action – pride, honour, and ambition. In general it is only hunger which can spur and goad them on to labour. The wisest legislature will never be able to devise a more equitable, a more effectual, or in any respect a more suitable punishment, than hunger is for a disobedient servant." Cited in Peter Mathias, "Leisure and Wages in Theory and Practice," in Peter Mathias, *The Transformation of England* (London: Methuen, 1979), p. 158.

[107] For a comprehensive overview of contemporary views on this doctrine, see E. A. Furness, *The Position of the Laborer in a System of Nationalism* (New York: Houghton Mifflin, 1920), Ch. 6.

Robert Fogel presents a picture of eighteenth-century Britain and France that leaves little room for industrious behavior among the poor because the available nutrition could support neither long nor strenuous work effort. People had long before adapted to this chronic state of affairs by adjusting their "biomass" (they were short and light) and by the measured pace of their labor and the frequency of their pauses from work. That is, the leisure they "enjoyed" was a bitter necessity.[108]

In Fogel's view, the only consumption to which British and French plebeians circa 1800 could reasonably aspire was sufficient caloric intake to become productive workers in the first place. These were poor societies that escaped only in the course of the nineteenth century from widespread hunger and malnutrition-induced premature death. Fogel argued that food availability per capita was such that, under certain assumptions about its distribution across income classes and the caloric needs for basal metabolism and bodily functions, there was insufficient nutrition available in England to support much sustained work for at least the lower quintile of the working population. In France, matters were even worse. He summarizes the situation as follows:

Individuals in the bottom 20 percent of the caloric distribution of France and England near the end of the eighteenth century lacked the energy for sustained work and were effectively excluded from the labor force. Moreover, even those who participated in the labor force had only relatively small amounts of energy for work.[109]

By Fogel's calculations, it was the lifting of this abysmally low nutritional ceiling in the nineteenth century that "explains 30 percent of the British growth rate since 1790." He supports his claim as follows:

The increase in the amount of energy available for work had two effects. It raised the labor force participation rate by bringing into the labor force the bottom 20 percent of consuming units of 1790 who had, on average, only enough energy for a few hours of slow walking. Moreover, for those in the labor force, the intensity of work per hour had increased because the number of calories available for work each day increased by about 50 percent.... The combined effect of the increase in dietary energy available for work, and the increased human efficiency

---

[108] Robert William Fogel, *The Escape from Hunger and Premature Death 1700–2100. Europe, America and the Third World* (Cambridge: Cambridge University Press, 2004). Before Fogel, nutrition-based interpretations of economic and demographic history were offered by Hermann Freudenberger and Gaylord Cummins, "Health, Work and Leisure Before the Industrial Revolution," *Explorations in Economic History* 13 (1976): 1–12; and Thomas McKeown, *The Modern Rise of Population* (New York: Academic Press, 1976).

[109] Fogel, *Escape from Hunger*, p. 33.

in transforming dietary energy into work output, appears to account for about 50 percent of British economic growth since 1790.[110]

In short, for Fogel the industrious revolution is a nineteenth- and twentieth-century event. It is the result of the lifting of a supply constraint: the supply of foodstuffs sufficient to sustain regular and heavy labor. Before 1800 we have no aspiring consumers; rather, we have malnourished workers, who are saved from their "nasty, brutish and short" lives of slow-paced, intermittent, unproductive labor by an otherwise unexplained, exogenous rise in nineteenth-century agricultural productivity.

Why is Fogel's argument of a binding nutritional constraint incorrect? There are three chief reasons, one economic, the second technical, and the third historical. First, if the nutritional constraint removed a substantial percentage of the potential work force from effective labor, we would expect the income elasticity of demand for foodstuffs to have been high, and to have been directed primarily to the cheapest sources of calories and nutrition. But studies of British consumption patterns have led to estimates of the demand elasticity for food in eighteenth-century England that vary between 0.63 and 0.70.[111] (For every 1 percent increase in income, food expenditures rose by 0.63 to 0.70 percent.) The highest income elasticities of demand were for the following commodities, starting with the highest: beer, dairy products, meat, and sugar.[112] This signals a rather strong interest in purchasing food, but not necessarily a strong interest in acquiring additional calories.

Consumer behavior in the eighteenth and early nineteenth centuries was not consistent with ordinary malnutrition, because the elasticity of demand for *calories* (as opposed to *food*) was, even in the worst economic times, no more than 0.45. A strong interest in more appealing, more processed and prepared, and more convenient food in this period is revealed by the significant rise of the "food-value multiplier" (the value

[110] Ibid., pp. 33–4.

[111] The higher estimate (which is statistically weak – one cannot rule out that the true elasticity is only 0.46) is offered by N. F. R. Crafts, "Income Elasticities of Demand and the Release of Labour by Agriculture During the British Industrial Revolution," *Journal of European Economic History* 9 (1980): 156–9. The lower estimate (which relates to the rural poor in a period of high prices, 1787–96) is from Gregory Clark, Michael Huberman, and Peter Lindert, "A British Food Puzzle, 1770–1850," *Economic History Review* 48 (1995): 215–37. Voth notes that the elasticities in contemporary Third World countries fall in the range of 0.7 to 0.9.

[112] Of these, only beer was what economists call a "superior good" – that is, where a 1 percent increase in income leads to *more* than a 1 percent increase in spending. Clark, Huberman, and Lindert, "A British Food Puzzle," p. 224.

of food products and beverages consumed relative to the value of under-lying foodstuffs) from 1.26 in 1695 to 1.43 in 1800 and 1.57 in 1850.[113] Indeed, it appears that nutritional quality in eighteenth-century Britain was inversely correlated to income growth – that is, that increased income tended to be used to acquire nutritionally inferior diets. The "logic" behind such perverse choices will be explored further in Chapter 4, but here it must be noted that it was choice more than scarcity per se that led to the poor nutritional state observed by the early nineteenth century.[114]

The second weakness of Fogel's argument is located in the methodology he used to conclude that the caloric intake of the lower income groups was inadequate to sustain labor. Fogel began with estimates of the average per capita calories availability to Britain and France as a whole and then distributed this stock of available food among income deciles. Food is dis-tributed among income groups less unequally than is income, of course: Fogel considered a range of Gini coefficients (measures of inequality) con-sistent with the need to leave the poorest decile with sufficient food for survival and settled on one that appears plausible.[115]

This methodology is suggestive and illuminating, but it is not robust. That is, small changes in any of the assumptions lead to large differences in the results. Hans-Joachim Voth explored these problems in detail.[116] To begin, there is uncertainty in the calculations of total food availability in France and Britain in 1800. In addition, one can question Fogel's assump-tion of symmetry in the distribution of food among income deciles (the caloric intake of richest decile is assumed to be as far above the national average as that of the poorest decile is below the average). Also doubtful is Fogel's assumption of a "hard line" between the nutritional needs of basal metabolism versus work energy, and the assumption that the caloric intake to support work is called upon every day of the week and year. The

---

[113] Ibid., p. 220.

[114] The consumer behavior of currently poor countries also fails to offer much support for the notion of workers caught in a "nutritional trap." Angus Deaton, in a review of Fogel's book, notes that tests of this theory have "consistently failed to provide support. In modern economies, even very poor ones, the trap cannot be binding; the 2,000 or so calories that can provide the means to escape can be bought with only a fraction of the daily wage. Angus Deaton, "The Great Escape. A Review of Robert Fogel's *The Great Escape from Hunger and Premature Death, 1700–2100*," *Journal of Economic Literature* 44 (2006): 110.

[115] Robert William Fogel, "New Sources and New Techniques for the Study of Secular Trends in Nutritional Status, Mortality, and the Process of Aging," *Historical Methods* 26 (1993): 5–43.

[116] Voth, *Time and Work*, pp. 161–72.

state of our knowledge in each of these dimensions simply does not allow for estimates of sufficient accuracy to yield useful results. Voth concluded, "Even minor changes to Fogel's assumptions lead to a reversal of one of his main findings, namely that a large section of Britain's poorer classes did not consume enough food to engage in more than very limited amount of work."[117]

Finally, we must note that Fogel's account of the "escape from hunger" relies a great deal on an unexplained, exogenous historical event: an abrupt rise in food production after 1790. What we know of the course of food production certainly confirms the straited circumstances of Britain, and most of Europe, in the decades around 1800. Population growth was then rapid, and unsettled international conditions helped make food prices high. But most of the eighteenth century had been blessed by low food prices and expanding production. The sustained growth of agricultural productivity in most of northwestern Europe was discussed earlier in this chapter. The chronology of Fogel's account takes no note of this but relies on a trend break's launching an acceleration of food production shortly after 1800, a trend break for which there is no evidence.

All of these reservations notwithstanding, it is clear that Fogel is grappling with a problem that is also central to this study: How is economic growth translated into improved well-being? His "escape from hunger," to which he attributes 50 percent of British growth since 1790, appears to be a *deus ex machina*. Even so, he noted that economic growth after 1790 yielded "only modest and uneven improvements in health, nutritional status, and longevity of the lower classes before 1890."[118] The *production* of more metal, fibers, and even food does not *by itself* translate into a longer and better life. To determine how these desired outcomes *can* be achieved, he directs our attention to the relationship between the individual human body and the economy: In Fogel's approach, nutrition and work are mediated by body mass. This study places its emphasis elsewhere: on the family as a producing and consuming unit that mediates – for better or for worse – between the market economy and the individual well-being of its members.

The productivity advances of the new technologies and organizational forms we know as the Industrial Revolution required many decades of maturation before they could powerfully affect overall economic growth. Individual wage workers in Europe as a whole faced declining real wages in most of the early modern era. Those in northwestern Europe fared

---

[117] Ibid., p. 170.   [118] Fogel, *Escape from Hunger*, p. 8.

somewhat better but experienced rising real earnings only exception-ally. Despite these evident obstacles to income growth, the long eigh-teenth century experienced substantial growth in production and trade and measurable improvements in material conditions. Economic growth is never explained simply; it is always the product of multiple forces. But in this period a major role must be reserved for the augmented sup-plies of market-oriented labor released by the households of northwest-ern Europe. There surely were times and places where this new labor was supplied under duress; but the dominant theme is one of households' redeploying their productive resources to secure new consumption goals. An industrious revolution preceded the Industrial Revolution.

4

The Industrious Revolution

Consumer Demand

The previous chapter explored the paths by which households became more industrious in the course of the long eighteenth century, devoting more of their labor to market-oriented activities. The concept at this study's core argues that this new industriousness was substantially motivated by new consumer aspirations. Is it possible to observe consumer behavior consistent with the industrious revolution hypothesis?

First a word is necessary about what we are *not* looking for. The new consumer demand was not a "consumer revolution," an exploding volume of purchased goods that jump-started the growth of production in the "leading sectors" of the Industrial Revolution. Indeed, it is striking how little the expansion of industrial production and the unfolding of consumer demand touch each other *directly* until the twentieth century. Nor was the new consumer demand driven primarily by emulation, where rising incomes allowed progressively lower socioeconomic strata to adopt, and be incorporated into, the material world of their social superiors.

Rather, the consumer demand of this era was associated with a broadened *choice* in the selection of "consumer technologies" whereby the ultimately consumed "Z-commodities" sought by various socioeconomic groups could be produced. An increased substitutability between the goods and the time inputs in consumption made possible substantial redistributions of the productive resources of the household at the same time as it encouraged renegotiation of the distribution of consumption resources within the household. That is, consumer demand developed through an interaction of market and household productive systems. In addition, the emergence of "incentive goods" – goods that responded persuasively to the wants of specific communities – acted as a focusing device, supporting the development of distribution networks in the face of high transaction costs. The interaction of household members with an expanded range of goods, and more numerous venues for purchase and consumption, led to the more frequent exercise of individuated choice. Experience and exposure led to an accumulation of consumption capital, consolidating in time the practices of consumption recognizable to us today.

This, in a nutshell, is my interpretation of the transformation of consumer demand associated with the industrious revolution as experienced in northwestern Europe and the North American seaboard in the long eighteenth century. What evidence exists to sustain such a vision?

Searching for the Early Modern Consumer

Probate inventories. The probate inventory is the place to begin the search, not only because it is a rich source of information about material culture but because the contemplation of its evidence of steadily richer, more diverse, and more refined material surroundings initially spurred my interest in explaining how such a phenomenon could be reconciled with the much more somber image of eighteenth-century economic life presented by the record of wage and price trends.[1] As we saw in Chapter 3, wage data, whether drawn from the ground zero of the Industrial Revolution or from provincial backwaters, give no grounds to believe that ordinary workers could do more than survive, and as the eighteenth century gave way to the nineteenth they show mostly distress and decline. Yet the historian who turns from the record of wage and price data toward the less aggregated and more heterogeneous historical data on the material surroundings of northwestern Europeans over the same period cannot help but be surprised at and puzzled by the optimistic impressions they give of long-term improvement, differentiation, and refinement.[2]

A considerable number of detailed regional studies now exist for colonial America (New England and the Chesapeake region), England,

---

[1] De Vries, "Between Purchasing Power and the World of Goods," pp. 89–107.

[2] For example, Peter King's analysis of the inventories of paupers in eighteenth-century Essex notes that "many historians, including those who have studied Essex, have portrayed this period as one of declining or static living standards among the poor." Yet King had to conclude that the inventories revealed something different: "The wealthier husbandman of the late seventeenth century had fewer goods than the poorer paupers of the late eighteenth century." Peter King, "Pauper Inventories and the Material Lives of the Poor in the Eighteenth and Early Nineteenth Centuries," in Tim Hitchcock, et al., eds., *Chronicling Poverty. The Voices and Strategies of the English Poor, 1640–1840* (New York: St. Martin's Press, 1997), pp. 179–80, 183.

Scotland, the Netherlands, Belgium, Germany, and France.[3] The motivating questions of investigators vary across these countries, as do the strengths and weaknesses of the inventories themselves. Moreover, the very richness of the inventories, each with scores, often hundreds, of entries, possess methodological challenges that no two investigators have resolved in just the same way. Yet wherever it proves possible to achieve a chronological coverage that spans the late seventeenth century to mid- or late eighteenth century, these studies have revealed a steady rise, generation by generation, of the number, range, and quality of material possessions. This was true of expansive, newly settled areas of North America, but also of declining provincial towns in Holland (Delft) and France (Chartres), and of a metropolis stripped of its economic vitality (Antwerp).

Johan Kamermans's study of a Dutch rural area (the Krimpenerwaard) quantified this growing material profusion: The average inventory of 1630–70 numbered 47 separate types of goods and 241 separate items; the averages for 1700–95 (holding socioeconomic categories constant) were 71 types of goods and 538 items. "As the number of different items rises," Kamermans concludes, "it is especially domains of exotic consumption

---

[3] A selection of the more important works includes Lois Green Carr and Lorena S. Walsh, "The Standard of Living in the Colonial Chesapeake," *The William and Mary Quarterly* 45, third series (1988): 135–59; Hester Dibbits, *Vertrouwd bezit. Materiële cultuur in Doesburg en Maassluis, 1650–1800* (Amsterdam: SUN Memoria, 2000); Peter Earle, *The Making of the English Middle Class* (London: Methuen, 1989); Mark Overton, Jane Whittle, et al., *Production and Consumption in English Households, 1600–1750* (London: Routledge, 2004); Benoît Garnot, *Un déclin. Chartres au XVIIIe siècle* (Paris: Editions de L.T.H.S., 1991); Benoît Garnot, *La culture matérielle en France aux XVIe, XVIIe et XVIIIe siècles* (Paris: Ophrys, 1995); Johan A. Kamermans, *Materiële cultuur in de Krimpenerwaard in de zeventiende en achttiende eeuw* (Wageningen: A.A.G. Bijdragen 39, 1999); Gloria L. Main and Jackson T. Main, "Economic Growth and the Standard of Living in Southern New England, 1640–1774," *Journal of Economic History* 48 (1988): 27–46; Ruth-E. Mohrmann, *Alltagswelt im Land Braunschweig* (Münster: Waxman, 1990); Stana Nenadic, "Middle-Rank Consumers and Domestic Culture in Edinburgh and Glasgow, 1720–1840," *Past and Present* 145 (1994): 122–56; Annik Pardailhé-Galabrun, *The Birth of Initimacy. Private and Domestic Life in Early Modern Paris* (Cambridge: Polity Press, 1991); Daniel Roche, *Le peuple de Paris. Essai sur la culture populaire au XVIIIe siècle* (Paris: Aubier Montaigne, 1981); C. Schelstraete, H. Kintaert, and D. de Ruyck, *Het einde van de onveranderlijkheid. Arbeid, bezit en woonomstandigheden in het land van Nevel tijdens de 17e en 18e eeuw* (Nevele: Heemkundig Kring "Het Land van Nevele, 1986); Anton Schuurman, *Materiële cultuur en levensstijl* (Wageningen: AAG Bijdragen 30, 1989); Lorna Weatherill, *Consumer Behavior and Material Culture in Britain, 1660–1760* (London: Routledge, 1988); Thera Wijsenbeek-Olthuis, *Achter de gevels van Delft* (Hilversum: Verloren, 1987).

goods, comfort, interior decoration, and dining table culture that assume a larger place in the household."[4] His description concerns a wholly rural district of farmers and villagers, and most of these improvements were achieved in a protracted period of falling agricultural prices.

The same trend toward a *"multiplication des objets"* is shown by Micheline Baulant's study of 1,200 probate inventories in northern France. Across the seventeenth and eighteenth centuries, the number of distinct items recorded per inventory grew between 47 and 82 percent, depending on the social category.[5] Lorna Weatherill's study of English probate inventories achieved its broad coverage of the "middling sort" (some 3,000 inventories) by focusing narrowly on 20 strategic goods, but she, too, found that over the period 1670–1730, "often presented as economically inactive," there were "remarkable instances of growth and change [in the ownership of goods]."[6] The percentage of her inventories recording the presence of saucepans, earthenware dishes, clocks, pictures, looking glasses, window curtains, and, of course, tea and coffee utensils all at least doubled over the period. Peter Earle's study of a rather more elevated London middle class in the same period documented "an almost revolutionary change in the types of clothing worn by both sexes" (Weatherill had not focused on clothing), and a major upgrading of furniture and interior decoration.[7] Inventories from the county of Kent, southeast of London, also reveal this "major upgrading." Overton and Whittle identified five specific new furniture types: court and press cupboards, chests of drawers, cabinets, and new fashions in tables and chairs. In the early decades of the seventeenth century, about 30 percent of inventoried households possessed any of these items; by the mid–eighteenth century, nearly 80 percent did so; over the same period, the median number of pieces of furniture doubled, from 12 to 24.[8] Chesapeake region and New England probate inventories also display a pattern of continual upgrading, so that there can be no question but that eighteenth-century colonials, even the

---

[4] Kamermans, *Materiële cultuur in de Krimpenerwaard*, pp. 137–8, 284.

[5] Micheline Baulant, "L'appréciation du niveau de vie. Un problème, une solution," *Histoire et Mesure* 4 (1989): 290.

[6] Lorna Weatherill, "The Meaning of Consumer Behavior in Late Seventeenth- and Early Eighteenth-Century England," in Brewer and Porter, eds., *Consumption and the World of Goods*, p. 209.

[7] Earle, *English Middle Class*, pp. 281, 300. The lower income limit for Earle's middle class was an annual income of 50 pounds sterling.

[8] Overton, Whittle, et al., *Production and Consumption*, pp. 90–1.

remote Yankee rustics studied by Gloria and Jackson Main, "were participating in what became a transatlantic revolution in consumer tastes."[9]

A dual pattern emerges from these heterogeneous studies. They all reveal a remorselessly creeping change toward greater material abundance, and each identifies, in its own way, rapid shifts, substitutions, and acquisitions that brought new consumption practices and new styles and fashions to specific communities and social classes. These consuming innovations did not remain localized but spread throughout the North Atlantic world, although the precise manner in which they were incorporated, or rejected, by social groups generated complex and dynamic patterns of cultural meaning, social differentiation, and market involvement.

The probate inventory is clearly a rich source, but it is not without its problems and limitations for the issues that concern us here. To begin, the temporal range of useable probate inventories sometimes limits their usefulness for this study. In France and parts of the Netherlands, inventories are abundant for most of the eighteenth century but are scarce in the seventeenth; in England they are plentiful at least in the late seventeenth century but quickly disappear in the course of the 1730s and 1740s.

While these limitations are an annoyance, a second feature is potentially much more disabling. Probate inventories ordinarily were drawn up only for decedents leaving sufficient moveable assets to make the exercise worthwhile. The social "depth" to which they reach is not everywhere the same, but only rarely comprehends true proletarians. Consequently, an argument for an industrious revolution among a laboring population can hardly be illustrated with most probate inventory data, when their coverage does not extend far below the middling sort. What they *can* show, however, is two broad trends in durable and semi-durable goods among the middle ranks: an increase in standards of domestic comfort, privacy, and refinement, and a shift toward "breakability" and obsolescence – that is, toward goods that depreciate quickly because of their materials and their embodied fashions.

Comfort. The first of these developments involved expenditures that made them largely inaccessible to the poorer half of the population until well into the nineteenth century. Indeed, it will become apparent in the

---

[9] Main and Main, "Economic Growth," p. 44. The frontier character of mid–seventeenth-century New England will exaggerate the transformation, but it remains striking to find from the probate inventories of Wethersfield, Connecticut, that its houses in the 1640s were furnished with no chairs (only stools and benches), while in the 1790s the average house held nearly sixteen. Kevin M. Sweeney, "Furniture and Domestic Environment in Wethersfield, Connecticut, 1639–1800," *The Connecticut Antiquarian* 36 (1984): 10–39.

following sections that consumer expenditures among the lower ranks constructed lifestyles that differed fundamentally from the new domesticity and respectability of the middling sorts. But, in a broad middle range the reorganization of space within homes unfolded in the century after the 1650s. The new forms of domestic comfort, which may first have been assembled in mid–seventeenth-century Dutch urban homes, was quickly introduced in England and France.[10] Brick construction replaced wood and lime; functional spaces became better defined, as drawing rooms and dining rooms appeared in middle-class homes and distinct bed chambers came to be identified.[11] All of this required space, of course, and was beyond the financial reach of the large majority. Yet even for those without space and without means, one can detect change, as when Annik Pardailhé-Galabrun reports that in the dwellings of humble Parisians beds became "less crowded" as most people came to have their own by the 1770s.[12] These interior spaces came to be filled with more, and more specialized, furniture. Pardailhé-Galabrun describes a transition from box chests and trunks toward closets and commodes – standing chests – in the 1720–60 period, tracing a transition made in Holland a century earlier.[13] Focusing on rural environments, Schuurman and Walsh emphasize the eighteenth-century diffusion of new items to produce heating and lighting, as well as the assemblage of dining furniture and related objects in support of social interaction.[14]

---

[10] Witwold Rybczynski, *Home. A Short History of an Idea* (New York: Viking Press, 1986), p. 77 and Ch. 3; Peter Thornton, *Seventeenth-Century Interior Decoration in England, France, and Holland* (New Haven, Conn.: Yale University Press, 1978). Thornton regards "true comfort, as we understand it" to have been a French invention of the seventeenth century.

[11] E. L. Jones and M. E. Falkus, "Urban Improvement and the English Economy in the Seventeenth and Eighteenth Centuries," *Research in Economic History* 4 (1979): 193–233; C. W. Fock, "Wonen aan het Leidse Rapenburg door de eeuwen heen," in P. M. M. Klep, et al., *Wonen in het verleden* (Amsterdam: NEHA, 1987), pp. 189–205.

[12] Annik Pardailhé-Galabrun, *The Birth of Intimacy* (Cambridge: Polity Press, 1991), pp. 81–2.

[13] Ibid., p. 110; on Dutch chests: Jan de Vries, "Peasant Demand Patterns and Economic Development," pp. 220–1; Hester C. Dibbits, "Between Society and Family Values. The Linen Cupboard in Early-Modern Households," in Schuurman and Spierenburg, eds., *Private Domain, Public Inquiry. Families and Life-Styles in the Netherlands and Europe 1550 to the Present* (Hilversum: Verloren, 1996), pp. 125–45.

[14] Anton Schuurman and Lorena Walsh, "Introduction," in Anton Schuurman and Lorena Walsh, eds., *Material Culture. Consumption, Life Style, Standard of Living, 1500–1900* (Milan: XI International Economic History Congress, 1994), pp. 7–20. A study of the Land van Nevele, a town and rural district in Flanders, similarly emphasizes that "In all levels of rural society *the urge to achieve comfort* makes itself felt [in the second half of the

Comfort, given the technologies of the time, also required labor. The market could not yet offer alternatives to goods requiring extensive household labor to provide ready access to water, illumination, heat, and hygiene.[15] Consequently, this domain of consumer demand remained one sharply bifurcated between households with servants and those without, and, indeed, those supplying their own children as servants to others. Consumer demand until the twentieth century consisted in a demand not only for goods but also for the services that only domestic servants could provide. Rather than being a relic of an earlier period, domestic servants were an object of intensifying demand.[16]

Yet, the search for comfort did generate new forms of demand, or, more commonly, it increased existing types of consumption, that extended across class boundaries. A good example is the keen interest in illumination, or, as Daniel Roche so nicely put it, "*le combat contre l'obscurité.*"[17] Early modern people lived in great darkness. The technologies to combat this changed in only modest ways until the nineteenth century, but in the seventeenth century consumer demand for window glass, mirrors, candles, and oil lamps all accelerated notably. It is a plausible hypothesis that the urbanization of this era, which was highly concentrated in the growth of a small number of very large cities, and the development of urban entertainments that created public spaces of a very tangible form, focused new attention on the benefits of illumination.[18] The improved oil-fueled street lantern developed by the painter-inventor Jan van der Heijden in 1663, and, perhaps more important, his detailed proposal for the organization of effective municipal street-lighting services, led to a rapid expansion

eighteenth century]. Furniture and the organization of domestic space were no longer confined to the utterly necessary; people wanted something more, something more pleasant, something more decorative." C. Scheltstraete, et al., *Het einde van de onveranderlijkheid*, p. 203 (emphasis in original). Stana Nenadic offers a specific example of the new place of (male) sociable furnishings in eighteenth-century Glasgow: "Household Possessions and the Modernizing City. Scotland, c.1720–1840," in Schuurman and Walsh, eds. *Material Culture*, pp. 147–60.

[15] All of these elements of comfort as discussed in Daniel Roche, *Historie des choses banales. Naissance de la consummation XVIIe–XIXe siècle* (Paris: Fayard, 1997), pp. 95–182.

[16] The demand for domestic servants is discussed in more detail in Chapter 5.

[17] Roche, *Historie des choses banales*, p. 138.

[18] Jan de Vries, *European Urbanization*, pp. 136–42. Hans-Joachim Voth's study of London time use makes it clear that Londoners (and other eighteenth-century urbanites?) did not live by the rising and setting of the sun. Their court testimonies identify 11:00 P.M. as the most common bedtime, while the length of night rest averaged well under seven hours. Such patterns of life caused Londoners to spend many waking hours in darkness. Voth, *Time and Work*, pp. 67–8.

of street lighting in Amsterdam, Paris (beginning in 1667, with 6,400 lanterns in use by 1740), London (where the Convex Lighting Company began operation in 1684), and many other cities.[19]

The demand for illumination, domestic and public, took the form of increased use of tallow and oil, and, of course, candlesticks and lanterns. The primary sources of lighting oil were vegetable oils (rape, linseed, and flax) and whale oil. The rapid growth of whaling in the seventeenth century was driven primarily by the demand for oil (the bones then being of secondary importance and the meat of no interest). The installation of seed-pressing mills and the expanded hunting of whales (from an annual catch by European whalers of under 300 whales until 1640 to well over 1,000 per year after 1670) generated an oil output that far exceeded the growth of population, and whose uses in cooking, soap, and lighting was led by the "battle against darkness."[20]

The nineteenth-century breakthroughs in illumination – urban coal gas beginning around 1800, kerosene after 1850, electricity beginning in 1882 – so radically reduced the cost of lighting as to make all that went before appear as trivial, part of a seemingly "motionless history."[21] But the alacrity with which all nineteenth-century lighting improvements were taken up is symptomatic of a social pressure to secure domestic comfort through illumination that had built up notably since the mid–seventeenth century.

Breakability. The second development, "breakability," refers to a broad and complex transformation of European material culture. The probate inventories reveal a portion of a much broader sphere of consumer behavior, one that characterized both the middle ranks and the lower orders: the gradual replacement of expensive, durable products possessing a high

[19] Auke van der Woud, *Het lege land. De ruimtelijke ordre van Nederland, 1798–1848* (Amsterdam: Meulenhoff, 1987), p. 414; Roche, *Histoire des choses banales*, p. 135; Voth, *Time and Work*, p. 67. Voth relates that London was long regarded as the worst-lit of the great cities of Europe. Lighting Acts of 1736 and 1738 brought improvement, and Paving Acts of the 1760s and 1770s led to more, such that the "bright lights" of London made a great impression on visitors.

[20] De Vries and van der Woude, *First Modern Economy*, pp. 257–9.

[21] So it appears in the clever and telling paper by William Nordhaus, "Do Real Output and Real Wage Measures Capture Reality? The History of Lighting Suggests Not," in Tim Breshnahan and Robert Gordon, eds., *The Economics of New Goods* (Chicago: University of Chicago Press, 1997), pp. 29–66. Nordhaus's data show little change in the unit cost of lighting from pre-history to 1800, after which it plummets. The merit of this article as a work of economics is considerable, but its historical investigation of the period between the invention of the Babylonian lamp and gas lighting is rudimentary and highlights the need for further study.

secondary market value by cheaper, less durable, more fashion-sensitive goods.[22] This might appear in contradiction to the development just discussed of the elaboration of a more refined, differentiated, and specialized material culture. In fact, the two – elaboration and cheapening – went hand in hand throughout the period. Examples are numerous and varied: Dinner plates evolved from pewter and wood to china and earthenware; drinking vessels similarly shifted from metal to glass and chinaware; furniture, to take a Low Countries example, reveals a shift from the "Spanish chair" (long-lasting, suited to repair and resale) to the more short-lived and more comfortable rush-seated chair; wall decoration shifts from paintings and tapestries to paper hangings. Finally, the best known of these shifts is revealed by the changing composition of wardrobes toward lighter woolens, linen, cotton, and mixed fibers, and to articles of apparel that embodied a shortened fashion life cycle.

Consider for a moment the new demand for the classic breakable item: crockery. Because ceramic objects are ubiquitous and ancient in their origins, one might wonder how a ceramics industry could be a new and dynamic focus of consumer demand. But potters long focused primarily on utilitarian objects such as storage vessels. By the sixteenth century they could offer tin-glazed ceramics and Mediterranean majolica. Yet, their characteristics did not make them demonstrably superior to alternatives, and most tableware continued to be made either of metal, usually pewter, or, more commonly, wood. Producing plates and dishes, cups and saucers with the necessary strength and finish required baking techniques and glazes that developed only in response to the example of Asian porcelain.

The story of the introduction to Europe of Chinese and, later, Japanese porcelain need not be retold here, except to take note of the intense interest shown in Europe for these new ceramic products. The importation of Asian porcelain by the Dutch East India Company (VOC), the first major importer, began at 50,000 to 100,000 pieces per year but rose, after 1630 to 200,000 pieces. The fall of the Ming dynasty disrupted supplies and caused the VOC to turn to Japan, but Chinese exports revived and reached much higher levels in the eighteenth century. By the end of the eighteenth century, the VOC had shipped some 43 million pieces of porcelain to Europe while all its rivals together had shipped an additional 30 million. Most of this total of more than 70 million pieces of exported porcelain

---

[22] A clear presentation of this position is offered in Bruno Blondé, "The Birth of a Consumer Society? Consumption and Material Culture in Antwerp, 17th and 18th Centuries" (unpublished paper, University of Antwerpen, 1997).

was produced in a single large industrial complex in and around the Chinese city of Jingdezhen.[23] When, in 1729, the VOC had established a permanent trading office in Guangzhou (Canton), it had sufficient access to this industrial center to provide models and drawings for copying by the potters as they labored to fill orders for "soup tureens, radish saucers, saltcellars, sauceboats, butter coolers, juice pourers, and mustard pots" to fill Dutch and other European cupboards.[24]

Imitating the hard paste Chinese porcelain required years of effort, but an intense if not obsessive elite interest in this lustrous product led to the establishment by Elector Augustus of Saxony of "arguably . . . the first research and development enterprise in history," bearing fruit in 1709 with the establishment of the Meissen porcelain works near Dresden.[25] It was followed by many others, almost all businesses producing luxury products under royal patronage.

The exquisite European porcelains were far more costly and delicate than the Chinese product that had inspired them; they did nothing to satisfy the broad consumer interest that had been awakened by the imported wares. This interest came from within the European ceramics tradition, seeking to develop products that approximated the functional features of Chinese porcelain and appropriated Asian-inspired decorative elements. The most successful seventeenth-century response to the new market opportunities was delftware, after Delft, the city in which production was concentrated. In 1650, fourteen workshops were active in Delft, and by 1670 there were thirty, much larger, workshops supplying an international market.[26]

The Dutch ceramic producers reached their peaks of production as the English began developing a fine-earthenware industry to exploit the latent demand for products with the right mix of price and quality just under the standard set by Chinese porcelain. Potteries of this type, concentrated in Staffordshire, more than tripled in number between the 1680s and 1750s, while production capacity, to judge by employment, grew more

[23] Peter Wilhelm Meister and Horst Reber, *European Porcelain of the Eighteenth Century* (Ithaca, N.Y.: Cornell University Press, 1983), p. 18.

[24] C. J. A. Jörg, "Porcelain for the Dutch in the Seventeenth Century," in Rosemary E. Scott, ed., *The Porcelain of Jingdezhen* (London: Percival David Foundation of Chinese Art, 1993), p. 187.

[25] Robert Finlay, "The Pilgrim Art. The Culture of Porcelain in World History," *Journal of World History* 9 (1998): 175.; Otto Walcha, *Meissen Porcelain* (New York: Putnam, 1981).

[26] De Vries and van der Woude, *First Modern Economy*, p. 308.

than six-fold in the century after 1680.[27] These developments in English ceramic production led to the development after 1730 of "creamware," a fine lead-glaze earthenware that approximated the attractive features of porcelain. Its potential was most fully exploited by the marketing and organizing genius of Josiah Wedgwood, whose new production facility of 1766, Etruria, was centered in a town, Burslem, where, according to Wedgwood himself, "there are 500 separate potteries for stoneware and earthenware. They provide employment for 7,000 and export to Liverpool, Bristol, Hull and from there to America and the West Indian colonies and every port in Europe."[28]

What began in Holland and quickly spread to England took somewhat longer to take hold in France, where:

Earthenware, even of the most common articles, did not begin to appear on Parisian tables until after 1720. Ceramics had not yet become part of daily life for most people before then, and objects of earthenware, such as pots, platters and cups, were used as decorative ornaments around the fireplace.[29]

In France, pottery factories begin to multiply after the 1720s. Farther east, new dining patterns diffuse more slowly still, certainly beyond the major cities. Sandgruber records a marked acceleration in the number of *steingutfabriken* in the Austrian lands only at the end of the eighteenth century and notes that their output reached only well-to-do consumers.[30]

Several probate inventory studies reveal the general pattern of development: From a mid–seventeenth-century preponderance of wooden trenchers and pewter plates (and many poorer households with no individual eating utensils at all), the rise of crockery in the second half of the seventeenth century is striking. In and around the Dutch town of Weesp (a small industrial and market center near Amsterdam), half of the town dwellers' inventories included porcelain in the 1650s, and half

[27] Lorna Weatherill, *The Pottery Trade and North Staffordshire, 1660–1760* (Manchester: Manchester University Press, 1971), pp. 1–9; Lorna Weatherill, "The Growth of the Pottery Industry in England, 1660–1815," *Post-Medieval Archaeology* 17 (1983): 15–46; Maxine Berg, *Luxury and Pleasure in Eighteenth-Century Britain* (Oxford: Oxford University Press, 2005), pp. 81–2.

[28] Quoted in Berg, *Luxury and Pleasure*, p. 129.

[29] Pardailhé-Galabrun, *The Birth of Intimacy*, p. 97. A study of elite consumption in provincial towns – two each in England and France – found that Chinese porcelain and deftware appeared with some frequency in late–seventeenth-century English households, but only after the mid–eighteenth century in similar French households. F.-J. Ruggiu, *Les Élites et les villes moyennes en France et en Angleterre (XVIIe–XVIIIe siècles)* (Paris: L'Harmattan, 1997), pp. 200–1.

[30] Sandgruber, *Die Anfänge der Konsumgesellschaft*, p. 382.

also possess delftware by the 1680s. By the 1690s about 20 percent of the farms possesed porcelain, but 75 percent had delftware. A pattern is set: Urban families prefer porcelain to delftware, while farm families prefer delftware, but many households own both. Thereafter, the issue becomes refinement and accumulation, and, unfortunately for delftware producers, one refinement that emerges after 1740 is English creamware, often in the form of sets of matching dishes, tea pots, and the like. By the 1780s Weesp's well-off residents leave behind, on average, 392 pieces of porcelain, and their less-well-off neighbors leave an average of 163, with an additional 30 pieces of delftware. The nearby farmers leave, on average, 64 pieces of porcelain, but now supplemented by 92 pieces of delftware.[31]

The inhabitants of Weesp and environs, with easy access to Amsterdam, were perhaps excessive in their appetite for crockery, but the basic pattern of diffusion is found throughout northwestern Europe.[32] The new tableware was not supplied by village potters. It was, in fact, a highly concentrated industry, not so much for technical reasons as to respond effectively to market demand. A durable, utilitarian object, defined primarily by its material, had become a "breakable" item of fashion expressed by design and finish.

Demand for Clothing

The demand for wearing apparel – from hats to shoes and everything in between – presents a special set of problems that deserves separate treatment. The probate inventory often lumps all forms of clothing together and sometimes lumps all textiles, whether clothing, curtains, or bed linens, into a single undifferentiated category.[33] But when the inventories do offer a full account of the wardrobes of the deceased, they pose a different problem, overwhelming the investigator in a mass of detail. In his 1695 effort

[31] Van Koolbergen, "De materiële cultuur van Weesp en Weesperkarspel," pp. 24–7.

[32] Bruno Blondé, "Tableware and changing consumer patterns. Dynamics of material culture in Antwerp, 17th–18th centuries," in J. Veeckman, ed., *Majolica and Glass from Italy to Antwerp and Beyond. The Transfer of Technology in the 16th–early 17th Century* (Antwerp, 2002), pp. 295–311; Overton and Whittle, et al., *Production and Consumption*, pp. 103–8; Weatherill, *Consumer Behavior*, p. 88.

[33] Weatherill, who studied thousands of English inventories, states that "clothing was not mentioned at all in about a fifth of them. . . . Only about half of them value clothes separately from cash and other personal possession." Lorna Weatherill, "Consumer Behavior, Textiles, and Dress in the Late Seventeenth and Early Eighteenth Centuries," *Textile History* 22 (1991), p. 297.

to calculate the value of English clothing expenditure, Gregory King listed no fewer than 90 separate categories of apparel.[34] However, it is in this detail that the most important developments in the demand for clothing are hidden.

Much of the transition from station-specific dress norms policed by sumptuary legislation to a competitive, fashion-driven dress was concentrated in this period. The story has earlier antecedents and varies in timing and speed of change by social class and country, but everywhere in western Europe the general trend was the same. In England and Holland the serious enforcement of sumptuary laws was abandoned by the early seventeenth century.[35] In France the privileges of fashionable dress were restricted to the appropriate elites with greater vigor in the seventeenth century. But even there:

By the late eighteenth century...the Parisian fashion culture had been transformed dramatically. Fashionable dress was no longer solely the privilege of the elite, but something in which men and women across a broad range of classes could indulge....[36]

Much contemporary discussion of the clothing revolutions identified the introduction of printed calicoes, and of fashions linked to cottons more generally, as the source of a new, irresistible, and democratizing force that altered behavior across the social spectrum. In 1697, not long after the introduction of printed calicoes, John Pollexfen supposed that their appeal had extended "from the greatest Gallants to the meanest Cook-Maids" all of whom now supposed that "nothing was...so fit to adorn their persons as the Fabricks of India."[37]

The celebration of the power of fashion – and the history of cotton, "fashion's favorite," is well stocked with comments of this sort – stands at the center of most accounts of a new consumer behavior in the long eighteenth century. But cotton is not the catalyst; it is the powerful accelerator of something that begins earlier, with linen. It is not too much of an exaggeration to characterize the apparel of the mid–seventeenth century

---

[34] N. B. Harte, "The Economics of Clothing in the Late Seventeenth Century," *Textile History* 22 (1991): 277–96.

[35] N. B. Harte, "State Control of Dress," in D. C. Coleman and A. H. John, eds., *Trade, Government and Economy in Pre-Industrial England. Essays Presented to F. J. Fisher* (London: Weidenfeld and Nicolson, 1976), pp. 132–65; Alan Hunt, *Governance of the Consuming Passions. A History of Sumptuary Law* (New York: St. Martin's Press, 1996).

[36] Jennifer Jones, "Coquettes and Grisettes. Women Buying and Selling in Ancién Regime Paris," in de Grazia and Furlongh, eds., *The Sex of Things*, p. 30.

[37] John Pollexfen, *A Discourse on Trade, Coyne, and Paper Credit* (London, 1697), p. 99.

as dominated by hues of black and brown, dark green and blue. Heavy woolens and leather "were hard wearing and could be handed down through generations."[38] In this drab sartorial world the white linen collar and expensively dyed woolens in red or bright blue formed the rare exceptions that underscored the exceptional status of their wearers. But all this was about to change: "A rather grim, hierarchic society gave way," according to Daniel Roche, "to a more colourful, shimmering universe."[39]

In this context a new interest in linen – for linen was not a new fabric – emerges, leading to a large expansion of production in proto-industrial zones throughout northwestern Europe and to a significant reduction in price.[40] Cause and effect are difficult to disentangle here, but the long-term expansion of linen production in northern France, Flanders, Westphalia, Scotland, and Ireland occurred in step with the development of new forms of dress and embellishment:

White shirts, white shifts, white caps and hoods, white handkerchiefs knotted round the neck became the emblem of respectability for the shop assistant as well as the maid servant, for the prosperous blacksmith, as well as the mistress of the middling household.[41]

Clean white linens were not so much a substitute for other garments as a sartorial innovation. The shirts, accessories, and especially linen undergarments were intended to be revealed in some way so as to "flash … to the world at large the wearers' commitment to concepts of cleanliness, their membership in a common community of respectable citizenry."[42] Although bed linens were not commonly displayed publicly, they, too – stored neatly in the new linen cabinets – possessed a similar symbolic value that warranted their accumulation in impressive quantities by many households.[43]

---

[38] Beverly Lemire, "Second-hand Beaux and 'Red-armed Belles'. Conflict and the Creation of Fashions in England, c. 1660–1800," *Continuity and Change* 15 (2000): 395.

[39] Daniel Roche, "Between a 'Moral Economy' and a 'Consumer Economy'. Clothes and Their Function in the 17th and 18th Centuries," in Robert Fox and Anthony Turner, eds., *Luxury Trades and Consumerism in Ancien Régime Paris. Studies in the History of the Skilled Workforce* (Aldershot, Hants.: Ashgate, 1998), p. 223.

[40] Carole Shammas, "The Decline of Textile Prices in England and British America prior to Industrialization," *Economic History Review* 47 (1994): 492–3.

[41] Lemire, "Second-hand Beaux," p. 395.

[42] Ibid., p. 400. On the fashion to expose undergarments, see C. W. Cunnington and Phyllis Cunnington, *The History of Underclothes* (London: M. Joseph, 1951).

[43] De Vries, *Dutch Rural Economy*, pp. 220–2.

England, which imported some 28 million yards of linen cloth from the continent around 1710 and itself produced an additional amount of low-quality linen, was consuming some 80 million yards by 1756, most of the increase imported from new production zones in Scotland and Ulster. By 1770 English domestic consumption reached 103 million yards – ranging from the finest "Holland" to "Manchester Coarse Linen."[44] The rise of mechanized cotton textile production after 1770 cut severely into the growth of linen production. Even so, the value of British linen output (in a period when prices were falling rapidly) rose at an annual rate of 1.64 percent from 1770 to 1830.[45]

Cotton cloth was also not an entirely new product for seventeenth-century Europeans, but the printed cotton cloth imported from India by the European trading companies definitely possessed a strikingly novel feature: brilliant colors. This is not to say the imported calicoes immediately conquered all. The early imports reflected the consumer preferences of their culture of origin, and it soon appeared that "Europe was attracted to Indian decorative textiles on account of their cheapness and technical excellence (especially their fast and brilliant dye-colours), *not* their qualities of design."[46] To convert an initial fascination with an exotic import into a lasting desire to incorporate printed cotton cloth into the wardrobe required adaptations of the Indian articles to make them comprehensible and attractive to European consumers. In this the style directives of the governors of the English and Dutch East India Companies eventually achieved the necessary "product innovation."[47] From the perspective of the British government, these companies did their work only too well, for the intense interest in printed cotton goods led to legislation prohibiting the importation of printed cottons for domestic use (in 1700) and a more comprehensive prohibition on the importation of nearly all cotton textiles in 1721.[48] Forbidden at home, British cotton imports were

[44] Jane Gray, "The Irish, Scottish and Flemish Linen Industries during the Long Eighteenth Century," in Brenda Collins and Phillip Ollerenshaw, eds., *The European Linen Industry in Historical Perspective* (Oxford: Oxford University Press, 2004), pp. 159–86; linen production in Ireland and Scotland, negligible in 1700, rose to a combined total of some 19 million yards by 1750, and 60 million yards by 1800.

[45] Phyllis Deane and W. A. Cole, *British Economic Growth, 1688–1959* (Cambridge: Cambridge University Press, 1963), p. 204.

[46] John Irwin, quoted in John Styles, "Product Innovation in Early Modern London," *Past and Present* 168 (2000): 136.

[47] The English company's efforts are described in Styles, "Product Innovation," pp. 132–40.

[48] England was not alone in prohibiting imports of cotton cloth. France enacted more than eighty pieces of legislation prohibiting imports and/or the wearing of imported cotton

diverted to continental markets, especially the Dutch Republic, which received two-thirds of all Indian textiles, printed and unprinted, originally shipped to England up to the 1740s.

As is well known, the combination of the consumer appeal of cotton cloth and British restrictions on the imported fabric encouraged the development of domestic cotton spinning, weaving, and printing industries. The importation of raw cotton (chiefly from Mediterranean production areas) grew from small beginnings around 1700, about one million kg per annum to Britain and France combined (about half to each), to over 13 million kg to the two countries by the mid-1780s: 5.0 million to France and 8.2 million kg to Britain. Britain pulled ahead as cotton spinning was mechanized beginning in the 1770s. By the 1850s Britain imported a stupendous 360 million kg of raw cotton while France, now a distant second, imported 76 million kg.[49] The cotton textile output data of these two countries are not commonly combined, because our attention is usually called to the divergence of these two countries brought about by Britain's early mechanization of cotton spinning. But joining their production data gives a fair impression of the overall growth of cotton textile consumption in northwestern European and North American markets: an average of 3.2 percent per annum from 1700 to the mid-1780s, and 5.1 percent per annum from then to the 1850s.

The contemplation of this swelling demand for cotton cloth set clever and aspiring producers to work on expanding productive capacity with, among other things, the new machines that stand at the heart of the Industrial Revolution. In rapid succession James Hargreaves's spinning jenny (patented in 1766), Richard Arkwright's water frame (1769), Samuel Crompton's spinning mule (1779), Edmund Cartwright's power loom (1786), and a steady stream of refinements and extensions on these inventions transformed the technical and organizational foundations of cotton cloth production.

With the successful mechanization of cotton spinning in the 1770s and the gradual mechanization of weaving thereafter, cotton cloth produced in

---

fabrics between the 1680s and 1740s. P. Leuillot, "Influence du commerce oriental sur l'économie occidentale," in Michel Mollat, *Sociètès et companies de commerce en Orient et dans l'ocean Indien* (Paris: SEVPEN, 1970), pp. 611–29.

[49] British data are drawn from B. R. Mitchell and Phyllis Deane, *Abstract of British Historical Statistics* (Cambridge: Cambridge University Press, 1969), pp. 177–83; French data from Jan Marczewski, "Some Aspects of the Economic Growth of France, 1660–1958," *Economic Development and Cultural Change* 9 (1961), tables 1 and 3; T. J. Markovitch, *L'industrie Française de 1789 à 1964* (Paris: Droz, 1964), p. 47.

England, and later elsewhere in Europe and North America, would revolutionize the textile industry. The Industrial Revolution supplied European consumers with cotton cloth in larger volume and at lower prices than previously had been thought possible. This stimulated demand, of course, but it did not originate the growing demand for cloth and clothing. As we have seen, long before these technological breakthroughs the growth of demand for linen and cotton had already been intense, supporting major increases in production in a pre-mechanized environment.

The contemplation of this swelling demand set the minds of inventors to thinking, but not theirs alone. It also activated the minds of political economists, leading them to new speculations about the infinite "wants of the mind" and the "exorbitant appetites of men" which will "dispose [them] to work, when nothing else will incline them to it."[50]

David Landes, in his classic *The Unbound Prometheus*, accounted for the onset of the British Industrial Revolution as follows: "[I]t was in large measure the pressure of demand on the mode of production that called forth the new techniques in Britain, and the abundant, responsive supply of factors that made possible their rapid exploitation and diffusion."[51] This is not to say that demand equals necessity, and necessity is the mother of invention. As Joel Mokyr emphasizes, most historical societies, most of the time, have not been technologically innovative. "Demand conditions may have affected the rate at which [the ideas leading to technological innovation] occurred, and may have focused them in a particular direction, but they did not determine whether a society would be technologically creative or not."[52] Still, a focusing device can be a powerful thing, and when demand is not focused exclusively by the passive influence of relative prices but by the insistently evolving "wants of the mind," it also possesses a measure of autonomy from the existing state of the productive system.

The centrality of clothing to the power of consumer demand in the long eighteenth century is related to its impact on overall household

---

[50] The quotations are from Nicholas Barbon and Sir Dudley North, both of whose observations addressed the phenomenon of Indian calicoes importation into England. See Joyce Appleby, "Ideology and Theory. The Tension between Political and Economic Liberalism in Seventeenth-Century England," *American Historical Review* 81 (1976): 499–515.

[51] David Landes, *The Unbound Prometheus. Technological Change and Industrial Development in Western Europe from 1750 to the Present* (Cambridge: Cambridge University Press, 1969), p. 77.

[52] Joel Mokyr, *The Lever of Riches. Technological Creativity and Economic Progress* (Oxford: Oxford University Press, 1990), p. 152.

expenditures. Was the propensity to spend on clothing such that this category gained relative to other objects of expenditure? In Paris, for example, we read that:

the wardrobes of Parisians of virtually all classes and positions had increased significantly in value, size and variety [across the eighteenth century]. Maids and shop girls sported cleaner and whiter blouses, cuffs, and stockings, while new, inexpensive, lightweight calicoes transformed the gray and brown wardrobes of the populace with splashes of color.[53]

The implicit claims made here are made explicitly in the quantitative studies of Daniel Roche, who shows that the value of wardrobes in Parisian probate inventories rose, between 1700 and 1789, both absolutely and relatively. Among the poorest households, with inventories valued below 500 *livre*, clothing rose from 7.5 to 16.0 percent of total value. Overall, the relative value of clothing doubled, reflecting a process of acquisition led by female apparel.[54] Provincial France followed these trends at a distance – the towns faster than the countryside, the rich more than the poor, women more than men. Nonetheless, Roche ventures the following estimates for urban France as a whole: "Between the end of the 17th century and the [end of] the 18th century, there was an increase of expenditure ... for all forms of consumption relating to clothes: 233 per cent in nominal expenditure for the nobility and the gentry, 215 per cent for wage earners. This increase was far higher than can be observed in respect to other articles of everyday use...."[55]

The diffusion of fashionable dress followed a different dynamic from that of durable goods. New items of house furnishings, for example, needed to be incorporated in existing dwellings and to an existing stock of furniture. The complementarities of material goods gave rise to a highly varied response on the part of consumers. The existing stock of goods offered resistance, as it were, to the infusion of novelty. In contrast, new clothing needs only a body, and in the absence of social or political regulation changes in fashion could spread quickly through the population.[56]

---

[53] Jones, "Coquettes and Grisettes," p. 30.
[54] Roche, *Histoire des choses banales*, p. 230.
[55] Ibid., p. 232; Roche, "Between a 'Moral Economy' and a 'Consumer Economy,'" p. 222.
[56] Cissie Fairchild, "Determinants of Consumption Patterns in 18th-Century France," in Anton Schuurman and Lorena Walsh, eds., *Material Culture. Consumption, Life-Style, Standard of Living, 1500–1900* (Milan: Eleventh International Economic History Congress, 1994), pp. 55–70. "Only a body" is a phrase that will appear a bit too uncomplicated for many readers, who know that dress, especially female attire, is often subject to rigorous external policing and, where this is not the case, is always subject to informal

The pace of fashion change was also augmented by a new flexibility introduced by the eighteenth-century proliferation of clothing accessories and decorative haberdashery to augment the standard construction of men's and women's dress. "Playing on, and varying, these components – shirts, handkerchief, stockings, and, for women, aprons, caps, and petticoats – created the whole difference and added novelty even to old apparel."[57]

The strategic position of clothing in consumer demand may well be related to its accessibility. With small, incremental purchases, people of modest means could still participate in a broad societal engagement with fashion and experience a new sense of change. Benoît Garnot captures this idea as he summarizes the consumer behavior of the somnolent and economically declining eighteenth-century provincial town of Chartres:

> Numerous habits of daily life change in eighteenth-century Chartres. The world of consumption is in the process of being born. The people of Chartres come to posses more and more goods. In number, in perishability [breakability?], in bright color, and in variety; these changes touch primarily *les objets léger* [the light/transitory objects] and much less *les infrastructures lourdes* [the heavy/durable infrastructure].[58]

Another declining city, but a much larger one, Antwerp, offers another view of this phenomenon. Antwerp lost its international commercial position, and a good deal of its population, in the course of the seventeenth century, but those who remained somehow found the means to follow fashion. Women's fashion shops, "boutiques à la mode," did not exist as such in 1660, but the city counted 61 such purveyors of fashion by 1700. As these and other clothing retailers grew in number, the dealers in second-hand clothing and other goods, *oudekleerkopers*, declined sharply both in number and relative economic standing.[59] Clothing was assuming a new, more prominent position in the spectrum of consumer spending.

History moves at different speeds, a truism well illustrated by the realm of consumer behavior. Moreover, once consumer aspirations are

---

social control. The point being made here is that in the time and place of the industrious revolution, the social space for sartorial innovation was larger than before and than elsewhere at the time.

[57] Lemire, "Second-hand beaux," p. 394.   [58] Garnot, *Un Déclin*, p. 226.

[59] Harald Deceulaer, "Urban Artisans and Their Countryside Customers. Different Interactions Between Town and Hinterland in Antwerp, Brussels and Ghent (18th Century)," in Bruno Blondé, E. Verhaute, and M. Galand, eds., *Labour and Labour Markets Between Town and Countryside (Middle Ages–19th Century)* (Turnhout: Brepols, 2001), pp. 218–35.

awakened, a lack of economic means blocking access to the "heavier" objects of desire will redirect that interest toward the "lighter" objects.

Related to the increased expenditure for clothing and the widening variety of available clothing is a major shift among lower-income groups toward buying clothing rather than cloth. In England "ready-to-wear apparel became a discernible and increasingly important part of the national clothing market ... " in the second half of the seventeenth century.[60] Simultaneously, ready-made accessories such as knitted stockings become common and a proliferation of small retailers supplied these goods in the towns while chapmen distributed them to even the remoter reaches of the countryside.[61] Consequently, when Gregory King in 1695 reckoned total household expenditures on textiles and clothing to form a quarter of total household expenditures, this already must have incorporated a sizeable value added for the tailoring and fabricating, selling and distributing of apparel.

A substantial portion of this shadow industry emerges from what had until recently been nonmarketed household production activity. (The labor supply side of this dual transformation was touched on in Chapter 3.) The simultaneous shift toward the purchase by plebian households of ready-made clothing (especially outer garments) and toward more intensive female engagement with garment production and retailing is, of course, consistent with an industrious household. A possible motivation for these parallel developments is found in a new desire to exercise personal choice as consumers in the new realm of fashion. This brings me to the final aspect of consumer demand for clothing in the long eighteenth century: its increasingly gendered character.

In 1695, when Gregory King set about estimating annual expenditures on 90 separate categories of apparel, his estimates did not betray a pronounced gendered propensity to spend on clothing. Only half the total value of clothing in his account could safely be distinguished by gender, and this amount was divided roughly equally between male and female apparel. Of the remaining half, several major items, such as hats, shoes, shirts, and stockings, may well have been predominantly male expenses (for example, King supposed that men's and boys' shoes accounted for 68 percent of the total value of leather used in shoe making), but the

---

[60] Lemire, *Dress, Culture and Commerce*, p. 54; Spufford, "The Cost of Apparel," p. 701.

[61] Thirsk, *English Policy and Projects*, pp. 6, 8; Margaret Spufford, *The Great Reclothing of Rural England. Petty Chapmen and Their Wares in the Seventeenth Century* (London: Hambleton Press, 1984).

overall impression one is left with is of rough equality in the values of male and female wardrobes. In estimates he made of his own household's expenditures, King assumed that the annual spending for his clothing was equal to that for his wife and that the expenditures for his maid equaled those for the boy in his employ.[62]

It is unlikely that a similar exercise made a century later would have worked with these same assumptions. Daniel Roche's probate inventory–based study of French dress and fashion in the *ancien régime* also begins around the time of Gregory King: 1685–1715. Roche reports that among wage earners, female wardrobes were valued at 88 percent of male wardrobes, that among artisans and shopkeepers, "sartorial refinement ... was more pronounced among women than men," and that among the bourgeoisie and nobility, female wardrobes were worth twice as much as male wardrobes. All in all, Roche concludes that "the sexual dimorphism of dress was not yet fundamental," even though he could discern the beginning of "a general change ... [and that] women were its architects in every milieu."[63]

By the 1780s his probate inventories showed wage-earning households possessing female wardrobes valued at 2.56 times those of male wardrobes, while artisans' and shopkeepers' wives spent twice as much on clothing as their husbands. "By the eve of the Revolution the pace of change had speeded up.... In all social categories, it was women who were chiefly responsible for circulating the new objects and the new values of a commercialized fashion and superfluous consumption."[64]

I can cite no quantitative evidence that male and female spending on clothing in Britain followed the same pattern, but there is no reason to doubt a similar trend. It is certainly consistent with the evidence released by the account books of a Lancashire farm family, kept by Richard and Nancy Latham of Scarisbrick between the 1720s and 1760s. Total expenditure on clothing rose sharply as the Latham children, especially the daughters, who worked as outwork spinners, grew older. John Styles relates,

This new spending was led by the unmarried daughters themselves, whose purchases also embraced luxury in a sense more familiar to eighteenth-century social commentators, in that they purchased stylish accessories and garments in addition

---

[62] Harte, "Economics of Clothing," pp. 277–96.
[63] Daniel Roche, *The Culture of Clothing. Dress and Fashion in the Ancien Regime* (Cambridge: Cambridge University Press, 1994), p. 504.
[64] Idem.

to practical, workaday items of clothing. Yet it is important to stress that the increase in family spending required to make all these new luxury purchases was small, no more than an extra 1s 8d a week, considerably less than the estimated weekly earnings of just one regularly employed outwork cotton spinner in the period. Relatively small shifts in family income could produce dramatic transformations in material culture.[65]

Additional confirmatory evidence is provided by the female servants in the employ of Robert Heaton, a Yorkshire farmer of the second half of the eighteenth century. He kept accounts of the wages paid to his servants, and how they spent their earnings. Styles summarizes the accounts as follows:

With only one exception, all Heaton's female servants devoted the bulk of what they spent out of their wages to purchase clothing. Moreover, a majority spent more than they earned, and they did so by borrowing from Heaton.[66]

These vignettes conform to a key assumption of Neil McKendrick's interpretation of the eighteenth-century "consumer revolution." This was fueled by the new money incomes of women and children, and in the case of women: "When a woman's wages went up the first commercial effects would be expected in the clothing industries and those industries which provided consumer goods for the home."[67]

What is most intriguing about this eighteenth-century advance in relative spending on female apparel is that it is not a once-and-for-all change. The rise of spending on female apparel is reversed, certainly below elite social levels, with the construction of a new household economy in the course of the nineteenth century. In 1899 a survey of working-class expenditure in York found female spending to stand only 4 percent above male spending on clothing, while a more extensive 1937–8 survey found male spending actually to exceed that of females in a variety of manual occupations.[68] A new rise in the ratio of female to male expenditures on clothing

---

[65] John Styles, "Custom or Consumption?" pp. 109–10.

[66] Ibid., p. 110.

[67] Neil McKendrick, "Home Demand and Economic Growth. A New View of the Role of Women and Children in the Industrial Revolution," in Neil McKendrick, ed., *Historical Perspectives. Studies in English Thought and Society in Honour of J. H. Plumb* (London: Europa Publications, 1974), pp. 199–200.

[68] Female spending was only 61 percent of male spending on clothing among agricultural workers, and as high as 87 percent for industrial workers. Richard Wall, "Some Implication of the Earnings, Income and Expenditure Patterns of Married Women in Populations in the Past," in Richard Wall, ed., *Poor Women and Children in the European Past* (London: Routledge, 1994), pp. 312–35.

would reemerge with a new industrious revolution in the second half of the twentieth century. These trends are discussed further in Chapter 5.

Materials, Styles, Costs

In the early seventeenth century, the members of every social class lived their lives in material worlds they inherited, surrounded by consumer goods they would not survive.[69] Recycled consumer durables supported an important trade in secondhand goods, including clothing. The decline of this trade was a gradual thing,[70] but it left an unmistakable mark on the probate inventories: the decline in the valuations of the goods of the deceased. Old goods depreciated faster in the course of the long eighteenth century because they wore out faster and they went out of fashion sooner.

Of course, another factor affecting inventory valuations in many cases was a decline in the original purchase price of goods. Mark Overton and Carole Shammas have both reported a long-term decline of the prices of consumer durables that preceded the technological innovations of the Industrial Revolution.[71] The falling cost of raw materials will have played a role in this as cheaper and less durable substances replaced costly woods, fibers, and metals. For instance, John Styles suggests that a substantial fall in the prices of wooden furniture between the 1660s and at least the 1720s was probably a consequence of the widespread use of imported softwoods.[72]

---

[69] Hester Dibbits, "Between Society and Family Values. The Linen Cupboard in Early-Modern Households," in Anton Schuurman and Pieter Spierenburg, eds., *Private Domain, Public Inquiry. Families and Life-Styles in the Netherlands and Europe, 1550 to the Present* (Hilversum: Verloren, 1996), pp. 125–45.

[70] For Scotland, Nenadic reports a post-1800 decline in the trade in used goods of all kinds, while Decleulaer's study of the regions around Brussels, Antwerp, and Ghent finds an eighteenth-century marginalization of traders in secondhand clothing (*oudkleerkopers*). Nenadic, "Middle-Rank Consumers and Domestic Culture," p. 134; Harald Deceulaer, "Consumptie en distributie van kleding tussen stad en platteland," *Tijdschrift voor sociale geschiedenis* 28 (2002): 439–68.

[71] Carole Shammas, "The Decline of Textile Prices in England and British America Prior to Industrialization," *Economic History Review* 47 (1994): 483–507; Mark Overton, "Prices from Probate Inventories," in Tom Arkell, Nester Evans, and Nigel Goose, eds., *When Death Do Us Part. Understanding and Interpreting the Probate Records of Early Modern England* (Oxford: Leopard's Head Press, 2000), p. 140. Overton's index of consumption goods prices falls by 25 percent between 1650 and 1674 and 1725 and 1749. In the same period, capital goods prices rise by 18 percent.

[72] John Styles, "Manufacturing, Consumption and Design in Eighteenth-Century England," in Brewer and Porter, eds., *Consumption and the World of Goods*, p. 538.

Was there also a widespread reduction in quality? This certainly must be acknowledged for the proliferation of what Cissie Fairchild calls "populuxe" goods: cheap copies of aristocratic luxury items, such as fans, umbrellas, snuffboxes, and stockings. Her study of lower-middle- and lower-class Parisian decedents in the period 1725–85 found only a small rise in average value over this interval of considerable price inflation, from 1,286 to 1,565 *livres*. "Yet," she continued, "because prices for many items favoured by consumers fell, the later inventories show more goods in greater variety than ever before."[73]

Still, it would be misleading to associate the characteristic of "breakability" too closely with lower quality. The shift from pewter to glass drinking vessels, wood tableware to earthenware, or thick leather to thin leather and cloth shoes often improved the functional attributes of an item even as it became less durable.[74] The new materials also eased the introduction of stylistic elements that emphasized the differentiation of taste and fashion by design and craftsmanship. This had the effect of shortening the fashion life cycle of a wide range of semi-durables. In both ways – physical and stylistic – the depreciation of goods was speeded, and the user necessarily became more a consumer and less an heir.

One might add here that purchases became more purely acts of consumption and less acts of "investment." Durable goods made of materials with a significant scrap or resale value were partly consumed (that is, they supplied a flow of inputs to the consumption technologies that produced the ultimately consumed Z-commodities) and partly held as a store of value. The important role played by pawn banks and traders in used goods in early modern society testifies to the often-strategic role of consumer goods as assets. To protect the value of such assets, one would be inclined to be hostile to changes in fashion that could erode their expected resale value. Today, most people, after a lifetime of frenetic consumer activity and prodigious expenditures, die with personal possessions of inconsequential resale value. Such wealth as they possessed will be found in financial assets and real property, not in their household possessions. The consumer behavior we associate with the industrious revolution required individuals to be able to separate the

---

[73] Fairchild, "The Production and Marketing of Populuxe Goods," p. 229.
[74] In a personal communication, Prof. Bruno Blondé observed that archeological excavations in Antwerp have produced shoes from the sixteenth and eighteenth centuries. The former almost always show signs of repair; the latter never do.

consumption-functions from the asset-functions of goods; that is, it required ready access to financial and other asset markets.[75]

This brings us to the heart of a phenomenon that reaches far beyond cups and saucers to define a new material culture. In the century after 1650, consumer priorities shifted from the standard of the material – the metal, the wood – to the standard of the workmanship.[76] That is, the appeal of an object was located less in its intrinsic value – the scrap value of the material – than in the appearance given to it in the processes of fabrication. Through inventive forms of imitation craftsmen learned to manipulate new materials, as Maxine Berg relates, to produce goods

made of cottons instead of silks, earthenware instead of porcelain, flint and cut glass, metal alloys and finishes such as gilt and silver plate, stamped brassware, japanned tinware and papier mâché, ormolu and cut steel instead of gold and silver, varnishes and veneers instead of exotic woods.[77]

To be sure, the developing skills in fashioning and finishing materials of great cost led, through the continued refinement of existing styles, to the production of masterpieces that continue to define the highest standards of European craftsmanship in ceramics, furniture, and every manner of *object d'art*. But these developing skills also faced in another direction: creating attractive "semi-luxuries" that "were endlessly variable, individualized and customized, fashionable and affordable."[78]

What may have begun with the seventeenth-century Dutch development of domestic furnishings that integrated society with common artifacts intended for many social classes, produced at varying levels of quality and cost (see Chapter 2), took on a new aspect in the course of the eighteenth century with the appearance, especially in Britain, of a broader range of "semi-luxuries" offered in a large variety of qualities and prices, and ever-changing patterns and styles.

The commercial writer Malachy Postlethwayt revealed a remarkably sophisticated marketing sensibility when he offered the following observations in *Britain's Commercial Interest Explained and Improved* of 1757:

   1. the generality of buyers are influenced and determined by the look of a thing, and its cheapness;

75 This distinction undergirds the argument of Helen Clifford, "A Commerce with Things. The Value of Precious Metalwork in Early Modern England," in Berg and Clifford, eds., *Consumers and Luxury*, pp. 147–68. This approach to consumer behavior will be developed in some detail in the dissertation of Harm Nijboer, University of Groningen.
76 Clifford, "A Commerce with Things," p. 148.
77 Berg, *Luxury and Pleasure*, p. 24.   78 Ibid., p. 113.

2. the purchase of a fine, solid, and well-finished thing is, as I may say, a piece of œconomy in rich people: consequently few ... are able to afford it. The interest of a society is plainly to sell to the greatest number [that is] profitable.

3. The luxury of buyers in general is excited by the lowness of price. The mechanic's wife will not buy a damask of fifteen shillings a yard; but will have one of eight or nine: she does not trouble herself much about the quality of the silk; but is satisfied with making as fine a shew as a person of higher rank or fortune.[79]

Postlethwayt's message was not simply to encourage production of cheap versions of aristocratic luxury goods, although there was a lively interest in such "populuxe" goods, but to call attention to the strategies necessary to address the consumer demand that could be uncovered below the "pricing points" of the conventional luxury trades. The new materials and techniques that yielded goods of greater "breakability" also offered variety, ranges of quality, and the incorporation of new design elements. This, in turn, connected ever more goods to faster cycles of fashion change. Maxine Berg offers a persuasive evocation of a new, and specifically British, world of consumer goods that recommended itself with the attributes of "'convenience,' 'ingenuity,' 'novelty,' 'taste,' and 'style.'"[80]

The probate inventory reveals itself as less than an ideal source from which to study consumer demand because it describes the *stock* of possessions at a point in time – a specific and often not typical point in time – rather than what most interests us: the *flow* of purchases that constitute consumer demand.[81] The probate inventories of the long eighteenth century reveal stocks of consumer durables whose valuations rise gradually, if at all, but the combination of speeded devaluations (reduced resale

---

[79] Malachy Postlethwayt, *Britain's Commercial Interest Explained and Improved*, 2 vols. ([1757] New York: Augustus M. Kelly, 1968), II, pp. 402–3.

[80] Berg, *Luxury and Pleasure*, p. 86. This model of a price-driven, differentiated "luxury" for sale to a socially broad market can be contrasted to the eighteenth-century French "empire of fashion" described by Michael Sonenscher as founded on rapid cycles of fashion change, in which prestigious goods sold at high prices could be sold at lower prices as they became outdated and were replaced in elite markets by the latest fashions. Michael Sonenscher, "Fashion's Empire. Trade and Power in Early 18th Century France," in Robert Fox and Anthony Turner, eds., *Luxury Trades and Consumerism in Ancien Régime Paris. Studies in the History of the Skilled Workforce* (Aldershot, Hants.: Ashgate, 1998), pp. 231–54.

[81] For a discussion of this issue, see Peter Lindert, "Probates, Prices and Preindustrial Living Standards," in M. Baulant, A. J. Schuurman, and P. Servais, eds., *Inventaires après-deces et ventes de meubles* (Louvain-la-Neuve, 1988), pp. 171–80.

value) and speeded depreciation (more frequent replacement) requires that much larger multipliers be applied to these stock values in order to translate them into measures of the flow of consumer demand. Moreover, the valuations of stocks of many "old fashioned" durable goods embodied a "wealth component" (hoards of metals and recyclables) that in later times was more likely to appear in the ownership of financial assets. Thus, Overton's finding that the median value of material goods recorded in English inventories doubled (rose 202 percent) between the 1640s and 1740s (after which English probate inventories all but disappear) masks a large growth in the number and variety of goods found in these inventories.[82] Average consumer prices declined by 25 percent over this century. If the durability (average useful life) of purchases fell by 33 percent (which is only an illustrative guess), the doubling of median valuation would be consistent with a four-fold increase in the value of per capita purchases ($2.02 * 1/0.75 * 1/0.67 = 4.03$).

The changing world of goods described by the probate inventories can be linked – without our being able precisely to quantify the link – to a rising volume of purchases: to increased demand relative to the stock of goods. Did the changing qualities of durable and semi-durable goods also influence the cultural and symbolic dimension of material possessions? On the face of it, the shortened fashion life cycles of clothing and home furnishings would seem to have given urban elites new means to use goods as signs and markers of their superior taste, continually reinforcing the barriers that define social hierarchy.[83] This is what Pierre Bourdieu's influential concept of "habitus" would predict. According to Bourdieu, this personal cultural inheritance (bearing comparison to Gary Becker's "consumption capital") is for the contemporary working classes little more than the learned outcome of their material situation. But for higher social classes, habitus is a roomier concept. They are not constrained by their material situation, it seems to Bourdieu, and are free to craft personal tastes as

[82] Mark Overton, "Household Wealth, Indebtedness, and Economic Growth in Early Modern England," *Economic History Review*, forthcoming. Overton's estimates are based on studies of more than 18,000 probate inventories in five English counties spanning the period 1550–1750. Median inventory values rose little in the century before 1650, a period of rising consumer goods prices. Median rather than mean values are cited because of the highly skewed nature of wealth holding. The median value (where half of all households have higher and half have lower inventory values) is a fairer representation of the broad base of households than the mean value, which is pushed to a much higher value by small numbers of very wealthy households.

[83] This view is supported by, among others, Muchembled, *Société et mentalités dans la France moderne*.

self-fashioning individuals. Thus, they have the cultural resources always to win the fashion game.[84]

But the same new material culture also made accessible to the middle ranks of society and, often, below the means selectively to appropriate features of elite consumption for their own purposes. Precisely because the world of goods became so large and varied, appropriation did not need to take the form of emulation. Instead, it generated a multiplicity of "taste groups," defined by clusters of goods and styles that confused, or diffused, any monotonic ordering of income with material possession.

The key to the new world of goods was choice. Thera Wijsenbeek uncovered and delineated these taste groups in her study of eighteenth-century Delft. She detected both innovative and traditional impulses in these "lifestyle" groups, but the power of these forces was not correlated strongly to income level or occupation. She observed:

As there did not exist official restrictions in the consumption behavior, in the sense of clothing regulations, and only some preachers tried – with the voice of those crying in the wilderness – to propagandize a severe Calvinistic life-style, all citizens had the freedom, within the boundaries of their financial possibilities, to choose their own status symbols and luxury goods.[85]

Her invocation of specifically Dutch social features raises the possibility that freedom of choice in the consumption realm was something "typically Dutch." But Cissie Fairchild's work on eighteenth-century France led her in the same direction, emphasizing the new importance of choice. "Social class did not, as it may have in earlier periods, dictate what people bought; instead they spent what they could afford on goods that expressed their social aspirations."[86] If the new "breakability" allowed the well-to-do to separate the consuming from the investing function and thereby become fashionable with a vengeance, it also gave new access to those below them to pursue their own consumer aspirations.

The Luxuries of the Poor?

"Luxury" was no longer what it once had been. It was being modernized under the impact of the practice of a broad class of consumers. Just how

---

[84] For critiques of Bourdieu, see Frank Trentmann, "Beyond Consumerism. New Historical Perspectives on Consumption," *Journal of Contemporary History* 39 (2004): 374–5; Colin Campbell, "Consumption. The New Wave of Research," pp. 63–4.

[85] Wijsenbeek, "A Matter of Taste. Lifestyle in Holland in the 17th and 18th Centuries," in Schuurman and Walsch, eds., *Material Culture*, p. 43.

[86] Fairchild, "Determinants of Consumption Patterns," p. 60.

broad that class was is not a question the probate inventories can answer, for reasons already discussed. But this factual darkness has not kept historians from opining that its breadth was not great. Weatherill, in her study of inventories of the middling sort, gained the impression that "the lower limit to the market for household goods" came before one descended the social hierarchy to the husbandmen and laborers.[87] She went on to claim that eighteenth-century Britain may have been a consumer economy, "but it was not a *mass* consumption economy.... There were limits, and those limits were reached at some point between the craftsmen and the small farmers."[88]

To Weatherill the glass was half empty; to Cary Carson, focusing his attention on domestic architecture and home furnishings in North America, the glass was half full. To him, the long eighteenth century witnessed a revolution in material life that was embraced by persons of nearly all social classes. He cites approvingly the Philadelphia antiquary John Fanning Watson, who, looking back from the 1820s, described the innovations of domestic fashion emerging after 1750 as distinguishing not rich and poor, but new-fashioned and old-fashioned. The "new fashion" was a material culture that supported sociability and domestic comfort. It took, of course, an elite form, but those of lesser means were not altogether excluded:

The scale was much reduced, the splendor diminished, the lines simplified, the materials cheapened. Yet one idea endured. That was the notion that virtually anyone could hold court in their own house by carefully observing prescribed conventions and correctly using a few pieces of standardized equipment. The goods could be purchased at popular prices and the manners learned from play, print, and publications.[89]

The probate inventories generally do not penetrate to the realm of manual workers, but there are exceptions. There were circumstances in which the English parish ordered inventories to be drawn up, and institutions, especially orphanages, found reason to do so when they took in newly

---

[87] Weatherill, "The Meaning of Consumer Behavior," p. 211.

[88] Weatherill, *Consumer Behavior*, p. 193. More strongly yet, Robert W. Malcolmson, *Life and Labour in England, 1700–1780* (New York: St. Martin's Press, 1981), claimed that the "expanding culture of consumerism ... was certainly not accessible to all: in fact, it was almost entirely inaccessible to the great majority of the nation's population" (p. 149).

[89] Cary Carson, "The Consumer Revolution in Colonial British America. Why Demand?" in Cary Carson, Ronald Hoffman, and Peter J. Albert, eds., *Of Consuming Interests. The Style of Life in the Eighteenth Century* (Charlottesville: University Press of Virginia, 1994), p. 642.

orphaned children or when they were the heirs of their deceased former charges. Peter King's study of a small number of English pauper inventories offers an intriguing glimpse into the material world of husbandmen and laborers which contradicts the view that humble people stood outside the new consumer society. In the late seventeenth century, they rarely possessed the clocks, books, candlesticks, lanterns, fire jacks, fenders, and other items that showed up at that time among the middling sort of mid-Essex, King's reference group. But a century later the material world of the poor had changed: The poor paupers of the late eighteenth century were materially better provided than the wealthier husbandmen of a century earlier:

The range of household goods that working people might expect to own expanded fairly rapidly in the century after 1700. . . . By the late eighteenth century the poor had reached beyond the 'middling sort's former ownership levels in relation to a small number of household items such as earthenware, tea-related goods, bellow and pokers.[90]

This more expansive view of the range of plebian consumer expenditure is reinforced in the research of Paul Glennie, who notes that the changing consumption expectations of harvest laborers had, by the mid–eighteenth century, brought about a change in the meals supplied by farmers. These payments in kind included "traditional elements like mutton, carrots and beer . . . [but] over half of the cost went on tea, sugar, coffee, chocolate, sago, biscuits and rum."[91]

The probate inventories of colonial Maryland analyzed by Lois Green Carr and Lorena Walsh offer a clear example of the eighteenth-century diffusion of new luxuries from the well-to-do to the poor.[92] In 1710–22 only the richest rural households in three Chesapeake tobacco counties (those with estate values in excess of 490 pounds sterling) possessed tea and teaware. And even then, less than half of the rich rural decedents possessed these goods. By 1768–77 tea and teaware were all but universal among the rich; they were present in 85 to 89 percent of households with inventory values above 490 pounds. But by then half the estates of modest

[90] King, "Pauper Inventories and the Material Lives of the Poor," p. 178.

[91] Glennie, "Consumption Within Historical Studies," in Miller, ed., *Acknowledging Consumption*, p. 174. Glennie is describing the food expenditures of a specific farm, that of William and Thomas Cox of Stansbourough, Hertfordshire, in the 1750s.

[92] Lois Green Carr and Lorena S. Walsh, "Changing Lifestyles and Consumer Behavior in the Colonial Chesapeake," in Carson, Hoffman, and Albert, eds., *Of Consuming Interests*, pp. 80, 87, 90, 98, 101.

households (valued at 50–225 pounds) possessed tea and teaware, as did 25 to 32 percent of the poorest households (with estates of under 50 pounds). Among urban dwellers in the Chesapeake (living in the small towns of Annapolis and Williamsburg), tea equipage was distributed highly unevenly in 1710–22. It was universal among the rich (estates 490 pounds and above), sporadically present among the middling sort, and absent entirely among the poor (estates of under 50 pounds). By 1768–77, it was all but universal among all classes except the poor, but even two-thirds of these under–50 pound households left items necessary for the consumption of tea. Within two generations in colonial America, tea had spread from being the indulgence of an urban elite to an everyday habit of all social classes in both town and country.[93]

A similar diffusion process is observable in the probate inventories of Antwerp, where Bruno Blondé's study distinguishes wealth classes by the number of rooms of the deceased's dwellings. Tea and tea paraphernalia are wholly absent from all households in 1680, are universal among the rich and present in 58 percent of the poorest households (those living in a single room) by 1730, and are universal among all classes in 1780. Blondé's data show coffee and its attributes following tea at a distance: In 1730 such goods are recorded in about three-quarters of rich households (at least 12 rooms), less than half of middling households (4 to 11 rooms), and very few of poorer households. By 1780 they are universal among the rich, present in more than 70 percent of the middling households, and present in 30–50 percent of poorer households. Chocolate, however, followed no such diffusion process: The substance was present among some of the richest households (at least 12 rooms) already in 1680, and its use spread to at least half of households with at least 8 rooms by 1730. But it had spread no further than this by 1780; indeed, what was uncommon among poor households in 1730 became even scarcer in 1780. Chocolate had defined itself as a product for the elite, and for them alone.[94]

In an ongoing study of Amsterdam social relations in the eighteenth century, Anne McCants reports on a sample of 914 inventories after death

---

[93] Another way of describing the diffusion of tea and teaware in the rural Chesapeake: Approximately 40 percent of the richest inventories (valued at more than 490 pounds) possessed these goods in 1710–22. By 1733–44, they are found in 36 percent of inventories valued between 226 and 490 pounds sterling. This level is reached by estates of 95 to 225 pounds by 1745–54, and by poorer estates, under 95 pounds sterling, by 1768–77. Carr and Walsh, "Changing Lifestyles."

[94] Bruno Blondé, "Toe-eigening en de taal der dingen. Vraag- en uitroeptekens bij een stimulerend cultuurhistorisch concept in het onderzoek naar de materiële cultuur," *Volkskunde* 104 (2003): 159–73.

drawn up by the municipal burghers' orphanage in the period 1740–82. These concern former orphans and Amsterdam burghers whose death left orphans to the institution's care.[95] Not all inventoried households were poor, but most were well below the wealth threshold for normal probate inventories, and this makes it possible to analyze the degree of penetration of consumer goods to the plebian ranks of Amsterdam. McCants ranked these goods in two ways: by the percentage of all inventories recording the presence of a given item, and by the median total value of the inventories in which the item appeared. Thus, the most basic possessions – say a bed or a cupboard – were so widely owned that the median inventory value of households containing such goods was very low. This method also highlights some distinctly plebian goods that were found *only* in very low-valued inventories. Likewise, only high-valued inventories possessed goods such as scientific instruments, gold jewelry, or equipment for the preparation of chocolate. In such a ranked list, it is striking that delftware, mirrors, coffee and tea wares, paintings, and tobacco wares were *both* widespread (that is, most households owned them) *and* had penetrated deeply into the lowest-valued inventories (that is, many poor householders owned them, too).

John Styles summarized English probate inventory research by noting that a block of household goods had spread among middling groups: clocks, prints, earthenware, cutlery, tea and coffee ware, and window curtains.[96] Among the Amsterdam orphanage inventories, heavily weighted to households *below* the middling level, all of these items were widespread: from 82 percent of households with window curtains,[97] 78 percent with tea and coffee wares, and 72 percent with delftware, to 39 percent with prints and 23 percent with timepieces. It does not appear that these new forms of consumer demand encountered a clear barrier preventing their diffusion from the middling to the manual working classes. Indeed, the authors of all the probate inventory studies of "declining" towns and social classes emphasize how those with stagnant or declining

---

[95] Anne McCants, "Poor Consumers as Global Consumers. The Diffusion of Tea and Coffee Drinking in the Eighteenth Century," *Economic History Review* (forthcoming). See also "The Not-so-Merry Widows of Amsterdam," *Journal of Family History* 30 (1999): 441–67.

[96] John Styles, "Manufacturing," in Brewer and Porter, eds., *Consumption and the World of Goods*, p. 537.

[97] On window curtains, see the intriguing discussion on the evolution of curtain fashions (colors and fabrics) among various social classes of eighteenth-century Delft in Thera Wijsenbeek-Olthuis, "The Social History of the Curtain," in Baulant, Schuurman, and Servais, eds., *Inventaires après-deces et ventes de meubles* (Louvain-la-Neuve: Academia, 1988), pp. 381–7.

incomes nevertheless reordered their consumption priorities to acquire at least the more accessible new commodities, new fashions, and new comforts.[98]

It became a standard insight of eighteenth-century political economists to remark that the new consumer desires had the power to cause people to deny basic necessities to themselves and their families. Sir James Steuart in 1767 described the plebian consumer as follows:

The desires which proceed from the affections of his mind, are often so strong, as to make him comply with them at the expence of becoming incapable of satisfying that which his animal oeconomy [basic needs] necessarily demand.[99]

These behavior patterns reappear in modern budget studies of newly developing economies and lend important support to my claim that the industrious revolution was a broadly based phenomenon.[100] The durable goods recorded in probate inventories may be said to have dominated the new consumption patterns of the middling sort, while they were necessarily a lesser – but not an absent – theme among the poor. We now turn to nondurables about which the probate inventories can offer only indirect evidence. Here the role of the plebian consumer was often of central importance.

Consumer Goods and Their Distribution

Colonial groceries. Because the probate inventories can take us only so far, one would like to examine consumer behavior directly, by measuring the volume and value of actual purchases. There is little hope that we can measure accurately the sales of the highly varied assortments of home furnishings and decoration, cooking and eating utensils, and the equally varied items of wearing apparel. Here the probate inventories remain our best hope. But at least a few of the nondurable consumer goods, which leave no direct trace in the inventories, can be measured because they were imported (paying import duties, if not smuggled) and/or were subject to excise tax. Happily, the most important objects of nondurable consumer

---

[98] Wijsenbeek, *Achter de gevels van Delft*; Garnot, *Un déclin*; Schelstraete et al., *Einde van de onveranderlijkheid*, pp. 198–9.

[99] Steuart, *Principles of Political Economy*, Ch. 21, pp. 313–14.

[100] In recent decades, when consumer durables such as domestic appliances began to spread among lower-income groups, nutrition tended to suffer. This was measured in detail in the Brazilian city of São Paulo in the decade after 1959. James, *Consumption and Development*, pp. 29–30.

expenditure in the long eighteenth century fall into these categories: sugar, tea, coffee, cocoa, raw cotton and imported cotton piece goods, and distilled spirits.

The elastic European demand for tropical products from Asia and the New World is a familiar theme of early modern history. On the face of it, the story appears rather uncomplicated: Once Europeans were exposed to new products of the East, they became eager consumers, and where production could be substantially augmented by the development of plantations in the Americas, the decline in price stimulated European demand for these novelties even more. There was something powerfully attractive about sweetened foods and caffeinated beverages, and something altogether irresistible about sweetened *and* caffeinated beverages. But such an approach naïvely ignores the importance of consumption clusters introduced in Chapter 1. New goods must be "recognizable" to the consumer and, hence, combinable with other elements of consumption practices in order to become widely and continually consumed. In short, the broad acceptance of these new products rarely is "self-explanatory" – it has a history.

Sugar was not a new commodity for Europeans. It had long been produced in the Mediterranean, and on Atlantic islands since the fifteenth century. Honey, a close substitute for sugar, was widely available all over Europe, and local supplies were supplemented by substantial imports from Russia and eastern Europe. The early growth of European sugar consumption was hardly explosive and was sensitive to relative prices. The acceleration and broadening of the demand for sugar after approximately 1650 was anything but inevitable. After all, China's urban populations had been introduced to both sugar and tea during the Sung dynasty (960–1279), but neither did they consume them together nor did consumption levels rise in the way they would in parts of Europe after 1650.[101] Europe as a whole, which then received annually something like 20 million kg

[101] Sucheta Mazumdar, *Sugar and Society in China. Peasants, Technology and the World Market* (Cambridge, Mass.: Harvard University Press, 1998), p. 29. Concerning the limited domestic market for Chinese sugar, Mazumdar observes: "A peasantry who by and large produced their subsistence needs and most of their own food and clothing did not have recourse to the market for consumer goods except for small items such as salt, soy sauce, matches, and a bit of oil. The market for Chinese sugar was to emerge overseas" (p. 59). This is definitely not the view of Kenneth Pomeranz, who sets mid–eighteenth-century sugar production (and consumption) at 1.7 to 2.25 kg per capita, with much higher levels in the east and south of the country. Kenneth Pomeranz, "Political Economy and Ecology on the Eve of Industrialization. Europe, China and the Global Conjuncture," *American Historical Review* 107 (2002), table 1.

of sugar, consumed ten times that amount by 1770, a figure that would double again in the following fifty years.[102]

Europeans did not know tea until the seventeenth century, when in 1610 the Dutch East India Company appears to have landed the first China tea in Europe. The company's directors explicitly ordered their merchants to purchase tea for the first time in 1637, but it remained a minor item, grouped with a variety of pharmaceuticals and exotica. Indeed, in 1667 the Governor General at Batavia sought to deflect criticism for the large amount of tea he had shipped home by pleading extenuating circumstances: "[We] had been forced to buy much tea in Fujian [South China] last year. We could not deal with this quantity within the Indies [i.e., sale within Asian markets] and have had to send a large part of it to the Fatherland."[103] It would take another twenty-five years before the English company sent tea to Britain on a regular basis.[104] But, when tea came to be incorporated into European social patterns and meal taking (see Chapter 1), the demand grew explosively, rising from negligible levels in 1700 to nearly one million kg per year by 1720. Then, with the opening of a direct tea trade from Canton, imports rose at a rate of 3.9 percent per year until the 1790s, when European consumption averaged 14.5 million kg annually.[105]

Coffee entered the Mediterranean region from its production zones in Yemen and became popular after 1650 among the rarefied social circles that frequented the coffee houses of major European cities.[106] As late as the 1690s, little coffee was produced outside Yemen, which exported annually no more than 9–10 million kg to all locations.[107] Western Europe

---

[102] Sugar production estimates. Robin Blackburn, *The Making of New World Slavery. From the Baroque to the Modern, 1492–1800* (London: Verso, 1997), pp. 109, 172, 403.

[103] *Generale Missive* 25 January 1667. Cited in Zhuang Guotu, "The Impact of the Tea Trade in the Social Economy of Northwest Fujian in the Eighteenth Century," in Leonard Blussé and Femme Gaastra, eds., *On the Eighteenth Century as a Category of Asian History. Van Leur in Retrospect* (Aldershot, Hants.: Ashgate, 1998), p. 195.

[104] Chaudhuri, *The Trading World of Asia and the English East India Company, 1660–1760* (Cambridge: Cambridge University Press, 1978), p. 538.

[105] Louis Demergny, *La Chine et l'occident. Le commerce à Canton au XVIIIe siècle* 3 Vols. (Paris: SEVPEN, 1964), I: 593.

[106] The first English coffee houses are thought to have been established in 1650. By 1663 London counted 82, clustered near the Royal Exchange; by 1673 coffee houses had spread to many provincial cities; by 1700 London held at least 500. Bryant Lillywhite, *London Coffee Houses* (London: George Allen and Unwin, 1963); Aytoun Ellis, *The Penny Universities; A History of the Coffee-Houses* (London, Secker and Warburg, 1956); Norma Aubertin-Potter and Alyx Bennett, *Oxford Coffee Houses, 1651–1800* (Kidlington: Hampden Press, 1987).

[107] Julius Norwich, *A History of Venice* (New York: Knopf, 1982), p. 18.

remained a minor destination for this coffee, consuming no more than one million kg as late as 1720. But thereafter, as coffee cultivation was taken in hand first by the Dutch on Java, then by the French on Reunion, followed by both nations on their Caribbean plantations, falling prices exposed a lively interest in the beverage. The European market for coffee grew even faster than for tea, reaching 50 million kg annually by the eve of the French Revolution.[108]

The demand for tobacco followed a somewhat different pattern from that for the other major tropical commodities. Sugar, tea, and coffee all took time to become "recognizable" to European consumers and to enter into dynamic consumption clusters. Once they did, production grew rapidly for an extended period. By comparison, tobacco found consumer acceptance much more quickly and almost as quickly reached a demand ceiling that would remain until the end of the nineteenth century (when the invention of the cigarette breathed new life, so to speak, into tobacco markets). The smoking of tobacco, perhaps because it could readily be introduced into existing tavern life, spread broadly soon after its early–seventeenth-century introduction to Europe. Some 300,000 kg of tobacco was sent annually, mainly to England and Holland, in 1634. Thereafter, production within Europe emerged to supplement New World shipments, with both sources supplying Europe with some 35 million kg by 1700.

To facilitate the smoking of all this tobacco, a clay pipe industry emerged, centered on the Dutch city of Gouda. These pipes, cheap but fragile, may have been the first genuine "throwaway" consumer item, the Bic lighter of their time. The industry grew to a peak around 1730, producing many hundreds of millions of pipes. While the shards can be found all over Europe, only a handful of intact examples remain.[109] One factor in the decline of the Gouda clay pipe industry may also have been a factor in the decelerating growth of demand for tobacco in the eighteenth century: the shift from smoking tobacco to using snuff. This form of ingestion may have reduced the per capita consumption of tobacco, although not necessarily the per capita cost. Total European demand grew gradually

---

[108] Jürgen Scheider, "The Effects on European Markets of Imported Overseas Agriculture. The Production, Trade, and Consumption of Coffee (15th to late 18th centuries)," in José Casas Pardo, ed., *Economic Effects of the European Expansion* (Stuttgart: Franz Steiner Verlag, 1992), pp. 283–306. The VOC transplanted Arabian coffee plants to Java in 1711. Within a few years the French had introduced them to the Indian Ocean island of Réunion and to the West Indian island of St. Domingue (Haiti). By 1718 coffee was also being produced in Suriname. In 1789 Haiti alone produced nearly 60 percent of all coffee entering international trade.

[109] De Vries and van der Woude, *First Modern Economy*, pp. 309–11.

in the course of the eighteenth century to reach approximately 60 million kg by 1790.[110]

These and other products of the East and West Indies – porcelain, silk, cotton cloth, drugs, spices, dyestuffs – all found their ultimate consumers in Europe (and North America) via complex networks of shippers, processors, distributors, and retailers. And with few exceptions these tropical products were consumers' goods rather than producers' goods. Consequently, the total value of the goods landed in Europe by the Asian trading companies and by traders with the Western Hemisphere will indicate in broad outline the course of consumer expenditure for these novel goods. As import volumes of these initially exotic commodities rose, prices fell – often spectacularly. Thus, while the imported *volume* of the chief commodities each sustained growth rates of between 2.5 and 4.0 percent over at least a century of expansion, the *value* of total colonial imports rose more slowly, at an overall rate of 1.6 percent per annum across the 140 years ending in the 1780s. See Table 4.1.

But a trend sustained for well over a century, even if "only" 1.6 percent, is no small matter. In the 1640s European consumption of non-European goods still consisted primarily of pepper, spices, and exotica and touched but lightly all but the most elite of consumers. By the 1780s European households (west of a line stretching from St. Petersburg to Vienna to Trieste) were consuming annually non-European goods valued (wholesale, at the ports) at some 8 Dutch guilders (or 14–15 English shillings) per household. The actual retail cost of these goods to the ultimate consumers will have been much greater, at least double these figures. Such expenditures sufficed to supply – in theory – the 120 million inhabitants of this "Europe" with an annual per capita supply of approximately 2.0 kg of sugar (5 gm per day – the contents of a sugar packet), 0.12 kg of tea (enough for a cup of tea per week), 0.42 kg of coffee (also, enough for a cup per week), and 0.50 kg of tobacco (about enough for a small pipeful every day for half the population of Europe).

---

[110] Data from Jacob Price, *France and the Chesapeake. A History of the French Tobacco Monopoly, 1674–1791, and of Its Relationship to the British and American Tobacco Trades*, 2 vols. (Ann Arbor: University of Michigan Press, 1973), p. 732; C. Lugar, "The Portuguese Tobacco Trade and Tobacco Growers of Bahia in the Late Colonial Period," in D. Alden and W. Dean, eds., *Essays Concerning the Socio-Economic History of Brazil and Portuguese India* (Gainesville: University Presses of Florida, 1977), p. 48; H. K. Roessingh, *Inlandse tabak. Expansie en contractie van een handelsgewas in de 17e en 18e eeuw in Nederland* (Wageningen: A. A. G. Bijdragen 20, 1976), pp. 42–7; Jordan Goodman, *Tobacco in History. The Cultures of Dependence* (London: Routledge, 1994).

TABLE 4.1. *Import value of intercontinental trade in Europe (thousands of guilders)*

Period	Asia	New world	Total	Per capita (in guilders)
1640s	12,000	[12,000]	24,000	0.32
1750s	52,000	88,000	140,000	1.50
1780s	63,000	171,000	234,000	2.03

In brackets: rough estimate.

Sources: Asia: Sales revenues of all Asian trading companies as cited in Jan de Vries, "Connecting Europe and Asia. A Quantitative Analysis of the Cape-route Trade, 1497–1795," in Flynn, Giráldez, and von Glahn, eds., *Global Connections and Monetary History, 1470–1800* (Aldershot, Hants.: Ashgate, 2003), pp. 82–93. New World: 1640s, estimate based on volumes of tobacco and sugar imports; 1750s and 1780s: import values (excluding precious metals) of Spain, Portugal, Britain, France, and the Netherlands as cited in de Vries and van der Woude, *The First Modern Economy*, p. 478, 499; Michel Morineau, *Incroyables gazettes et fabuleux métaux* (London and Paris: Cambridge University Press, 1985), p. 487.

Of course, none of these commodities were distributed in this fashion, equally over the surface of Europe. They were landed at the Atlantic ports of the chief colonial powers and from there distributed in complex ways shaped by transport costs, tariff policies, and consumer demand. Our knowledge of consumption levels by region and social class is still far from adequate, but the bits of available evidence for the eighteenth century are summarized in the appendix to this chapter. These, observations, in turn, are summarized, in Table 4.2, in a sketch of approximate late–eighteenth-century consumption levels.

Immediately apparent from a perusal of Table 4.2 is the highly unequal distribution of sugar and tea, and the relatively broad distribution of coffee and tobacco. In the late eighteenth century the British consumed nearly half of all the sugar sent to Europe; consumption levels in Britain were more than ten times higher than in the "rest of Europe" taken as a whole. Likewise, Britain then attracted to itself more than 60 percent of all the tea shipped to Europe, substantially more than its own East India Company succeeded in landing at British ports. France, which imported large amounts of both sugar and tea, consumed relatively little, re-exporting most of both to Amsterdam and Hamburg, from where they were processed and distributed to northern European markets. Sugar consumption outside northwestern Europe was largely confined to urban markets. Paris accounted for a quarter of total French consumption in 1787, while

TABLE 4.2. *Sketch of the European distribution of sugar, tea, coffee, and tobacco: Per capita consumption circa 1780s*

	Europe	Britain	Netherlands	Rest of Europe	to Baltic
Sugar	2.00 kg	9.0	4–5.0	0.8	1.0
Tea	0.12 kg	0.7	0.5	0.05	–
Coffee	0.42 kg	0.05	2.8	0.4	0.37
Tobacco	0.50 kg	0.7	2–3.0	0.4	0.16–0.48

Column 1, for Europe as a whole, expresses the per capita supply of each commodity based on estimates of total shipments to Europe (plus an estimate of European production of tobacco). The estimated consumption in Britain and the Netherlands is subtracted from this supply to estimate the per capita supply for the rest of Europe. The final column, for the Baltic littoral, is shown for comparison.

Sources:
Sugar: Blackburn (1997), pp. 109, 172, 403.
Tea: Lenman (1990), p. 57; Dermigny (1964), I: 539.
Coffee: Smith (1996), pp. 183–214.
Tobacco: Goodman (1993), pp. 177–8; Price (1973), p. 732; Lugar (1977), p. 48.

Vienna by itself in the 1780s accounted for half of all the sugar consumed in the Austrian crown lands.[111]

Coffee was distributed rather differently. Here, the French and Dutch were the major suppliers. Britain, which imported coffee at a level approximating the European per capita average, re-exported nearly all of it to the continent, primarily Germany and the Netherlands.[112] There, consumption spread quickly to both city and countryside in the Netherlands, both north and south, and in other parts of northern Europe.[113] But elsewhere

[111] The estimate of Parisian consumption was made by Antoine Laurent Lavoisier. See Woodruff D. Smith, *Consumption and the Making of Respectability* (London: Routledge, 2002), p. 100. In the late 1810s, Benoiston de Châteauneuf estimated sugar consumption in Paris at 7.5 kg. This left 0.6 kg available per Frenchman outside Paris. Martin Breugel, "A Bourgeois Good? Sugar, Norms of Consumption and the Labouring Classes in Nineteenth Century France," in Scholliers, ed., *Food, Drink and Identity*, p. 103. On Vienna, see Sandgruber, *Die Anfänge der Konsumgesellschaft*, pp. 206–8.

[112] S. D. Smith, "Accounting for Taste. British Coffee Consumption in Historical Perspective," *Journal of Interdisciplinary History* 27 (1996): 183–214. Smith explains the apparent British preference for tea over coffee as a direct consequence of "a fiscal system that effectively reversed the relative costs of the two beverages. The British political economy strangled coffee drinking at its inception through tax measures that reflected the strength of the West India sugar planters, no less than the might of the East India Company" (p. 214).

[113] In 1740 Holland gathered information on consumer behavior with a view to reforming its excise taxes, the Republic's largest source of public revenue. The Fiscal Commissioner, Meester Gerard de Normandie reported: "It is readily apparent that the drinking of

it appears to have remained primarily an urban taste: In the 1780s, Paris consumed coffee at ten times the French average, Vienna at three times the Austrian average.[114]

Finally, tobacco was geographically the most equally distributed of all the commodities under investigation here, with important markets in the Mediterranean and the Levant, although it appears to have found a particularly congenial consumer environment on the shores of the North Sea.[115] In addition, the French national average may obscure significant regional differences, because most of the French tobacco monopoly's ten manufactories were located in northern France, near Paris.[116] In general, however, both the relative ease of distribution and the highly individualized character of its consumption caused tobacco use to spread readily to lower social classes and rural consumers.

It appears that irregular concentric circles of consumption intensity emanated from a North Sea epicenter, where British consumption of colonial groceries stood at several times the European average, and that of the Netherlands at something like 2 to 4 times that average. The Baltic littoral, benefiting from an intense maritime trade with the North Sea ports, may have consumed colonial goods at approximately the European average. The Sound Toll registers record a ten-fold rise in the weight of all colonial goods entering the Baltic between 1700–9 and 1770–9. In the 1780s, 8 percent of all coffee and 5 percent of all sugar entering Europe found its markets via this route. Only 3 percent of the tobacco shows up in the

coffee and tea in our land has broken through in such a manner that there are not only very few households to be found wherein these substances are not consumed, but also that the excessive consumption of coffee and tea has inflicted significant damage to the excise on beer. There are hardly households to be found among those of modest means where coffee and tea is not consumed to excess." Netherlands State Archives, Den Haag, Staten van Holland, nr. 4013 Verbaal aan den Gecommitteerde Raden door Mr. Gerard de Normandie, Commis Fiscaal van de Gemeenelands Middelen. Bevindingen van 1740.

[114] Coffee consumption in pre-Revolutionary Paris from Lavoisier. See note 110. On Vienna, see Sandgruber, *Die Anfänge der Konsumgesellschaft*, p. 137. Indeed, in rural Austria the regular consumption of coffee appears to be a post–World War II achievement. H.-G. Haupt, *Konsum und Handel. Europa im 19. und 20. Jahrhundert* (Göttingen, 2002), p. 25.

[115] Norwegian tobacco consumption reached 2.5 pounds per capita by 1760, declining thereafter to about 1.5 pounds per capita circa 1815. Fritz Hodne, "New Evidence on the History of Tobacco Consumption in Norway, 1655–1970," *Economy and History* 21 (1978): 118–20.

[116] Price, *France and the Chesapeake*, pp. 411–12. The importation, processing, and sale of tobacco was in the hands of a monopoly company from its establishment in 1674 until its abolition by the Revolution in 1791. On the eve of the Revolution, the company sold annually 7 million kg of tobacco, 80 percent of it in snuff form.

Sound Toll registers in these years, which almost certainly understates tobacco use in the region.[117] The potential market reached in this way – extending into Germany, Poland, and Russia – numbered in the tens of millions, but it is unlikely that more than a very small part of this volume penetrated deeply into eastern Europe. If this is true, the populations of Sweden, Finland, the Baltic States, and northern Poland and Germany (perhaps 10 million people circa 1780) will have consumed at the rates shown in Table 4.2.[118]

Most colonial products had a value to weight ratio that could support overland transportation for considerable distances, but there is little evidence to suggest that eastern zones became major markets. Indeed, as one leaves northwestern Europe, consumption of tea, coffee, and sugar quickly becomes an elite and urban matter. As for Iberia and the Mediterranean region, little can be said with confidence, but there is no evidence that the area significantly increased the levels of consumption of coffee and sugar over what had been supplied from Levantine sources before the rise of the Atlantic empires. Overall, while the new non-European products will have touched daily life in eastern and southern Europe but lightly, they were in regular use by the bulk of the populations of northwestern Europe, while in England they appear to have absorbed some 10 percent of the annual income of lower-class households by the late eighteenth century.[119]

The epicenter of the colonial goods market was located in northwestern Europe, with lower levels of demand as one moved east and south in Europe. But the colonies also consumed colonial goods, most notably the rapidly growing settler societies of British North America. Even when faced with the despised Townshend duty on tea, colonial Americans between 1770 and 1773 purchased some 150,000 kg of tea annually from

---

[117] The 1.9 million kg of tobacco passing the Sound in 1784–9 may show the effects of the American Revolution on supplies and English-Scottish distribution networks. Earlier in the century, Dutch suppliers alone shipped over 2 million kg to the Baltic, and earlier still, in 1706, they shipped some 7 million kg to Scandinavia and the Baltic. For a review of the available evidence, see Roessingh, *Inlandse tabak*, pp. 408–55.

[118] Hans Chr. Johansen, "How to Pay for Baltic Products?," Fischer, McInnis, and Schneider, eds., *The Emergence of a World Economy 1500–1914* (Wiesbaden: F. Steiner, 1986), Vol. I, pp. 123–42. The trade volume cited here excludes the colonial trades of Denmark and Sweden. Nor is any account taken of overland trades from centers such as Hamburg and Amsterdam. Johansen makes no reference to tea. Presumably, it was sent to the Baltic in quantities too small to be included in his study of "colonial products which according to weight were the most important" (p. 129).

[119] Inferred from data in Carol Shammas, *The Pre-Industrial Consumer in England and America* (Oxford: Oxford University Press, 1990), p. 136.

British merchants. These official figures alone are good for 0.08 kg per (non-native) inhabitant of North America,[120] but smuggling, especially from Dutch traders, greatly increased the true level of consumption, perhaps to half the very high English consumption level.[121] After the Revolution, tea appears to have made way for coffee; in the decades after 1790, coffee consumption averaged 0.73 kg per capita, well above the European average.[122] The colonists consumed sugar at a rate exceeded only by the mother country (6.4 kg per capita in the 1770s) and a large amount of imported rum besides. Overall, the Jeffersonian farmers on their frontier holdings appear to have had more recourse to the market to buy sugar, tea, and coffee than did most Europeans.

The influx of colonial goods was no marginal phenomenon. It reorganized the structure of meals and the timing of meal taking;[123] it attracted

---

[120] Breen, *The Marketplace of Revolution*, p. 300.

[121] Shammas, *Pre-industrial Consumer*, pp. 83–5.

[122] William Rorabaugh, *The Alcoholic Republic. An American Tradition* (Oxford: Oxford University Press, 1979), pp. 100–1.

[123] In the Netherlands, the shift from the "two-meal system" common to much of Europe in the early modern period to a three- or four-meal system began earlier than in most other parts of Europe – before the introduction of tea and coffee. But those commodities redefined the concept of breakfast in the Netherlands, and sped the replacement of meals based on porridges and pancakes, which were very labor intensive, with meals based on tea or coffee and bread. Jozien Jobse-van Putten, *Eenvoudig maar voedzaam. Cultuurgeschiedenis van de dagelijkse maaltijd in Nederland* (Nijmegen: SUN Memoria, 1995), pp. 260–68.

In Jan Luikens, *Het Leerzaam huisraad* (Amsterdam, 1711), the text accompanying his illustration of a family seated around a table, partaking of coffee, entitled "Het Thee en Koffy-gereedschap" [tea and coffee equipment], reads as follows:

De ouden hielden zich te vreden,	The older [generation] took satisfaction
Mits dat zy tweemaal op een dag,	with gathering twice per day
Den t'zaamenvoeg der tafel deeded,	together at the table.
En vierden zo dien ommeslag.	So they marked the passing day
Maar jongertyd, in onze dagen,	But now a day, in our time,
Heeft deze maat verdubbeleerd,	this pace has been doubled,
En tot een eiders welbehaagen	and to the satisfaction of all
De viermaal tafeling geleerd.	[we have] learned to table four
	times [per day].

See Hester Dibbits, *Vertrouwd bezit*, pp. 162–3 (my translation).

For Germany, "the crucial changes in our meal system were not initiated merely by urbanisation and industrialisation after the middle of the nineteenth century. The proto-industrialisation in the countryside was in general more important for this alteration. [This is] correlated with the appearance of food and meal innovations: potatoes, beet sugar, chicory coffee, and spirits.... " Hans J. Teuteberg, "Food Consumption in Germany since the Beginning of Industrialisation. A Quantitative Longitudinal Approach,"

poor and remote householders to retail shops, the only source of these goods; it increased the utility of cash income, the only way to acquire these goods; and it fundamentally reoriented the fiscal regime of England, and to a lesser extent the Netherlands and France, as they learned to levy import tariffs and excise taxes on commodities exhibiting such high income elasticities of demand.[124] The declining relative prices of colonial goods are often noted, but the rising fiscal charges on their consumption did much to hide this from the consumer. Patrick O'Brien reckoned that the various taxes and tariffs on sugar, tobacco, and tea, plus wine, spirits, and beer, accounted for about 60 percent of total British public revenue by 1788–92.[125] In the course of the eighteenth century, the shifting consumer behavior buoyed excise tax receipts, causing them to rise from 29 percent of total British tax receipts in 1696–1700 to 51 percent of a vastly larger total in 1791–5.[126] The British effort to extend such a fiscal regime to the American colonies led to consumer boycotts, demonstrative resistance (the Boston Tea Party of 1774), and revolution.[127]

Old consumer goods. Before considering what could have motivated ordinary householders to undertake such a far-reaching renovation of their quotidian lives, a few words must be said about the changing consumption of "old commodities," for the reorganization of consuming practices was not confined to the colonial groceries; these had to be fitted into larger systems of consumption that included well-established staples.

in Baudet and Van der Meulen, *Consumer Behavior and Economic Growth in the Modern Economy*, p. 235. "The British ritual called 'tea' was one of two major meals invented or radically revised in the late-seventeenth and early eighteenth century that centered around the consumption of overseas imports and that possessed important social and cultural meanings for its participants. The other was breakfast...." Smith, *Consumption*, p. 172.

Concerning France, Colin Jones observes: "The consumption of sugar, tea, coffee, and chocolate rose dramatically and this was not simply a reflection of increased elite use; for *café au lait* was well on its way to becoming the breakfast of the urban labouring classes; and was probably penetrating the countryside as well." Colin Jones, "Bourgeois Revolution Revivified," in Colin Lucas, ed., *Rewriting the French Revolution* (Oxford: Oxford University Press, 1991), p. 90.

[124] Carole Shammas, "The Eighteenth-Century English Diet and Economic Change," *Explorations in Economic History* 21 (1984): 258.

[125] Patrick K. O'Brien, "The Political Economy of British Taxation, 1660–1815," *Economic History Review* 41 (1988), p. 11, Table 5.

[126] Martin Daunton, "The Politics of Taxation, 1815–1914," in Donald Winch and Patrick O'Brien, eds., *The Political Economy of British Historical Experience, 1688–1914* (Oxford: Oxford University Press, 2002), pp. 318–50; Robert M. Kozub, "Evolution of Taxation in England, 1700–1815. A Period of War and Industrialization," *Journal of European Economic History* 32 (2003): 363–88.

[127] This, in a nutshell and without the necessary caveats, is the argument of T. H. Breen in *The Marketplace of Revolution*.

Alcoholic drinks experienced a major reorganization in the course of the long eighteenth century. Everywhere, wine consumption was tending to decline, and the same was true in most places for beer consumption as well.[128] This was partly a response to the rise of tea and coffee, but even before the use of caffeinated beverages had escaped the medicinal sphere, the traditional alcoholic drinks faced competition from distilled spirits. While distilling was not altogether new to the long eighteenth century, the migration of this process from the traditional wine distillates (brandy) to grain distillates (gin and whiskey) and the sugar-based rum made distilling of all sorts one of the leading growth industries of the long eighteenth century. The industrious revolution floated like a cork on an expanding pool of alcohol, and unlike wine and beer, which were often locally produced and consumed, distilled spirits were internationally traded commercial products, just as sugar, tea, and coffee were.[129]

French brandy had supplied Dutch and the Baltic markets well before the mid–seventeenth century. It was, indeed, war-related disruptions of access to French brandy that stimulated the late–seventeenth-century development of grain distilling in Holland. But in the long run, brandy consumption grew substantially: English imports increased fourteen-fold

---

[128] English beer consumption fell from 33 gallons of strong beer and 17 gallons of small beer per capita in 1688, to 21 gallons and 11 gallons, respectively, by 1751, and a total of 17.9 gallons in 1833. Peter Mathias, *The Brewing Industry in England, 1700–1830* (Cambridge: Cambridge University Press, 1959), p. 375. In the Dutch Republic, brewing capacity rose to the 1670s, although domestic per capita consumption may not have been rising. Thereafter per capita consumption, which is roughly estimated at 200 liters around 1675, fell steadily to only 40 liters in 1800. Richard Unger, *A History of Brewing in Holland 900–1900* (Leiden: Brill, 2001), pp. 222–84; de Vries and van der Woude, *First Modern Economy*, pp. 320–1.

 Parisian wine consumption drifted downward from 120 liters per capita in 1711–14, to 110 liters in the 1750s, to 95 liters in 1789. Lyon data reveal a similar trend. T. E. Brennan, *Public Drinking and Popular Culture in Eighteenth-Century Paris* (Princeton, N.J.: Princeton University Press, 1988), p. 190. English and Dutch wine consumption was always much lower but also tended to decline. Annual data are highly sensitive to international conditions and tariff policies, which could disrupt access to the large French production centers, but by the early nineteenth century both countries consumed in the vicinity of 2 to 3 liters per capita while in the late seventeenth century the figures may have been double these amounts. John V. Nye, "The Myth of Free Trade. Britain and Fortress France," *Journal of Economic History* 51 (1991): 23–46; de Vries and van der Woude, *First Modern Economy*, pp. 584–85.

[129] Erik Aerts, et al., eds., *Production, Marketing and Consumption of Alcoholic Beverages Since the Late Middle Ages* (Leuven: Leuven University Press, 1990). The distilling of spirits in Europe appears to date from the twelfth century, but only after the mid–seventeenth century do technical changes in production, cheaper raw materials, and an elastic demand combine to generate an explosive growth of production and consumption.

between 1684–6 and 1743–6. After a hiatus, foreign demand for brandy grew again from the late 1750s, while domestic French markets also expanded.[130] Even more dramatic was the growth of the Dutch *jenever* industry. From small mid–seventeenth-century beginnings, demand grew to support some 90 gin distilleries by 1700, mostly in towns near the ports of Amsterdam and Rotterdam. In the eighteenth century the number and average size of Dutch distilleries continued to grow rapidly, to 175 in 1736, the peak of the "gin age," and after a hiatus, they grew again after 1770 to reach 245 distilleries by 1816. Dutch distilling capacity supplied domestic markets with 15 liters per capita in 1831–5, and probably not too much less around 1800, when the province of Friesland taxed *jenever* at the rate of 12.5 liters per capita. Yet, more was exported than consumed at home, supplying most of the Southern Netherlands' spirits consumption of 6 liters per capita in 1800 as well as markets in the Baltic, Iberia, and the Americas.[131]

The rise of English spirits consumption is a complex story of competing substances: gin, rum, brandy, and whiskey. The rapid growth of gin consumption to the 1730s confronted elite observers with a compelling example of Mandeville's thesis that private vices offered public benefits. In this era of very low grain prices, the rising demand for grain-based drink buoyed the incomes of landowners and accounted for one-quarter of public revenue.[132] But to most observers, the benefits of this spectacle of unleashed plebian appetites could not weigh against the evident self-destructiveness and societal harm that came in the wake of these new consumer wants. Restrictive legislation was enacted in 1736 and again in 1751. This had the desired effect of moderating gin consumption, but imported brandies and rum quickly filled the void until a new wave of domestic spirits production pushes per capita consumption to new heights after 1780. Domestically produced gin supported a consumption of 0.4 liters in the 1680s, 2.0 liters by 1722, and more than 5 liters by the 1740s. Imported spirits raised total consumption well above this level, such that by 1751 there were said to be no fewer than 17,000 gin shops in and around London alone.[133]

[130] L. M. Cullen, *The Brandy Trade under the Ancien Régime* (Cambridge: Cambridge University Press, 1988), pp. 18, 47.

[131] De Vries and van der Woude, *First Modern Economy*, pp. 322–4, 481; Chris Vandenbroeke, *Agriculture et Alimentation dans les Pays-Bas Autrichiens* (Gent-Leuven, 1975).

[132] Jonathan White, "The 'Slow but Sure Poyson'. The Representation of Gin and Its Drinkers, 1736–1751," *Journal of British Studies* 42 (2003), p. 38.

[133] Lee Davidson, "Experiments in the Social Regulation of Industry. Gin Legislation, 1729–51," in Lee Davidson, et al., eds., *Stilling the Grumbling Hive. The Response to Social and Economic Problems in England, 1689–1750* (New York: St. Martin's Press, 1992),

Rum, a by-product of sugar refining, is difficult to track in detail, but for a time it was a key commodity of the Atlantic economy. McCusker estimated rum consumption in the American colonies on the eve of the Revolution at 16 liters per capita. After the Revolution, rum declined in importance, only to be replaced by whiskey distilling. In the American colonies, as in the highlands of Scotland and other remote locations, the distillation of grains (and maize) was a strategy of industrious households to render their crops commercially profitable, and to enter more fully into the market economy. Rorabaugh, who chronicles this development in the young American republic, estimates that the per capita consumption of spirits peaked at 15 liters (4 gallons) by 1830. Earlier, in 1810, he calculated, "Americans were spending two percent of their personal income on distilled spirits."[134]

In a complex pattern, alcohol consumption rose substantially across the long eighteenth century throughout northwestern Europe and the American colonies. The consumption of beer and wine declined, but the types of beer drunk and the increasing resort to public venues probably tended to increase the per-unit expenditures on beer.[135] The same tendency appears in Paris, where the consumption of wine declined slightly over the course of the eighteenth century. But it was increasingly drunk in cafés and *guinguettes*: 3,000 in Paris by 1750, or one per 200 inhabitants.[136] Distilling was a growth industry of the long eighteenth century, and nearly everywhere total alcohol consumption reached levels by the early nineteenth century that would not be reached again until recent decades, if ever.

Finally, we can consider the staff of life: bread. Both England and northern France experienced a large shift in the course of the eighteenth century from the "lesser grains" and unbolted wheat breads toward fine wheat bread. Gregory King reckoned that wheat made up only 20 percent of total English bread consumption in 1688. By 1800 wheat accounted for 66 percent of English grain consumption, and even more in southern

pp. 25–48. Earlier, in 1725, 6,000 places selling "strong waters" were counted in the same area, the Bills of Mortality, which defined the London metropolitan area. John J. McCusker, "The Business of Distilling in the Old World and the New World during the Seventeenth and Eighteenth Centuries. The Rise of a New Enterprise and Its Connection with Colonial America," in John J. McCusker and Kenneth Morgan, eds., *The Early Modern Atlantic Economy* (Cambridge: Cambridge University Press, 2000), p. 202.

[134] Rorabaugh, *The Alcoholic Republic*, pp. 64–5, 89; John J. McCusker, "The Business of Distilling in the Old World and the New World," p. 202.

[135] Peter Clark, *The English Alehouse. A Social History 1200–1830* (London: Longmans, 1983), pp. 292–3.

[136] Brennan, *Public Drinking and Popular Culture*, p. 76.

England.[137] Fernand Braudel supposed that the French had led the way in "a wheat bread revolution," but in truth it was a broader movement, which Hollanders passed through in the seventeenth century and the (northern) French and (southern) English experienced in the eighteenth century.[138] Bolted (sifted) wheat bread was, and was perceived by consumers to be, a very different product from other types of bread.[139] The bread yield per bushel of grain was far lower, making fine wheat bread much more expensive per pound than the coarser loaves, and it was much more likely to be bought from a baker than prepared at home. Yet, even as grain prices tended upward in the second half of the eighteenth century, the drift of demand toward the most expensive breads continued. This consumer behavior endured the scolding of reformers and faced regulation by officials who sought to force the consumption of coarser wheat breads in order to increase the available bread supply.[140] In 1801, after noting that half the bread consumed in London was bought the same day and eaten hot, Parliament enacted the Stale Bread Act, forbidding the sale of fresh (warm) bread. This measure "was said to have reduced metropolitan consumption by a sixth."[141]

This minor event in the annals of curious legislation reveals to us a characteristic of the fine wheat loaf that is the key to its eighteenth-century popularity: When supplied warm and fresh from the baker's oven it was a

[137] E. J. T. Collins, "Dietary Change and Cereal Consumption in Britain in the Nineteenth Century," *Agricultural History Review* 23 (1975): 105.

[138] Fernand Braudel, *Civilization and Capitalism. 15th–18th centuries*, Vol. 1, *The Structures of Everyday Life. The Limits of the Possible* (New York: Harper & Row, 1981), p. 137. "Wittebroodskinderen" (white bread children) was a seventeenth-century Dutch term roughly equivalent to "yuppie." J. J. Voskuil, "De weg naar Luilekkerland," *Bijdragen en mededelingen van de geschiedenis der Nederlanden* 98 (1983), p. 476.

[139] E. J. T. Collins, "Why Wheat? Choice of Food Grains in Europe in the Nineteenth and Twentieth Centuries," *Journal of European Economic History* 22 (1993): 7–38. Collins describes the general tendency in all European countries for rye, barley, oats, millet, buckwheat, and maize to yield their place in the diet to wheat. The timing of wheat's rise to dominance varied by country – earlier in northwestern Europe, later in eastern Europe – but everywhere the texture, color, taste, and digestibility of wheat came to be preferred by consumers. "Its singular advantage is as a bread-making material, in that it alone contains sufficient gluten to make possible the raising of the loaf" (p. 26). Indeed, "until recent times, when the nutritional benefits of other grains and of wholemeal breads were rediscovered, medical opinion came out strongly in favour of wheat as the perfect grain and the raised loaf as the most desirable human grain food" (p. 34).

[140] Christian Petersen, *Bread and the British Economy, c. 1770–1870* (Aldershot, Hants.: Scolar Press, 1995), pp. 105–6; Steven Kaplan, *The Bakers of Paris and the Bread Question, 1700–1775* (Durham, N.C.: Duke University Press, 1996), pp. 536–9.

[141] Roger Wells, *Wretched Faces. Famine in wartime England, 1763–1803* (New York: St. Martin's Press, 1988), pp. 29, 218.

"convenience food." Bread made of other grains was often baked in large batches and purchased once or twice a week. Indeed, the standard Dutch rye loaves weighed from 3 to 6 kilograms. Wheat bread quickly became stale, so gaining access to its desirable qualities depended critically upon professional bakers and a dense network of retail outlets.[142]

Retail networks. One feature all these new forms of consumption had in common was – expressed in the terms of our model – the heavy weight of purchased goods (x) in the final form of Z-consumption. Relatively little household labor entered into the new forms of consumption. Indeed, much of it did not occur primarily within the household at all. Consumers came to depend much more on retail shops and venues of sociable consumption than had been the case under the consumption patterns of earlier times. Indeed, the century after 1650 can fairly be said to have witnessed a retailing revolution. Retailing, like so many services, has not received sufficient attention from economic historians, but the scraps of available evidence support the view that the 1650–1750 century witnessed a major shift from markets, fairs, and direct, guild-controlled artisanal sales toward retail shops and peddlers. At first, retail shops appear to supplement the fairs and market of the market towns. Carole Shammas's investigation of the locational patterns of English retailing found that "virtually every town of this sort had a shop by 1700." Thereafter, she traces the spread of retail shops beyond the traditional market towns to villages where they sold "small amounts of a wide variety of goods."[143] Peddlers may be thought to be an alternative to such a profusion of shops, but they seem to have complemented each other more than they competed – perhaps because they sold different goods. The number of peddlers grew with the increase in small retail outlets.

This spatial thickening of retailing networks allowed for far more frequent purchases than the old market town–based system of periodic markets, and a new way of living for many households. This development has been interpreted, most notably by Mui and Mui, as a "supply-side" achievement: Technical improvements in transportation, a rising population density, and rising incomes created an environment in which shops could supply retailing services at lower cost than alternative forms of distribution. This thesis is not compelling, because the era in which the retail networks took decisive shape was not, in fact, notably affected by any of these changes. In the century after 1650 the population in northwestern

---

[142] Collins, "Why Wheat?" pp. 34–5.
[143] Shammas, *The Pre-Industrial Consumer*, p. 248.

Europe was quite stagnant, income growth was modest at best, and most significant transportation investments (canals, turnpike roads) came later. Households reoriented their consumer behavior to make heavy use of shops *despite* their high cost, not because of major supply-side reductions in the transactions cost of retailing.

At the upper ends of retailing, the emergence of fashionable shops clustering together in retailing districts established the social as well as the economic spaces that served to codify the fashion cycles, spread information, and focus consumer aspirations. This was no "natural" development. Maxine Berg says of the London shopping streets, first around St. Paul's Cathedral and in Westminster, later at Piccadilly and St. James's, that they

emerged out of the weakness of corporate controls in London; the livery companies [guilds] retreated from efforts to control production methods. Production processes were dispersed, and division of labour allowed many masters in luxury trades to become retailers, relying almost entirely on subcontracting.[144]

The escape from guild controls that allowed for a separation of the sale of craft goods from the place of production had profound consequences for the organization of production – a well-studied topic – but it also allowed for a reorganization of retailing – a development that we take too much for granted, for in many parts of Europe the persistence of corporate power delayed the emergence of modern retail shops.[145]

Excise records allow Mui and Mui to estimate that England possessed one retail shop per 52 inhabitants in 1759. They believe the density must have been much lower in 1688, at the time of Gregory King's social arithmetic exercises.[146] For the Netherlands, no national estimates are available, but regional data reveal a comparable density of shopkeepers: 1 per 50 in Holland's cities in 1742; 1 per 66 in the rural Krimpenerwaard in 1795.[147] In the Southern Netherlands, the mercers guilds controlled retail shop keeping. Here, too, the number and variety of shops grew, such

---

[144] Berg, *Luxury and Pleasure*, p. 261.

[145] The physical transformation of provincial towns to make them suitable settings for new consumption aspirations and practices is another dimension of the retailing revolution that deserves further investigation. Beckett and Smith describe how "urban renewal and consumer preference went hand in hand in post-Restoration Nottingham." John Beckett and Catherine Smith, "Urban Renaissance and Consumer Revolution in Nottingham, 1688–1750," *Urban History* 27 (2000): 48.

[146] Hoh-Cheung Mui and Lorna H. Mui, *Shops and Shopkeeping in Eighteenth-Century England* (Kingston and Montreal: McGill–Queen's University Press, 1989), pp. 135–47.

[147] De Vries and van der Woude, *First Modern Economy*, p. 581; Kamermans, *Materiële cultuur in de Krimpenerwaard*, pp. 33–4.

that Antwerp, its declining commercial fortunes notwithstanding, came to have 1 mercer per 26 inhabitants by 1690, and a remarkable 1 per 16 in 1773.[148] While the French took some pleasure in contrasting their society from that "nation of shopkeepers" across the *Manche*, they too were moving in this same direction as a swelling volume of domestic trade imparted "a more consumerist outlook on everyday life."[149]

The overall volume of French trade quintupled between the death of Louis XIV and the Revolution, and between three-quarters and four-fifths of this took place within the home market. Although the retailing network lacked the sophistication of that of England, a great many localities witnessed "the rise of the shopkeeper."[150]

No quantitative data stand at our disposal for North America, but by the 1750s a recently arrived German clergyman could express amazement that "already, it is really possible to obtain all the things one can get in Europe in Pennsylvania, since so many merchant ships arrive there every year."[151] Pennsylvania was not the only colony with ready access to imported goods. Beginning in the 1740s Glasgow merchant houses opened what were called "Scotch stores" throughout the Chesapeake region. Staffed by British resident factors, these places purchased tobacco "and, in return, supplied the less affluent planters of the region with a variety of imported goods. . . . The stores represented a brilliant innovation. As a contemporary observed, the factors opened up the Atlantic economy to 'the common People . . . who make up the Bulk of the Planters.'"[152]

---

[148] Bruno Blondé and Ilja van Damme, "Consumer and Retail 'Revolutions'. Perspectives from a Declining Urban Economy, Antwerp, 17th–18th Centuries" (Unpublished paper, University of Antwerpen, 2005). Not every member of the mercers guild owned and operated a retail shop, although it appears that most did. Other cities of the region were rather less densely seeded with shops, to judge again from the membership rolls of the mercers guilds. In the second half of the eighteenth century the small cities of Lier and Turnhout averaged one mercer per 26 inhabitants, but for larger cities, such as Leuven, Mechelen, Brussels, and Ghent, the ratios stood at 35, 96, 128, and 155, respectively. In these cities, the mercers guilds did not control all aspects of retailing.

[149] Jones, "Bourgeois Revolution Revivified," p. 95.

[150] Ibid., p. 88. Jones cites Jonathan Dewald, *Point-Saint-Pierre* (Berkeley: University of California Press, 1987), pp. 20–1.

[151] T. H. Breen, "'Baubles of Britain'. The American and Consumer Revolutions of the Eighteenth Century," *Past and Present* 119 (1988): 73–104; T. H. Breen, "Narrative and Commercial Life. Consumption, Ideology, and Community on the Eve of the American Revolution," *The William and Mary Quarterly* 50 (1993): 471–501.

[152] Breen, *Marketplace of Revolution*, p. 123. The term *planter* refers here to farmers of nearly every description, not only the owners of large plantations with numerous slave laborers.

From the mid–eighteenth century onward, the striking fact of American colonial material culture was not its self-sufficient rusticity but its market dependence. Almost everywhere, American settlers sought to produce commodities for the market so that they might acquire the goods of European – principally British – manufacture. Between 1720 and 1760 the number of weekly newspapers published in the Colonies grew from 3 to 22, and these papers found eager readers in part because of the information they supplied about new products available in the developing network of retail outlets that stretched along the entire seaboard and penetrated deep into the interior, unifying a sprawling and diverse region with common consumption practices. Both consumer information and the goods themselves reached colonists, however humble and rustic, throughout the vast expanse of North America occupied by the mid–eighteenth century. It also reached and affected colonists whose religious principles were founded on thrift, simplicity, and charity. By the 1740s, the Quakers of Pennsylvania were as much in need of a Great Awakening as were the Calvinists of New England. In neither case did a new-found spirituality slow the refinement and enlargement of their material cultures.[153]

The official statistics of eighteenth-century British exports are an imperfect source, but they reveal an unmistakable general trend. Between the mid-1740s and the 1760s the "official values" of exports to mainland North America rose from 872,000 pounds sterling per year to 2,006,000, and further to 4,577,000 in the peak year of 1771. Colonial Americans – overwhelmingly agricultural and spread across a vast expanse of territory – were then parting with at least a tenth of their annual income to acquire British imports.[154]

T. H. Breen argues that this broadly shared consumption practice became the means to communicate shared political grievances. "Since Americans from Savannah to Portsmouth purchased the same general range of goods, they found that they were able to communicate with each other about a common experience."[155] Breen's interpretation focuses attention on the sociability and the signaling that are part and parcel of

---

[153] Quaker views on material prosperity are discussed in David E. Shi, *The Simple Life. Plain Living and High Thinking in American Culture* (Oxford: Oxford University Press, 1985), pp. 28–49.

[154] The import and income data are discussed in John McCusker and Russell Menard, *The Economy of British North America, 1607–1789* (Chapel Hill: University of North Carolina Press, 1985), pp. 279–80. The per capita consumption estimate is made by Carole Shammas, "How Self-Sufficient was Early America?" *Journal of Interdisciplinary History* 13 (1982): 247–72. See also Breen, *Marketplace of Revolution*, pp. 54–60.

[155] Breen, *Marketplace of Revolution*, p. 15.

market-based consumption. Consumption is often held to be a private – and selfish – act, but it cannot occur without public acts of purchase and display, and the utility of the new forms of consumption of this era was much enhanced by the social signals they transmitted, which, in turn, depended on shared knowledge imparted by the information systems of a commercial society. Consumer boycotts (against the Stamp Act [1765], the Townshend Act [1767], and the Tea Act [1773]) became the common coin of political protest on the eve of the American Revolution. Breen stresses the "utter novelty" of this form of protest: "No previous rebellion had organized itself so centrally around the consumer."[156] This could occur, he goes on to argue, because "American colonists discovered a means to communicate aspirations and grievances to each other through a language of shared experience [the experience of consumption]."[157] The sheer magnitude of this "shared experience" was substantial, because the colonial population, which grew more than eight-fold between 1700 and 1773 (when it stood at 2.2 million), increased its share of a rapidly growing volume of British trade from under 6 to nearly 26 percent of all British-produced exports.[158]

Joining the new multitude of retail shops spreading throughout the Atlantic world were establishments of commercialized sociability, entertainment, and leisure. At the higher social levels we see the coming together of the complex of urban assemblies, coffee houses, concert halls, and theatres that drew genteel leisure from the private into a public, and commercialized, sphere.[159] At the plebian level, the focus shifted to cockfights, animal baiting, prizefighting, and other sports – all of which, similarly, were taking a commercialized form.[160] And everywhere there were taverns, beer stalls, gin shops, *guinguettes*, and cabarets. If the new sporting and betting venues were masculine to a fault, the proliferating drinking establishments, often operated by women, "were increasingly patronized by women attracted to the growing availability of spirits, especially gin, and music and dancing."[161]

The owners of this growing multitude of shops established them, often, to earn a bit of extra cash; their patrons paused to spend there the extra

---

[156] Breen, "Narrative of Commercial Life," p. 486.

[157] Breen, *Marketplace of Revolution*, p. 14.

[158] McCusker and Menard, *Economy of British North America*, pp. 279–80.

[159] Peter Borsay, *The English Urban Renaissance. Culture and Society in the Provincial Town, 1660–1760* (Oxford: Oxford University Press, 1989).

[160] Gareth Steadman-Jones, "Working-Class Culture and Working-Class Politics in London, 1870–1900. Notes on the Remaking of a Working Class," *Journal of Social History* 7 (1974): 460–508.

[161] Shoemaker, *Gender in English Society*, pp. 274–5.

cash they had earned in order to participate in new consumption practices. The turnover of this multitude of shops will, on average, have been very modest. Many must have been the part-time undertakings of our "industrious" households, serving literally as the pantries of a consuming public unable to purchase goods in large quantities and/or dependent on credit that only retailers with local knowledge could provide.

Credit featured prominently in industrious consumerism, just as it does in our modern consumer era. Indeed, credit probably played a larger role then, even in petty retailing, for the simple reason that small coins were scarce (and not sufficiently small!).[162] In addition, the highly seasonal character of production and trade caused financial settlements to be concentrated in annual or semi-annual cycles. The harvest cycle continued to dominate this pattern of annual reckoning, in which cash changed hands only to settle net obligations, after all other transactions of the previous period had been cancelled out. But urban economies shared many of the same features. In Amsterdam and several other Dutch cities May 1 was the traditional contract date for the rental of houses and All Saints day, November 1, was the semi-annual settlement date for rents. These two dates also marked the start of semi-annual employment contracts for servants.[163] On these dates, as payments were made – or defaulted on – a human "reshuffling of the deck" took place, as families moved to better, or to cheaper, lodgings, and servants went to new employers, or left to marry or otherwise strike out on their own.

Inevitably, credit was needed to make such a cash-short economy function. Consequently, few participants in the early modern market economy were *only* debtors or *only* creditors. People of every income level were enmeshed in extensive networks of lending and borrowing, their total debts tending to rise with their assets.[164]

---

[162] On the general problem of the shortage of cash and the role of credit in early modern England, see Craig Muldrew, "'Hard Food for Midas'. Cash and Its Social Value in Early Modern England," *Past and Present* 170 (2001): 78–120. He expressed as follows the stress under which the English economy was being placed: "Gold and silver were not the water upon which the vessel of the economy floated; they were the anchor which was becoming increasingly corroded by the currents of economic change" (p. 89).

In many urban areas of Britain one could purchase the same bread at three different prices (or, more commonly, at the same price, but for progressively smaller loaves): ready money bread (paid by cash), tally bread (bought on credit), and hucksters bread (sold in the streets). Wells, *Wretched Faces*, pp. 21, 28.

[163] Clé Lesger, *Huur en conjunctuur. De woningmarkt in Amsterdam, 1550–1850* (Amsterdam: Amsterdamse Historische Reeks No. 10, 1986), pp. 26–9.

[164] This pattern is described for Amsterdam in Jan de Vries, "The Republic's Money. Money and the Economy," *Leidschrift* 13 (1998): 7–30.

But, of course, credit served other functions as well: It supported those temporarily without means, but it also underwrote consumers whose desires swelled faster than their means. More properly, it performed these functions for the creditworthy.

Who was creditworthy? Only in the past half-century has most credit been removed from the world of face-to-face, personal relations. Lenders in the long eighteenth century took tangible collateral (pawns) or had personal knowledge of the debtor, leading to relationships of obligation and reciprocation. Some historians, inspired by the anthropology of gift exchange, have supposed that credit was not so much an economic contract as it was a cultural act in which creditworthiness had at least as much to do with power relations and community standing as with an ability to repay the debt.[165] Today's borrower, whose creditors are almost all institutional abstractions, may need to be reminded of the socially charged character of the personal debt relationships of earlier times, but it does not follow, as some historians suggest, that these transactions were not primarily rational, commercial agreements. It does follow that the determination of creditworthiness depended very much on local knowledge of personal characteristics and family reputation. Overall, the retailing system advanced faster than the monetary regime; the new patterns of consumption depended on credit arrangements to address limitations that otherwise would have stymied the elaboration of new material cultures.

The restricted availability of information about creditworthiness tied consumers to local retailers and to pawnshops, ancient institutions that found a new market niche in this era. Anne McCants's studies of

---

[165] Anthropologists, following Marcel Mauss, have long emphasized the strategic role of gift exchange – routine, socially enforced gift giving – in the maintenance of social relations within "traditional" societies. Some historians count early modern Europe among these traditional societies, where credit, instead of being the life blood of a capitalist economy, is blurred with gifts and constitutes, as Pierre Bourdieu puts it, a social "attack on the freedom of one who receives it. . . . It creates obligations, it is a way to possess, by creating people obliged to reciprocate. Credit, rather than being an instrumental contract, acts as a cultural force, embedding its participants in binding social and symbolic relations."

According to Craig Muldrew, Tudor and Stuart England still possessed such an "economy of obligation." "There was not as yet an important social distinction between the utilitarian world of economics and the more 'subjective' social world of feelings and events." Craig Muldrew, *The Economy of Obligation. The Culture of Credit and Social Relations in Early Modern England* (Basingstoke: Macmillan, 1998), p. 65. See also Margot Finn, *The Character of Credit. Personal Debt in English Culture, 1740–1914* (Cambridge: Cambridge University Press, 2003), pp. 4–11. Finn argues that credit remained more a cultural than an economic concept in England until the eve of World War I.

eighteenth-century plebian Amsterdam households reveal a widespread use of the city's municipal pawn bank, the Bank van Lening, at least above the level of the very poorest families. One needed to possess a pawn-worthy asset. Thus, it appears the purchase of semi-durables depended on shop credit, while the pawn bank saw the overextended households through the vicissitudes of daily life, providing liquidity at short notice.[166] Credit of these types stood behind the alacrity, noted by John Styles, with which humble consumers gained access to the objects of their desire: "What is especially striking about the consumption habits of the eighteenth-century labouring poor is their capacity to respond to accessible innovations."[167] Gin, cotton clothing, and the observation of teatime come to mind as "accessible innovations." Via credit, the plebian consumer could act on what Sir James Steuart called "the little objects of ambition," the desires, as he put it, "which proceed from the affections of his mind."[168] The role of credit had earlier attracted the attention of Defoe, who characteristically moderated any tendency to moralize with a strong appreciation of the beneficial economic consequences of plebian abundance:[169]

How many thousands of families wear out their cloaths before they pay for them, and eat their dinner upon tick with the butcher? Nay, how many thousands who could not buy any cloaths, if they were to pay for them in ready money, yet buy them at a venture upon their credit, and pay for them as they can?

Here we confront the high transaction costs that ordinarily impeded the shift toward specialized production and consumption. The high markups of retailers were a major theme of Sir Frederick Morton Eden's critique of the new household economy in his *State of the Poor* of 1797. He organized

---

[166] McCants, "Goods at Pawn," pp. 213–38; "Petty Debts and Family Networks," pp. 33–50.

[167] Styles, "Manufacturing Consumption and Design," p. 538.

[168] Steuart, *Principles of Political Economy*, ch. 21, pp. 315, 313. Objects of ambition are not always material goods. Karl Marx's aspiration to complete *Capital* forced him periodically to pawn his household furniture and silver, and also his overcoat, in order to gain the cash to satisfy his creditors. However, he could not gain admission to the reading room of the British Museum without the overcoat. Redeeming this pawn had his highest priority, perhaps spurring him to industrious behavior. It is striking that he concentrated his famous critique of capitalism on production, writing almost nothing about the perhaps personally painful topic of credit. See Peter Stallybrass, "Marx's Coat," in Patricia Spyer, ed., *Border Fetishisms. Material Objects in Unstable Spaces* (New York: Routledge, 1998), pp. 183–207; Craig Muldrew, "'Hard Food for Midas'. Cash and Its Social Value in Early Modern England," *Past and Present* 170 (2001): 78–120.

[169] Defoe, *The Compleat English Tradesman*, p. 410.

his investigation as a comparison of northern and southern rural laboring families: The former retained, in his view, old patterns of self-provisioning, while the latter depended on retailers for their food, clothing, and most everything else.[170] His pioneer budget studies showed these poor households spending more than 11 percent of their earnings on sugar, treacle, and tea. The high prices they willingly paid, often for foods of inferior nutritional quality, caused him to conclude that the poverty problem of southern England was founded on improvident spending rather than on inadequate earnings.[171] If only plebian Englishmen returned to the simpler ways of their forefathers – still observable in the remote corners of the land – they would live better. His remedy ignored the interrelated character of the consumption patterns he deplored and their relationship to the productive system that, presumably, he found more estimable. An earlier, midcentury observer saw this relationship more clearly, when he declared that "[A]lmost the whole Body of the People of *Great Britain* may be considered either as the Customers *to*, or the Manufacturers *for* each other."[172]

Conclusion

The industrious revolution that began in the late seventeenth century increased consumer demand, but equally important was the way it changed the composition of consumption. The new consumer behavior cannot, in my view, be understood simply as so many marginal adjustments to changes in relative prices. Nothing in the movement of wages and prices experienced by the affected societies made inevitable the new consumption regime observable by the second half of the eighteenth century. Rather, it should be seen as a jump from an old to a new state, requiring simultaneous changes in the productive organization of the household and its desired "consumption bundles." The new regime formed the context in which the Industrial Revolution unfolded rather than being itself a creation of that sequence of events.

---

[170] Carole Shammas supports Eden's assessment of the labourers' market dependence. "By the end of the early modern period many English labouring families bought nearly their entire diet – apart from garden produce – on the market from the baker, the butcher, the grocer or whoever sold the tea, sugar, butter, milk, four, bread, and meat in the locality. The more prepared the food the better, so that fuel would not have to be expended in cooking it." Shammas, *Pre-Industrial Consumer*, p. 145.

[171] Eden, *The State of the Poor*.

[172] Tucker, *Instructions*, pp. 245–6. Quoted in Göran Hoppe and John Langton, *Peasantry to Capitalism. Western Ostergotland in the Nineteenth Century* (Cambridge: Cambridge University Press, 1994), p. 29.

This new consumption regime was not uniform across social classes. The two sources I have relied on to chart the changes tend to illuminate consumption of two distinct, though overlapping, ranges of society. For those with some sort of property and/or the ability to keep domestic servants, the new forms of consumption were integrated into a domestic setting that featured greater comfort, domestic sociability, symbols of respectability, and steps toward the acknowledgment of privacy. Developing side by side with this luxury of the middling sort, and overlapping in some respects, was a plebian consumer culture in which the domestic setting played a subordinate role. Many domestic comforts were simply not accessible to households that supplied, rather than kept, servants.

They pursued, instead, the cultivation of sociability outside the home, used the widened choice in food and drink to simplify meal preparation, and shifted from jointly consumed to more individuated forms of consumption. In all these developments, the long-term needs of the household had a relatively low priority. Indeed, it appeared to anxious observers from Eden to Engels and Le Play that the household was increasingly rudderless: a zone of contention rather than a unit with a common purpose. Multiple income earners meant multiple voices in consumption that in its extreme form could assume a "struggle for the breeches," which is how Anna Clark describes London's "metropolitan libertine culture" with its high demand for public consumption to the neglect of household needs.[173] Outside the Great Wen, matters were not much different, according to Hans Medick, who described western Europe's proto-industrial cottages as places where "the long-term needs of the household had a low monetary priority. By contrast, the demand for public consumption in the monetary sphere was extraordinarily high."[174] And this demand tended to be *individual* demand. Pastor Franz Weizenegger, in reflecting on his home visitations in Austria's Vorarlberg, a center of rural industry, wrote in 1839:

When the pastor [*Seelsorger*] expresses concern over vanity and splendid garments where they barely have bed linens and foodstuffs, but one sees scattered about festive clothing, smoking pipes and timepieces, the parents excuse themselves with the obdurate statement that the children earned the money themselves. . . . In this way, there are as many separate purses [*Nebenkassen*] as there are workers in the family.[175]

---

[173] Anna Clark, *Struggle for the Breeches. Gender and the Making of the British Working Class* (Berkeley: University of California Press, 1995), pp. 25–30.
[174] Medick, "The Structure and Function of Population Development under the Protoindustrial System," in Kriedte, Medick, and Schlumbohm, eds. *Industrialization Before Industrialization*, p. 91.
[175] Quoted in Sandgruber, *Die Anfänge der Konsumgesellschaft*, p. 375.

These observations about disorder in the household speak in generalities, or about the failings of parents, but the chief object of scrutiny in critiques of this sort was nearly always the family's wife and mother. The industrious revolution had as its social pendant female earning power that affected the terms of marital unions.[176] The increased bargaining power of women also exposed them more than before to male default. If the rising rate of prenuptial pregnancy reveals something of the broadened scope for unions based on "romantic love" rather than property (rising from 15 to nearly 40 percent of the first pregnancies of English women between the 1670s–80s and 1810s),[177] the rise of illegitimate births is a direct measure of the concomitant risk of male default (rising from 1.0 percent of all births in the 1650s to 5.3 percent in the 1800s, reaching a peak of nearly 7 percent in 1850, before declining sharply).[178]

Once married, women found their attachment to labor and commodity markets increasingly associated by elite observers with poor nutrition,[179] infant death,[180] stunted growth,[181] and disorderly homes.[182] The

---

[176] John Gilles, *For Better, For Worse. British Marriages, 1600 to the Present* (Oxford: Oxford University Press, 1985), pp. 181–2; Edward Shorter, *Making of the Modern Family* (New York: Basic Books, 1975).

[177] P. E. H. Hair, "Bridal Pregnancy in Rural England in Earlier Centuries," *Population Studies* 20 (1966–7): 233–43.

[178] Peter Laslett, "Introduction," in Peter Laslett, Karla Oosterveen, and Richard M. Smith, eds., *Bastary and its Comparative History* (Cambridge, Mass.: Harvard University Press, 1980), pp. 13–19; see also Adrian Wilson, "Illegitimacy and Its Implications in Mid-Eighteenth Century London," *Continuity and Change* 4 (1989): 103–64.

[179] Clark, Huberman, and Lindert, "A British Food Puzzle," p. 234. The puzzle addressed here is the gap between food output (and net imports) and final food consumption. The authors account for the difference by a growing consumption of foods that have endured extensive transportation, processing, and marketing costs. See also Shammas, *Pre-Industrial Consumer*: "The abysmal dietary situation of the early nineteenth century industrialization period...may well have had its origins a century earlier" (p. 145).

[180] W. R. Lee, "Women's Work and the Family. Some Demographic Implications of Gender-Specific Rural Work Patterns in Nineteenth-Century Germany," in Hudson and Lee, eds., *Women's Work and the Family Economy*: "Female economic activity is generally associated with an early start to harmful supplementary feeding, a termination of breast feeding, and higher infant mortality and morbidity" (p. 61).

[181] The relative importance of the multiple determinants of net nutritional status remains a matter of debate. See Hans-Joachim Voth, "Height, Nutrition, and Labor. Recasting the 'Austrian Model,'" *Journal of Interdisciplinary History* 25 (1995): 627–36; John Komlos, "Shrinking in a Growing Economy? The Mystery of Physical Stature During the Industrial Revolution," *Journal of Economic History* 58 (1998): 779–802; Richard Steckel, "Stature and Living Standards," *Journal of Economic Literature* 33 (1995): 1903–40.

[182] David Weir, "Parental Consumption Decisions and Child Health During the Early French Fertility Decline," *Journal of Economic History* 53 (1993): 259–74. On human capital formation, see David Mitch, "The Role of Education and Skill in the British

consumption clusters fostered by the needs and aspirations of the industrious household stimulated demand in sectors that, with few exceptions, had no strong links to the leading sectors of the Industrial Revolution.[183] Richard Steckel, in pondering the decline in antebellum American stature, mused that "a particular type of prosperity may have accompanied industrialization while other aspects of the standard of living deteriorated." Likewise, Nicholas Crafts, addressing British income growth during the industrialization, emphasized that this "peculiar type of prosperity" would rank poorly in a Human Development Index.[184]

Against all these negative features of the plebian version of the industrious household and its consumer behavior stood the positive achievement: the exercise of choice across a widened array of available goods to construct consumption clusters with the appeal to activate intensified market production. Through the increased offer of labor and specialization, this supported an extensive growth of the economy, and through the focused demand on certain "incentive goods" it speeded the construction of distribution and retailing systems that supported an intensified division of labor.

The new forms of consumer behavior that emerged after the mid–seventeenth century in northwestern Europe, and the new organization of the household economy that went with them, were instrumental in setting the stage for the Industrial Revolution, but they were not immediately transformed by that great supply-side event. The same consumer patterns persisted well into the nineteenth century. Indeed, the chief effect of the speeded economic growth brought about by the Industrial Revolution may well have been to enlarge the social classes that kept servants, which had long divided society into two distinct spheres of material culture. This complex was disrupted and transformed after 1850, by a new revolution in the household economy and its relations to the market economy.

Industrial Revolution," in Joel Mokyr, ed., *The British Industrial Revolution* (Boulder, Colo.: Westview Press, 1993), pp. 241–79.

[183] Sara Horrell, "Home Demand and British Industrialization," *Journal of Economic History* 56 (1996): 561–604.

[184] Richard Steckel, "Stature and Living Standards in the United States," in Robert Gallman and John Wallis, eds., *American Economic Growth and Standards of Living Before the Civil War* (Chicago: University of Chicago Press, 1992), p. 294; N. F. R. Crafts, "Some Dimensions of the Quality of Life During the British Industrial Revolution," *Economic History Review* 50 (1997): 617–39. The Human Development Index is an indicator of social well-being that includes income per head, life expectation at birth, and measures of educational attainment.

Appendix: Per Capita Consumption of Selected Commodities

Sugar	Date	Per capita consumption
England	1670s	c. 1.0 kg.
	1700–9	2.6
	1720–9	5.0
	1750–9	7.5
	1770–9	10.5
Great Britain	1784–6	7.7
	1804–6	9.3
	1834–6	9.2
	1844–6	9.6
Belgium	c. 1800	1.65[a]
	1850–4	3.0
Brussels	1760	1.65
Netherlands	c. 1750	3.75[b]
	c. 1820	5.5
France	1730–4	0.45
	1784–7	0.85
	1788–90	0.95
	1810–19	0.95
	1830	2.0
Paris	1787	4.9
	1815–19	7.5
Austria (Crown Lands)	1780	0.15
	1800	0.4
	1830	1.0
British North America (13 colonies)	1770s	7.6
Baltic Littoral[c]	1784–9	1.0

[a] plus 0.90 kg syrup
[b] plus syrup, amount unknown
[c] Supplies passing through the Danish Sound for consumption in Sweden, Finland, northern Germany, Poland, and Russia. I assume these supplies serve markets totaling 10 million consumers.

Sources:
England: Sheridan (1973), p. 22; Mokyr (1988), p. 75.
Great Britain: Davis (1979), p. 45.
Belgium: Vanderbroeke (1975); Segers, et al. (2002), p. 100.
Brussels: De Peuter (1999).
Netherlands: de Vries and van der Woude (1997), p. 327; Kooi (2001), p. 141.
France: Toutain (1971), p. 2016; Breugel (2001), pp. 99–118; Stein (1980), pp. 5–6.
Paris: Stein (1980), pp. 5–6.
Baltic: Johansen (1986), pp. 123–42, 197.
British North America: Walsh (1992), p. 238.

Appendix (Continued)

Tobacco	Date	Per capita consumption
England	1669	0.42 kg.
	1698–1702	1.05
	1748–52	0.88
	1794–6	0.51
	1814–36	0.44
Netherlands	1700–9	1.96–2.86
Maastricht	1670s	0.5
	18th century	1.5
France	1789	0.26
Norway	c.1760	1.14
	c.1815	0.68
Baltic Littoral	1784–9	0.16–0.48
Austria (Crown Lands)	1780	0.5
	1800	0.79
	1850	0.88
British North America (13 colonies)	18th century	1.0–2.5

Sources:
England: Shammas (1990), p. 79; Nash (1982), p. 367.
Netherlands: Roessingh (1976), pp. 236–48.
Maastricht: Steegen (1998), p. 178.
France: Price (1973), pp. 411–12.
Norway: Hodne (1978), pp. 118–20.
Baltic: Johansen (1986), pp. 123–42. (See note 99.)
Austria: Sandgruber (1982), p. 197.
British North America: Shammas (1990), p. 78.

Appendix (Continued)

Coffee	Date	Per capita consumption
England	1699–1701	0.05 kg.
	1749–51	0.05
	1785–7	0.03
	1801	0.03
	1841	0.23
Netherlands	1770s	2.8
Maastricht	1728–30	0.8[a]
Friesland	1711	0.07
Friesland	1786	2.8
Belgium	1790	0.5
	1850–4	4.0
Brussels	1760	0.55
France	1781–9	0.24
	1815–24	0.24
	1825–35	0.29
Paris	1787	1.9
Baltic Littoral	1784–9	0.37
Austria (Crown Lands)	1780	0.04
	1800	0.05
Vienna	1783	5.0
United States	1790–1825	0.73

[a]In 1729–30, consumption in rural hinterland was negligible; in 1750, rural consumption was equal to that of the city of Maastricht.

Sources:
England: Smith (1996), p. 185; Burnett (1989), pp. 15–17.
Netherlands: Voskuil (1988), pp. 77–83.
Maastricht: Jansen (1997), pp. 48–55.
Friesland: Anon. (1786), p. 28.
Belgium: Vandenbroeke (1975); Segers, et al., (2002), p. 101.
Brussels: De Peuter (1999), p. 111.
France: Toutain (1971), p. 1975.
Paris: Lavoisier (1988), p. 141.
Baltic Littoral: Johansen (1986), pp. 123–42.
Austria: Sandgruber (1982), p. 197.
United States: Rorabaugh (1979), pp. 100–1.

Appendix (Continued)

Tea	Date	Per capita consumption
England	1722	0.28
	1750–9	0.5
	1784–6	0.61
	1804–6	0.79
	1834–6	0.86
	1844–6	0.84
Netherlands	1780s	0.5–0.9
Friesland	1711	0.04
	1760	0.40
	1791	0.90
Maastricht	1729–30	0.2–0.25
	1760	0.4–0.5
Belgium	1720–9	0.045
	1850–4	0.01
Brussels	1760	0.10
France	1825–34	0.03
	1835–44	0.04
British North America (13 Colonies)	1773	0.34
United States	1835–50	0.36

Sources:
England: Davis (1979), pp. 45–6; Mokyr (1988), p. 75.
Netherlands: Voskuil (1988), pp. 77–83.
Friesland: *Vergelijking van de voornaamste imposten* (Leeuwarden, 1786), p. 28.
Maastricht: Jansen (1977), pp. 48–55.
Belgium: Parmentier (1996), p. 110.
Brussels: De Peuter (1999), p. 111.
France: Toutain (1971), p. 1975.
United States: Rorabaugh (1979), p. 99.

Appendix (Continued)

Spirits	Date	Per capita consumption
England	1680s	0.35 liters
	1710s	1.5
	1722	1.9
	1740s	c.6.0
	1833	3.5
Netherlands	1790	7.0
	1831–5	15.0
Utrecht (Prov.)	1790–8	6.0
Friesland	1767	7.0
	1800	12.5
Groningen (Prov)	1790	7.0
Belgium	c.1800	6.0
	1850–4	8.4
Brussels	1760	9.0
France	1780–9	0.9
	1825–34	0.9
Paris	1711–14	3.6
Paris	1787	9.0
British North America (13 colonies)	1770	13.25
United States	1830	14.8
	1850	3.8

Sources:
England: Mathias (1959), p. 375; Mitchell and Deane (1969), pp. 355–6; Cullen (1988), p. 18.
Netherlands: Burema (1953), pp. 177–8.
Friesland: *Vergelijking van de voornaamste imposten* (Leeuwarden, 1786).
Belgium: Vandenbroeke (1975); Segers, et al. (2002), p. 101.
Brussels: De Peuter (1999), pp. 109–11.
France: Toutain (1971), p. 1974.
Paris: Brennen (1988), p. 189.
United States: Rorabaugh (1979), pp. 232–3.

5

The Breadwinner–Homemaker Household

Introduction

Toward the middle of the nineteenth century, as the new industrial capabilities brought about by the Industrial Revolution made themselves felt with increasing force throughout northwestern Europe and North America, consumer behaviors had constructed two distinct forms of household economy. Among a growing class of servant-keeping households, a broad array of goods, most owing little directly to the Industrial Revolution itself, brought increasing domestic comfort, fashion, and variety to the middling classes and above. Below these middling classes matters were very different. Here, where the truly industrious households were most numerous, the consumer behaviors that had been developing since well before the Industrial Revolution were viewed by elite observers with concern and even horror. With their multiple income earners, vestigial household production, and individuated consumer aspirations, working-class families appeared to be both dysfunctional and disintegrating. Whether one turns to Frederic Le Play in France, Frederich Engels in England, or Wilhelm Heinrich Riehl in Germany, the founders of family sociology offered the same basic diagnosis: A traditional "family economy" where all members worked together in support of a common enterprise was being undermined by industrial capitalism.[1] As E. P. Thompson so evocatively put it, under industrial capitalism "[t]he family was roughly

[1] Eric Richards, "Women in the British Economy Since about 1700. An Interpretation," *History* 59 (1974): 343. See also Katherine Lynch, *Family, Class, and Ideology in Early Industrial France. Social Policy and the Working-Class Family, 1825–1848* (Madison: University of Wisconsin Press, 1988), p. 56; Janssens, *Family and Social Change*, pp. 1–10.

torn apart each morning by the factory bell," and the resulting centrifugal forces led its members toward selfish behaviors that began with deplorable consumer preferences, the insubordination of children, the neglect of the home by wives and mothers, and ultimately the dissolution of family ties.[2] The process set in motion by the inexorable forces of industrial society, according to most theories of the family, has continued since then in a linear path, resulting in the eviscerated, vestigial families of today.

There are two major problems with this scenario. The first, discussed in detail in the earlier chapters of the study, is that the characteristics of the household economy so often attributed to the functional requirements of industrial society in fact predate the rise of modern industry. The industrious households of the mid–nineteenth century had been developing their peculiar features for two centuries, beginning well before the first factory bells summoned the first industrial workers from their cottages. To be sure, the industrious household had both its positive and negative features, and industrial society added a new dimension to these features. Moreover, the consumer aspirations developed in the eighteenth century faced an increasingly hostile economic environment in the first half of the nineteenth century, when both price and employment volatility was severe. Much industrious behavior was then defensive, and the pathologies of the industrious household were accentuated, as infant health deteriorated, literacy stagnated, and the average height attained by young adults shrank. But, all in all, the idea that the industrial system undermined the integrity of a family economy is a myth.

The second problem, which will be explored in this chapter, is that there was no linear process of family decomposition dating from this period. The fears of a Le Play in the 1850s foreshadow the fears of family sociologists in the early twenty-first century, but in between, for at least one hundred years, the household economy took on a very different form. The industrious revolution ended, and the same broad geographic zone that had led in its earlier development now led in new household strategies that resulted in what will here be called the breadwinner–homemaker household.

The new household economy shifted from an emphasis on market production and multiple earners to an emphasis on specialization within the household. Its guiding principles were neatly summarized as follows by a Baltimore charity organization in 1897: "The man must provide the means of subsistence, the woman must transmute this provided means

[2] Thompson, *Making of the English Working Class*, p. 416.

into a home, and the children should learn at school."[3] These same three points are central to the more elaborate definition offered by Angélique Janssens, whose "male breadwinner family" is

...a model of household organization in which the husband is the sole agent operating within the market sector, deploying his labour in order to secure the funds necessary to support a dependent wife and children. In exchange, the wife assumes responsibility for the unpaid labour required for the everyday reproduction of her husband's market work, such as cooking, cleaning and laundering. In addition, she provides for the intergenerational reproduction of labour: the bearing and raising of children. Through this parental division of labour, the children are exempted from productive activities until a given age and are provided with time for education and personal development.[4]

The ideals of this form of household economy were not put in place overnight; their achievement proceeded in stages. The withdrawal from paid labor of the wife and mother took precedence over the withdrawal of children. Indeed, in the nineteenth century child labor was often intensified to achieve this first, essential feature of the breadwinner–homemaker household.[5] Later, as household investment in education grew more important, married women returned to the labor force as their children grew older. Both forms of non–adult male labor fit the logic of the breadwinner–homemaker household.

But what brought about this sea change in the organization of the household – especially, of the working-class household? A substantial literature addresses this question, finding answers in the reemergence of patriarchy, the "needs" of capitalism, and structural features of economic change that reduce employment opportunities for women and children. These arguments and their merits will be considered in due course. However, they all assume that the household changes its form in response to external forces, whether these are economic, technical, or cultural. I argued earlier that the industrious household took shape as the consumer aspirations of the household itself evolved, leading to intensified market-oriented labor. I will argue here that the emergence of the breadwinner–homemaker household has a similar explanation: The reorganization of the working

---

[3] The Baltimore Charity Organization School, 1897, cited in S. J. Kleinberg, "Children's and Mothers' Wage Labor in Three Eastern U.S. Cities, 1880–1920," *Social Science History* 29 (2005): 53.

[4] Angélique Janssens, "The Rise and Decline of the Male Breadwinner Family? An Overview of the Debate," in Janssens, ed., *Rise and Decline*, p. 3.

[5] Hugh Cunningham, "The Decline of Child Labour. Labour Markets and Family Economies in Europe and North America Since 1830," *Economic History Review* 53 (2000): 409–10.

class household after 1850 was motivated in part – a very large part in my view – by a shift in the consumer aspirations of the family.

Consumer Capital Accumulation and New Consumer Aspirations

The most striking and novel feature of the new objects of consumer desire that defined the breadwinner–homemaker household is also unexpectedly ironic. As the productive powers of the Western industrializing economies grew as never before, the defining characteristic of the new objects of desire was their "unpurchasability." The meaning of this unlovely term may be clarified by referring to the vocabulary introduced in Chapter 1: The elasticity of substitution between time and goods needed to secure the desired Z-commodities was very low. After the mid–nineteenth century, real wages began to rise substantially and permanently, which, *ceteris paribus*, would have induced a substitution away from household time and toward goods in the production of the consumed Z-commodities – an intensification of the old industrious household. But, simultaneously, consumers began to shift demand toward a set of Z-commodities that could be achieved only via heavy inputs of household labor. They could not be purchased "off the shelf." To state my case more provocatively: The major advances of living standards that we associate with modern society were achieved not *directly* by industrial and market production but *indirectly* by the household, which diverted goods produced by the market sector toward consumption objectives they would not have served "naturally."

The new consumer aspirations had the power to override the countervailing market forces because they formed a complex of consumption goals that could not readily be achieved separately but required a larger household strategy so they might be secured as a cluster. They included improved health, better nutrition, and better housing. Each of these rather broad categories can be further refined to identify goals such as access to pure water and sewer facilities and reduced exposure to germs; or more elaborate equipment for the storage and preparation of food, and more varied diet; or domestic comfort, effective heating and ventilation, privacy, and symbols of social respectability. They formed a complex not because each and every element was, in fact, equally essential to achieve the ultimate goal of a longer, healthier, more comfortable life but because they were perceived to facilitate these goals and to signal to others the commitment to achieve them. Consumption is a means of satisfying our material needs and wants, but it also signals our larger intentions to others, which offers social advantages (then usually known as "respectability") as well as performs a coordinating function in the construction of new consumer clusters.

Health was a major focus of household consumption in this period, and it is worth pausing for a moment on the question just how economic growth (higher per capita income) leads to improved health. Until the mid–eighteenth century there is little evidence that high-income groups enjoyed a longer life expectancy than the bulk of the population. The state of knowledge was such that it was not possible simply to purchase better health. Income and longevity began to show some positive correlation in the century after 1750, but this "cross-sectional" correlation does not appear within social groups across time. Overall English life expectancy at birth rose, or rather recovered, across the eighteenth century, but after the 1820s it showed no further gains of note for more than forty years.[6] Moreover, the heights attained by children born from the 1820s to the 1850s actually tended to decline.[7] This deterioration is often explained as the effect of the unhealthful urban and industrial environments to which growing numbers were exposed in the course of industrialization. This negative force presumably overwhelmed the more positive effects of higher incomes. Thus, exogenous, or social, factors were more powerful than endogenous, household-level factors. But a fuller account may need to consider the deleterious health effects of the consumption decisions of plebian households, which led, among other things, to nutritional deterioration even as incomes rose.[8]

Students of the nineteenth-century mortality decline are by no means in agreement as to the primary cause. The view held by Fogel (and, before him, by McKeown) ascribes much importance to improved nutrition, itself

[6] Wrigley and Schofield, *The Population History of England*, pp. 534–5.

[7] Roderick Floud, Kenneth Wachter, and A. Gregory, *Height, Health and History. Nutritional Status in the United Kingdom, 1750–1890* (Cambridge: Cambridge University Press, 1990); Komlos, "Shrinking in a Growing Economy?" pp. 779–802; Paul Johnson and Stephen Nicholas, "Male and Female Living Standards in England and Wales, 1812–1857. Evidence from Criminal Height Records," *Economic History Review* 48 (1995): 470–81. Johnson and Nicholas found that mean attained height for those born between the early 1820s and mid-1850s declined from 65.5 to 64.5 inches for males and from 62.0 to 60.5 inches for females.

[8] Carole Shammas mused that "The abysmal dietary situation of the early nineteenth-century industrialization period ... may well have had its origins a century earlier." *Pre-Industrial Consumer*, p. 145. She notes that apparent malnutrition went together with a large percentage of total income spent on nonfood items and concludes that "If they had unlimited resources no doubt they would have combined their taste for the new commodities with more cheese and meat. When forced to choose, though, they preferred the sugar, tea, butter, and bread" (p. 146).

a direct result of economic growth, especially in the agricultural sector. But this seems unpersuasive by itself because the elasticity of demand for food was, for so long, much greater than the elasticity of demand for nutrition. That is, until well into the nineteenth century consumers did not use their extra food expenditures primarily to improve their nutrition.[9] Nor does it appear that the fall in infant mortality, when it began at length at the end of the nineteenth century, was strongly correlated with the income of the family.[10]

Another approach, advanced most vigorously by Simon Szreter, emphasizes the impact of the public health movement. "Economic growth in itself had no inherently health-enhancing properties." Improved health requires "collective political decisions...specifically aimed at utilizing the population's increased wealth for explicitly health promoting objectives...."[11] Szreter emphasizes the spread of municipally provided infrastructure providing sewer drainage and water supplies and the

---

[9] Clark, Huberman, and Lindert, "The British Food Puzzle." See also Shankar Subramanian and Angus Deaton, "The Demand for Food and Calories," *Journal of Political Economy* 104 (1996): 133–62.

[10] R. I. Woods, P. A. Watterson, and J. H. Woodward, "The Causes of Rapid Infant Mortality Decline in England and Wales," *Population Studies* 42 (1988): 343–66; 43 (1989): 113–32. "The relationship between infant mortality and income was by no means straightforward. They do not explain timing or rate of change" (p. 364).Late–nineteenth-century medical officers believed they had linked high infant mortality to the employment of mothers. Their findings led to the 1891 Factory Act, prohibiting mothers from working within one month of delivery. Sir George Reid's study of mothers working in the Staffordshire potteries determined that only 10 percent of these mothers breast-fed their infants, while 74 percent of nonworking mothers did so. Artificial feeding was then linked to diarrheal diseases. Reid went on to accuse these women of working not out of necessity (their husbands were often skilled artisans, fully employed) but out of intemperance and financial mismanagement. That is, their consumption preferences still exhibited the patterns of the industrious–plebian rather than the breadwinner–homemaker household. Clare Holdsworth, "Women's Work and Family Health. Evidence from the Staffordshire Potteries, 1890–1920," *Continuity and Change* 12 (1997): 103–28. See also W. R. Lee, "Women's Work and the Family. Some Demographic Implications of Gender-Specific Rural Work Patterns in Nineteenth-Century Germany," in Hudson and Lee, eds., *Women's Work and the Family Economy*, pp. 50–75. Lee interprets German infant mortality data in the light of evidence from developing economies, concluding that "There is increasing evidence from studies of so-called Third World economies that infant care and nurture during the late pre-natal and early post-natal period, although affected by cultural norms, is primarily a function of the mother's economic activities and non-household roles....Female economic activity is generally associated with an early start to harmful supplementary feeding, a termination of breast feeding, and higher infant mortality and morbidity" (p. 61).

[11] Simon Szreter, "Mortality and Public Health, 1815–1914," in Digby, Feinstein, and Jenkins, eds., *New Directions*, Vol. 2, p. 147.

professionalization of Britain's medical officers of health. These had their greatest impact in the final third of the nineteenth century, when the modern decline in mortality could well and truly begin.

The relationship between the public *provision* of sanitation and public health services and public *demand* for these services is a complex issue that I will not enter into except to note that consumer demand is not limited to privately supplied goods and services; there is also a demand for "public goods." In the nineteenth-century political context it is usually assumed that public health was supplied "from above" to a public not fully cognizant of its benefits, and even against its will. But just as the earlier deterioration of health and nutrition was not entirely a product of the external environment, so the late–nineteenth-century improvement was not entirely the result of paternalistic measures. Szreter adds to the two public interventions in support of better public health a third factor: a shift in popular attitudes toward personal hygiene and a new cooperative posture with respect to the preventive health agencies.[12] That is, the reform movement "from above" could bear fruit in the late nineteenth century because it met with a new positive response "from below." It is this happy conjuncture that I wish to explore a bit further. Just as new private consumer goods succeed when innovative producers meet actively seeking consumers, so public goods have their greatest impact when reform-minded politicians face citizens with Z-commodity aspirations that are enhanced by public goods. Without this pressure from below, elite projects of plebian uplift and redemption cannot bear much fruit.

The plebian industrious household that took shape in the course of the long eighteenth century placed little emphasis on consumption patterns designed to increase domestic comfort, nutrition, and health. The new consumption technologies introduced in this period substituted purchased goods for household labor. We have seen how factory workers in the early nineteenth century

could survive without doing much housework at all. They and their families existed off wheaten bread and potatoes, washed down with tea or coffee, and lived, for the most part, in filthy houses.[13]

---

[12] This is documented in the case of working-class London by A. Hardy, *The Epidemic Streets. Infectious Disease and the Rise of Preventive Medicine* (Oxford: Oxford University Press, 1993).

[13] Caroline Davidson, *A Woman's Work Is Never Done. A History of Housework in the British Isles, 1650–1950* (London: Chatto and Windus, 1982), p. 184.

Household time allocations tended in this direction, but so did expenditures on goods, such as kitchen equipment, that were complementary to the attainment of higher standards of domestic life.

In many rural cottages and in the tenemented houses where many poor town-dwellers lived there was only an open fireplace, and not always enough fuel for that. In these circumstances the stewpot, the frying-pan and the kettle were the main cooking utensils, especially when housewives worked on the land, in factories or at domestic industries. "Convenience foods" such as bought bread, tea and cheese were not so much luxuries as necessities, and meat...was usually bacon which could be quickly fried, rather than butcher's meat, which required stewing or roasting.[14]

Little time was spent washing up after meals when utensils were limited to "the communal cooking pot or bowl – and this itself was rarely washed." Hufton's account of French cottages and tenements concludes with the observation that "domestic chores preoccupied no one," while in Germany, the reformer Victor Hubor found the "homes" of working people unworthy of that name: "The man who contrives to exist with his wife and children [in such a dwelling] cannot lay claim to be head of the family; he is simply the biggest pig in the sty."[15] Nor were elite observers impressed with the parenting efforts of working mothers. Sir Charles Shaw declared Manchester factory women in the 1840s to be "totally unequal to fulfill any domestic duty," routinely leaving babies and young children in the care of neighbors, neglecting to clean, and preferring to take meals at the ale house rather than cook.[16]

With the quality of housing itself matters were no different. In a new study by Gregory Clark based on a large sample of houses let by English charities, no trend toward higher average quality (as measured by house size, size of garden, and presence of plumbing and sanitary drainage) could be detected before 1850. Indeed, after 1810 Clark finds that housing costs rose relative to other goods and that people substituted away from housing toward consumer goods.[17]

---

[14] Derek J. Oddy and John Burnett, "British Diet Since Industrialization. A Bibliographical Study," in Teuteberg, ed., *European Food History*, p. 32. See also Martin J. Daunton, *House and Home in the Victorian City. Working Class Housing, 1850–1914* (London: Edward Arnold, 1983).

[15] Hill, *Women, Work, and Sexual Politics*, p. 110; Olwen Hufton, "Women and the Family Economy in Eighteenth Century France," *French Historical Studies* 9 (1975):1–22; Victor Hubor, as cited in Seccombe, *Weathering the Storm*, p. 55.

[16] Cited in Davidson, *A Woman's Work*, p. 205.

[17] Gregory Clark, "Shelter from the Storm. Housing in the Industrial Revolution, 1550–1909," *Journal of Economic History* 62 (2002): 489–511.

Ultimately, very few household resources of money and time were directed toward enhanced nutrition, cleanliness, and comfort because of a third factor: what contemporaries conventionally called "ignorance." This, in my view, is an unhelpful term, if only because it narrows the possible explanations of change to accounts of social and moral uplift effected by the paternalistic efforts of more enlightened classes.

It is more illuminating to approach the issue from the perspective of the accumulation by individuals of consumption capital (that is, relevant past consumption and experience) and social capital (information and the influence of peers).[18] The knowledge and beliefs shaped by these factors will affect whether and how individuals act to secure particular Z-commodities, the ultimate consumption objectives. In a recent study of household production and consumption of "health services," Joel Mokyr sought to formalize the interaction of knowledge and belief. The state of "expert knowledge" ("the degree to which best practice captures the true effect of [a good or practice] X_i on health") can vary between a full understanding of the impact of X on health and no reliable knowledge at all. An individual's actual belief and practice, similarly, could vary in the extent to which it lags behind the best practice as understood by experts regarding a particular good. Mokyr proposed a quantitative expression to capture the states of expert knowledge concerning a good i (A_i) and popular practice of individual j with respect to good i (ε_{ij}). A_i can vary between 1 (full, reliable knowledge) and 0 (no reliable knowledge about the health benefit of X_i). ε_{ij} measures the extent to which an individual's consumption practices lag behind best practice regarding good i. The less the lag, the lower the value of ε_{ij}.[19]

$A_i - \varepsilon_{ij}$ measures the degree to which consumer j is aware of and believes that an array of goods (X_i) achieves improved health. The value of this expression could exceed 1, in which case consumers have exaggerated expectations concerning the efficacy of particular goods: Such goods will be overconsumed. The further the value falls below 1, the greater will be the underconsumption (from the perspective of societal best practice – hence, the imputation of ignorance), because the individual is unable or unprepared to accept and internalize "expert knowledge." It is important to emphasize that this unwillingness may not be attributable to ignorance.

---

[18] Gary Becker, *Accounting for Tastes* (Cambridge, Mass.: Harvard University Press, 1996), pp. 4–5.

[19] Joel Mokyr, "More Work for Mother? Knowledge and Household Behavior, 1870–1945," *Journal of Economic History* 60 (2000): 7.

It may reflect uncertainty: The translation of a particular form of consumption into better health may be too unpredictable, disputed, or invisible. It may reflect the conflicting influence of other desired consumption objectives: You know that x is good for you, but consuming it requires consuming less of y, which you desire even more for other reasons. It follows, then, that the extent to which the expression $A_i-\varepsilon_{ij}$ approaches 1 is partly a reflection of the persuasiveness with which best practice is communicated, and partly a reflection of the extent to which best practice is compatible with, or even reinforces, other desired consumption objectives.

In the realm of "health consumption" the nineteenth century experienced a knowledge revolution. This greatly increased the value of A, in Mokyr's notation, and the task of persuading families of the truth and value of the new knowledge was, as is well known, a major achievement of the age. The revolution was begun as a sanitary and hygienic movement that emerged from the statistical explorations in the late eighteenth century and culminated in advances in epidemiology that exposed connections between consumption patterns, personal habits, and disease. It was followed by the confirmation of the germ theory of disease. After 1865 bacteriology demonstrated the value of improved cleanliness, which shifted responsibility for the health of household members from an unknowable providence into the province of the homemaker. Finally, nutritional science advanced through the discovery of vitamins and minerals and knowledge of their effects on the body. It established a link between good diet and the defense against infectious diseases.

Mokyr is impressed by the speed with which the new knowledge was diffused and accepted throughout the population, as revealed by the speed by which mortality fell as a result of preventive measures (i.e., before the advent of antibiotics that actually could "cure" diseases). This suggests that most people altered their household consumption as they were persuaded of the efficacy of new consumer technologies to improve health. He calls this the "tightness of knowledge" – that is, the degree of correspondence between available knowledge and the willingness of people to act on it.

I suspect there was something else in play contributing to the success of the health revolution. The observed "tightness of knowledge" is not only a product of "persuasiveness" in an intellectual sense, for this alone is often far from sufficient to change behavior. It is also a product of the compatibility of the newly recommended consumption practices with other desired forms of consumption. As I argued in Chapter 1, consumption takes place in clusters: complementary elements, each of which affects the utility derived from consumption of the others. It follows that a consequential new type of consumption does not arise in isolation but emerges in concert with other dimensions of consumption that together have the ability to establish what we today might call a "lifestyle." The integration of new health consumption in the late–nineteenth-century household occurred as part of a larger pattern of consumption involving housing and domestic comfort, diet and meal patterns, as well as hygiene and housekeeping.

The health-related improvements went hand in hand with a major shift of expenditure to better housing. Clark, who could measure no improvement in average English housing quality between the 1640s and the 1840s, reports a more than 50 percent rise in his quality index between 1850 and 1909. Indeed, throughout northwestern Europe, the percentage of household expenditures devoted to housing rose substantially in this period.[20] However, no small portion of this new expenditure was directed toward forms of domestic consumption that had little to do with any objective measure of improved well-being.

The parlor, or front room, offers a classic example. Middle-class observers often despaired over the shrine-like wastefulness of this new interior space. One such observer of 1910, Margery Loane, ridiculed the rules of the working class parlor:

The blinds must not be drawn up because the carpet will fade; the gas must not be lighted because it will blacken the ceiling; the windows must not be opened because the air may tarnish the frame of the looking glass; the chimney must be blocked up, lest the rain should fall and rust the fender. Finally, the door must be locked on the outside.[21]

Could it be that the bulk of increased plebian expenditure on housing after 1850 was entombed in symbolic spaces of no practical use to the family? Or were these fussy formal rooms actually symbols of respectability that signaled to the family members as well as to outsiders the household's commitment to the larger consumption cluster? That is, social

---

[20] Hartmut Kaelble, *Industrialisation and Social Inequality in Nineteenth Century Europe* (Leamington Spa: Berg Publishers, 1986), pp. 112, 117; Christian Topalov, *Le Logement en France* (Paris: Presses de la Fondation nationale des sciences politiques, 1987); p. 131; Nicholas Bullock and James Reed, *The Movement for Housing Reform in Germany and France, 1840–1914* (Cambridge: Cambridge University Press, 1985), p. 304; Daunton, *House and Home.*

[21] Margery Loane, *The Queen's Poor. Life as They Found It* (London: Edward Arnold, 1910), pp. 22–3.

respectability, domestic comfort, and personal hygiene were bound together in a consumption complex. The consumer acted to appropriate those elements still valued by posterity because they were part of a total package that held strong contemporary appeal – but included elements that have not survived the evolving tastes of advanced circles.

As noted earlier, a conspicuous feature of all these new consumer aspirations was that *either* they could not be achieved primarily via the purchase of market-supplied goods, *or* the new expenditures on purchased goods (and public goods) required a major new commitment of complementary household labor in order to be transformed into the desired consumption objectives.

The open hearth, requiring labor-intensive forms of cooking, was supplemented after the 1750s by the open range, a relatively cheap cast-iron range, which facilitated simpler meal preparation and the shift toward purchasing semi-prepared foods. These ranges were said to be nearly universal in humble dwellings by the 1830s, and their diffusion was certainly encouraged by the reduced cost of coal and iron brought about by the Industrial Revolution.[22] The more expensive closed range, ending the need for a suspended pot, came next and permitted the maintenance of a cleaner kitchen and the preparation of a wider variety of prepared foods. But even more important was the introduction of the gas cooker, which diffused rapidly with the introduction of metered gas supplies in the 1880s. By 1901 one-third of British homes possessed gas cookers, which could be rented.[23]

New standards of home and personal cleanliness could not hope to spread to servantless homes without improved water supplies. Piped water caused consumption to rise to a level – more than 12 gallons per head – that made regular washing and cleaning possible. Closely linked to this late–nineteenth-century spread of piped water supplies was the growth of soap consumption. British per capita soap consumption stood at 3.1 lb. in 1791 and rose at a rate of 0.94 percent per annum from then to the 1830s, where after the growth of consumption it accelerated to 2.3 percent per annum for the next fifty years, when, in 1881 consumption stood at 14 pounds per capita, and first reached a mass market.[24] At this time French per capita soap consumption stood at only 6 lb. But neither water

[22] Davidson, *Woman's Work*, p. 60. [23] Ibid., pp. 67–8.
[24] Vögele, *Urban Mortality Change*, p. 206. In Germany, where available data record only private expenditures, the trend of soap consumption is flat until the 1870s but more than triples in the following forty years.

nor soap in a house makes it, or its inhabitants, clean. The application of labor – to heat the water, and apply the soap in washing and scrubbing – is essential. There was little scope for a substitution of goods for labor in either meal preparation or house cleaning in this period. Indeed, the opposite was more likely to be the case as standards rose in the face of the new possibilities – and new motivation – to achieve better health and greater cleanliness.

Of course, for those with sufficiently high incomes, substitution was possible by purchasing the labor of domestic servants. We have noted already that one of the principal consumption effects of the economic growth brought about by the first century of British industrialization was an increased demand for domestic servants, whose numbers grew absolutely up to 1911 (when 35 percent of all employed women worked in service) and whose relative numbers rose steadily to 1891, when they constituted 16 percent of the total labor force. In Germany 23 percent of employed women worked in domestic service at its peak in 1895, while in the Netherlands the figure was 31 percent as late as 1930 (many of them from Germany).[25] In France, some 15 percent of all late–nineteenth-century households employed at least one domestic servant. In the United States there were more domestic servants in relation to households in the inter-war years than ever before.[26]

Households that kept servants developed forms of domestic comfort and acted to introduce higher standards of cleanliness much earlier than other households. The strong nineteenth-century demand for servants suggests that the appeal of labor-intensive domestic and health consumption also continued to increase among the well-to-do. In contrast, the social classes that had released their family members to work as servants, and had neither servants themselves nor the labor of older children to act in their stead, clearly could not hope to follow the servant-keeping classes in their domestic arrangements, even in pale imitation – hence the stark difference in the household arrangements of plebian and middling-class families through the long eighteenth century.

---

[25] Janneke Plantenga, *Een afwijkend patron. Honderd jaar vrouwenarbeid in Nederland en (West-) Duitsland* (Amsterdam: SUA, 1993), p. 61.

[26] Theresa M. McBride, *Domestic Revolution. The Modernisation of Household Service in England and France, 1820–1920* (London: Croom Helm, 1976), p. 34; George Stigler, "Domestic Servants in the United States, 1900–1940" (NBER occasional paper no. 24, 1946). McBride estimates that "a quarter of all French and English women probably served as domestic servants for a period of time in the nineteenth century" (p. 119).

Explaining the Breadwinner–Homemaker Household

After midcentury this longstanding social gulf separating the orientation of consumer aspirations begins to narrow. It would take nearly a century for the stark distinctions in the domestic arrangements of servant-keeping and servant-supplying households to fade away, or nearly so, but in retrospect we can state that the construction of a new household economy among the working class is launched after 1850 that would allow these families to acquire a newly accessible cluster of consumption objectives. One might describe these new developments as a form of emulation: The lower orders emulated their social superiors in the ordering of their domestic arrangements so as to achieve a state of "respectability." In its historical context, this much-abused term served to link the various elements of the consumption cluster I have referred to; it served as a codification of emulation that converted it from "foolish mimicry" to a reform of lifestyle. Respectability served as a guide to households as they negotiated the move from one consumption cluster to another.

The invocation of emulation for such a consequential change begs the question of why one would enter onto such a path, and why then? Perhaps the timing is explained by the term *newly accessible*. Newly accessible in what sense? Is this simply a question of rising income's bringing a range of goods within reach of new consumer groups for the first time? That is only part of the story, because a rising income brings *many* things into reach for the first time. Moreover, a larger income was, by itself, not enough to make effective use of goods requiring labor-intensive consumption technologies. The new consumption cluster also required a redeployment of household resources. It required a conscious and coordinated effort, which brings us back to the claims with which I introduced this chapter.

"Accessibility" required two things: money income and household labor time. It also required basic family decisions about priorities, because the expenditure patterns of existing income needed to change, and the labor force participation of family members also needed to be revised. Once household income reached a certain level – passed a threshold (estimated by Joanna Bourke at weekly earnings of 21 to 30 shillings in Victorian Britain) – the family could reach a higher level of total utility by withdrawing the labor time of women, especially married women, from market labor and redeploying it as household labor to produce the labor-intensive triad of domestic comfort, nutrition, and health services.[27] Until

---

[27] Joanna Bourke, "Housewifery in Working-Class England, 1860–1914," *Past and Present*, 143 (1994), p. 176. Vögele appears to make a similar point, although he does not refer

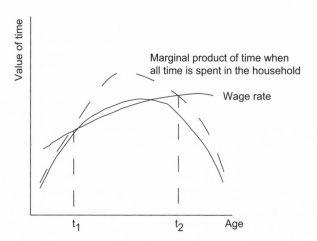

FIGURE 5.1. Life-Cycle Variation in the Value of Time for Women.

breadwinner incomes rose yet further, this redeployment of labor also required a continued emphasis on the market labor of children. To some extent child labor was substituted for that of adult women in the creation of the breadwinner–homemaker household.[28]

A diagram illustrates the income threshold concept: Figure 5.1 shows the time path over the life course of the marginal productivity of women's household labor time and the market wage rate. These two measures of productivity differ fundamentally. While the wage-rate curve is, of course, exogenous to the household, the productivity curve of household work is not. Its shape is affected over time by accumulated consumption capital and changes in the substitutability of goods for household labor in meeting consumption objectives (the consumption technologies). It is also affected by the level of total household money earnings, because purchased goods are complementary to household labor and directly affect its productivity. Between the first and second half of the nineteenth century a growing

---

to threshold incomes, when he concludes his comparative study of nineteenth-century German and British urban mortality change by observing that "At some stages of economic development . . . additional family income [from women's paid labor] improved the survival changes of infants, while in others it increased the risks for mother and child." *Urban Mortality Change*, p. 135.

[28] Carolyn Tuttle, *Hard at Work in Factories and Mines. The Economics of Child Labor during the British Industrial Revolution* (Boulder, Colo.: Westview Press, 1999), p. 75. Bourke, "Housewifery in Working-Class England," p. 176. Both argue that children's wages rose relative to those of adult women in the 1840s–1860s. This is probably not as important as the changing ratio of the market wages of women relative to the productivity of their household labor as total family income rose.

proportion of laboring families found that they were in a position to benefit from a new division of labor within the household and capture the higher productivity of wives once they could secure for the family the new consumption complex that would have been unattainable via their market income.[29]

The economic foundation of the breadwinner–homemaker household is specialization. While the specialized skills a man and a woman bring to a marriage can vary and are certainly not in every case highly differentiated beyond those rooted in biology, the logic of this household form dictates that the participants will both benefit from the continued cultivation of their complementary skills within marriage. Thus, the ultimate consumption of Z-commodities that two persons could achieve singly, Z_f and Z_m, will be less than their combined output: Z_{mf}.[30] The difference, attributable to the specialization made possible within the household, will be larger or smaller according to the consumption technologies used by the household in converting purchased goods into the ultimately consumed Z-commodities and by the efficiency with which these are deployed. Consumption technologies vary over time, depending on the substitutability between purchased and home-produced consumption. The strength of

[29] The reader contemplating Figure 5.1 may wonder about two of its features. Is it credible to suppose that household productivity between ages t_1 and t_2 actually rises so high? An answer of sorts is provided by the contemplation of the conundrum of our times, the difficulty of securing "affordable quality childcare." Without subsidy, satisfactory care for young children is beyond the reach of many workers. That is, it costs more than many workers earn. Second, why is this figure devoted to the wages and productivities of women only? The economist could respond by observing simply that this productivity in household labor can, in theory, be achieved differently, so long as *someone* specializes. (See Becker, *A Treatise on the Family*, p. 30, who claims that "Specialization in the allocation of time and in the accumulation of human capital would be extensive in an efficient family *even if all members were biologically identical*" [emphasis added].). Sheilagh Ogilvie approaches this issue more directly: "Women's work is distinguished from that of men by the superior household productivity of females, a consequence of both biology and socialization. Because women take into account their productivity in the household as well as in alternative market occupations in deciding how much time to allocate to the market... female employment reacts very sensitively to demographic and institutional changes altering the rewards of different uses of time." Ogilvie, "Women and Proto-Industrialisation," p. 76. Future changes in socialization could, to some degree, alter the shape of the curves of Figure 5.1. At present, however, the presence of a child increases the household time of mothers far more than of fathers, even when the market earnings of the mother are greater than those of the father. Offer, *Challenge of Affluence*, pp. 319–20.

[30] Gary Becker puts it this way: "M[ale] and F[emale] gain from marriage because t_m and t_f [the time of a male and a female, respectively] are not perfect substitutes for each other or for goods and services supplied by market firms...." Gary S. Becker, "A Theory of Marriage. Part I," *Journal of Political Economy* 81 (1973): 819.

the breadwinner–homemaker household in the era of its pre-eminence is directly related to the high value of household production time in producing the desired forms of Z-commodities. The second factor, efficiency, varies among households, and within them as the members' commitments to specialization increase their productivity. Being a skilled consumer requires effort, knowledge, and calculation, which together determined the "productivity of consumption": the amount of utility created per unit of household time devoted to the transformation of goods into ultimate consumption. An interesting aspect of efficiency (familiar to any parent preparing a meal for a family with children) is the optimal selection of items of consumption for redistribution to other members of the household. The greater the heterogeneity of preferences among members of the household, the more difficult it is to achieve high efficiency.[31]

Critics of the breadwinner–homemaker household model often claim that the unpaid labor of the homemaker is systematically undervalued, and that the wife's confinement to the "private sphere" of the household denies her the external options (opportunity costs) that could strengthen her bargaining power in household decision making. However, the position of the homemaker is rather different when the space between Z_f and Z_m on the one hand and Z_{mf} on the other is large.[32] The presence of this valued resource binds members to the household and gives those active in household production a stronger voice in determining its specific form and allocation.

Contemporaries expressed an understanding of the newly unfolding household economy, although their comments are inevitably rendered unpalatable to us by the paternalistic sauce in which they typically were drenched. Henry Higgs's study of working-class household budgets in 1893 led him to the observation that good housekeeping was the crucial variable which could "turn the balance of comfort in favour of one

---

[31] Consumption efficiency is comparable to the theory of "X-efficiency" developed by Harvey Leibenstein. For discussion, see James, *Consumption and Development*, pp. 186–9.

[32] The ability of a household to achieve greater total Z-commodities than the sum of its individual members is not primarily the result of economies of scale. It is the complementarity of the household's members that accounts for most of the gain. Following Becker once again, "the "shadow" price of an hour of t_f to a single M[ale] – the price he would be willing to pay for t_f – would exceed w_f, and the "shadow" price of t_m to a single F[emale] – the price she would be willing to pay for t_m – would exceed wm. Both gain from marriage because M then, in effect, can buy an hour of t_f at w_f and F can buy an hour of t_m at w_m, lower prices than they would be willing to pay." Becker, "A Theory of Marriage," p. 819. t_f and t_m are the time of the female and male, respectively; w_f and w_m are the wage rates available to female and male labor, respectively.

workman whose wages are much below those of another."[33] Likewise, Charles Booth, in his 1891 survey of London, included poor household management (he spoke of "drunken or thriftless wives") as one of his nine causes of poverty, while Seebowm Rowntree's highly influential 1902 study of poverty made a fundamental distinction between "primary poverty," caused by insufficient income, and "secondary poverty," caused by the mismanagement of family income.[34] Helen Bosanquet's 1906 study, *The Family*, also placed great emphasis on the competence of the wife, whose influence rendered useless, in her view, any statistical "poverty line." A later commentary put it as follows:

The increased prosperity of working class households from the 1860s was created not only by higher wages, but also by improved housewifery. Households containing employed women lacked "domestic or material comfort" compared with those containing full-time housewives.[35]

From the mid–nineteenth century on, a steady stream of elite observers decried the rudimentary and inadequate homemaking activities of the industrious households of the working class and pressed for reform. But was the pressure for change all from above? Anna Clark, in her study of British working-class life, detected "a popular understanding, even in communities where female factory work was well established, that it was often better for the household as a whole if the women did not work. The reduction in money income was compensated for by the value of domestic labor, while material benefits could still be expected from [informal and incidental market activities]."[36] She described mid–nineteenth-century textile and other factory towns as exhibiting two distinct working-class cultures:

In the one, couples retained the rough, crude vitality of the old culture, socializing in a larger community setting, drinking and fighting together in public; in the other, a few disciplined men tried to pull themselves out of poverty, saving the

---

[33] Henry Higgs, "Workmen's Budgets," *Journal of the Royal Statistical Society* 56 (1893): 225–85.

[34] Charles Booth, *Life and Labour of the People of London* ([1891] New York: Augustus Kelly, 1967); B. Seebohm Rowntree, *Poverty. A Study of Town Life* (London: Macmillan, 1902), Chapter 5.

[35] Tuttle, *Hard at Work*, p. 177. This line of thought culminated in the home economics movement of the first half of the twentieth century. Its key message was: "It does not matter so much just how many dollars are in the pay-envelope, as it does what those dollars actually secure and bring into the life of the worker." Benjamin R. Andrews, *Economics of the Household* (New York: Macmillan, 1924), p. 34.

[36] Clark, *Struggle for the Breeches*, p. 133.

money they would otherwise drown in drink by spending their evenings at home with their wives.... [37]

The historical literature on this transformation is deeply divided. Jane Humphries approaches the breadwinner–homemaker family as the product of a strategy understood to benefit the family as a whole, and as a creation of the working class acting on the basis of its own material interests rather than being subject to the imperative of external forces.[38] More common, however, is the view of Wally Seccombe, who describes its emergence within the working class as the result of the imposition of patriarchy to restabilize family life in a form that suited the new needs of industrial capitalism. He, too, concluded that "a family's living standard was *not* reducible to its income. The quality of domestic labour exerted in converting wages into the means of subsistence made a very considerable difference in the consumable product, whether it was a hot meal, clean clothes or a warm bed."[39] This seeming endorsement of the new household economy is reinforced in the conclusion of Seccombe's detailed study, where he reflects on the mature breadwinner household of the early twentieth century with the observation that

Where the breadwinner was steadily employed and decently paid, where women could concentrate on their domestic duties... family households provided their members with better living conditions than their predecessors had ever been able to achieve.

Seccombe then steps back from the implications of this reasoning. Recalling that the breadwinner household is, after all, a product of patriarchy and of political and cultural reaction, he hastened to conclude that "the reasons for this success were only obliquely due to the form itself, and might have been achieved under different arrangements."[40]

This claim, which Seccombe does not further develop or defend, is one I very much doubt. The household was then, and would remain well into the twentieth century, the essential production unit for many of the ultimately consumed goods and service. The market supplied no acceptable substitutes for most of them. In some cases, this was still technically impossible; in others the quality of the market alternative was low or it was unverifiable (that is, principal-agent problems stood in the way of entrusting

[37] Ibid., p. 255.
[38] Jane Humphries, "Class Struggle and the Persistence of the Working-Class Family," *Cambridge Journal of Economics* 1 (1977): 241–58.
[39] Seccombe, *Weathering the Storm*, p. 152.   [40] Ibid., p. 206.

many services to nonfamily members). Consequently, a division of labor within the household was the only feasible route to enter the realm of this consumption cluster for families of modest income. What people wanted to consume was not what the industrializing economy made available; in the face of this reality the household remained – or, rather, it once again became – an important site of production in urbanizing and industrializing societies.

Was the Breadwinner–Homemaker Household a Voluntary Achievement?

The breadwinner–homemaker household that emerged after 1850 and ruled for a century does not now enjoy a good reputation. Seccombe discounted its acknowledged achievements because it was the product of "forces of cultural restoration," a reestablished patriarchy that was oppressive to women, imprisoning married women in particular in a separate sphere: unequal, inferior, and degrading. From this perspective, reinforced by the knowledge that contemporary families are organized very differently, it is not surprising that an explanation of the breadwinner–homemaker household that emphasizes the intentions and aspirations of its members – of both sexes – is difficult for many to accept. And, indeed, a large literature now exists that offers very different explanations than that proffered here for the evolution of family forms in the course of the nineteenth century.

The key claim of all alternative approaches to the history of the household as an economic unit is that women – married women – did not withdraw but were excluded from market labor. Historians have explained this forcible breakup of earlier household forms, featuring the industrious market-oriented labor of men and women, adults and children, by invoking a variety of social forces. One explanation attributes the change to the generalized *needs of capitalism* as an economic system. The developing organization and technology of both agriculture and industry reduced the demand for female labor (or redefined lines of work as inherently "male") while new and higher standards in the realm of the "reproduction of labor-power" required the domestication of the wife. The first claim (reduced demand for female labor) is based on the belief that capitalism and market systems impose by their inner logic a deterioration of the economic position of women. Men monopolize wage labor and market production because only they can act alone in the public sphere. Thus, as capitalism breaks up the artisanal and peasant production units in which women had long worked side by side with men, work migrated from the family sphere and entered the market – that is, the public sphere – where women could not readily follow. Bridget Hill argues in this way and understands "the process of transformation and almost complete undermining of the family economy [to have] extended over a long period of time . . . further in 1750 than 1700, and further still in 1800."[41] She also asserts that "the sexual division of labour rigidified as the capitalist division of labour becomes more refined and job specialization increases."[42] Keith Snell, Eric Richards, and Janet Thomas, among others, share this position with Hill, but few accounts explain *why* capitalism has this interest, or *why* technology has this inherent tendency.[43]

Of course, the expulsion of women from the labor force can also be approached as an empirical question. The question is then whether it is the demand or supply curve that is doing most of the shifting. The clearest evidence of a decline in women's participation in paid labor is found in the (English) agricultural sector. Harvest labor in particular saw a large diminution of female participation in the century before 1850. This appears to be a phenomenon unique to England in this period; indeed, in many parts of northwestern Europe during this time, the spread of new crops and intensified forms of small-scale agriculture tended to have the opposite effect, increasing the demand for women's labor.[44] But even in England, the non-agricultural sectors do not offer much evidence in support of the female expulsion thesis. In assessing the evidence, Margaret Hunt concluded that the common assumption "that middling women dropped out of gainful employment sometime in the course of the eighteenth century" is based primarily on the prescriptive literature of the time and is not supported by direct evidence.[45] Amanda Vickery was similarly critical of claims based largely on ideals rather than on actual behavior, while Maxine Berg, focusing on industrial employments, concluded that "women workers [in manufacturing] played a greater part over the whole course of the eighteenth century than they had done previously and were

[41] Hill, *Women, Work and Sexual Politics*, p. 47.
[42] Catherine Hall, *White, Male, and Middle Class. Explorations in Feminism and History* (Cambridge: Polity Press, 1992), p. 133.
[43] Janet Thomas, "Women and Capitalism. Oppression or Emancipation?" *Comparative Studies in Society and History* 30 (1988): 534–49; Snell, *Annals of the Labouring Poor*, p. 22; Richards, "Women in the British Economy," p. 347.
[44] W. R. Lee, "Women's Work and the Family. Some Demographic Implications of Gender-Specific Rural Work Patterns in Nineteenth Century Germany," in Hudson and Lee, *Women's Work and the Family Economy*, pp. 59–60.
[45] Hunt, *Middling Sort*, pp. 125–6.

to do in the later stages of industrialization."[46] Finally, the most comprehensive quantitative study of women's labor market participation, based on working-class budget studies, found adult women's participation rates hovering around a very high 60 percent as late as 1841–5, falling to 45 percent in the following twenty-year period.[47] Overall, there appears to have been some decline in female participation in agriculture, but rising participation in other sectors. When the limited extent and unreliability of the data on women's labor force activities are taken into account, it is difficult to be fully confident of any conclusion, but a cautious one would be that there is little evidence to support an aggregate reduction of either supply or demand before the mid–nineteenth century – that is, during the classic century of the Industrial Revolution and the capitalist transformation of agriculture. The decline came later.

A related "needs of capitalism" argument emphasizes capitalism's needs for new, improved forms of labor reproduction. Here, however, the temporal scene shifts to the very end of the nineteenth century. Deborah Valenze's book *The First Industrial Woman* argues that the needs of the system then made the project of civilizing the working-class female a central concern of industrial society.[48] It is an argument Wally Seccombe found attractive and he elaborated upon it, claiming that "it was the new demand for labour characteristic of the second industrial revolution that fostered the shift from an extensive to an intensive mode of consuming labour power."[49] Apart from the fact that causal mechanisms linking capitalism to family forms remain unspecified in these works, a basic problem of timing tends to undermine their plausibility. Just as there is little evidence for the posited eighteenth-century decline of women's work until after 1850, so the presumed demands of a new reproductive regime could not have had their effects until at least a generation after the new breadwinner–homemaker household system began to take shape.

---

[46] Maxine Berg, "What Difference," p. 40. Elsewhere, Berg concludes: "The identification of a great transition in women's working lives with the advent of industrialisation seems on present evidence to be an impossible task. But perhaps it is after all a chimera of simplistic linear notions of Marxist historiography." Maxine Berg, "Women's Work, Mechanization and the Early Phases of Industrialization in England," in R. E. Pahl, *On Work* (Oxford: Basil Blackwell, 1988), p. 91.

[47] Horrell and Humphries, "Women's Labour Force Participation and the Transition to the Male-Breadwinner Family, 1790–1865," *Economic History Review* 48 (1995): 98.

[48] Deborah Valenze, *The First Industrial Woman* (Oxford: Oxford University Press, 1995), p. 185.

[49] Seccombe, *Weathering the Storm*, p. 82.

A second explanation of the removal of women from paid work emphasizes the role of men, especially working-class men and their trade unions, sometimes supported by capitalists (but now more for cultural reasons – a shared allegiance to patriarchy – than for strictly economic reasons). The economic system itself sets the process in motion: Economic development raises male wages. Men then use this increased income to buy, as it were, a desired consumption good: patriarchy. Louise Tilly recently put it this way:

With the coming of the Industrial Revolution, men's higher wages earned outside the household undergirded their stronger bargaining power early on, while women's increasingly incommensurate contribution [household labor] was most often ignored and discounted. This advantage translated into ever more favorable (for men) outcomes of cooperation and bargaining...The advantage that men acquired varied according to their class position,...but the outcome across the economy and in the household, of early male superiority in both entrepreneurship and the industrial workplace...was redefined social relationships, including a revised notion of gender roles.[50]

A variant of this argument holds that the breadwinner–homemaker household – forcing women out of the labor market and back into the home – was actually the achievement of working men and trade unionists in opposition to middle-class ideology (which was liberal, and opposed to the regulation of women's contractual rights). Thus Wally Seccombe argued that it was the product of a labor movement, "in the wake of the defeat of Chartism and Owenite Socialism, reacting in a narrow exclusionist fashion to the very real threat which the mass employment of women as cheap labour represented to the job security and wage levels of skilled tradesmen."[51] This "real threat" did not impress Heidi Hartmann, who insisted that talk of a breadwinner wage was an excuse for men to monopolize skilled work in the workplace and dominate their wives at home.[52] Elaborating on this theme, Sonya Rose explained male behavior as motivated by males' need to define their identity in a strife-ridden social environment. Their response was to assert their "maleness" rather than

---

[50] Louise Tilly, "Women, Women's History, and the Industrial Revolution," *Social Research* 61 (1994), p. 133.

[51] Wally Seccombe, "Patriarchy Stabilized," *Social History* 11 (1986), p. 55.

[52] Heidi Hartmann, "Capitalism, Patriarchy and Job Segregation by Sex," *Signs* 1 (1976): 137–69.

their "working-classness," shoring up their position in terms of masculine identity rather than in economic terms.[53]

Finally, we can add the voice of Anna Clark, who holds that it was precisely radical trade unionists who embraced the breadwinner household as a means of addressing some of the sexual tensions within the working-class home. The strategy of pursuing domesticity at the expense of egalitarianism (gender egalitarianism) appealed to women, with the "promise to replace a hard-drinking artisan who neglects his family with a respectable patriarch who brought home the bacon." It was a male strategy, but not one imposed from above, whether by capitalists or middle-class reformers.[54]

What all these arguments have in common is a conviction that women were *pushed* out of the paid labor force. Whether because of the requirements of capitalism, or because of a socially constructed redefinition of gender roles, whether by the bosses or by trade unionists and male workers, separate spheres emerged to define the lives of men and women, and women were dispatched into a "domestic void," there to pass their days in housework and child rearing. Such work might have real value, but in an increasingly market-based society it existed in a sphere that was not only separate but isolated and, hence, as Tilly put it, "ignored and discounted" by the larger society. Nor is it only the market that devalues the work performed within the domestic void. In a recent survey of English family history, prominent historians pronounce household labor to be a dead weight loss:

> There is little a homemaker can do to increase income. Rather, activities done within the home, from cooking and interior decorating to embroidery, making music, and constructing models are seen as non-working and given amateur status.... On the whole, as sociologist Dorothy Smith has written, "the house constitutes a dead end. The surplus above subsistence which enters it does not pass beyond into productive activities."[55]

Not only was the work of the housewife "a dead end," but wives and children as well now lived their lives in households governed and guided by patriarchal power, which imposed an unequal distribution of family

[53] Sonya Rose, "Gender Antagonism and Class Conflict. Exclusionary Strategies of Male Trade Unionists in Nineteenth Century Britain," *Social History* 13 (1988): 191–208.
[54] Anna Clark, *The Struggle for the Breeches. Gender and the Making of the British Working Class* (Berkeley: University of California Press, 1995), pp. 218–19.
[55] Davidoff et al., *The Family Story*, pp. 85–6.

resources, leading to the undernourishment of wives and children, and an overallocation of resources to the "social spending" of males. Their personal expenditures on drinking, smoking, and gambling, taken out of the hides of their dependents, gave solace to a male honor rendered fragile by the alienation of factory labor. The working-class family was an unhappy, hopeless place, oppressed by rapacious capitalists on the outside and insecure patriarchs on the inside.[56]

Assessing the Explanations

We now have two general models of the breadwinner household. One sees it as a product of a renewed patriarchy, constructed, literally, on the backs of women – excluding them from the labor force, imposing alien standards of domesticity and respectability to the point of creating fetishes of household cleanliness, and enforcing unequal distributions of household resources and power. The other, which I seek to advance in this book, sees it as entered into by the joint decisions of couples and for the general benefit of the family – specifically, for the achievement of consumption patterns that improved the health, comfort, and, ultimately, the human capital endowments of working people at a time when the goods available for purchase on the market could not, by themselves, deliver such consumption objectives. How can we assess the relative merits of these competing models? Any such assessment will require coming to terms with the ways in which the family engages with the market, and with the internal economy of the family – with how decisions are made in the allocations of individual functions and resources.

  1. *The labor market and the family.* An influential feminist interpretation of nineteenth-century market engagement relies on the concept of "separate spheres." It rests on the notion that the "family economy" of peasants and artisans, supported by the pre-capitalist institutions of guilds, manors, and corporate community regulation, was eroded by the expansion of market-based economic relations, which led, in turn, to a progressive separation of life activities into distinct private (female, home-based) and public (male, market-based) spheres. We have already, in Chapter 3, had occasion to critique the idealist concept of the "family

---

[56] This account will strike the reader as overdrawn, but it follows faithfully the positions staked out in L. Orem, "The Welfare of Women in Labouring Families. England, 1860–1950," in Mary S. Hartman and Lois Banner, eds., *Clio's Consciousness Raised. New Perspectives on the History of Women* (New York: Harper & Row, 1974), pp. 226–44.

economy." The most that can be said for it is that the "golden age" it posits of men and women working together in largely self-sufficient households must be located in a very distant, if not a mythic, past of England and northwestern Europe.[57]

Of more immediate importance, the separate spheres concept makes the fatal assumption that the market (the male/public sphere) is isolated from the activities of the private sphere of the housewife and household. It is this assumption that allows adherents of the concept to speak so readily of the devalued – even valueless – character of housework, because it is assumed to exist in complete isolation from the market. The intellectual origins of this assumption can be located in the theory of peasant economic behavior developed by the Russian economist Chayanov.[58] In his view, the peasant household deployed its resources (labor and land) independently of the market, guided instead by the size and composition of the household over the course of the family life cycle. Market signals were of no importance in making these decisions. In the 1970s, Louise Tilly and Joan Scott appropriated Chayanov's model of the peasant economy to posit the existence more generally of a pre-capitalist family economy. Shortly thereafter Hans Medick sought to extend this model to the households of proto-industrial workers. So it came to pass that women engaged in household labor rather than market labor were thought to have entered into the equivalent of some remote and backward Russian village, rather than to participate in a division of labor for the achievement of the maximum household utility *given the relative prices of labor and goods, and given the consumption technologies* available to produce the desired consumption package. Which is to say only that the family labor resources dedicated to household production have an opportunity cost, and the goods and services produced with those resources have shadow prices. One need not believe that ordinary householders calculate these values to the penny in order to accept that the market penetrates the household, and that the household, in turn, responds to market conditions. And, while family labor can rarely be shifted between the household and the market with complete short-term flexibility, responding in a carefully calibrated manner to every marginal change in conditions, neither is the family a

[57] Besides the sources cited in Chapter 3, see Ogilvie, "Women and Labour Markets," pp. 25–60. Ogilvie argues that the corporate institutions that are thought to protect "family economy" do more to restrict the range of economic activities available to women than the market institutions that are asserted to undermine the position of women.

[58] A. V. Chayanov, *The Theory of Peasant Economy*, D. B. Thorner and B. Kerblay, et al., eds. (Homewood, Ill.: R. D. Irwin, 1966).

TABLE 5.1a. *Female labor force participation rates, 1846–1930*

Country	1846–49 total	1909–10 Total	Married	1930 non-agric
Great Britain	30	25[b]	10	5
Netherlands	24	15	5	2
Belgium	38	29	19	10
France		33	20	13
U.S.A.	25[a]	19[b]	5	
Germany			12	7

[a] 1870s
[b] 1890

TABLE 5.1b. *Labor force participation by marital status, circa 1900*

	Single	Married	Date
Great Britain (ten largest cities)	75	15	1911
(total)	69	10	
Netherlands	39	5	1899
United States	41	5	1890
France	52	38	1896
Germany (total)	29		1925
(excl. family enterprise)	7		

Source: H. A. Pott-Buter, *Facts and Fairy Tales about Female Labor, Family and Fertility* (Amsterdam: Amsterdam University Press, 1993); C. Golden *Understanding the Gender Gap* (Oxford: Oxford University Press, 1990); Geyser, "Die Frau im Beruf"; J. Vögele, *Urban Mortality Change in England and Germany, 1870–1913* (Liverpool: Liverpool University Press, 1998), pp. 125–31; Pat Hudson and W. R. Lee, *Women's Work and the Family Economy* (Manchester: Manchester University Press, 1990), p. 21.

realm of economic irrationality, wasting labor on valueless activities and ignorantly undervaluing its output simply because it does not carry a market-determined price sticker.

The reallocation of labor between the market and household sphere was real and substantial, and it largely took the form of a change in the deployment of the labor of married women. At the most aggregate level there is little evidence that this reallocation began before the 1840s, and the timing will not have been the same in every region and every occupational category. But, throughout northwestern Europe and the United States, the transition was largely concentrated in the second half of the nineteenth century. Table 5.1 brings together summary data. The adequacy of census categories and tabulations in this area leave much to be desired,[59] and I would not want to insist on the literal accuracy of these numbers, but the trends and patterns are likely to be reliable and are consistent with other types of data. Women's labor force participation declined, and the decline was accounted for overwhelmingly by married women, who by the early twentieth century were highly unlikely to be regularly employed in market labor. In contrast, the labor force participation of young women and girls tended to increase over this period, stimulated by the growing demand for domestic servants, which around 1910 accounted for between 25 and 40 percent of *all* female employment in northwestern Europe and the United States. Indeed, in the Netherlands, women under twenty-five (nearly all unmarried) accounted for half of all female employment until after 1960. The overall downward trend in women's labor force participation is found everywhere, but the level remained substantially higher in France and Belgium than in Britain, the United States, and the Netherlands. The effects of a large peasant sector on these rates explain a substantial part of the difference.[60] By 1930, the participation of married women in the labor force (excluding the agricultural sector) ranged from 13.4 percent in France and 10.1 percent in Belgium to 8 percent in the United States, 7 percent in Germany, 5 percent in Great Britain and Sweden, and only 2.2 percent in the Netherlands.[61]

[59] In the century after 1850 the female market labor we wish to have recognized in labor force participation data can be divided into three parts. The first is work for others, in which case one is employed and receives a wage. The second is work in one's own business, in which case one is self-employed and earns profits. Recording the first is straightforward, while recognizing the second often depends on the adequacy of census questions. The third category, work assisting other family members in a family business, normally does not provide personal monetary compensation. Its inclusion in labor force data is most uncertain, undermining comparisons both across countries and across time.

[60] Paul Klep analyzed the occupational data for Belgium and the Netherlands at the provincial level in 1846–9 and 1909–10. After he accounted for the size of "peasant" sectors in each province, a significant part of the difference in national-level female labor force participation rates disappeared. Where agricultural and proto-industrial home production prevailed, women's work persisted. As incomes grew, specialization advanced, urbanization rose, and provincial rates of female labor force participation declined, especially for married women. Urbanization was related to a rise in the labor force participation of young unmarried women. P. M. M. Klep, "Female Labour in the Netherlands and Belgium, 1846–1910" (unpublished working paper, Katholieke Universiteit Nijmegen, 1978).

[61] Hettie A. Pott-Buter, *Facts and Fairy Tales about Female Labor, Family and Fertility. A Seven-Country Comparison, 1850–1990* (Amsterdam: Amsterdam University Press, 1993), p. 199; U.S. data, inferred from Goldin, *Understanding the Gender Gap*, Tables 2.1, 2.2, and 2.9. The German data are for 1925 and refer to women employed by

Any argument that this trend was driven by forces excluding women from the labor market must be consistent with the timing of the phenomenon and the concentration of this change among married women. Arguments based on "the needs of capitalism," apart from being vague, are weak with respect to timing, because industrial capitalism appears to have "needed" women as it developed up to the mid–nineteenth century, but not thereafter. The many variants of the argument that women's work has been transformed from something abundant and satisfying to something ghettoized and demeaning – from a golden age to separate spheres – all have in common a linear process of change linked in some way to the impact of a capitalist-market economy. Yet this "impact" remains undefined and unjustified.

To summarize: The golden age never existed; the separate spheres are fundamentally mischaracterized; the driving force of changing household organization is located at least as much within families and their aspirations as in the economy and its imperatives. Many existing critiques of the academic comfort food of separate spheres have established its factual inconsistencies; here I seek to provide an alternative explanation for the new household economy.[62] But there remains another interpretation to be considered: that based on a reasserted patriarchy.

2. *The practice of patriarchy*. The breadwinner–homemaker household's close association with patriarchy places it in a bad odor in contemporary society. It is a commonplace of women's history and family history that patriarchy, and ideologies of male supremacy more generally, had existed for centuries. Patriarchy was, so to speak, endemic to European culture, a resource to be drawn upon and an ideal to be invoked as the occasion required.[63] Consequently, prescriptive and normative literatures

someone other than their husbands. Of 3.7 million married women (with husbands present) working in the labor market, only 850,000 worked for nonhusband employers. Karen Hausen, "The German Mother's Day, 1923–33," in David Sabean and Hans Medick, eds., *Interest and Emotion* (Cambridge: Cambridge University Press, 1984), pp. 371–414. The role of women in agriculture increased in this period, as many men entered industry, leaving wives to tend to their peasant holdings.

[62] Critiques include Amanda Vickerey, "Golden Age to Separate Spheres? A Review of the Categories and Chronology of English Women's History," *Historical Journal* 36 (1993): 383–414; Colin Creighton, "The Rise of the Male Breadwinner Family. A Reappraisal," *Comparative Studies of Society and History* 38 (1996): 310–37; Robert Shoemaker, *Gender in English Society, 1650–1850. The Emergence of Separate Spheres?* (London: Longman, 1998).

[63] Katrina Honeyman and Jordan Goodman, "Women's Work, Gender Conflict, and Labour Markets in Europe, 1500–1900," *Economic History Review* 44 (1991): 608–28. Citing Heidi Hartmann, these authors refer to a structural–cultural propensity to (re)assert

of all sorts can be expected to have drawn upon this common cultural legacy. Such invocations are also plentiful in the eighteenth century, when family practice clearly differed from such norms in important respects. It is therefore important to inquire into the *practice* of the breadwinner–homemaker household in the century after 1850, to determine the extent to which the patriarchal norms so often invoked actually describe how households actually functioned.

This task requires that we attempt to peer into the "black box" that is the family. How does the family determine who will work, who will study, and who will stay home? How does it decide how to distribute its consumption resources among its members, and what form that consumption will take? These issues were introduced in the first chapter, and I will not rehearse the full story here. It is enough for present purposes to recall that the approach outlined there offers a *prima facie* case in support of the view that the adult male is likely to gain significant decision-making power in the breadwinner household.

Household decision making can take the form of a single "intelligence" (not necessarily a single person) that decides altruistically (but not paternalistically) for the benefit of all family members. In this model, *the neoclassical pooled household model*, the family members place all income, from whatever source, into a common pool from which it is allocated according to a single objective function, intended to maximize the utility of all family members. Alternatively, the household can be seen as consisting of individuals each with his or her own utility function. Here, in *the bargaining model*, the common enterprise continues only so long as members are better able to maximize their individual utility within rather than outside the household. The family members have "threat points," and they bargain with one another to achieve their individual objectives. Their bargaining power depends on their alternatives, and individual market earnings are an important desideratum in assessing those alternatives. A bargaining model need not assume – and I do not assume – that the household is viewed by its members in wholly instrumental terms. Between the substantialist concept of the family as an indecomposable realm of altruism and the insistence that individuals and their self-interests form the only unit of analysis, there is space to see individuals deriving affective as well as material benefit from the family unit and engaging in what Amartya Sen called cooperative conflict. Where economic gains to cooperation exist, the conflict (bargaining) over the allocation of resources normally

patriarchy – the "sex-gender system" – that is called upon as needed to legitimate rules defining the acceptable gender division of labor in the workplace.

concerns "choice among the set of efficient cooperative arrangements" rather than all-or-nothing struggles.[64]

Conceptually, and econometrically, a simple exercise can identify which of these two models is at work within the black box: If the neoclassical pooling model is operative, the only factor determining the household's pattern of consumption will be the *amount* of total income; the *sources* of that income will have no influence on the decisions. If a bargaining model obtains, the consumption patterns will also be influenced by the individual *source* of the income.[65] This, indeed, is precisely what we found at work in the unfolding demand patterns of eighteenth-century industrious households: Multiple earners gave rise to tension over the distribution of household earnings. The bargaining model appears to capture well the actual dynamics of the industrious household, but does it continue to apply to the breadwinner–homemaker household, where something approaching a pooled income controlled by a "single decision-making entity" is the evident goal? The bargaining model suggests that as the adult male becomes very nearly the sole source of household money income, he will become inordinately influential in deciding its disposition: He will act as a patriarch and place his own consumption values – *his* preferences for himself and for others – above the preferences held by his wife and children. Is this, in fact, how the breadwinner–homemaker household functioned?

The first thing we need to know is just how dominant the earnings of the adult male actually were in the total household budget. Working-class household budget studies offer the best information on this question, and by the late nineteenth century, when the breadwinner household was well established, such studies had become quite numerous. Budget studies before the mid–nineteenth century were fewer in number, smaller in scope, and less reliable in execution, but they can help to give some indication of the change in the composition of household income over the course of the century.

The earliest such exercises are the well-known budget studies of English agricultural laborers by Sir Frederick Morton Eden and the Reverend

---

[64] On the family as a "realm of altruism," see Paul A. Samuelson, "Social Indifference Curves," *Quarterly Journal of Economics* 70 (1956): 1–22; Becker, *Treatise on the Family*, Ch. 8: "Altruism in the Family," pp. 277–306. For critiques of the substantialist concept of the household, see Sabean, *Neckerhausen*, pp. 97–8; Hartmann, "The Family as the Locus of Gender, Class and Political Struggle," pp. 366–94. On cooperative conflict, see Amartya Sen, "Economics and the Family," *Asian Development Review* 1 (1983): 14–26.

[65] Shelly Lundberg and Robert A. Pollak, "Bargaining and Distribution in Marriage," *Journal of Economic Perspectives* 10 (1996): 27.

David Davies, conducted in 1795 and 1789–90, respectively. These studies, supplemented by the unusually thorough 1790 survey of Corfe Castle, a Dorset village, give a picture of poor families in a period of very high price and, hence, of widespread economic distress.[66] In about 80 percent of the surveyed households of all these studies, wives contributed to cash income, although not very much, while in about half of the households children contributed. The size of that contribution was clearly affected by the age of the oldest children. Taken together, the wives and children contributed on average about 20 percent of household consumption. These surveys did not deal well with supplementary (i.e., nonwage) incomes, which may help explain why expenditures exceeded recorded income in 78 percent of the surveyed households. Indeed, in these deficit households, expenditures exceeded income by an average of nearly 25 percent. Most of these deficits point to unrecorded income rather than to rising indebtedness. If this unrecorded income can be attributed to the activities of the wives and children – and Jane Humphries makes a strong case that their gathering, scavenging, processing, and petty trading activities were often important to family well-being – the total contributions of husbands may have stood at no more than 60–67 percent of the total.[67]

Humphries and Horrell's analysis of English household budget studies allows us to pursue the pattern of household earnings from the pioneering work of Eden and Davies up to 1865. We have already considered their findings in Chapter 3, focusing on the earnings of wives and children. Here we consider the 1,190 budgets of husband–wife households they assembled and analyzed to focus on the earnings of male heads of households. Their earnings range between 55 and 68 percent of total household money earnings until 1840, where after they rose to 81–83 percent in 1846–65. Breadwinner earnings varied by the age of the household head: Over the entire period, those in their twenties earned 90 percent of household income; in their thirties they earned 75 percent, and in their forties and fifties household heads accounted for little more than 60 percent of total income. Wives' money earnings varied between 5 and 10 percent throughout, while most of the difference was made up by the earnings of children. While wives' contributions tended to decline as children's

---

[66] The following discussion is based on Sokoll, "Early Attempts at Accounting the Unaccountable," pp. 34–60.

[67] Jane Humphries, "Enclosures, Common Rights, and Women. The Proletarianization of Families in the Late Eighteenth and Early Nineteenth Centuries," *Journal of Economic History* 50 (1990): 17–42.

TABLE 5.2. *Belgian budget studies*

	1853	1891	1928/9
Percentage of households recording income other than that of the male breadwinner			
Wife	84	11	20
Children	89	86	35
Other	77	28	
All three sources	60	4	
Percentage of total income from each source:			
Husband	51.5	65.6	70.2
Wife	10.1	1.2	3.7
Children	22.4	31.4	16.2
Other	15.8	1.8	9.9

Source: G. Alter, *Journal of Interdisciplinary History* 15 (1984): 255–76; 1928–9: Pieter Scholliers, "Family Income, Needs and Mothers' Wages. A Critical Survey of Working Class Budget Inquiries in Belgium, 1853–1929," in Toni Pierenkemper, ed., *Zur Okonomik des privaten Haushalts* (Frankfurt: Campus Verlag, 1991), pp. 145–81.

earnings rose, "the cut back is modest in relation to the increase in child earnings."[68]

Across the Channel, an impressive 1853 budget study of Belgian working-class families revealed a broadly similar pattern of income contribution by family member. Table 5.2 presents the data as summarized by George Alter. Here, too, family income in 1853 depended on multiple sources of income, and in this more industrialized setting the husband's wage income accounted for only half of the total. The "other" category – nonwage income – is explicitly accounted for in this survey, but the actual sources of income remain a bit mysterious. Alter cites one contemporary observer to the effect that "Every worker has a pastime producing a poor supplementary income: piercing pipes, ... making bird cages, making furniture at home at night, becoming a barber or shoemaker, etc., etc."[69] Thus far the industrious household, where, as a contemporary worried, only the law of "self preservation" – of all against all – could prevail,

---

[68] Sarah Horrell and Jane Humphries, "The Origins and Expansion of the Male Breadwinner Family. The Case of Nineteenth-Century Britain," in Angélique Janssens, ed., *International Review of Social History* 42 (1997), Supplement 5: *The Rise and Decline of the Male Breadwinner Family?*, pp. 31–7.

[69] George Alter, "Work and Income in the Family Economy. Belgium, 1853 and 1891," *Journal of Interdisciplinary History* 15 (1984): 268.

because "the family income is not earned by a common head, nor does it flow from a common source."[70]

The same Table 5.2 shows that the second half of the nineteenth century brought much change in Belgium, and, as we shall see shortly, elsewhere as well. By 1891 only 4 percent of surveyed households drew income from the full complex of sources characteristic of 1853. The husband's role as provider had expanded, his share of total income rose from half to two-thirds, but what is perhaps even more noteworthy is the extent to which the wage labor of children had expanded as that of their mothers contracted. "The breadwinner–homemaker household" is an awkwardly long name, but it is not long enough to reveal the role that child labor played, alongside rising adult male wages, to make possible the redeployment of women's labor from the market to the home.

Before we turn to the labor of children, the "withdrawal" of married women from market labor needs some further exploration. The sharp decline in such labor reported for Belgium between 1853 and 1891 required some growth of the breadwinner's earnings. Recall the threshold model, described in Figure 5.1, which related the withdrawal of married women's market labor to the increase of breadwinner earnings above a threshold level. It follows from such a model that not everyone could construct the breadwinner–homemaker household simultaneously. This is evident from the investigation of Louis Varlez at the turn of the twentieth century into the earnings of working class families whose breadwinners worked in four industrial sectors in the Belgian city of Ghent: cotton textiles, linen, metallurgy, and artisanal crafts. Around 1900 women married to men active in cotton and linen textiles, where male earnings were low, were much more likely to be employed than those married to men active in metallurgy and as artisans, where earnings were higher. Moreover, the wives of textile workers were more likely to toil in factories rather than in (the much lower paid) shopkeeping and other home-based enterprises preferred by the others. Patricia Van den Eeckhout's analysis found that these divergent work and earnings patterns led to a remarkable equalization of total household earnings across these industrial sectors. She observed that if the wives of the better-paid artisans and metal workers "had realized the same work effort" as those of the textile workers, their total family income would have been much higher. Why did these married women not work more? Her answer was that "neither

[70] Cited in John Rule, *The Labouring Classes in Early Industrial England, 1750–1850* (London: Longman, 1986), p. 180.

metal workers nor artisans were prepared to *pay that price....* Other than financial considerations seemed to carry more weight, such as the pride of the male breadwinner to be seen to be earning enough to save his wife from taking a job, let along a factory job."[71] Our model of the breadwinner–homemaker household leads to a fundamentally different interpretation. The "price" the better-paid workers were unwilling to pay was not simply one of a wounded patriarchal pride; it was the value of the home-produced consumption that gave them a different, and superior, standard of living than the still "industrious households" of the textile workers. This household production was of value to the breadwinner, of course, but also to the larger, lifecycle strategy of his entire household, which leads us back to the position of children in this household type.

These Belgian householders (or was it the patriarchs?) evidently found women's household labor to be more valuable than the education of their children, for the withdrawal of women's labor from the market was not immediately accompanied by a similar withdrawal of the labor of children.[72] In this they were far from unique. A remarkable survey of industrial workers' incomes conducted by the U.S. Commissioner of Labor in 1889–90 recorded household incomes and their sources for seven industrial categories in the United States and five western European countries (the United Kingdom, Belgium, France, Germany, and Switzerland). These data – 6,784 U.S. and 1,707 European household budgets – were gathered in such a way that we can identify the income sources across the family life cycle, as measured by the age of the male head.[73] Figures 5.2 and 5.3 reveal the overall pattern of the household sources of income across the family life cycle. In both the United States and the five European countries,

---

[71] Patricia Van den Eeckhout, "Family Income of Ghent Working-Class Families ca. 1900," *Journal of Family History* 18 (1993), p. 109. Emphasis added.

[72] French families thought similarly: In the brief period 1907–14 wives' contributions to household income fell from 11.7 to 5.4 percent while children's wages grew from 10.0 to 18.5 percent of household income. Tilly and Scott, *Women, Work and Family*, pp. 176–77, 185, 199. Claudia Goldin's study of Philadelphia households in 1880 revealed a similar pattern: "The higher the father's wage, the lower the probability of the child's participation in the labor force." But, Goldin adds, the rise of the breadwinner's wage first withdrew wives from the labor force. Only later did the children withdraw. Claudia Goldin, "Household and Market Production in Families in a Late Nineteenth-Century American City," *Explorations in Economic History* 16 (1979): 124.

[73] The fullest presentation of the data is in Michael R. Haines, "Industrial Work and the Family Life Cycle," *Research in Economic History* 4 (1979): 289–356.

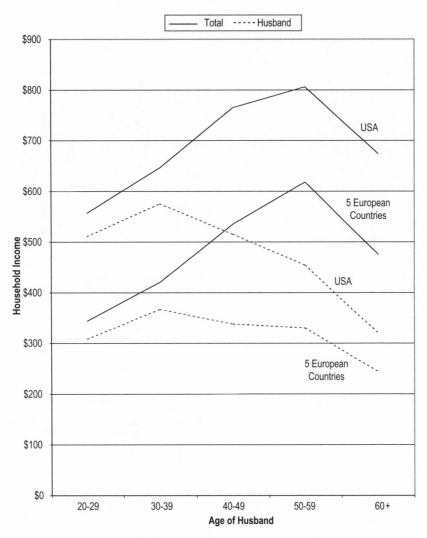

FIGURE 5.2. Household Income ($ U.S.), 1889–90 Industrial Survey.

husbands' wage earnings accounted for nearly 90 percent of total house-hold earnings when the families were young – when the male heads were in their twenties and thirties. But, as breadwinners in industrial employ-ments entered their forties, their earnings began to fall – rather steeply in the United States, more gradually in Europe. Total household income rose despite this, as the breadwinner's children began entering the labor force;

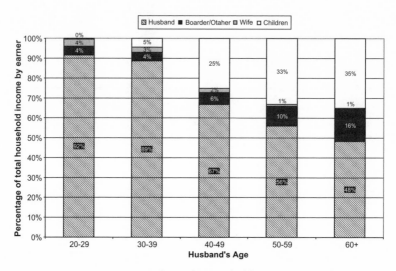

FIGURE 5.3a. 1889–90 Industrial Household Income: United States.

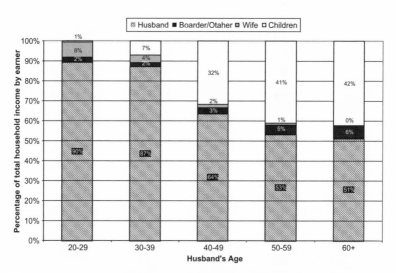

FIGURE 5.3b. 1889–90 Industrial Household Income: Europe.

by the time breadwinners were in their fifties, their children contributed 30 percent of household income in the United States and 40 percent in Europe.

At no point in the family life cycle did wives and mothers contribute substantial wage earnings, although in the American case nonwage income rises to more than 10 percent as the family ages, much of which can be attributed to the business activities of women, especially in retailing and renting rooms to boarders.[74]

The earnings of children loomed large in the breadwinner–homemaker household. Large but strategic – for children, especially daughters, were not sent indiscriminately into the labor markets. Goldin's analysis of child labor in Philadelphia in 1880, by linking employment to data on family structure, reveals the broad patterns of household labor deployment: (1) the higher the father's earnings, the less children worked for wages; (2) the presence of boarders or working relatives led to the daughters' staying home; (3) where the oldest child is a son, he was sent to work and a younger sister remained in the home, but where the oldest is a daughter, she stayed home if there were younger children; and, (4) if there was no mother present, the daughter remained in the home. Which children worked, and at what age they started work, was related to the household structure, birth order, and the earnings of the head.[75] These decision rules sought simultaneously to optimize family income *and* household production of the ultimately consumed Z-commodities.

If we follow the development of the breadwinner–homemaker household into the first half of the twentieth century, this dependence on the labor of children fades. Compulsory schooling and the extension of secondary education did much to withdraw younger children from the labor force, while rising adult male wages did much to make this withdrawal financially possible.[76] But compulsory schooling did not end the economic contribution of children to the household economy.

---

[74] It takes a special effort today to appreciate the scope of boarding-house accommodations in the breadwinner era. Goldin found that 14 percent of all white households in 1880 Philadelphia included boarders (although the 1880 census for Philadelphia counted less than 1 percent of households as having a female boarding-house keeper). Goldin, "Household and Market Production," pp. 111–31.

[75] Idem.

[76] Surveys of American urban workers reveal the following pattern of household income supplementation by source, for native-born and Irish-born household heads:

	Native born		Irish born	
	1874	1901	1874	1901
Wife	3.2%	0.7%	2.3%	1.9%
Children	24.0	5.3	84.2	12.1
Boarders and lodgers	N.A.	25.8	N.A.	36.9

John Modell, "Patterns of Consumption, Acculturation, and Family Income Strategies in Late Nineteenth-Century America," in Tamara Hareven and Maris Vinovskis, eds., *Family and Population in Nineteenth-Century America* (Princeton, N.J.: Princeton University Press, 1978), p. 218.

TABLE 5.3. *Women's labor force participation rates: 1890–1960*

	Belg.	Neth.	France	U.K.	USA
All women, above the age of 14/16					
1890	29	15	33	25	19
1930	24	19	37	27	24
1940			38		27
Married Women (to 65–9 years of age)					
1890					5
1900	19	5	20	13	6
1930	16	6	26	11	12
1940					15
1960	20	6	31	32	31

Source: H. A. Pott-Buter, *Facts and Fairy Tales about Female Labor, Family and Fertility* (Amsterdam: University of Amsterdam Press, 1993); Susan Carter, et al., eds. *Historical Statistics of the United States* (Cambridge: Cambridge University Press, 2006), Tables Ba 345, Ba431.

A Belgian budget study for 1927–8, which can be set beside those already introduced for the nineteenth century, reveals that the percentage of wives contributing wage income doubled relative to 1891 (see Tables 5.1 and 5.2). Their earnings were not large, but they may also have been chiefly responsible for the large increase in nonwage income achieved over this same interval. Table 5.3 summarizes the trend across the first half of the twentieth century. The pace of women's return to the labor force varies considerably by country, which is not surprising given the substantial importance in this period of law and public policy in shaping women's work. Overall, however, it is the movement of married women back to the labor force, usually later in life, that dominates the total female participation rates in this period.

To return to the question of patriarchy within the household: This brief survey of the composition of household earnings should suffice to demonstrate that the impression given by static analysis – of households supported overwhelmingly by the pay packets of the husband and father – is modified in important respects when the family is observed across the life cycle. The economic well-being, if not the very viability, of the breadwinner household depended on the earnings of children. Now, some readers may be deeply skeptical that a bargaining model can realistically capture relations between husband and wife in this period, but I do not believe the same reservations will obtain in applying such a model to the relations between children and parents. Maintenance of the loyalty of children – in a material sense – is an important theme in the study of the nuclear family forms that long were dominant in northwestern Europe. The early departure of children from the homes of proto-industrial workers, exploiting their earning power to live independently and marry early, was a major source of anxiety in centers of rural industry.[77] Even among agricultural families with important tangible resources to distribute to children via inheritance, the phenomenon of "child default" appears to have been a growing problem in the nineteenth century.[78] How much more challenging must have been the task of binding children to the propertyless, proletarian family. Helen Bosanquet anxiously asked,

Is it the case that when the family has no property, or only property of such a nature that each member can, if he will, walk away with his share in his pocket, the family ceases to be a reality? Or are there other forces and connecting links which preserve its strength, though in another form?[79]

In fact, there *were* "connecting links." The breadwinner–homemaker household could maintain the loyalty of children to the family as a pooled economic unit more effectively than had the less cohesive industrious family or, ironically, than many families endowed with transferable assets. There are several dimensions to this issue. First, we must consider how long children actually remain physically in the parental home. The departure of children to work in service and apprenticeship was a longstanding feature of the nuclear family regime. In the nineteenth century, the rising demand for domestic servants caused girls to leave home even earlier

[77] The demographic theories of proto-industrial development emphasize this issue. See Rudolf Braun, *Industrialisierung und Volksleben. Veränderungen der Lebensformen unter Einwirkung der verlaginustriellen Heimarbeit in einem ländlichen Industriegebiet (Züricher Oberland) vor 1800* (Erlenbach-Zürich: Eugen Rentsch Verlag, 1960); Franklin Mendels, "Proto-Industrialization, the First Phase of the Industrialization Process," *Journal of Economic History* 32 (1972): 241–61; David Levine, *Family Formation in an Age of Nascent Capitalism* (New York: Academic Press, 1977).

[78] "Child default" refers to children who default on an implicit contract to provide for aging parents in return for receipt of an inheritance at the death of the parents. This implicit contract was characteristic of rural landowning families. As non-agricultural opportunities became more plentiful and more attractive, adult children might forgo the wait for land (and obligation to care for parents). This is thought to stand behind the early decline in fertility experienced in the United States beginning after 1800. Roger Ransom and Richard Sutch, "Did Rising Out-Migration Cause Fertility to Decline in Antebellum New England? A Life-Cycle Perspective on Old-Age Security Motives, Child Default, and Farm-Family Fertility," California Institute of Technology Social Science Working Papers, no. 610 (April 1986); Paul David and William Sundstrom, "Old-Age Security Motives, Labor Markets, and Family Farm Fertility in Antebellum America," *Explorations in Economic History* 25 (1988): 164–97; Laurence J. Kotlikoff and A. Spivak, "The Family as an Incomplete Annuities Market," *Journal of Political Economy* 89 (1981): 942–63.

[79] Helen Bosanquet, *The Family* (London: Macmillan, 1906), p. 203.

than had been common before. Because their earnings at home were not likely to equal their subsistence costs, parents had no reason to resist this departure, and Snell offers evidence that the average age of leaving the parental home for girls in England fell from 17 in the eighteenth century to just under 15 by 1860. For boys the trend moved in the opposite direction, as, over time, service and apprenticeship figured less prominently in their work lives. Over the same time period the mean age at which boys left their parental homes rose from 14.6 to nearly 16.[80] This trend continued after 1860, and by the early twentieth century children of both sexes tended to remain home longer than they ever had before. In 1959, 90 percent of English children still lived at home two years after leaving school.[81]

A second question is: How much of the income of children, whether living at home or in service, was contributed to the family income pool? That is, did children living apart from their families continue to be part of the pooling regime? The answer in the case of girls appears to be yes, a large portion of their money income was remitted; and in the case of children of both sexes living at home, the contribution was very large. An early twentieth-century survey of the U.S. Bureau of Labor reported that sons gave 83 percent of their earnings, and daughters 95 percent, to their parents.[82] In Britain, similar patterns are reported, although once boys reached age eighteen they tended to shift to a fixed payment for room and board, now retaining much more of their income, while girls remained more fully integrated within the household economy.[83] This is a pattern that lasted to the mid–twentieth century in Britain, when working children continued to live in the parental home and contribute much of their income to the family pool.[84]

These last observations lead us to the third and final question: Why did older children, earning higher wages than earlier had been common, remain home longer and participate in the income pool of the patriarchal family? Michael Anderson's study of mid–nineteenth-century Preston revealed that, contrary to the expectation of contemporary observers, children earning relatively high wages in factories were more likely than others

---

[80] Snell, *Annals of the Labouring Poor*, pp. 332–7.

[81] Cunningham, "The Decline of Child Labour," p. 423.

[82] Cited in Tamara Hareven, *Family and Kin in Urban Communities, 1700–1930* (New York: Franklin Watts, 1977), p. 198.

[83] Leonore Davidoff, "The Family in Britain," in F. M. L. Thompson, ed., *Cambridge Social History of Britain*, Vol. 2, (Cambridge: Cambridge University Press, 1990), p. 122.

[84] Cunningham, "The Decline of Child Labour," p. 423.

to remain home. He reasoned that they did so because their earnings "allowed them to enter into relational bargains with their parents on terms of more-or-less precise equality."[85] If children with the wherewithal to leave now more commonly remained home, participating in the household economy, we must conclude that they found it to be advantageous to do so.[86] What advantages did they find in prolonging their subjection to a reasserted patriarchy?

To answer this question we must return to the other relational dyad of the breadwinner household: that between husband and wife. Here the radical specialization of functions characteristic of the breadwinner household, and the vanishingly small female monetary contribution to household money income, is commonly held up as evidence of the wife's diminished bargaining power. But this was not Helen Bosanquet's interpretation of the breadwinner household as she observed it in 1906. To her this was a regime to harness the adult male to work for a higher good than he could – or would – endeavor to attain on his own: "Nothing but the combined rights and responsibilities of family life will ever raise the average man to his full degree of efficiency, and induce him to continue working after he has earned sufficient to meet his personal needs."[87] These "combined rights and responsibilities" featured a division of labor in which, as Bosanquet elaborated with her rather ferocious directness, wives "expect to have, and they get, the entire management of the family income." Did they, in fact?

The struggle over household resources played itself out over a long time period, and the pace of change was by no means everywhere the same, but

[85] Michael Anderson, *Family Structure in Nineteenth-Century Lancashire*; Tuttle, *Hard at Work*, note 131.

[86] Seccombe poses this question in *Weathering the Storm*. He saw that it was advantageous to parents to keep their working children at home as long as possible, but, he mused, "The reasons for their evident success in this regard are not so clear, given that they lacked the carrot and stick of substantial property inheritance. Why did the great majority of proletarian youth remain under their parents' roofs, subject to their domestic authority, until marriage?" (p. 62). Seccombe reviews several possible reasons (love for parents, employment uncertainty, employers' displeasure) before turning to another topic. The conundrum becomes less daunting when one approaches the household from a bargaining perspective. Children with earnings have bargaining power. Tuttle, in *Hard at Work in Factories and Mines*, predicates her analysis on the assumption that "The welfare of children who work for wages depends on the outcome of negotiations with their parents" (p. 55). Such young people had a voice in determining their standard of living. Those whose future depended on inheriting the property of their parents had much less. Their options were loyalty or default. And, default was a real option for growing numbers, especially in the nineteenth century.

[87] Bosanquet, *The Family*, pp. 202, 222.

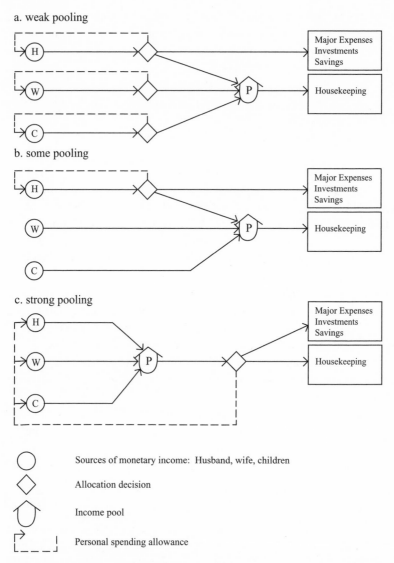

a. weak pooling

b. some pooling

c. strong pooling

○   Sources of monetary income: Husband, wife, children

◇   Allocation decision

⬠   Income pool

⌐→⌐   Personal spending allowance

FIGURE 5.4. 1889–90 Industrial Household Income: 5 European Countries.

the direction of change is not in question: The "weak pooling system" of the industrious household was replaced by the "strong pooling system" of the breadwinner household. The three panels of Figure 5.4 illustrate the essential changes. They involved a move toward (1) the remittance of a larger portion of income by contributing household members, (2) a shift of the decision about the size of the personal allowance to persons other than the beneficiary, and (3) the (re)definition of decision-making authority over the pooled income.

Income pooling goes to the heart of the household as an economic unit. Before turning to each of the three changes in practice that characterize the breadwinner–homemaker household, it should be emphasized that income pooling is far from a universal family practice. In many societies, today as in the past, it is not even very common. An alternative to pooling includes a gender-based division of responsibility, where husbands and wives have separate spheres of responsibility to be covered by their own earnings, without regular transfers between them. Another is an individualized system whereby members enter into pools temporarily and for restricted purposes as their resources permit. Income pooling has long been common among European nuclear families, but the range of expenditures covered (only regularly recurring household expenditures, durable goods, investments, inheritable assets?) varies substantially, as does, of course, the locus of decision making about the expenditures and the distribution of consumption.

The construction of the breadwinner–homemaker household with a strong pooling regime involved the following steps:

Remittance. An investigation of 1850 concluded that English working men spent one-third to one-half of their earnings on themselves, with the percentage rising in inverse relation to the earnings of the worker.[88] It was in this context that the Chartist T. B. Smith could admonish his male followers to abandon their "destructive selfishness:"[89]

Look at the tattered gowns of your wife, at the frockless and shoeless children who are crawling on the floor, at the almost coalless grate, and the nearly breadless cupboard, and then look at the well-filled tobacco pouch, and the flowing pint, and blush at your own delinquencies.

Late in the century, a retention of about 20 percent of one's pay packet was thought closer to the norm, and this conforms with the results of a detailed study of income pooling in the immediate post–World War II years in Glasgow. The percentage of earnings given over to the wife for management rose with the size of the family and declined with the size of the breadwinner's pay packet but fell below 75 percent only among

---

[88] G. R. Porter, "On the Self-Imposed Taxation of the Working-Classes in the United Kingdom," *Journal of the Royal Statistical Society* 13 (1850): 364.

[89] T. B. Smith, *English Chartist Circular* 1 (1841), p. 160. Cited in Seccombe, *Weathering the Storm*, p. 249.

the best-paid workers.[90] A broader British study of 1961 still found that 16 percent of breadwinners handed their entire pay over to the wife while 70 percent remitted a household allowance. By this date another option was to establish a checking account with joint access, which was used by 14 percent of households.[91] Still, more important than the practice of establishing a household allowance was the manner in which decisions were made about its existence, size, and range of responsibilities.

Allowance. At issue, when all is said and done, was *who* was put on an allowance? The breadwinner might "dole out" housekeeping money to his wife as she requests or begs and he agrees. A stronger commitment to the household could lead to the breadwinner's paying a "wife's wage," a fixed allowance, to cover the operating costs of the household. The size of this allowance was commonly related to the normal, or minimum, earnings of the breadwinner, allowing him to retain windfalls and other exceptional earnings. In both these arrangements, the breadwinner is certainly a patriarch – in the first an arbitrary and undependable one; in the second a figure who retains resources, and presumably attendant responsibility, for all expenditures except the sphere explicitly reserved for the homemaker.[92]

But a third system appears to have been regarded as normative by the end of the nineteenth century, where the breadwinner (and child earners as well) deposited, "tipped up," all their pay with the wife (and mother), who then returned a sum for spending money. The breadwinner was now the one on allowance, and the ceremonies in which earnings were handed over and allowances paid were often public and transparent.[93] These British practices were also encountered by early–twentieth-century investigations into American wage earners' household practices, where it was the wife "who doles out spending money according to the needs and earnings of each."[94]

---

[90] Michael Young, "Distribution of Income Within the Family," *The British Journal of Sociology* 3 (1952): 310.

[91] Jan Pahl, *Money and Marriage* (London: Macmillan, 1989), p. 50.

[92] In the first half of the twentieth century, before the spread of joint checking accounts and other forms of greater transparency, the "wife's wage" allowance system was more common the higher the breadwinner's income. Thus, as a 1917 study put it, as total income increased, "the proportion controlled by the wife diminished till often she becomes simply the beneficiary of the husband." Cited in Viviana Zelizer, *The Social Meaning of Money* (New York: Basic Books, 1994), p. 177.

[93] Davidoff, "Family in Britain," p. 113.

[94] Louise B. More, *Wage-Earners' Budgets* (New York: Henry Holt, 1907), as cited in Zelizer, *The Social Meaning of Money*, p. 177. An allowance system controlled by the

Authority. This last form of pooling, which gained ground as the nineteenth century came to an end, clearly shifted much if not all the authority over the disposition of household income from the husband (whose only job is to "bring home the bacon") to the wife. On the basis of his study of English working-class autobiographies, Vincent concluded (in conformity with Bosanquet's insistence) that "the wife was in charge of the household budget."[95]

The focus of attention here is on the household operating budget. It remains possible that male, or joint, responsibility was retained over funds earmarked for long-term, durable purchases, savings, and investment decisions. For example, the growing consumer demand for a "decent" burial led millions of Britons to contract burial insurance policies. By 1914 such policies were more numerous than the population of Britain, and by 1936 the annual premiums reached more than 66 million pounds.[96] Decisions about such financial commitments may well have been made differently than decisions about day-to-day expenditures. But daily reality in a "tipping up" household was not what one would ordinarily describe as patriarchal.

Another approach to testing the patriarchal practice of the breadwinner–homemaker household is to focus not on inputs and their control but on outcomes. Did this household form, in fact, result in distinct lifestyles for its members, coddling the patriarch and subordinating and degrading the homemaker and the children?

An anthropological approach to the family would pay attention to ritualized practices such as common meals. Are these occasions to reaffirm the commitment of all participants to the household as a joint enterprise, or are there, for example, seating and serving priorities that define different standards of living for different family members?[97] At this point one can do little more than speculate.

Without direct knowledge of distributional practices, it is the outcomes on which we must focus. One possibly revealing outcome is human

---

wife is also confirmed in Leslie Tentler's study of working class women in the period 1900–13, *Wage-Earning Women* (Oxford: Oxford University Press, 1982).

[95] David Vincent, *Bread, Knowledge and Freedom: A Study of Nineteenth Century Working-Class Autobiography* (London: Methuen, 1981), p. 53.

[96] Paul Johnson, *Saving and Spending. The Working-class Economy in Britain, 1870–1939* (Oxford: Oxford University Press, 1985), pp. 16–18. Total annual premium income rose from 0.7 million pounds in 1870 to 19 million in 1910 and 66 million in 1936.

[97] Seccombe, *Weathering the Storm*, p. 155; Baud, "Familienetwerken," pp. 123–47.

stature. The height of human beings is fully determined during the years before adulthood, most of which are spent subject to the allocation decisions of one's parents. Reasoning thus, David Weir investigated French height data to determine whether they supported the hypothesis that food scarcity in an industrializing society would induce parents to divert nutritional resources away from children (because the adults could benefit more directly and immediately from these resources). His conclusion, based on male height data, was that French children did indeed suffer such a diversion early in the nineteenth century (still the era of the industrious household) but that this pattern was undone late in the century (as the breadwinner household was consolidated).[98]

Stephen Nicholas and Deborah Oxley peered more deeply into the phenomenon of parental discrimination by studying the height records of more than 6,000 English and Irish female convicts transported to Australia. Their concern was to detect patriarchy in practice, by testing for a gender-based differential allocation of nutrients and care.[99] They found that the attained heights of female convicts, especially rural English convicts, deteriorated relative to the trend for males among birth cohorts stretching from 1790 to 1825. They could add to this finding a second outcome: relative deterioration of female literacy over the period in which these birth cohorts were being raised and, presumably, educated.

They found that there was "a pro-male bias in the allocation of household resources by the late eighteenth century" lasting to about 1840. Because they assumed that only a patriarchal household could produce such an unhappy result, they concluded that "Our data support the pessimist case, but place the emergence of the male breadwinner half a century earlier [than it is conventionally thought to emerge]."[100] Less ideologically committed investigators might have resisted the temptation to shift the timing of the rise of the breadwinner household to conform with their findings of discriminatory behavior. Their own evidence shows the objectionable behavior receding as the breadwinner household in fact became more common.

---

[98] David R. Weir, "Parental Consumption Decisions and Child Health During the Early French Fertility Decline, 1790–1914," *Journal of Economic History* 53 (1993): 259–74.

[99] Stephen Nicholas and Deborah Oxley, "The Industrial Revolution and the Genesis of the Male Breadwinner," in Graeme Snooks, ed., *Was the Industrial Revolution Necessary?* (London: Routledge, 1994), pp. 96–111. The study is based on 2,926 English-born and 3,370 Irish born female convicts transported to Australia between 1826 and 1840.

[100] Ibid., p. 111.

But, before drawing conclusions of our own, another, more broadly studied outcome should be considered: sex differentials in mortality. Investigations of adult mortality by sex have reported evidence of excess female mortality in late–eighteenth- and early–nineteenth-century England, Germany, France, and Ireland.[101] Ascribing economic causes to these patterns is by no means simple, because maternal mortality is a complicating factor. Moreover, in Germany excess female mortality appears to have been most pronounced among the middle class and landowning peasants rather than among wage earners and the poor. What all of these studies have in common, however, is a diminution or disappearance of these differentials in the second half of the nineteenth century.

One study of sex differentials in mortality reported the opposite trend: a sharp increase in excess male mortality, most pronounced in cities, and peaking in the 1820–50 period, before disappearing in the second half of the nineteenth century. Gunnar Fridlizius found this pattern in Sweden, sufficiently far afield from the region of our chief concern to be ignored were it not for the substance of his analysis. He determined that the most important general factor "is undoubtedly the enormously large consumption of alcoholic beverages, which from the beginning of the nineteenth century to the middle of the century was larger than in any other period in Swedish history."[102] Fridlizius argued that the propensity to devote increases in real income to an enlarged consumption of alcohol was particularly high in the early stages of modern income growth. "In fact, in the emerging consumer society, the liquor industry became the industrial flagship."[103] After midcentury a long-term decline in the consumption of alcohol set in, bringing with it a disappearance of the urban–rural, and the male–female differentials in mortality.

In this respect Sweden's experience was perhaps extreme, but not unrepresentative of trends in the United States, England, and the Netherlands.

---

[101] Stephen Klasen, "Marriage, Bargaining, and Intra-household Resource Allocation. Excess Female Mortality among Adults During Early German Development," Harvard Ph.D. dissertation, 1994; Arthur Imhof, *Lebenserwartungen in Deutschland vom 17. bis 19. Jahrhundert* (Weinheim: VCH Verlagsanstalt, 1990); Robert Kennedy, *The Irish. Emigration, Marriage, and Fertility* (Berkeley: University of California Press, 1973); Dominique Tabutin, "La Surmortalité feminine en Europe avant 1940," *Population* 33 (1978): 121–48.

[102] Gunnar Fridlizius, "Sex-Differential Mortality and Socio-Economic Change. Sweden, 1759–1910," in Anders Brändström and Lars-Göran Tedebrand, eds., *Society, Health and Population During the Demographic Transition* (Stockholm: Almqvist and Wiksell Internatonal, 1988), p. 244.

[103] Ibid., p. 259.

In all these countries the consumption of alcohol, especially spirits, rose to a peak in the first half of the nineteenth century. Eighteenth-century alcohol consumption in the American colonies stood well above European levels, the region being awash in (traded) rum and (home-produced) cider. The Revolutionary War disrupted rum supplies, but soon thereafter domestic whiskey more than replaced the declining supply of rum, as "technological improvements in distillation increased the output of distilled spirits, [and] western settlers began to turn large quantities of surplus corn into cheap, abundant whiskey."[104] The new American republic was "The Alcoholic Republic" according to one historian of the period, as "after 1800 . . . the total quantity of alcohol consumed from all sources increased until it reached a peak of nearly four gallons [14.8 liters] per capita in 1830. This rate of consumption was the highest in the annals of the United States."[105] In the young United States as in Sweden, distilled spirits were a leading industry of early economic modernization, and in America too, its rise went paired with a striking decline in life expectancy and other measures of health.[106] American alcohol consumption declined rapidly from the peak values of the 1830s and continued a steady downward trend to prohibition (although not the actual cessation of alcohol consumption) in 1920.

In Britain, alcohol consumption peaked later, in 1875–9, and fell thereafter into the 1930s. The decline was not small: In the 1930s British per capita consumption of spirits stood at only 20 percent of its 1870 peak, and beer consumption at 62 percent.[107] The Netherlands exhibited the same pattern of declining alcohol consumption: from a composite 6 liters of pure alcohol per capita in 1876–9 to a low point in 1936–9, and again

---

[104] William J. Rorabaugh, *The Alcoholic Republic. An American Tradition* (Oxford: Oxford University Press, 1979), p. 61. The economic importance of whiskey in the early American republic was such that it became the first object of domestic taxation by the federal government. This excise on whiskey led directly to the Whiskey Rebellion of 1794, the first major challenge to the authority of the government established under the Constitution of 1787.

[105] Rorabaugh, *Alcoholic Republic*, p. 10.

[106] In the United States, life expectancy at age ten, which had risen to above fifty-six years in the 1780–94 period, fell thereafter to below forty-eight years in the 1850s. Robert Fogel, "Nutrition and the Decline in Mortality Since 1700. Some Preliminary Findings," in Stanley Engerman and Robert Gallman, eds., *Long-Term Factors in American Economic Growth* (Chicago: University of Chicago Press, 1986), pp. 439–527; Steckel, "Stature and Living Standards in the United States," in Gallman and Wallis, eds., *American Economic Growth*, pp. 265–308.

[107] D. J. Oddy, "Food, Drink and Nutrition," in Thompson, ed., *Cambridge Social History of Britain, 1750–1950*, Vol. 1, p. 265.

in 1956–60, when it stood at 2 liters, a decline to a third of the peak level.[108]

If the new discipline of the income-pooling household set more restrictive boundaries on this classic male vice, it appears also to have affected expenditures for which women are thought to have a certain weakness. The tendency over the course of the eighteenth century for female wardrobes to be valued much more highly than male wardrobes – over twice as high in French probate inventories – was reversed in the nineteenth century. By the end of the nineteenth century, Rowntree's budget studies of York show a rough equality of expenditure by gender. In a more comprehensive study of English industrial workers, Lees found that more was spent on men's clothing in locations of heavy industry, while more was spent on women's clothing in textile districts. She supposed that the higher money earnings of textile workers' wives, who were more likely than other married women to work for wages, take in boarders, and so on, granted them an entitlement to a greater share of family income.[109] A still more broadly based spending survey of 1937–8 found spending on male clothing actually to exceed that on female apparel in a variety of manual occupations. Overall expenditures on female clothing were 86 percent of expenditures on male clothing. Finally, the total value of ready-made clothing sold in the U.K. in 1936 was roughly equally divided between male and female, as were the expenditures of recipients of clothing coupons in the war year 1941–2.[110] In the first quarter of the twentieth century, the United States exhibited the same general gendered pattern of expenditures on clothing: More was spent on clothing for men than for women in 1900, while approximate gender equality was reached at the eve of World War I.[111]

What all these studies of outcomes highlight is the concentration of the greatest inequalities in the intra-household distribution of resources, and the greatest consumption of the adult male's poison of choice during the final decades of the industrious household era, with its multiple wage earners, individuated consumption pattern, and weak provision of common

[108] Centraal Bureau voor de Statistiek, *Jaarcijfers. 85 jaren* (The Hague: Staatsuitgeverij, 1985).

[109] Lynn Hollen Lees, "Getting and Spending. The Family Budgets of English Industrial Workers in 1890," in John M. Merriman, ed., *Consciousness and Class Experience in Nineteenth Century Europe* (New York: Holmes and Meier, 1979), p. 180.

[110] Richard Wall, "Some Implications of the Earnings, Income and Expenditure Patterns of Married Women," pp. 312–35.

[111] Susan Carter, et al., eds., *Historical Statistics of the United States* (Cambridge: Cambridge University Press, 2006), Table Cd10–12.

goods and services. The emergence of the breadwinner–homemaker household in the course of the second half of the nineteenth century was associated with, and I believe causally associated with, the diminution of malignant intra-household resource differentials and the gradual reduction of the percentage of family income devoted to the classic male vices. The "patriarchy" of these male breadwinners was akin to the "monarchy" of the crowned heads of twenty-first-century European states – more show than substance.

Why was the breadwinner so restricted in the exercise of his typical patriarchal prerogatives? The bargaining model of household decision making would predict that the wife's diminished contribution to the household's earned income would correspondingly diminish her influence. As her options outside the household vanish, so her "threat point" becomes remote and ineffectual. Historical studies that emphasize the wife's increasingly weak position invoke her marginal position in the market economy, especially her inability to be self-supporting. But this had also been true in earlier centuries. Eighteenth-century women who devoted so much of their labor to proto-industry, agriculture, retailing, urban services, and the like earned more than they consumed only in exceptional, and usually not very appealing, circumstances. Their earnings influenced consumption patterns at the margins and affected household decision making, but they rarely elevated wives to positions of autonomy, let alone authority.

To grasp what was happening in the second half of the nineteenth century, the bargaining model must consider not only the household's money income but also the value of the consumed "Z-commodities." The new consumption technologies of the breadwinner–homemaker household caused the utility of consumption to become substantially greater than the utility of the money income, if consumed directly, as it were. Moreover, contrary to some feminist historians' claims rehearsed earlier that nonmarket Z-commodities are devalued and denigrated (because of their confinement to the despised "private sphere") and even worthless in fact, it now seems clear that the behavior of household members attested to the opposite. Children remained longer in breadwinner homes, the source of desired common goods, than in industrious homes with their more vestigial domestic sphere. Husbands gradually took on the yoke prescribed for them by the redoubtable Helen Bosanquet, handed over their pay packets, and restricted their personal expenditures.

In return, household members gained access – more or less according to a combination of total household income and the efficiency of the homemaker in converting resources into Z-commodities – to the goods and services we associate with a successful, modern society. During industrialization, the household became more rather than less important as a productive unit because the market economy was rarely able to produce and distribute more than the "raw materials" for a higher standard of living, or, more exactly, for the standard of living to which people aspired. Increased gross national product did not translate into better health and nutrition or greater domestic comfort, unless households converted the purchased raw materials into finished products. Indeed, the specific manner in which economic growth as conventionally understood was translated into standards of living depended on the household, and in ways not reducible in a deterministic way to the unfolding of the market economy. The withdrawal of the labor of married women in the face of rising wages and increased consumer choice bears direct testimony to the attractive power of the new consumer clusters that have been the focus of this chapter. The strategic role of the wife and mother in supplying these ultimately consumed commodities is what gave the homemaker a substantial bargaining power in the household despite the diminution of market involvement, and despite the reassertion – far more apparent than real – of patriarchy.

The contemporary vestiges of the breadwinner–homemaker household suffer the condescension of contemporary historians and other social scientists, who often suppose themselves to be liberated from a structure of Western society as long lasting as it was suffocating. It deserves a more serious scholarly treatment. Far from eternal, it was literally a moment in Western family history. Far from suffocating, it was, in its prime, a powerful vehicle of modernization and economic advance. It was the indispensable producer of many of the final consumption commodities that we continue to associate with the finest achievements of modern society. Far from becoming a "haven in a heartless world," it emerged as the site of the coordinated action and division of labor sought to exploit the new opportunities and parry the new risks generated by the market economy unfolding beyond its doors.

6

A Second Industrious Revolution?

In the twentieth century all this would change. Upper-class foreshadowings early in the century became a broadly based social trend after the 1950s, questioning both the value of the common goods provided by the breadwinner–homemaker household and the justice and rationality of the division of labor on which the production of those goods depended. A new industrious revolution emerged in whose grip we continue to live today.

Similarities and Differences

The basic facts are familiar. Expressed in the terms of the household models used in this study, the past generation has witnessed (1) a vast expansion of the number of households with multiple earners, (2) a pronounced redeployment of labor time from household to market production, (3) the introduction of consumption technologies that are much less intensive in their use of household labor, (4) reduced income pooling, and (5) the shift of consumer preferences toward services, public consumption, and individuated consumption. Each of these features has parallels in the industrious revolution of the long eighteenth century and involves the household in similar decisions about consumption objectives and the means to achieve them.

Yet, these similarities notwithstanding, it is obvious that the modern context of household decision making differs significantly from that in the centuries before 1850. To begin with, the state now encroaches on household decisions far more than in the past. While state policy, broadly conceived, was not without influence in the past (prohibitions or taxes on certain forms of consumption, restrictions on women's labor), the "second" industrious revolution unfolds in societies where the state shapes labor force participation strongly and directly via education policy, child labor laws, pension policy, and, perhaps most significantly, through the taxation of earned income. Together, these state policies influence the timing of entry and departure from the labor force and the forms of participation in the time in between. These policies differ considerably from one country to another.

Second, state policy now influences the organization of the household economy itself through its redistribution of income among households and, at times, within them. As noted in Chapter 1, income support for families in various situations and phases of the life cycle are nothing new for the "fragile" nuclear families of Western societies. Institutions to support and, when necessary, replace the family-based household long predate the rise of modern industrial societies, and the modern state insurance programs that emerged from the late nineteenth century onward reflect clearly and directly the public interest in protecting the specialization within the breadwinner–homemaker household that was simultaneously its source of strength and its point of vulnerability to economic fluctuations.[1] But the elaboration of the welfare state since the 1950s, while a logical extension of much older traditions, has interacted with individual behavior to provide an alternative to traditional household forms in most Western societies.[2] This alternative, "marriage to the state," establishes a new form of household economy, with neither the specialization of the breadwinner–homemaker regime nor the potential resourcefulness of the industrious household.[3] Thus, modern state policy constrains the spread

[1] W. H. Beveridge, *Report on Full Employment in a Free Society* (London: HMSO, 1944); Susan Pedersen, *Family, Dependence, and the Origins of the Welfare State. Britain and France, 1914–1945* (Cambridge: Cambridge University Press, 1994).
[2] The relationship between the perceived uncertainty of marriage by women and their political preference for political parties that support expansion of welfare expenditures in both the United States and Europe is explored in Lena Edlund and Rohini Pande, "Why Have Women Become Left-Wing? The Political Gender Gap and the Decline in Marriage," *Quarterly Journal of Economics* 1 17 (2002): 917–61; Lena Edlund, Laila Haider, and Rohini Pande, "Unmarried Parenthood and Redistributive Politics," *Journal of the European Economics Association* 3 (2005): 95–119.
[3] British households reported the following sources of income in 1986:

Income source	Man	Woman	State benefits	Other
Married couple, no children	60	36	2	2
Single woman, no children	–	83	12	5
Married couple, two children	74	13	9	4
Single woman, two children	–	26	51	23

Cited in Stein Ringen, *Citizens, Families and Reform* (Oxford: Oxford University Press, 1997), p. 94.

of "industrious households" in ways that had not been possible in earlier times.

More generally, the state encourages the consumption of many goods and services – "merit goods" – either by subsidy or direct public provision (education, health care, child care, housing, cultural consumption, specific foods). Finally, certain services are provided directly, bypassing the household to benefit specific family members (usually mothers and/or children).[4] Here, again, state policies vary substantially in the specificity and scope of their taxation and provision of goods and services, but they are usually sufficient to reduce measurably the autonomy of the household as an economic unit.

A third factor that powerfully alters the specific character of a second industrious revolution is the transformed demographic setting in which it functions. This study has not pursued the demographic variables of marriage (leading to the formation of new households) and fertility (in the past simultaneously a dimension of consumption and of household income) as aspects of household decision making. While this simplification may be defended before the mid–nineteenth century, the demographic transition that unfolded thereafter powerfully affected household size and structure. It gave the breadwinner–homemaker household a different aspect in the twentieth century (fewer children, less child labor, more state payments for child rearing) than in the nineteenth yet culminated in a striking "Indian summer" of the breadwinner–homemaker household in the baby boom phenomenon of the immediate post–World War II years. The new fertility decline beginning in the 1960s and accelerated by new contraceptive technologies has played an important role in shaping the new industrious household, its supply of market labor, and its patterns of consumer demand.[5] What follows is not an effort to explain fully the new consumer behavior and related family forms of the past fifty

---

[4] A notable example is the British Child Allowance. This program sought to alleviate child poverty by providing income support for the family as a whole, the money being paid to the usually male head of household. The program was revised in 1980 to provide income directly to the mother of the children who qualified the family for the benefit. Clearly, the British government did not believe that household expenditures were governed by a neoclassical income pooling model. The program was predicated on the belief that the mother's bargaining power over household consumption would increase if the benefit went to her, and that this power shift was likely to benefit the children. For a discussion of the change, see Shelly J. Lundberg, et al., "Do Husbands and Wives Pool Their Resources? Evidence from the United Kingdom Child Benefit," *Journal of Human Resources* 32 (1997): 463–80.

[5] Claudia Goldin, "The Quiet Revolution That Transformed Women's Employment, Education, and Family," *American Economic Review* 96 (2006): 1–21.

years. My purpose here is more modest: to identify those features of the modern household economy that bear comparison with the past. Precisely because the contemporary situation is so often regarded as a fundamentally new departure, without historical precedent, such an historicizing effort may help illuminate our present condition and its possible future development.

Alternative Explanations: Structural and Cultural

Perhaps the greatest recommendation for entertaining my conceit that contemporary family developments can be compared to the experience of the long eighteenth century is the evident weaknesses of the two arguments commonly invoked to explain modern changes in the relationship of the household and its consumer behavior to the market economy. The first supposes that society is experiencing a long historical transition from extended families to nuclear families and on to individualism (radical or expressive individualism), which necessarily brings with it the progressive weakening of family ties and disinvestment from family commitment. This transition is directly linked to economic development and the associated growth of cultural complexity.[6] Models of this sort stood behind the anxiety expressed by the mid–nineteenth-century sociologists who decried the destabilized family of the first industrious revolution.[7] These sociologists ascribed the weakness of the family – its growing inability to command the loyalty of its members to a common enterprise – to the direct effects of early industrialization, but in the twentieth century sociologists elaborated a structural-functionalist analysis to predict what now seems to stand at the gates: the final "de-institutionalization" of the family.[8]

Economists are less inclined than sociologists to look back before their own youth. In their hands, a century-long sociological "transition" becomes a radical alternation of the past generation. Gary Becker's economic theory of the family has proved very useful to this study, but his

---

[6] David Popenoe, "The Family Condition of America. Cultural Change and Public Policy," in Henry J. Aaron, Thomas E. Mann, and Timothy Taylor, eds., *Values and Public Policy* (Washington: Brookings Institute, 1994), pp. 81–112. See also Popenoe, *Disturbing the Nest*, ch. 3.

[7] Frederic Le Play, *Les ouvriers Européens* (Paris: Imprimerie impériale, 1855; 2nd ed., Tours, Alfred Mame et fils, 1877–9).

[8] Contemporary calls to action include Popenoe, *Disturbing the Nest*; James Q. Wilson, *The Marriage Problem. How Our Culture Has Weakened Families* (New York: Harper-Collins, 2002). The Parsonian approach is described in Chapter 1 of the present volume.

own application of his fruitful insights was confined to the events of "the past three decades" when "the family in the Western world has been radically altered – some claim almost destroyed."[9] Becker's acolytes do not stray far from this vision of a stable "traditional" family regime undermined by a shriveling economic role of the family "as the market and the state supplemented or replaced more and more family functions."[10]

The second and related argument holds that Western countries have experienced a cultural transition from a "traditional" society in which "religious, ethical and communal values and institutions restrain individualism and materialism" and, hence, suppress consumer culture, to one in which no available cultural resources are capable of resisting the beguiling attractions of an acquisitive and materialist culture.[11] Material goods, endowed with enhanced powers, now confront a modern man who has been shorn of traditional cultural defenses. Deskilled by the modern factory, alienated by modern capitalism, and set adrift by the collapse of traditional religion, modern man feels compelled to fill the empty spaces of the soul with fantasy, distraction, ostentation, and (the promise of) luxury.[12] Between the individual consumer–worker and the beguiling opportunities of the marketplace, only the tattered remnants of a household economy remain as a dim reminder of how people once structured their lives. And to some it is a remnant over which no tears need be shed, for the family is necessarily a terrain of conflict that inhibits self-actualization, especially for women.[13] To yet others no tear need be shed because it is the fate of the modern, soulless consumer ultimately to be transformed into the willful postmodern consumer, whose self-fashioning, individualized consumption promises liberation from – is even an antidote to – the alienation brought about by the capitalism that, ironically, is itself consumerism's progenitor.[14]

[9] Becker, *Treatise on the Family*, p. 1.
[10] Shelly J. Lundberg and Robert Pollak, "The American Family and Family Economics," *Journal of Economic Perspectives* 21 (2007): 3–26.
[11] This is the argument of David Horowitz, *The Morality of Spending*, p. xxi. Horowitz goes on to argue that the transition from a traditional to a modern society took place in the United States between 1880 and 1920: "In the late nineteenth century a shift started from self-control to self-realization, from the work of the producer, based on the values of self-denial and achievement, to a consumer culture that emphasized immediate satisfaction and the fulfillment of the self through gratification and indulgence" (pp. xxvi–xxvii).
[12] This pastiche is drawn from elements found in the work of Pierre Bourdieu, T. J. Jackson Lears, and Colin Campbell. See also Cross, *Time and Money*, pp. 154–83.
[13] See, for example, Hartmann, "The Family as the Locus of Gender, Class and Political Struggle."
[14] Miller, "Consumption as the Vanguard of History. A Polemic by Way of an Introduction."

Variants of these arguments have stood behind historians' declarations of consumer revolutions since the eighteenth century. The factual weaknesses of these linear models I have sought to highlight in the preceding chapters. The industrious revolution began well before the rise of modern industry and led to forms of household organization and consumption that cannot be reduced to the supply of the products of modern industry. Nor is there any linear process of family change or consumer behavior traceable across the centuries since the initial rise of modern industry. Moreover, the cultural interpretation of consumption addresses an era of high modernism that is now past, and whose consumer aspirations, in retrospect, it explains poorly. Critical cultural interpretations are capable of teaching us little more than contempt for consumers just below our own level of taste and income – which is to say that the cultural critique of consumerism does not stand apart from but is very much a part of a consumer society: It is primarily a training course for the aspiring elite consumer. And as for today, what does it really have to say about the ironic consumers inhabiting the recycled warehouses and gentrified slums of a post-industrial society? The theoretical weakness of these arguments is located, I believe, in an inadequate appreciation of the ongoing vital functions of the family as an economic unit across changing market economic environments. This is not to claim that its actions are all for the good – far from it – but simply to affirm that the household economy remains, despite everything, the location of major decisions that jointly solve problems of consumer aspiration and the deployment of time among various forms of work and leisure.

Characteristics of the Second Industrious Revolution: Supply of Labor

The dismantling of the breadwinner–homemaker household has affected the supply of labor to the market by all types of family members: men, women, and children, although at first glance there is nothing about the labor force participation of men over the past fifty years that deserves to be described as "industrious." In all Western countries, including the United States, men have come to work less than before, following a gently downward-sloping long-term trend. Thus, in the United States, 85 percent of all men, age sixteen and over, were employed or sought employment in 1955, while participation stood at only 80 percent in 1970 and has since fallen to 75 percent. This decline is driven in large part by a major increase in post–age sixty-five retirement. When the focus is restricted to males aged sixteen to sixty-four, U.S. male labor force participation stood at

80 percent in 2000. Participation declined more sharply in Europe. However, here too there are important distinctions: In "Germanic" Europe no country falls below 94 percent of the U.S. rate of male labor force participation, while in the Europe of Romance languages, none reaches higher than 90 percent of the U.S. rate.[15]

The work week has also declined over this fifty-year period: little, if at all in the United States, where the forty-hour week was already common in 1950, but much more in Europe, where forty-four to forty-eight hours per week then prevailed, and where legislation has reduced the standard work week below forty hours in most countries. Hours *actually* worked, as opposed to the statutory work week, have fallen less and remain at above forty hours per week for full-time workers in nearly all European countries.[16] When the decline in hours, a rise in part-time employment, and the lengthening of vacation time are combined with the decline in participation, the total postwar decline in lifetime labor hours is substantial, especially in Europe, although nearly all of the reduction had been achieved by the 1980s. In 1960 the annual hours worked per year for full time workers varied between 1,950 and 2,150 in western Europe, well above the 1,780 hours of the United States. In 1995, all were below the U.S. level of 1,625 hours per year, mostly by fifty to one hundred hours.[17] Thus, while annual hours fell by 8–9 percent in the United States, they fell, from a much higher initial level, by 20–25 percent in most western European countries.

Yet, the decline in labor force participation, and much of the decline in annual hours of work, can be reconciled to the industrious revolution concept: Men enter the labor force, on average, later than before because of prolonged education and leave earlier because of earlier retirement. For example, in the Netherlands in 1950 the mean age of school leaving was

---

[15] OECD, *Employment Outlook*, June 1998. "Germanic Europe" refers to the Scandinavian countries, all German-speaking countries, the Netherlands, and the United Kingdom. The countries of Romance language, for this purpose, are Belgium, France, Spain, Portugal, and Italy.

[16] In 2004, the average collectively agreed normal weekly hours in the 15 (pre-expansion) member states of the European Union was 37.9 hours; the actual, or usual, work week for full-time employees in the same countries was 40.8 hours for men and 38.7 hours for women.

[17] Angus Madisson, *Monitoring the World Economy, 1820–1992* (Paris: OECD, 1995); Bart van Ark and Robert H. McGucklin, "Perspectives on the Global Economy. The Euro's Impact on European Labor Markets," The Conference Board Europe, Report Number 1236–99-RR (1999).

16.4 while retirement before age 65 was rare. By 2001, the mean age of school leaving had risen to 20.8 and the mean retirement age had declined to 61.4.[18] In between these labor market landmarks, in the prime working age range, the reduced labor force participation by men is modest, part-time work has grown primarily to accommodate increased labor force participation by women, and the effective (as opposed to the statutory) hours of full-time workers have declined little since the 1980s.[19] Lurking behind these averages, however, is a significant difference between the annual hours of work of lower-skilled workers, which *have* declined, and those of better-educated workers, which have tended to increase.[20]

The overall pattern is consistent with a reorganization of the working year and the working career to support a life of high consumption. Consumption requires leisure – or consumption time – as well as income, and "quality consumption" requires substantial blocks of time rather than, say, an extra fifteen minutes of leisure per day. The second industrious revolution might take as its motto "Work hard, play hard."

These generalizations are intended to cover developments in both North America and northwestern Europe. Yet the perception is widespread that there has been a fundamental parting of the ways in recent decades, leading to a leisure-rich Europe and a work-obsessed United States. While Europeans lounge at terrace cafés sipping fine wines, Americans rush from work to Wal-Mart and back again. Thus, if there is a second industrious revolution, it does not apply to "Old Europe." As noted above, both Europe and the United States have the common experience of increased labor force participation, more dual-earner households, and fewer hours

[18] Robert Selten and Pieter Al, "Nederlanders zijn minder gaan werken," *Sociaal-economische trends* (205): 14–21. The average retirement age for the 15 pre-expansion member states of the European Union in 2003 was 61.7.

[19] The Netherlands has seen a particularly great reduction in hours and days of work by most measures, but when the total volume of work is related to the population aged twenty to sixty-one (the effective working age population), hours of work per capita (whether working or not) are as high today as in 1950, when the six-day work week of a society rebuilding from World War II was very much focused on work rather than on leisure. Selten and Al, ibid., calculate the annual hours per *potential* worker at 1,094 in 2001 versus 1,056 in 1950.

[20] Mary T. Coleman and John Pencavel, "Changes in Working Hours of Male Employees, 1940–1988," *Industrial and Labor Relations Review* 46 (1993): 262–83. Mean annual hours of labor for white men, aged 16–64, stood at 2,018 in 1950 and 2,114 or 2,012 in 1988, depending on the data consulted. However, the hours of male workers with a high school education or less declined by 109 hours over this same period, while the figure for those with at least 16 years of education rose by 156. This pattern is also observed in western Europe. See note 39.

devoted to household labor. These are the essential characteristics of the industrious household.

Where they differ is in the marginal choice of leisure over income by Europeans as productivity has increased in recent decades. A portion of the difference is accounted for by the differing constraints and incentives established by tax policy and other laws. How much is thus explained remains in dispute. Edward Prescott believes tax policy accounts for all of the difference, while other studies find that tax rates explain a substantial portion of the difference, but usually less than half.[21] But a difference in the preference for leisure, when that leisure is really "consumption time," is not a difference that undermines the concept of the industrious household. It suggests, instead, some difference in the ultimate Z-commodities that motivate households in the two regions.

The centerpiece of the new industrious household is, of course, the rise in the paid labor force participation of women. This is hardly surprising, because changes in women's work have substantially shaped all of the developments in household organization considered in this study. As Sheilagh Ogilvie put it (in considering the work of women in seventeenth-century Germany): "[Because] women are often located close to the boundary between market work and household work, female employment reacts very sensitively to demographic and institutional changes altering the rewards of different uses of time."[22] In the course of the twentieth century, educational, technological, as well as demographic and institutional, changes set in motion one of the central social and economic transformations of our times. While the phenomenon is familiar to all, it is worth pausing briefly over the data on women's labor force participation to call attention to some specific features of this phenomenon.

A slowly rising trend in the overall female labor force participation rate can be detected in many Western countries already in the first half of the twentieth century (see Table 6.1). Two world wars had both temporary and permanent effects on women's employment in some countries, but this trend was driven primarily by increased market work by young unmarried women (whose participation rates rose while those of young men, increasingly undergoing more prolonged schooling, fell) and by older married women, whose (re)entry to the labor force often compensated for the

---

[21] Olivier Blanchard, "The Economic Future of Europe," *Journal of Economic Perspectives* 18 (2004): 3–26; Edward C. Prescott, "Why Do Americans Work So Much More Than Europeans?" *Federal Reserve Bank of Minneapolis Quarterly Review* 28 (2004): 2–15.

[22] Ogilvie, "Women and Proto-Industrialization in a Corporate Society," p. 76.

TABLE 6.1. *Female labor force participation rates (ages 15–64), 1955–2000*

	Neth.	Belg.	France	Ger.	U.K.	U.S.A.
1955		34	46		46	38
1960	26	36	47	47	49	40
1965	38	46	47	51	44	
1970	30	40	49	46	51	58
1975	31	43	51	48	55	53
1980	38	48	54	50	57	60
1985	41	49	56	53	61	64
1990	53	52	57	56	65	70
1995	59	56	59	62	67	71
1999	64	56	61	62	68	74
% increase	146	65	33	32	48	95
Married women (ages 15–64), 1960–90						
1960	7	24	31	36	32	30
1990	47	[50]	53	54	59	64
% increase	571	108	71	50	84	113

Source: Pott-Buter, *Facts and Fairy Tales* (Amsterdam: University of Amsterdam Press, 1993); OECD, Manpower Statistics (Paris, 1963); OECD Labour Force Statistics (Paris 1987; Paris 2000), Netherlands and Germany: Siv Gustafsson, "Public Policy and Women's Labor Force Participation: A Comparison of Sweden, West Germany, and the Netherlands, in T. Paul Schultz, ed., *Investment in Women's Human Capital* (Chicago: University of Chicago Press, 1995), p. 99. U.S.: Mishel, Bernstein, and Bourshey, *The State of Working America 2002/03* (Ithaca, N.Y.: Cornell University Press, 2003), p. 398; Claudia Goldin, *Understanding the Gender Gap* (Oxford: Oxford University Press, 1990).

declining contributions of children and was, as discussed in Chapter 5, consistent with the basic logic of the breadwinner–homemaker household.[23]

After the mid–twentieth century, the rate of increase accelerated and was pushed forward by new factors, factors that directly affected the nature of the household economy. In these recent decades the rise in female labor force participation has been driven primarily, often exclusively, by the growing participation of married women, especially married women with children. In 1960 American married women aged twenty to

[23] Pott-Buter, *Facts and Fairy Tales*, pp. 317–18. Between 1940 and 1960 the overall labor force participation of women in the United States rose from 28 to 37 percent. Women twenty to thirty-four were slightly less likely to have paid employment in 1960 than in 1940. The increase in labor supply was accounted for overwhelmingly by women under twenty and over forty-five. In this period, labor force participation doubled among women aged forty-five to sixty-four.

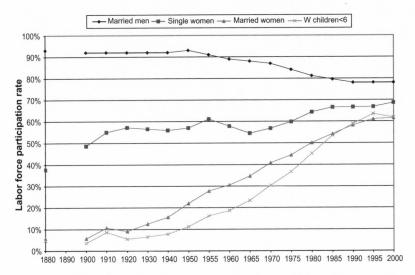

FIGURE 6.1. Labor Force Participation Rates by Sex and Marital Status, 1880–
2000.

forty-four were employed at half the rate of unmarried women of the
same age. By the 1990s, the differential between the participation rates
of married and unmarried women was only 10 percent.[24] In 1950, only
12 percent of married women with children under the age of six were in the
paid labor force; in 2000, 64 percent were working.[25] Figure 6.1 shows
the overall trends for men and women, and married men and women,
across the twentieth century in the United States.

It is particularly revealing to trace the changing labor market behavior of women by birth cohorts – that is, to follow the work experience of
women born in a given period through the course of their lives. Figure 6.2
displays the labor force participation rates of United States women in five-
year age cohorts beginning with women born in 1901–5. The women of
this cohort reached age fifteen in 1916–20 (World War I), thirty in 1931–5
(the Great Depression), forty in 1941–5 (World War II), and sixty-five
in 1966–70 (the Vietnam War/cultural revolution). They married and
formed households in the heart of the breadwinner–homemaker regime,
and while a changing environment later in their lives may have opened
new work opportunities, the labor market skills they were able to develop

[24] Lawrence Mishel, Jared Bernstein, and Heather Boushey, *The State of Working America.*
2002/03 (Ithaca, N.Y.: Cornell University Press, 2003), p. 398.
[25] Carter, et al., *Historical Statistics of the United States*, Table Ba 581.

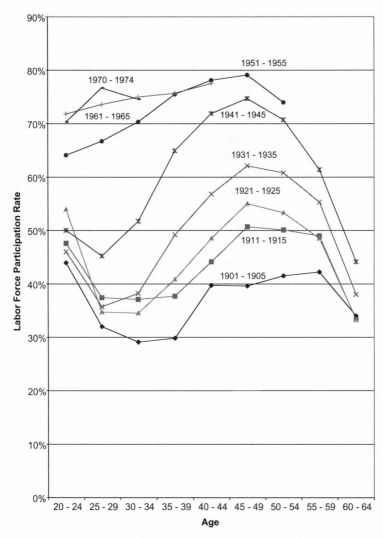

FIGURE 6.2. U.S. Women's Labor Force Participation by Birth Cohorts, since 1901.

early in life and the specialized households to which they had made commitments early on will strongly have influenced their later labor market participation. Figure 6.2 shows that 44 percent of women born in 1901–5 worked in their early twenties (when most were still unmarried), and that with marriage and child bearing they withdrew from paid labor, such that under 30 percent of all women in their thirties (during the 1930s) worked. As children grew up (and World War II and the postwar boom created new employment opportunities), some of these women reentered the labor force, but participation never far exceeded 40 percent, before old age and retirement reduced the rates again.

This pattern – substantial work before marriage, withdrawal with marriage and the raising of young children, gradual (re)entry to the labor force after age forty, followed by retirement – continued to characterize successive cohorts of women through those born in the 1930s. Employment in youth increased slightly, and, cohort by cohort, (re)entry employment became more pronounced, but the sharp drop in labor participation during the ages of family formation remained.

The cohort of women born in 1941–5 (who reached age twenty-five in 1966–70 and age sixty in 2001–5) pioneered in a profound transition. They were the last cohort of American women to withdraw from the labor force for purposes of family formation (although in a more muted form than earlier), and the first substantially to increase their participation in the labor force in later years. Their work participation after age forty would not be significantly bettered by later cohorts.

Women born after 1950 (who reached age twenty-five in 1976–80 and age fifty in 2001–5) were the first to follow a pattern of labor force participation over the life course in which the labor force participation dip associated with child bearing and child rearing disappeared completely. Their labor force participation in youth (ages twenty to twenty-four) was far higher than that of earlier cohorts (even though they were also much more likely to undergo extended schooling), and labor force commitment strengthened with each passing five-year period thereafter, peaking at nearly 80 percent when in their forties.

Cohorts that followed that of 1951–5 continued to increase the level of early adult labor force participation, but they have not significantly exceeded the levels reached by the 1951–5 cohort in maturity, and cohorts currently in their thirties may come to exhibit some retreat from the recent high-water marks.[26]

Just as in the past a determined minority of women worked in every age category, so today a distinct minority of women are not in the labor force

[26] Goldin, "The Quiet Revolution," pp. 1–21. Goldin considers whether a "natural rate" of female labor force participation was reached by the 1990s, and whether the "revolution" is being reversed in the years after 2000. Her provisional conclusion is that current evidence of reversal is transitory, a product of the business cycle rather than more fundamental factors. Cyclical factors certainly can obscure long-term trends, but the cohort patterns displayed in Table 6.2 give little reason to believe that the labor force participation rates of women will rise significantly in the absence of new structural changes. See also Chinhui Juhn and Simon Pooter, "Changes in Labor Force Participation in the United States," *Journal of Economic Perspectives* 20 (2006), p. 44.

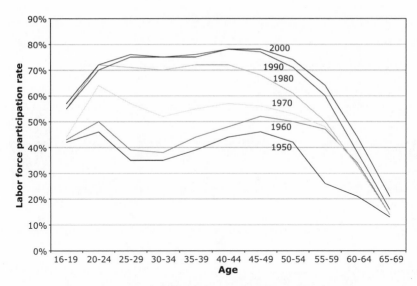

FIGURE 6.3. Female labor force participation: United States.

at any given age. But the "life cycle dip" is gone, and has been gone since the 1970s. When labor force participation is viewed in cross-sectional data (showing age-specific labor force participation rates at a given time), as shown in Figures 6.3 and 6.4, the experience of different cohorts are combined, and they continue to show some residual dual-peak pattern, but what they show most clearly is the enormous growth in the supply of female labor over the course of the past generation.

Yet another way to make the same point is revealed by the British data of Figure 6.5, which tracks labor force participation by age category over time. The rise in female participation between 1971 and 2000 is accounted for entirely by women aged twenty-five to fifty-four, and by students aged sixteen to twenty-four. I will return to the latter finding below, but note here that labor force participation over this thirty-year period rose by 67 percent among twenty-five- to thirty-four-year-olds, 25 percent among thirty-five- to forty-four-year-olds, and 20 percent among forty-five- to fifty-four-year-olds. Changes among older women and younger women no longer undergoing schooling show no upward trend over this period.[27] The rise in their labor force participation had taken place earlier in the twentieth century.

[27] Joanne Cutler and Kenny Turnbill, "A Disaggregated Approach to Modelling Labour Force Participation," External MPC Unit Discussion Paper No. 4 (Bank of England, 2001).

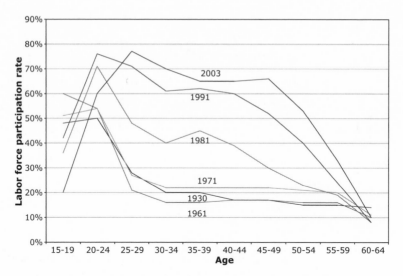

FIGURE 6.4. Female labor force participation: Netherlands.

The net effect of these changes has been gradually to reduce marital status and especially the care of young children as important determinants of women's labor force participation. The data displayed in Table 6.2 suggest that there is now little difference in the labor force participation of married women vis-à-vis that of other women.[28] As we shall see below, this generalization is subject to an important proviso (concerning part-time work and social-class differences), but it does confirm that the breadwinner–homemaker household is now a special taste. Where it had been most dominant circa 1900–50 (in the United States, the United Kingdom, and the Netherlands), it has retreated most sharply circa 2000. Its place has been taken by an industrious, dual–wage-earner household. Or, perhaps one should say a multiple–wage-earner household, for the labor of household dependents also took on new dimensions in the second half of the twentieth century.

The labor force participation rates of children – teenagers – are difficult to summarize, and even more than in the case of women, part-time

[28] The presence of children remains the strongest determinant of female labor force participation, but its influence is much weaker than in the past. Thus, in 1975, the labor force participation of married women with children age six or under was 74 percent, and for women with children under three is was 65 percent, of the rate for all women aged sixteen to sixty-four. In 2000 the figures were 88 percent and 82 percent, respectively. Bureau of Labor Statistics, *Women in the Labor Force. A Databook* Report 973 (Washington: U.S. Department of Labor, 2004).

TABLE 6.2. *Labor force participation of married women as percentage of all women, by country, 1960–90*

	Netherlands	Belgium	France	Germany	U.K.	U.S.A.
1960	0.269	0.667	0.660	0.766	0.653	0.750
1990	0.887	0.962	0.930	0.964	0.908	0.914

Labor force participation of married women as percentage of never married women, by age cohort. United States, 1960–99.

	20–24	25–34	35–44	45–64
1960	0.547	0.456	0.531	0.600
1999	0.897	0.884	0.900	0.946

Sources: See Table 6.1.

employment complicates the story, making it difficult to find data that are comparable across countries and across time. But the general pattern of the past thirty years has been for teenage employment to rise – by participation rate and by average number of hours per year – *in the face of* the simultaneous rise in secondary and postsecondary school enrollment rates. In the United States, the employment of sixteen- to nineteen-year-olds declined until the early 1960s, when it stood at 52 percent for boys and 35 percent for girls. This decline was associated with rising school attendance, but despite the continued rise in school attendance after the 1960s youth employment began a rather irregular rise: modest for boys, but substantial for girls, whose labor force participation reached 50 percent by 1995.[29] By 1998, 36 percent of high school students and half of all full time university students were employed.[30] Another study reports that 57 percent of fourteen-year-olds worked for money (a looser definition than that used by the U.S. Department of Labor in the above-cited study) in 1998.[31]

In the Netherlands, a 1984 survey among full-time secondary school students found that 53 percent of boys and 37 percent of girls aged fifteen

---

[29] Carter, *Historical Statisitcs of the United States*, Figure Ba-D; Tables Ba 528; Ba 544. For additional data on teenage employment, see Juliet Schor, *The Overworked American* (New York: Basic Books, 1991), p. 25–6.

[30] The employment rate was 45.1 percent for university students aged eighteen to nineteen; 53.1 percent at twenty to twenty-one, and 55.3 percent at twenty-two to twenty-four. *Wall Street Journal,* 15 September 2004.

[31] *New York Times,* 1 August 1999.

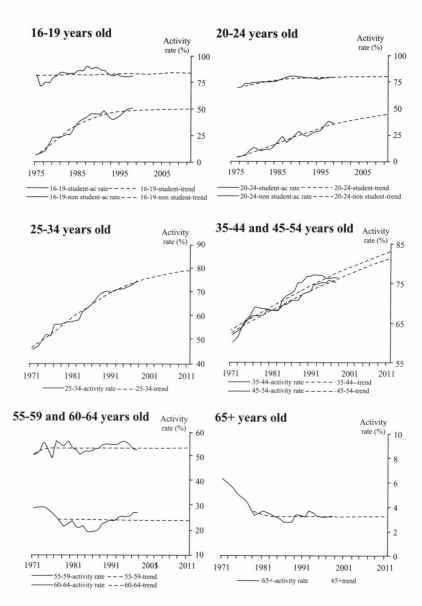

FIGURE 6.5. British trends in female labor force participation. (Source: Joanne Cutler and Kenny Turnbill, "A Disaggregated Approach to Modelling Labor Force Participation," External MPC Unit, Discussion Paper No. 4 [Bank of England, 2001], p. 21.)

to nineteen held jobs of some type. A 1991 survey found the rates to be the same for boys, but 45 percent of girls. A broader 1996 survey found that 75 percent of all school attendees aged twelve to nineteen worked at some point in the course of that year, and 47 percent reported paid work at the time they were surveyed, during a normal school week. They averaged nine hours of paid employment per week.[32]

Figure 6.5 displays British data that distinguish the labor force participation of students and nonstudents among those aged sixteen to nineteen and twenty to twenty-four. The patterns are similar for both males and females: Nonstudents in both age categories were heavily engaged in market labor throughout the 1975–2000 period. For students, the story is fundamentally different. In 1975 (when they formed a smaller percentage of their age cohort) students were almost entirely absent from the paid labor force. By 2000 (when students bulked larger among all sixteen- to twenty-four-year-olds) their labor force participation had grown to 50 percent for sixteen- to nineteen-year-olds and over 30 percent for students aged twenty to twenty-four.

The net effect of these trends has been a large increase in the hours of market labor per household, as the household has shifted from a breadwinner to an industrious (multiple earner) form. Among U.S. households formed by married couples, the percentage with only one wage earner (usually the husband) fell from 57 percent in 1960 to 18 percent in 2000 while the percentage with husband and wife both working rose from 26 to 60. Households with husband, wife, and yet other members of the household in the labor force rose from 6 percent to 13 percent.[33] In the much shorter span of 1992–2004, Dutch households with only one wage earner declined from 50 to 32 percent of all households with two adults present.[34]

Overall, in the United States, married couples aged 25 to 54 increased their combined annual paid labor by 354 hours between 1979 and 1999. In the longer interval 1968–2000, couples without children at home

[32] Findings for 1991 and 1996 are drawn from Nationaal Scholierenonderzoek carried out by NIBUD, and reported in NRC *Handelsblad*, 18 January 1992 and 27 December 1997. Data for 1984 from Pott-Buter, *Facts and Fairy Tales*, pp. 152–3.
[33] Rose M. Rubin and Bobye J. Riney, *Working Wives and Dual-Earner Families* (Westport Conn. and London: Paeger, 1994), p. 28; Bureau of Labor Statistics, *Women in the Labor Force*.
[34] Johan van der Valk, "Arbeidsdeelname van paren," *Sociaal-economische trends* (2005): 27–31.

increased their combined paid labor by 10 hours per week (from 58 to 68), while couples *with* children at home increased theirs by 11 hours per week (from 53 to 64) in the same interval.[35]

A frequently discussed consequence of this second industrious revolution is the increasing income inequality between the shrinking category of single-earner households and the growing number of dual-income households. Of course, if the vast majority of households were either single-earner or dual-earner, these work patterns would not by themselves be a source of inequality. It is the transition period, when there are sizeable numbers of both household types, which exhibits the most intense inequality. But the inequality does not stop with this "composition effect" because the transition to a new household type does not proceed at the same pace among all social categories. Before 1960 the average number of hours worked tended to decline as incomes rose (thereby moderating inter-household income inequality), but since then the relationship between hours worked and earnings per hour has been reversed. Low earners are now less likely than high earners to be part of dual-income households, and among dual-income households, low earners have increased their hours of employment less than high earners.[36]

The second industrious revolution has intensified income inequality in yet another way. Across the second half of the twentieth century, married couples became much more homogeneous in their levels of educational attainment. Men who had not completed high school became increasingly likely to marry women with similarly low educational attainments; women with bachelor's degrees or better grew increasingly likely to marry men educated to a similar level.[37] This process of social sorting echoes a similar process at work during the first industrious revolution. As female literacy rates in northwestern Europe gradually rose to a rough parity with those of men (between circa 1750 and 1850), the tendency for illiterate men to marry illiterate women (and vice versa) grew steadily stronger. In the Netherlands around 1850, marriages of two illiterates were from five to eight times more frequent than would be predicted by random association. A century earlier, when the number of illiterates was larger,

---

[35] Lawrence Mishel, Jared Bernstein, and Sylvia Schmidt, *The State of Working America 2000/2001* (Ithaca, N.Y.: Cornell University Press, 2001), p. 98.

[36] Dora Costa, "The Unequal Work Day. A Long Term View," *American Economic Review* 88 (1998): 330–4; "The Wage and Length of the Workday. From the 1890s to 1991," *Journal of Labor Economics* 18 (2000): 156–81.

[37] Robert D. Mare, "Five Decades of Educational Assortative Mating," *American Sociological Review* 56 (1991): 15–32.

the tendency for partners to select each other on the basis of literacy was much weaker.[38]

The intensified socioeconomic sorting of the first industrious revolution probably decreased inter-household income inequality because the industrious mode of labor market participation was most pronounced among the less well-off. But in the second industrious revolution the more rigorous sorting by educational attainment has intensified income inequality. Until the 1960s the marriage of a highly educated woman to a similarly educated man tended to reduce differences in household income, because marriage disproportionately reduced the labor force participation of educated women. Today, the higher the educational attainment of the wife, the higher are her hours of paid labor, thereby amplifying inter-household income differences.[39] In 1968 the total hours worked by college-educated couples in the United States exceeded by seven hours per week those of couples where both had failed to complete high school; by 1995 the gap had grown to twenty-five hours and was still twenty hours in 2001.[40] In the Netherlands, couples with postsecondary education worked a combined ten hours per week more than couples with vocational educational attainments in 2003. This is caused by the fact that among women living with partners, 81 percent with academic degrees participate in the labor force, while only 38 percent of women with vocational school diplomas and 25 percent of women without secondary school diplomas did so.[41] A broadly similar pattern is found in the United States, where in 1990,

---

[38] Ad van der Woude, "Alfabetisering als gezinsgeschiedenis," in Ad van der Woude, *Leven met geschiedenis. Theorie, praktijk en toepassing van historische kennis* (Amsterdam: Balans, 2000), pp. 225–94. In nineteenth-century England a similar process of social sorting is evident on the basis of the social background of the fathers of brides and grooms. Kendell's Q, a measure of sorting, rises from 0.38 to 0.73 between the 1830s and 1890s for the marriages of unskilled workers, and from 0.68 to 0.92 for skilled workers over the same interval. David Glass, *Social Mobility in Britain* (London: Routledge & Kegan Paul, 1966).

[39] Mary T. Coleman and John Pencavel, "Trends in Market Work Behavior of Women Since 1940," *Industrial and Labor Relations Review* 46 (1993), p. 661. Intensifying this effect is a major change in the likelihood of college-educated women to marry in the first place. Until 1970, U.S. women with at least a bachelors degree were significantly less likely to be married than women with lesser educational attainments. In the twenty-first century their likelihood to be married is notably higher than that of less-educated women. The relationship has reversed. Lundberg and Pollok, "The American Family," p. 10.

[40] Michael Hout and Caroline Hanley, "The Overworked American Family. Trends and Nontrends in Working Hours, 1968–2001," Survey Research Center Working Paper, University of California at Berkeley, June 2002.

[41] Labor hours of couples calculated from data in Van der Valk, "Arbeidsdeelname van paren," pp. 27–31. For data on labor force participation by educational level, see

47 percent of women with less than twelve years of education were in the labor force while 82 percent with at least four years of postsecondary education were employed.[42]

Household Production, Consumption, and Internal Distribution

Just as in the first industrious revolution, the new industrious families have necessarily reduced substantially their household production of goods and services. The hours devoted to housework and childcare declined over the past thirty to forty years, although there is much debate about the extent of the decline. Detailed time use studies carried out by Stafford and Juster show that women aged twenty-five to forty-four reduced housework from forty-five to thirty-three hours per week between 1964 and 1982, while they increased their hours of paid work from fifteen to twenty-five. The two trends roughly offset each other.[43] More recently, a six-country study found a decline of 1 to 1.5 hours per day in routine domestic work from the 1960s through the 1980s.[44]

The overall economic impact of such a reallocation of labor time cannot have been small, for even though measurements of nonmarket production are open to debate about the proper shadow prices, there is little argument that the breadwinner–homemaker household had accounted for a large portion of the value of final consumption. We noted earlier Gary Becker assertion that

Families in all societies, including modern market-oriented societies, have been responsible for a sizeable part of economic activity – half or more – for they have

Johan van der Valk and Annemarie Boelens, "Vrouwen op de arbeidsmarkt," *Sociaal-economische trends* (2004): 19–25.

[42] Carter, et al., eds., *Historical Statistics of the United States*, Tables Ba 515–18.

[43] F. Thomas Juster, "A Note on Recent Changes in Time Use," in Juster and Frank P. Stafford, *Time, Goods, and Well-being* (University of Michigan, Survey Research Center, 1985), p. 326.

[44] Johnathan M. Gershuny and John P. Robinson, "Historical Changes in the Household Division of Labor," *Demography* 25 (1988): 550. The decline of between 365 and 547 hours per year in routine domestic work is independent of the effects of rising opportunity costs and decreasing child-raising time. Another study by Gershuny records a decline in household work by women aged 20–60 from 217 minutes per day in 1961 to 162 minutes in 1985. Time spent in housework declined for both the growing number of working women and the declining number of women not in the paid labor force. The same study showed a rise in the time spent by men in household tasks over the same period, but the increase (23 minutes per day) could make good only a minor portion of the reduction in women's housework. Cited in Patricia Hewitt, *About Time. The Revolution in Work and Family Life* (London: Rivers Oram Press, 1993), p. 53.

produced much of the consumption, education, health, and other human capital of the members.[45]

One effort to measure the value of the home-produced and home-provided portion of total consumption, Stein Ringen's estimate for the United Kingdom in 1986, simply multiplied the hours of household work by the wage of a housekeeper. To this value of household production he added the value of cooperation in the use of shared resources, by weighting the second adult in a household at 0.7 of the first, and children at 0.5 of the first adult. (Thus, each member of a family of two adults and two children enjoys the utility of the adult head's resources at only 68 percent of the per capita cost of these resources.) Under these assumptions Ringen calculated that household production augmented effective household income by 58 percent, while the value of shared resources increased it by an additional 35 percent. The combination of the two augmented the value of household consumption to a bit more than total family money income – a finding consistent with Becker's expectation. Under these assumptions, Ringen concluded that the curtailment in household labor hours and the decline in average household size over the decade preceding 1986 reduced real income by 8 percent.[46] Measured over a longer period, this effect would have been significantly larger.[47]

Arguably more important than the change in total household income over the past forty or so years is the change in the composition of consumption and the change in the portion of total consumption redistributed within the households. The intra-household redistributive function has diminished as a larger share of the income of multiple earners is not

[45] Becker, *Treatise on the Family*, p. 303.
[46] Ringen, *Citizens, Families and Reform*. The reduction of the value of shared services may also be grasped by considering that the average adult in the United States will spend under 40 percent of his or her life in a household with spouse and children under conditions prevailing in 2000 while such an adult in the conditions of 1960 spent 62 percent of a lifetime in such a household. Susan Cotts Watkins, et al., "The Demographic Foundations of Family Change," *American Sociological Review* 52 (1993): 47–84.
[47] An analysis of time use in the United States over the period 1960–86 estimated the imputed value of household work (excluding child care) for men and women. In 1960 the income derived from household work accounted for 50 percent of the combined total income (market- and household-based) of men and women. In 1985 it accounted for only 33 percent. While money income of men and women combined over this period rose at an annual rate of 3.5 percent (driven by the rapid growth of women's money incomes), total income (market plus household production) rose at an annual rate of only 2.3 percent. Victor R. Fuchs, *Women's Quest for Economic Equality* (Cambridge, Mass.: Harvard University Press, 1988), pp. 79–80.

pooled and used for common consumption. This is most obviously true in the case of the earnings of children.

Under the breadwinner–homemaker regime, child labor played a strategic part in the pooled income of the household. In this context a notable characteristic of the new industrious household is the dissipation of the Dickensian aura surrounding the labor of adolescents via the almost total disappearance of income pooling. In Britain, Cunningham found that "The 1940–50s mark a shift from children handing over most or all of their earning to their parents to keeping most or all, giving a token sum for room and board." By the 1990s, he went on to note, that of "young people aged 13–18 who work, only one percent did so because it was 'essential for making ends meet for my family.'"[48] Hardly any child and youth earnings are pooled but are instead spent directly by the earner on personal expenditures. Matters are no different in the Netherlands, where a 1997 survey found that secondary school students disposed fully over their own earnings, devoting most to clothing, going out, alcohol, and music. However, the other side of the coin of the rise of the self-financing "teenage consumer" is a significant reduction of parental commitment to the intra-household redistribution of income in support of what had earlier been thought to be core expenditures on children, especially for clothing and postsecondary education.[49]

Not only is less income pooled, but the income that *does* support the household as a whole enters into consumption technologies that economize on the use of household labor. Both trends – reduced pooling and reduced production of items of common consumption – tend to promote individuated consumption and to favor perishable goods and services over durables and investment. In this respect consumption patterns in the second industrious revolution appear to many observers to differ in their social impact from those of the long eighteenth century. Then, individuated, nonhousehold-based consumption was often associated with new forms of sociability. The intensification of consumption brought with it an intensification of communication, leading to the sharing of a common discourse. So "social" was consumption then that it could become political,

[48] Cunningham, "The Decline of Child Labour," pp. 423–4.
[49] *NRC Handelsblad*, 27 December 1997. A survey of school attendees aged twelve to nineteen found that parents paid the full cost of room and board and insurance in over 80 percent of cases, but less than 40 percent of expenditures on clothing, school articles, vacations, and travel. A 1999 survey of American undergraduate students reports that nearly half the students enrolled full time also work full time, and they expect little if any financial support from parents. *New York Times*, 15 January 2000.

leading, in T. H. Breen's view, to the outbreak of the American Revolution. The individuated consumption patterns of the contemporary era certainly have fed the explosive growth in the patronage of restaurants and coffee houses – eminently sociable forms of consumption. But to some political scientists the new industriousness seems to lead to "bowling alone" and the decay of "social capital." The combination of intensified market labor and individual consumption is thought to lead to a constriction of social networks and, in the view of Robert Lane, a rise in the incidence of clinical depression.[50]

Whether sociable or not, the era since 1950 has reversed the long-term trend toward reduced alcohol consumption. Britain and the Netherlands regained their peak nineteenth-century levels or more by the 1980s while American alcohol consumption doubled between 1935 and 1950 and 1976 (from five to ten liters of absolute alcohol per capita, although this remains well below the levels prevailing during the nineteenth century "era of good feeling").

Another tendency toward more individuated consumption is observable in the large decline in the household preparation and joint consumption of meals. The percentage of American respondents (married men and women aged twenty-five to fifty-four) answering positively to the question "our family usually eats dinner together" fell from 44 percent in 1977 to 26 percent in 1998.[51] More generally, "eating out" in all its forms rose from 25 percent of total household food expenditures in 1950–4 to 45 percent in 1990–4. In Britain, the same trend is observed, although from a lower base. In consequence, the time devoted to food preparation in the home by women fell by half between the 1960s and 1995 (from 120 to 60 minutes per day), a decline only partially compensated for by an increase for men from 9 to 35 minutes.[52]

We can also note that in this period the large gender differential in spending on clothing that had emerged in the course of the eighteenth century, only to disappear in the century after 1850, has been fully restored.

[50] Robert Putnam, *Bowling Alone. The Collapse and Revival of American Community* (New York: Simon and Schuster, 2000); Robert Lane, "Friendship or Commodities? The Road Not Taken. Friendship, Consumerism, and Happiness," *Critical Review* 8 (1994): 521–54; Robert Lane, *The Loss of Happiness in Market Democracies* (New Haven, Conn.: Yale University Press, 2001).

[51] DDB Life Style Survey, 1975–1998, reported in Dora L. Costa, "Understanding the American Decline in Social Capital, 1952–1998," *Kyklos* 56 (2003): 17–46.

[52] Offer, *Challenge of Affluence*, pp. 146–7, 158. The time survey, which is the work of Jonathan Gershuny, controls for the changes in the incidence of women's employment and motherhood.

In Britain, expenditures for women's clothing exceed those for men by 25 percent in 1953 and by 72 percent in 1991, while in the United States, clothing expenditures for women exceed those for men by 65 percent around 1940 and again around 1950 but rose to exceed expenditure on male clothing by 89 percent in 1990–3 and 93 percent in 2001–4.[53]

In Britain, a 1980 revision of the Child Allowance (state support for families with children) directed state payment to the mother rather than to the household head, usually the father. If all family income, regardless of source, is pooled, this change should have had no effect on family expenditures. The new policy was predicated on the assumption that this was not, or no longer commonly, the case and that mothers would spend the child benefit differently than fathers. Experience revealed this to be true. After the change, expenditures on children's clothing rose, but spending on women's clothing rose even more, and the effect was stronger the more children in the household. In families with two children, the female–male spending ratio on clothing was 1.33 before the new policy and 1.60 in 1980–90; in three-child families, the ratio rose from 1.27 to 1.77.[54]

The decline in household-produced consumption has also been encouraged by technological developments and improvements in the organization and delivery of services that have enhanced the substitutability of market-provided for household-produced forms of consumption. For example, securing better health had long been associated with the production within the household of a number of goods – cleanliness, nutrition, and domestic comfort. Health came, as it were, as a by-product of these goods, and householders may well have "overproduced" them because of the difficulty in measuring accurately where diminishing returns set in. Because undershooting could have fatal consequences, the bias toward overproduction was substantial.[55] Joel Mokyr speculates that the introduction of antibiotics after 1945 "removed part of the responsibility for health from the household." One could now purchase "a set of 'pure' health goods that conveyed health exclusively, rather than as a byproduct

[53] Wall, "Some implications," p. 329; Carter, et al., eds., *Historical Statistics of the United States*, Tables Cd 163–5; Bureau of Labor Statistics, Consumer Spending Survey as reported in the *Wall Street Journal*, 15 September 2004.

[54] Shelly J. Lundberg, et al., "Do Husbands and Wives Pool Their Resources?"

[55] Today, we face this sort of dilemma most acutely with respect to the details of diet. The nutritional and medical consequences of food intake are both significant and subject to much debate. As a consequence, extreme responses to the available information are common, and what Mokyr calls the "tightness of knowledge" is far from tight.

of the consumption of other goods and the production of cleanliness."[56] If infectious diseases could be cured with antibiotics, housework lost some of its value to the "consumer."

This is an illustration of the increased substitutability between goods and household labor in the securing of the ultimately consumed Z-commodities. What could not be bought "off the shelf" in the nineteenth century had become available in commercialized forms by the late twenti-eth century. The "mechanization" of homemaking via electric appliances offers an interesting example, as does the growth of commercial services providing specialized alternatives to the work once performed by domestic servants.

Electrical appliances – vacuum cleaners, clothes washers, water heaters, electric irons, refrigerators – are commonly preceded with the adjective *labor saving*, and it is generally assumed that they were taken up quickly by housewives eager to liberate a portion of their labor from the prison of the home. Yet, when the diffusion of these appliances is studied with some care, the demand for them before the 1950s proves to have been remarkably limited. They were far from irresistible. Bowden and Offer summarize their study of appliances as follows:

We have traced the diffusion pattern for a range of consumer durables in the United States and United Kingdom from the 1920s to the present day.... Irons, refrigerators, washing machines, water heaters, and vacuum cleaners all took decades to diffuse through society. Both irons and refrigerators took over two decades to enter the majority of households, while the water heater, washing machine, and vacuum cleaner reached only a 20 percent ownership level in the same time. The vacuum cleaner, the washing machine and the water heater took 40, 30, and 33 years, respectively, to reach 50 percent ownership levels.[57]

In neither Britain nor the United States did the diffusion of most new household appliances proceed far beyond the income groups that had customarily employed domestic servants and that continued to do so throughout the inter-war period. The new appliances appealed to such households not because of their potential to replace domestic servants but because they increased servants' productivity.[58] Households without

---

[56] Mokyr, "More Work for Mother," p. 20.

[57] Sue Bowden and Avner Offer, "The Revolution that Never Was," in Victoria de Grazia and Ellen Furlough, eds., *The Sex of Things. Gender and Consumption in Historical Perspective* (Berkeley: University of California Press, 1996), p. 247.

[58] Ronald Tobey, *Technology as Freedom. The New Deal and the Electrical Moderniza-tion of the American Home* (Berkeley: University of California Press, 1996), p. 177. In the United States the number of domestic servants rose from 1.4 million in 1920 to

servants might well have been attracted to their labor-saving features, but other products made even more compelling claims on the incomes of such households in the inter-war period, new goods that fit better into the overall logic of the breadwinner–homemaker household. In this period, demand grew faster for household furniture and fittings than for other major categories of expenditure and, most tellingly, the new electrical appliance that *did* diffuse rapidly through *all* social classes was the radio. Bowden and Offer note that the "time saving" household appliances diffused slowly in this period, while the "time using" leisure appliances (radio before World War II, television thereafter) diffused with lightning speed. Introduced in 1922, the radio was found in 66 percent of British households by 1930.[59] Before the 1960s, the radio was a "common good," supplying services consumed by the family as a unit, much as household furniture served the entire family.

The relative appeal of these forms of consumption shifted later in the twentieth century, as the breadwinner–homemaker household began to unravel. Then, new labor-saving appliances (electric washing and drying machines, dishwashers, microwave ovens) *did* diffuse quickly and through all social classes, and the time-using leisure appliances (radios, television, music and entertainment delivery systems in their many variants) strengthened their appeal as they became more personalized. The erosion of social capital is often ascribed to the pernicious, isolating effects of television viewing, but when introduced in the environment of the breadwinner–homemaker household, television was a "common good," supplying family entertainment; if the same technology today has become an agent of social isolation, the reasons should be sought from the demand side at least as much as from the supply side. Individuated consumption and economizing on the household production of consumption, key features of the industrious household, reemerged in the late

2.4 million in 1939, faster than the growth of the number of households. By 1939 there was one domestic servant per 11.5 households. Servant numbers rose until the 1930s in Britain and the Netherlands as well, although not with the exuberance of the United States.

[59] Bowden and Offer, "The Revolution That Never Was," pp. 247–51. Tobey's detailed study of radio ownership in Riverside, California, reveals its diffusion to 80 percent of households in upper-income neighborhoods by 1931–5. Middle-income areas were close behind, reaching 82 percent by 1936–9, while laboring and nonwhite neighborhoods reached 80 percent by 1941–5. Tobey, *Technology and Freedom*, p. 178. The continuing emphasis on common goods in household consumption is revealed by the large increase in British spending on household furnishings and fittings, which rose by 52 percent between 1924 and 1937; in the same period, expenditures on clothing rose only 16 percent.

twentieth century to redefine the relative utility of a broad range of commodities, including appliances. The medium of television is "consumed" differently in the second industrious revolution than it was when it was introduced during the "Indian summer" of the breadwinner–homemaker household.

Where machines cannot substitute for household labor, commercially provided services sometimes can. The greatest challenge in achieving substitutability of commercial services for the home-produced alternative is overcoming a variant of the "principal-agent" problem. That is, the appeal of hired providers of domestic services is limited by a lack of confidence that others (one's agents) will perform the contracted functions to the standards one requires, or with the care and dependability one would expect of another family member. This concern – lack of trust – is most acute in questions affecting childcare. A definition of unpaid work – that is, household labor – is that "it is possible to pay a third party to engage in the activity yet still gain the same utility from it."[60] The elasticity of substitutability in many household activities has been limited by the fact that utility is often substantially reduced when it is delivered by third parties.[61] Clearly, the affective qualities that characterize the relations among family members contribute significantly to the utility derived from many household activities. Still, whether because of an erosion of these affective qualities, or an increase in the relative quality of commercial services, or both, the elasticity of substitutability across a large range of activities has increased in recent decades. As a result, many previously nonmarket services, especially involving child care and meal preparation, are now lodged firmly within the market economy.

The increased substitutability between market and home production that has speeded the contraction of the household sector is partly the

---

[60] Gershuny and Robinson, "Historical Changes in the Household Divison of Labor," p. 544.

[61] Suspicion of the quality of market-supplied substitutes for traditional household-supplied services is notably absent in the case of restaurant-supplied meals. Here, instead of careful scrutiny, we find consumers who appear oblivious to the differences between home and commercial meal preparation. Up to two-thirds of the increase in U.S. adult obesity between 1984 and 1999 can be attributed to the growth in the per capita number of fast-food and full-service restaurants. The rise in average hours worked by mothers can account for as much as one-third of the growth of obesity among children in certain types of families. S. Y. Chou, M. Grossman, and H. Saffer, "An Economic Analysis of Adult Obesity. Results from the Behavioral Risk Factor Surveillance System," *Journal of Health Economics* 23 (2004): 565–87; P. M. Anderson, K. F. Butcher, and P. B. Levine, "Maternal Employment and Overweight Children," *Journal of Health Economics* 22 (May 2003): 477–504.

product of new technologies. But most household services remain highly labor intensive, and the new substitutability depends also, perhaps primarily, on an increasing inequality in the distribution of income. In many cases, the services that have come to replace so much household production reconstitute in a commercialized form the old institution of domestic service that had divided the material life of social classes so long and so sharply until the twentieth century. The social chasm standing between the households that hired servants and the much larger number that supplied them was reinforced by starkly differing material cultures. Consumption habits that spanned this divide were rare.

One of the most novel features of the consumer aspirations of the breadwinner–homemaker era was the growing convergence of the material cultures of what came to be called – perhaps in subconscious recognition of this fact – the upper and lower middle classes. As domestic servants became a thing of the past for all but a rarefied stratum, a broadly shared "do it yourself" material culture emerged after World War II that today is viewed with boundless condescension. Yet, it represented what can now be seen as a brief historical moment of broad household commensurability in material cultures and in the consumption technologies by which ultimate consumption was secured.[62]

The new industrious revolution of recent decades has reversed this equalizing trend.[63] It rests on a foundation of "reconstituted servanthood" of nannies, housecleaners, au pairs, gardeners, pool men, and the providers of commercialized household and personal services of all kinds. If the servantless household in which the breadwinner–homemaker era culminated placed a heavy domestic burden on the homemaker (whatever her income level), the new industrious revolution is advancing hand in hand with a rising inequality in incomes and forms a major source of

---

[62] I use the term "commensurability" rather than "equality." Large differences remained between the qualities of specific articles of consumption of different income classes; what became more similar was the consumption technologies by which they were converted into Z-commodities.

[63] Jill Rubery, et al., *Women and European Employment* (London: Routledge, 1998). The authors argue that a collective (state-subsidized) rather than a private provision of household services could diminish or eliminate this tendency toward greater inequality. They describe the United States and the United Kingdom as follows: "Many services such as food preparation, laundry and cleaning, and some care services are marketed and retail opening hours are relatively long. These services are provided by women in low-wage, private sector employment." They contrast this with the example of the Nordic countries, where "many care services have been collectivised and are carried out by women employed in the public sector [where wages are much higher]" (p. 203).

demand for migrants from poor to rich countries.[64] Once again, as in the long eighteenth century, plebian lifestyles are diverging from those of the better sort.

Commercial services to care for children are now common, even though concerns about their quality and cost continue to generate anxiety and dissatisfaction. No comparable market-based substitutes have arisen to provide services in the support of husbands and their careers. This gap in the market may help account for the recent sharp erosion of the so-called "marriage premium." This longstanding, often-noted but somewhat mysterious characteristic of the breadwinner–homemaker household refers to the substantial earnings premium enjoyed by married male workers. That is, married men earned more than single men after controlling for other variables (such as education, health, job longevity) that influence labor market compensation. In 1976, the average wage of married men exceeded those of never-married men by 13 percent overall but was higher for older than for younger married men.[65] Marriage premiums of this magnitude are a robust finding of labor economics going back to the late nineteenth century.[66] Several hypotheses seek to explain the existence of the marriage premium, including discriminatory behavior by employers in favor of married men, assortive selection (i.e., systematic but unobserved differences between those men who marry and those who don't), and differences in how married and unmarried men prefer to be compensated. However, the explanation most consistent with the evidence remains that marriage makes men more productive, and that this higher productivity is a consequence of specialization within marriage.

It is, therefore, of particular interest that this durable historical labor market artifact has shown substantial erosion in recent decades, as specialization within marriage has become less pronounced. In 1976, the marriage premium took the form of a steepening of the wage profile of married men over time. The longer one had been married, the higher the premium, suggesting a positive return to marital tenure rather than simply

---

[64] Many service industries crucial to the industrious household have an international character. The second largest source of foreign exchange to the economy of the Philippines is derived from the remittances of female service workers abroad. The Filipinas employed as nannies and housekeepers for working American parents often have children of their own at home, who are cared for by yet other hired women.

[65] Jeffrey S. Gray, "The Fall in Men's Return to Marriage. Declining Productivity Effects or Changing Selection?," *Journal of Human Resources* 32 (1997): 482–4; Daniel Kermit, "The Marriage Premium," in Tommasi and Ierulli, ed., *New Economics of Human Behavior* (1995), pp. 113–25.

[66] Goldin, *Understanding the Gender Gap.*

to the state of being married. By 1993, no premium attributable to years of marriage could be detected, suggesting a fall in the productivity-enhancing attributes of marriage. Jeffrey Gray, in analyzing this shift, concludes that

The observed fall in the marriage wage premium is very sensitive to the degree of household specialization taking place.... These results suggest that the decline in the productivity effects of marriage results from less specialization taking place in marriage rather than any decrease in the return to specialization.... The returns to specialization actually increased slightly over the 1980s, as a wife's labor market activity had an increasingly negative impact on her husband's marriage wage premium.[67]

The details of the new industrious household vary considerably from country to country, and to a lesser extent by social class, but the essential features are common to most of western Europe and North America: the replacement of the breadwinner by multiple-earner households, a substantial reduction in household-based production and the associated specialization of household members, an enhanced substitutability of market- and household-produced goods, and a diminution of intra-household redistribution.

Conclusion

What is driving the second industrious revolution? I have argued that the industrious revolution that unfolded gradually after 1650 linked an intensification of market labor by the household to new consumer aspirations – what contemporaries called an "awakening of the appetites of the mind." Many of these new aspirations reflected individual appetites, and, over time, the multiple voices within the household put pressure on its integrity, but under the conditions of the times the execution of new patterns of consumer demand required household-level strategies. It is an understatement to say that the developments of the recent past are not often viewed in this way.

The new industriousness is generally explained as the result of one of three distinct and largely incompatible forces. A popular explanation for the increased labor force participation and increased hours of labor focuses on a combination of a sharp deceleration in individual earnings growth in the 1973–96 period and increased wants, stimulated not so much by the mind as by advertising. Several recent books deplore a turn

[67] Gray, "Fall in Men's Returns to Marriage," p. 502.

away from leisure and toward frenetic consumerism. With titles such as *The Two-Income Trap, The Overworked American, The Overspent American, The Time Bind,* and *The Second Shift,* they chronicle in various ways an increase in market labor and a diminution of household and leisure time brought about by a growing economic pressure on middle-class families.[68]

A second approach focuses on the labor force participation of married women and attributes its rise to the increased earnings power of women that flows from the combined effects of increased education and the market opportunities created by the long-term expansion of the service sector.[69] This increased earnings power gives rise to both income and substitution effects, with the latter eventually dominant.[70] Women substitute away from household activities, child bearing, and child raising in order to capture the now-enlarged economic benefits of market labor. Thus, marriage, fertility, and consumption behavior all appear to be driven by autonomous rises in the demand for and supply of female labor.

In the first approach, "the market" places households in a bind, putting new pressure on women; in the second, the market is a liberating force, placing new options and opportunities before women. A third approach denies that market forces are primarily responsible for these changes: Cultural transformation – affecting norms and values – brings about behavioral change in the marketplace. Either it starts with cultural change – invoking the exogenous rise of the new feminism and other events of the 1960–70s – or it ends there, by noting that regression studies of women's labor force participation leave large, unexplained residuals after the measurable effects of education, relative wages, the incidence of marriage, the number and spacing of children, and the like have been taken into account.[71] From this perspective, the only thing limiting a faster

---

[68] Schor, *The Overworked American;* Juliet Schor, *The Overspent American* (New York: Basic Books, 1998); Arlie Hochschild, *The Time Bind* (New York: Metropolitan Books, 1997); Elizabeth Warren and Amelia Warren Tyagi, *The Two-Income Trap. Why Middle-Class Mothers and Fathers Are Going Broke* (New York: Basic Books, 2003).

[69] For a succinct and influential formulation of this view, see Becker, *Treatise on the Family,* p. 55. For a recent summation of this approach, see Goldin, "The Quiet Revolution."

[70] The higher the degree of substitutability between market-purchased goods and home production, the stronger will be the substitution effect. Jacob Mincer, "Labor Force Participation of Married Women," in National Bureau for Economic Research, *Aspects of Labor Force Economics* (Princeton, N.J.: Princeton University Press, 1962), p. 46.

[71] A recent example of the latter is Jan Dirk Vlasblom and Joop J. Schippers, "Increases in Female Labour Force Participation in Europe. Similarities and Differences," Tjalling C. Koopmans Research Institute Discussion Paper Series nr. 04-12 (Utrecht University,

abandonment of old household forms is the pace at which public policies can be adapted to accommodate the new cultural norms.[72]

In this study I propose placing the developments of the past half-century in the same context of interaction between work and consumption that I have explored in the long-term developments of the household since the mid–seventeenth century. Without denying that new developments in education, technology, government policy, and fertility control have played important roles in shaping household forms and the allocation of household time in the past century, I do wish to question whether the lines of causation find their origins is these variables. The speed and force of change in these variables, I argue, are related to decisions made within the household itself about the ultimately consumed commodities, the choice of consumption technologies used to achieve them, and the specialization of tasks among household members to carry out these goals.

The accumulation of consumption capital, through the very experience of consumption and from other sources of information, periodically focuses individual preferences around new consumption clusters that commonly require adjustment in household organization for their realization. The adjustment process generates intra-family tensions, as individual preferences are negotiated with the household economy, leading to the expansion or contraction of time devoted to household production. Over time, at the outer limits of this historical oscillation, the household has appeared sometimes as something formidable – a mighty bulwark or a suffocating prison – or, conversely, it appears as a pathetic vestigial remnant of the real thing, retaining perhaps its basic biological functions but stripped of significant productive or redistributive activities. While critiques of the stultifying family are plentiful and jeremiads abound that bemoan the desiccated, deinstitutionalized family, the historical reality in Western societies has long been located somewhere in between these extremes: relatively simple, open family-based households, vulnerable to external shocks and influences, that are nevertheless responsible for a substantial amount of nonmarket production. The amount of that production, and the commitments to specialized functions within the household by its members, has varied – this book has sought to describe

---

2004). "We come to the conclusion that norms and values in society changed in such a way that the working wife has become more and more the standard in all European countries."

[72] Rubery, et al., *Women and European Employment*, offers a catalogue of policy changes to unblock what the authors hold to be a frustrated supply of female labor to the marketplace.

the historical paths of that variation – but this household production and internal redistribution has always been crucial for the well-being of all members, most obviously for those whose market earnings are low or non-existent.[73]

Maintaining a viable relationship between the household and the market in the twenty-first century requires an acknowledgment of the dual character of the household emphasized in this study: its role in both production and consumption. The challenge for the household as a unit of production is familiar to us. It is centered on the tension between, on the one hand, the individual commitments to market labor and, on the other, the time needed for household production of the ultimately consumed commodities. The household sector benefits, just as does the market economy, from commitment and specialization. Thus, the question before us is this: Can an effective internal division of labor emerge that does not deny to half or more of the household's members the development of their full human potential?

The challenge for the household as a unit of consumption is centered on the formulation of consumption aspirations. This is less familiar, because of the common assumption that consumption practices are broadly determined by the development of the economy. Individual consumer choice has only a circumscribed role in responding to the specific productive offerings of the economy over time. The burdens of this study have been to challenge the simple assumption that economic growth is directly and unproblematically linked to increased well-being and to call attention to the central role of the household in strategizing consumption goals. The extent to which growth leads to increased well-being depends largely on the household's strategies.

The more our consumer aspirations require extensive household production to transform purchased goods into the objects of final consumption, the more motivation household members should feel to solve the household specialization and commitment problem that confronts us now. Is it realistic to envision a future in which a new complex of consumer

---

[73] It is a commonplace that children are at a disadvantage in competition for public funds relative to the other main category of dependents, the elderly. In the household, children as a group tend to suffer the more market-oriented is the household economy. The reason, as Stein Ringen puts it, is that children are "consumption efficient" (i.e., the marginal cost of supporting an additional child is relatively low) but they are not "market efficient" (the opportunity cost of parental time is large). Samuel Preston, "Children and the Elderly. Divergent Paths for America's Dependents," *Demography* 21 (1984): 435–57; Ringen, *Citizens, Families and Reform*, p. 55.

aspirations serves to advance rather than undermine the human potential of household members active in its production?

An irony of the present time is that there is great professed interest in types of ultimate consumption that the market does not supply directly. This was true of the nineteenth century as well, when a keen interest in health, comfort, and respectability led to an expansion of household production to secure what could not be purchased "off the shelf." Household production expanded to achieve the new objectives of the time. At present, the role of the household – as opposed to the individual and the state – in achieving the often professed desires for educated children and environmental quality and sustainability, to give some examples, is a distinctly underdeveloped object of study.[74]

Many "family pessimists" suppose that any redirection of time away from the market and toward the household must itself make use of direct market incentives. If one accepts the claim that the household's production has no value unless it is validated by the market, the question then becomes: How "can a market be created that will send the right signals to parents about the social value of investing in children?"[75] This leads to advocacy for public measures that shore up "traditional" household consumption patterns via subsidies, tax incentives, and the like, proposals that accept the view that only the intervention of a benevolent state can save households from their inherently self-destructive preferences.[76]

What, then, does the future hold in store? Historians generally proceed with the implicit mission of accounting for why things are the way they

---

[74] I hesitated to include "sustainability" because of its irritatingly vague meaning, but in its time "respectability" suffered from a similar indeterminateness, a product of its reference to a broad consumption complex. Sustainability may become the new respectability.

[75] Burggraf, *The Feminine Economy and Economic Man*, p. 6.

[76] At the high-water mark of the breadwinner–homemaker household, a debate was launched in the United States over a perceived imbalance between private and public consumption. In his *Affluent Society* John Kenneth Galbraith spoke of private affluence and public penury. Now, a half-century later, the provision of many important public goods continues to suffer neglect, even though public spending has grown substantially relative to national income. Today, these public goods must compete with a broad array of consumption needs that in the past were met by the household economy. Between 1959 and 1996 transfer payments to individuals grew from 2.7 percent of average family incomes to nearly 10 percent, and rose from 19 percent of all government revenues to 44 percent. In short, public goods have come to compete with transfer payments more than with private consumption. These payments certainly have enabled many households headed by the elderly to function independently, but no one would argue that they have restored viability to the economies of households with working-age heads. Data from Frank Levy, *The New Dollars and Dreams. American Incomes and Economic Change* (New York: Russell Sage Foundation, 1998), pp. 34, 50.

are, while social scientists purport to go a step further and predict the future. I have sought to indicate that historians have misinterpreted how we, as consumers, became as we are while I have also been critical of the linear models common to much social science prognostication. However, they are certainly correct to emphasize that there is no turning back. This study has sought to demonstrate that historical consumption has been a dynamic phenomenon, charting a far from linear process of change. It will not cease to do so in the future. But this is not to say that the path forward is clearly marked or wholly determined. To be sure, our choices are heavily constrained by the accretions of experience. We stand more than waist-deep in the routines of daily life and the impedimenta of our material world. But what economists have come to call the "path dependence" that commits us to particular technologies, consumer clusters, lifestyles – in short, that binds us to particular, powerful, and compelling solutions to the complex coordination issues we face in managing all aspects of daily life – is not perpetual and eternal. Periodically, events converge to speed the depreciations of long-accumulated stocks of capital – physical, human, and social capital – and encourage the construction of new institutions to coordinate our activities. The catalysts of such transformations are various, but they include our own strategies to more fully achieve the ultimately consumed commodities that give us satisfaction (utility), and that have been the focus of attention in this book. Households will continue to be central to the development of these strategies, by both helping shape aspirations and devising the means to attain them.

Bibliography

Abel, Wilhelm. *Agricultural Fluctuations in Europe from the Thirteenth to the Twentieth Century* ([1935, 1966] London: Methuen, 1980).

Aerts, Erik, Louis M. Cullen, and Richard G. Wilson, eds. *Production, Marketing, and Consumption of Alcoholic Beverages since the Late Middle Ages* (Leuven: Leuven University Press, 1990).

Akkerman, Tjitske. *Women's Vices, Public Benefits. Women and Commerce in the French Enlightenment* (Amsterdam: Het Spinhuis, 1992).

Allen, Robert. "Economic Structure and Agricultural Productivity in Europe, 1300–1800," *European Review of Economic History* 3 (2000): 1–25.

"The Great Divergence in European Wages and Prices from the Middle Ages to the First World War," *Explorations in Economic History* 38 (2001): 411–47.

Alter, George. "Work and Income in the Family Economy. Belgium, 1853 and 1891," *Journal of Interdisciplinary History* 15 (1984): 255–76.

Anderson, Michael. *Family Structure in Nineteenth-Century Lancashire* (Cambridge: Cambridge University Press, 1971).

"New Insights into the History of the Family in Britain," in Anne Digby, Charles Feinstein, and David Jenkins, eds., *New Directions in Economic and Social History*, Vol. 2 (London: Macmillan, 1992), pp. 125–35.

Approaches to the History of the Family, 1550–1914, second ed. (Cambridge: Cambridge University Press, 1995).

Anderson, Michael, Frank Berchhofer, and Jonathan Gershuny, eds. *The Social and Political Economy of the Household* (Oxford: Oxford University Press, 1994).

Anderson, Michael, Frank Berchhofer, and Jonathan Gershuny. "Introduction," in Anderson, Berchhofer, and Gershuny, eds., *The Social and Political Economy of the Household*, pp. 1–16.

Anderson, P. M., K. F. Butcher, and P. B. Levine. "Maternal Employment and Overweight Children," *Journal of Health Economics* 22 (2003): 477–504.

Andrews, Benjamin R. *Economics of the Household* (New York: Macmillan, 1924).

Anon. *Considerations on Policy, Commerce and Circumstances of the Kingdom* (London, 1771).

Appleby, Joyce. "Ideology and Theory. The Tension Between Political and Economic Liberalism in Seventeenth-Century England," *American Historical Review* 81 (1976): 499–515.

"Consumption in Early Modern Social Thought," in Brewer and Porter, eds., *Consumption and the World of Goods*, pp. 162–73.

Arkell, Tom, Nester Evans, and Nigel Goose, eds. *When Death Do Us Part. Understanding and Interpreting the Probate Records of Early Modern England* (Oxford: Leopard's Head Press, 2000).

Aubertin-Potter, Norma, and Alyx Bennett. *Oxford Coffee Houses, 1651–1800* (Kidlington: Hampden Press, 1987).

Bairoch, Paul. *Cities and Economic Development* (Chicago: University of Chicago Press, 1988).

Barbon, Nicholas. *A Discourse of Trade* (London, 1690).

Baud, Michiel. "Familienetwerken, redistributie van inkomen, en migratie," in Baud and Engelen, eds., *Samen wonen, samen werken?*, pp. 123–47.

"Huishouden, gezin, en familienetwerk," in Baud and Engelen, eds., *Samen wonen, samen werken?*, pp. 11–33.

Baud, Michiel, and Theo Engelen, eds. *Samen wonen, samen werken? Vijf essays over de geschiedenis van arbeid en gezin* (Hilversum: Verloren, 1994).

Baudet, Henri, and Henk van der Meulen, eds. *Consumer Behavior and Economic Growth in the Modern Economy* (London: Croom Helm, 1982).

Baulant, Micheline. "Le salaire des ouvriers du bâtiment à Paris de 1400 à 1726," *Annales Economies, Sociètès, Civilisations* 26 (1971): 463–83.

"L'appréciation du niveau de vie. Un problème, une solution," *Histoire et Mesure* 4 (1989): 267–302.

Baulant, Micheline, Anton J. Schuurman, and Paul Servais, eds. *Inventaires après-deces et ventes de meubles* (Louvain-la-Neuve: Academia, 1988).

Becker, Gary S. "A Theory of the Allocation of Time," *Economic Journal* 75 (1965): 493–517.

"A Theory of Marriage. Part I," *Journal of Political Economy* 81 (1973): 813–46.

"A Theory of Social Interactions," *Journal of Political Economy* 82 (1974): 1063–94.

A Treatise on the Family (Cambridge, Mass.: Harvard University Press, 1981; enlarged ed., 1991).

Accounting for Tastes (Cambridge, Mass.: Harvard University Press, 1996).

Becker, Gary S., and Robert T. Michael. "On the New Theory of Consumer Behavior," in Gary S. Becker, ed., *The Economic Approach to Human Behavior* (Chicago: University of Chicago Press, 1976), pp. 131–49.

Becker, Gary S., and George J. Stigler. "De Gustibus non est Disputandum," *American Economic Review* 67 (1977): 76–90.

Beckett, John, and Catherine Smith. "Urban Renaissance and Consumer Revolution in Nottingham, 1688–1750," *Urban History* 27 (2000): 31–50.

Bennett, Judith. "History That Stands Still. Women's Work in the European Past," *Feminist Studies* 14 (1988): 269–83.

Benson, John. *The Penny Capitalists. A Study of Nineteenth-Century Working-Class Entrepreneurs* (New Brunswick, N.J.: Rutgers University Press, 1983).

The Rise of Consumer Society in Britain, 1880–1980 (New York: Longman, 1994).

Benson, John, and Gareth Shaw, eds. *The Evolution of Retail Systems, c. 1800–1914* (Leicester: Leicester University Press, 1992).

Berg, Maxine. "Women's Work, Mechanization and the Early Phases of industrialization in England," in R. E. Pahl, ed., *On Work. Historical, Comparative and Theoretical Approaches* (Oxford: Basil Blackwell, 1988), pp. 61–94.

"In Pursuit of Luxury. Global History and British Consumer Goods in the Eighteenth Century," *Past and Present* 182 (2004): 85–142.

Luxury and Pleasure in Eighteenth-Century Britain (Oxford: Oxford University Press, 2005).

Berg, Maxine, and Helen Clifford, eds. *Consumers and Luxury. Consumer Culture in Europe, 1650–1850* (Manchester: Manchester University Press, 1999).

Berg, Maxine, and Elizabeth Eger, eds. *Luxury in the Eighteenth Century. Debates, Desires and Delectable Goods* (London: Palgrave Macmillan, 2003).

Berkeley, Bishop George. *Querist*, 3 vols. (Dublin, 1735–7).

Berry, Christopher J. *The Idea of Luxury. A Conceptual and Historical Investigation* (Cambridge: Cambridge University Press, 1994).

Beveridge, W. H. *Report on Full Employment in a Free Society* (London: HSMO, 1944).

Bienefeld, M. A. *Working Hours in British Industry. An Economic History* (London: Weidenfeld and Nicolson, 1972)

Bianchi, Marina. "Introduction," in Bianchi, ed., *The Active Consumer*, pp. 1–18.

"Taste for Novelty and Novel Tastes," in Bianchi, ed., *The Active Consumer*, pp. 64–86.

Bianchi, Marina, ed. *The Active Consumer. Novelty and Surprise in Consumer Choice* (London: Routledge, 1998).

Blackburn, Robin. *The Making of New World Slavery. From the Baroque to the Modern, 1492–1800* (London: Verso, 1997).

Blanchard, Oliver. "The Economic Future of Europe," *Journal of Economic Perspectives* 18 (2004): 3–26.

Blom, H. W. "Political Science in the Golden Age. Criticism, History and Theory in Dutch Seventeenth-Century Political Thought," *The Netherlands Journal of Sociology* 15 (1979): 47–71.

Blondé, Bruno. "Domestic Demand and Urbanisation in the Eighteenth Century. Demographic and Functional Evidence for Small Towns of Brabant," in Peter Clark, ed., *Small Towns in Early Modern Europe* (Cambridge: Cambridge University Press, 1995), pp. 229–49.

"The Birth of a Consumer Society? Consumption and Material Culture in Antwerp, 17th and 18th Centuries" (unpublished, University of Antwerpen, 1997).

"Tableware and Changing Consumer Patterns. Dynamics of Material Culture in Antwerp, 17th–18th Centuries," in J. Veeckman, ed., *Majolica and Glas from Italy to Antwerp and Beyond. The Transfer of Technology in the 16th–Early 17th Century* (Antwerp, 2002), pp. 295–311.

"Toe-eigening en de taal der dingen. Vraag- en uitroeptekens bij een stimulerend cultuurhistorisch concept in het onderzoek naar de materiëcultuur," *Volkskunde* 104 (2003): 159–73.

Blondé, Bruno, and H. Greefs. "Werk aan de winkel. De Antwerpse meersenieers. aspecten van de kleinhandel en het verbruik in de 17de en 18de eeuw," *Bijdragen tot de geschiedenis* 84 (2001): 207–29.

Blondé, Bruno, Peter Stabel, Jon Stobart, and Ilja van Damme, eds., *Buyers and Sellers. Retail Circuits and Practices in Medieval and Early Modern Europe* (Turnhout: Brepols, 2006).

Blondé, Bruno, and Ilja van Damme. "Consumer and Retail 'Revolutions'. Perspectives from a Declining Urban Economy, Antwerp, 17th and 18th Centuries," (unpublished, University of Antwerpen, 2005).

Bloom, Ida. "Changes in Women's Work and Family Responsibilities in Norway Since the 1860s," in Pat Hudson and W. R. Lee, eds., *Women's Work and the Family Economy*, pp. 157–79.

Bluestone, Barry, and Stephen Rose. "The Enigma of Working Time Trends," in Golden and Figart, eds., *Working Time*, pp. 21–37.

Blumer, Herbert. "Fashion. From Class Differentiation to Social Selection," *Sociological Quarterly* 10 (1969): 275–91.

Booth, Charles. *Life and Labour of the People of London* ([1891] New York: Augustus Kelly, 1967).

Borsay, Peter. *The English Urban Renaissance. Culture and Society in the Provincial Town, 1660–1760* (Oxford: Oxford University Press, 1989).

Bosanquet, Helen. *The Family* (London: Macmillan, 1906).

Boserup, Ester. *The Conditions of Agricultural Growth* (Chicago: University of Chicago Press, 1965).

Women's Role in Economic Development (New York: St. Martin's Press, 1970).

Bourdieu, Pierre. *Distinction. A Sociological Critique of the Judgment of Taste* ([1979] Trans. Richard Nice. London: Routledge & Kegan Paul, 1984).

Bourke, Joanna. "Avoiding Poverty. Strategies for Women in Rural Ireland, 1880–1914," in Henderson and Wall, eds., *Poor Women and Children in the European Past*, pp. 292–311.

"Housewifery in Working-Class England, 1860–1914," *Past and Present* 143 (1994): 167–97.

Bowden, Sue, and Avner Offer. "The Technological Revolution That Never Was. Gender, Class, and the Diffusion of Household Appliances in Interwar England," in de Grazia and Furlough, eds., *The Sex of Thing*, pp. 244–74.

Braudel, Fernand. *Civilization and Capitalism, 15th–18th Century. The Structures of Everyday Life. The Limits of the Possible* (New York: Harper & Row, 1981).

Braun, Rodolf. *Industrialisierung und Volksleben. Veränderungen der Lebensformen unter Einwirkung der verlaginustriellen Heimarbeit in einem ländlichen Industriegebiet (Züricher Oberland) vor 1800* (Erlenbach-Zürich: Eugen Rentsch Verlag, 1960).

Breen, T. H. "An Empire of Goods. The Anglicization of Colonial America, 1690–1776," *Journal of British Studies* 25 (1986): 467–99.

"'Baubles of Britain'. The American and Consumer Revolutions of the Eighteenth Century," *Past and Present* 119 (1988): 73–104.

"Narrative of Commercial Life. Consumption, Ideology, and Community on the Eve of the American Revolution," *William and Mary Quarterly* 50 (1993): 471–501.

The Marketplace of Revolution. How Consumer Politics Shaped American Independence (Oxford: Oxford University Press, 2004).

Brennan, T. E. *Public Drinking and Popular Culture in Eighteenth-Century Paris* (Princeton, N.J.: Princeton University Press, 1988).

Breugel, Martin. "A Bourgeois Good? Sugar, Norms of Consumption and the Labouring Classes in Nineteenth Century France," in Peter Scholliers, ed., *Food, Drink and Identity. Cooking, Eating, and Drinking in Europe Since the Middle Ages* (Oxford: Berg, 2001), pp. 99–118.

Brewer, John, and Roy Porter, eds. *Consumption and the World of Goods* (London: Routledge, 1993).

Briggs, Asa. "Work and Leisure in Industrial Society," *Past and Present* 30 (1965): 96–102.

Broadberry, Stephen, and Bishnupriya Gupta. "The Early Modern Great Divergence. Wages, Prices and Economic Development in Europe and Asia, 1500–1800," *Economic History Review* 59 (2006): 2–31.

Brunner, Otto. "Das 'Ganze Haus' und die alt-europäische Ökonomik" (1958), in Otto Brunner, *Neue Wege der Verfassungs- und Sozialgeschichte* (2nd ed., Gottingen: Vandenhoeck und Ruprecht, 1968), pp. 103–27.

Bullock, Nicholas, and James Read. *The Movement for Housing Reform in Germany and France, 1840–1914* (Cambridge: Cambridge University Press, 1985).

Bureau of Labor Statistics. *Women in the Labor Force. A Databook* Report 983 (Washington: U.S. Department of Labor, 2004)

Burggraf, Shirley P. *The Feminine Economy and Economic Man. Reviving the Role of Family in the Post-Industrial Age* (Reading, Mass.: Addison-Wesley, 1997).

Burnett, John. *Plenty and Want*, 3ed ed. (London: Routledge, 1989).

Calvin, John. *Institutes of the Christian Religion* ([1536 edition] Atlanta: John Knox Press, 1975).

Cameron, Rondo. *A Concise Economic History of the World* (Oxford: Oxford University Press, 1989).

Campbell, Bruce, and Mark Overton. "Productivity Change in European Agricultural Development," in Bruce Campbell and Mark Overeton, eds., *Land, Labour and Livestock. Historical Studies in European Agriculture* (Manchester: Manchester University Press, 1991), pp. 1–50.

Campbell, Colin. *The Romantic Ethic and the Spirit of Modern Consumption* (Oxford: Basil Blackwell, 1987).

"Consumption. The New Wave of Research in the Humanities and Social Sciences," *Journal of Social Behavior and Personality* 6 (1991): 57–74.

Carr, Lois Green, and Lorena S. Walsh, "The Standard of Living in the Colonial Chesapeake," *William and Mary Quarterly* 45 (1988): 135–59.

"Changing Lifestyles and Consumer Behavior in the Colonial Chesapeake," in Carson, Hoffman, and Albert, eds., *Of Consuming Interests*, pp. 59–166.

Carson, Cary. "The Consumer Revolution in Colonial British America. Why Demand?" in Carson, Hoffman, and Albert, eds., *Of Consuming Interests*, pp. 483–697.

Carson, Cary, Ronald Hoffman, and Peter J. Albert, eds. *Of Consuming Interests. The Style of Life in the Eighteenth Century* (Charlottesville, Va.: University Press of Virginia, 1994).

Chaudhuri, K. N. *The Trading World of Asia and the English East India Company, 1660–1760* (Cambridge: Cambridge University Press, 1978).

Chayanov, A. V. *The Theory of Peasant Economy*, D. B. Thorner and B. Kerblay, et al., eds., The American Economic Association Translation Series (Homewood, Ill.: R. D. Irwin, 1966).

Chou, S. Y., M. Grossman, and H. Saffer, "An Economic Analysis of Adult Obesity. Results from the Behavioral Risk Factor Surveillance System," *Journal of Health Economics* 23 (2004): 565–87.

Clark, Alice. *Working Life of Women in the Seventeenth Century* ([1919], reprint, New York: A. M. Kelly, 1968).

Clark, Anna. *The Struggle for the Breeches. Gender and the Making of the British Working Class* (Berkeley: University of California Press, 1995).

Clark, Gregory. "Productivity Growth without Technical Change in European Agriculture before 1850," *Journal of Economic History* 47 (1987): 419–32.

"Factory Discipline," *Journal of Economic History* 54 (1994): 128–63.

"Farm Wages and Living Standards in England, 1670–1869," *Economic History Review* 54 (2001): 477–505.

"Shelter from the Storm. Housing in the Industrial Revolution, 1550–1909," *Journal of Economic History* 62 (2002): 489–511.

Clark, Gregory, Michael Huberman, and Peter T. Lindert, "A British Food Puzzle, 1770–1850," *Economic History Review* 48 (1995): 215–37.

Clark, Gregory, and Ysbrand van der Werf, "The Industrious Revolution or Calvinist Middle Ages?" *Journal of Economic History* 58 (1998): 830–43.

Clark, Jonathan. *Our Shadowed Present. Modernism, Postmodernism, and History* (Stanford, Calif.: Stanford University Press, 2004).

Clark, Peter. *The English Alehouse. A Social History, 1200–1830* (New York: Longman, 1983).

Clifford, Helen. "A Commerce with Things. The Value of Precious Metalwork in Early Modern England," in Berg and Clifford, eds., *Consumption and Luxury*, pp. 147–68.

Coats, A. W. "Changing Attitudes to Labour in the Mid-Eighteenth Century," *Economic History Review* 11 (1958–9): 35–51.

Coclanis, Peter A. "The Wealth of British America on the Eve of the Revolution," *Journal of Interdisciplinary History* 21 (1990): 245–60.

Cohen, Lizbeth. "Citizens and Consumers in the United States in the Century of Mass Consumption," in Daunton and Hilton, eds., *The Politics of Consumption*, pp. 203–21.

Coleman, Donald C. "Proto-industrialization. A Concept Too Many," *Economic History Review* 36 (1983): 435–48.

Coleman, Mary T., and John Pencavel, "Changes in Working Hours of Male Employees, 1940–1988," *Industrial and Labor Relations Review* 46 (1993): 262–83.

"Trends in Market Work Behavior of Women Since 1940," *Industrial and Labor Relations Review* 46 (1993): 653–76.

Collier, Frances. *The Family Economy of the Working Classes in the Cotton Industry, 1784–1833* (Manchester: Manchester University Press, 1964).

Collins, Brenda, and Philip Ollerenshaw, eds., *The European Linen Industry in Historical Perspective* (Oxford: Oxford University Press, 2004).

Collins, E. J. T. "Dietary Change and Cereal Consumption in Britain in the Nineteenth Century," *Agricultural History Review* 23 (1975): 97–115.

"Why Wheat? Choice of Food Grains in Europe in the Nineteenth and Twentieth Century," *Agricultural History Review* 22 (1993): 7–38.

Corneo, Ciacoma, and Oliver Jeanne, "Conformism, Snobbism, and Conspicuous Consumption," *Journal of Public Economics* 66 (1997): 55–71.

"Demonstrative Consumption, Rivalry and Development" (unpublished paper, Jena Workshop on "Escaping Satiation," 11–13 Dec. 1997).

"Segmented Communication and Fashionable Behavior," *Journal of Economic Behavior and Organization* 39 (1999): 371–85.

Costa, Dora. "The Unequal Work Day. A Long Term View," *American Economic Review* 88 (1998): 330–4.

"The Wage and Length of the Workday. From the 1890s to 1991," *Journal of Labor Economics* 18 (2000): 156–81.

"Understanding the American Decline in Social Capital, 1952–1998," *Kyklos* 56 (2003): 17–46.

Cowan, Ruth Schwartz. *More Work for Mother* (New York: Basic Books, 1983).

Crafts, N. F. R. "Some Dimensions of the Quality of Life During the British Industrial Revolution," *Economic History Review* 50 (1997): 617–39.

"Income Elasticities of Demand and the Release of Labour by Agriculture During the British Industrial Revolution," *Journal of European Economic History* 9 (1980): 156–9.

Crafts, N. F. R. and C. K. Harley, "Output Growth and the Industrial Revolution. A Restatement of the Crafts–Harley View," *Economic History Review* 45 (1992): 703–30.

Creighton, Colin. "The Rise of the Male Breadwinner Family. A Reappraisal," *Comparative Studies in Society and History* 38 (1996): 310–37.

Cross, Gary. "Worktime and Industrialization. An Introduction," in Gary Cross, ed., *Worktime and Industrialization. An International History* (Philadelphia: Temple University Press, 1988), pp. 3–20.

A Quest for Time. The Reduction of Work in Britain and France, 1840–1940 (Berkeley: University of California Press, 1989).

Time and Money. The Making of Consumer Culture (London: Routledge, 1993).

Crowley, John. "From Luxury to Comfort and Back Again. Landscape Architecture and the Cottage in Britain and America," in Berg and Eger, eds., *Luxury in the Eighteenth Century*, pp. 135–50.

Cullen, L. M. *The Brandy Trade under the Ancien Régime. Regional Specialisation in the Charente* (Cambridge: Cambridge University Press, 1988).

Cunningham, Hugh. "The Employment and Unemployment of Children in England c. 1680–1851," *Past and Present* 126 (1990): 115–50.

"The Decline of Child Labour. Labour Markets and Family Economies in Europe and North America Since 1830," *Economic History Review* 53 (2000): 409–28.

Cunnington, C. W., and Phyllis Cunnington. *The History of Underclothes* (London: M. Joseph, 1951).

Cutler, Joanne, and Kenny Turnbill. "A Disaggregated Approach to Modelling Labour Force Participation," External MPC Unit Discussion Paper No. 4 (London: Bank of England, 2001).

Daniel, K. "The Marriage Premium," Ierulli and Tommasi, eds., *New Economics of Human Behavior*, pp. 113–25.

Daunton, Martin. *House and Home in the Victorian City. Working Class Housing, 1850–1914* (London: Edward Arnold, 1983).

"The Political Economy of Taxation, 1815–1914," in Donald Winch and Patrick O'Brien, eds., *The Political Economy of British Historical Experience, 1688–1914* (Oxford: Oxford University Press, 2002), pp. 319–50.

Daunton, Martin, and Matthew Hilton, eds., *The Politics of Consumption. Material Culture and Citizenship in Europe and America* (Oxford and New York: Berg, 2001).

David, Paul, and William Sundstrom. "Old-Age Security Motives, Labor Markets, and Family Farm Fertility in Antebellum America," *Explorations in Economic History* 25 (1988): 164–97.

Davidoff, Leonore. "The Family in Britain," in F. M. L. Thompson, ed., *The Cambridge Social History of Britain, 1750–1950*, Vol. 2 (Cambridge: Cambridge University Press, 1990), pp. 71–130.

Davidoff, Leonore, and Catherine Hall. *Family Fortunes. Men and Women of the English Middle Class 1780–1850* (London: Hutchinson, 1987).

Davidson, Caroline. *A Woman's Work Is Never Done. A History of Housework in the British Isles, 1650–1950* (London: Chatto and Windus, 1982).

Davidson, Lee. "Experiments in the Social Regulation of Industry. Gin Legislation, 1729–51," in Lee Davidson, et al., eds., *Stilling the Grumbling Hive. The Response to Social and Economic Problems in England, 1689–1750* (New York: St. Martin's Press, 1992), pp. 25–48.

Davin, Anna. "Child Labour, The Working-Class Family, and Domestic Ideology in 19th Century Britain," *Development and Change* 13 (1982): 633–52.

Davis, Ralph. *The Industrial Revolution and British Overseas Trade* (Leicester: Leicester University Press, 1979),

Deane, Phyllis, and W. A. Cole. *British Economic Growth, 1688–1959*, second ed. (Cambridge: Cambridge University Press, 1969).

Deaton, Angus. "The Great Escape. A Review of Robert Fogel's *The Great Escape from Hunger and Premature Death, 1700–2100*," *Journal of Economic Literature* 44 (2006): 106–14.

Deceulaer, Harald. "Urban Artisans and Their Countryside Customers. Different Interactions Between Town and Hinterland in Antwerp, Brussels and Ghent

(18th Century)," in Bruno Blondé, E. Verhaute, and M. Galand, eds., *Labour and Labour Markets Between Town and Countryside (Middle Ages–19th Century)* (Turnhout: Brepols, 2001), pp. 218–35.

"Consumptie en distributie van kleding tussen stad en platteland," *Tijdschrift voor geschiedenis* 28 (2002): 439–68.

Defoe, Daniel. *The Compleat English Tradesman*, 2 vols. (London, 1726–7).

A Plan of the English Commerce (London, 1728).

de Grazia, Victoria. "Changing Consumption Regimes," in de Grazia and Furlough, eds., *The Sex of Things*, pp. 11–24.

de Grazia, Victoria, and E. Furlough, eds. *The Sex of Things. Gender and Consumption in Historical Perspective* (Berkeley: University of California Press, 1996).

Dejongh, G., and E. Thoen. "Arable productivity in Flanders and the former territory of Belgium in a long term perspective," in Van Bavel and Thoen, eds., *Land Productivity and Agro-Systems in the North Sea Area* (Turnhout: Brepols, 1999), pp. 30–65.

Dekker, Rudolf. "'Private Vices, Public Virtues' Revisited. The Dutch Background of Bernard Mandeville," *History of European Ideas* 14 (1992): 481–98.

de la Court, Pieter. *Welvaren der stad Leyden* ([1659, in manuscript] The Hague: F. Driessen, 1911).

de la Court, Johan and Pieter. *Politieke Discoursen* 2 vols. (Amsterdam, 1662).

Fables Moral and Political, With Large Explications, 2 Vols. ([original ed., *Zinrijken Fabulen*, Amsterdam: [1685] London, 1703).

de Marchi, Niel. "Adam Smith's Accommodation of 'Altogether Endless' Desires," in Berg and Clifford, eds., *Consumers and Luxury*, pp. 18–36.

Demergny, Louis. *La Chine et l'occident. Le commerce à Canton au XVIIIe siècle* 3 Vols. (Paris, SEVPEN, 1964).

de Peuter, Roger. *Brussel in de achttiende eeuw* (Brussels: VUB Press, 1999).

de Vries, Jan. "Boserup as Economics and History," *Peasant Studies Newsletter* 1 (1972): 45–50.

"Peasant Demand Patterns and Economic Development. Friesland, 1550–1700," in William N. Parker and Eric L. Jones, eds., *European Peasants and Their Markets* (Princeton, N.J.: Princeton University Press, 1975), pp. 205–66.

European Urbanization, 1500–1800 (London: Methuen, 1984).

"Art History," in de Vries and Freedberg, eds., *Art in History, History in Art*, pp. 249–82.

"Between Purchasing Power and the World of Goods. Understanding the Household Economy in Early Modern Europe," in Brewer and Porter, eds., *Consumption and the World of Goods*, pp. 85–132.

"The Labour Market," in Karel Davids and Leo Noordegraaf, eds. *Economic and Social History in the Netherlands* (Amsterdam: NEHA, 1993), pp. 55–78.

"The Industrial Revolution and the Industrious Revolution," *Journal of Economic History* 54 (1994): 249–70.

"An Employer's Guide to Wages and Working Conditions in the Netherlands, 1450–1850," in Carol S. Leonard and B. N. Mironov, eds., *Hours of Work and Means of Payment. The Evolution of Conventions in Pre-Industrial*

Europe (Milan: Eleventh International Economic History Congress, 1994), pp. 47–64.

"The Republic's Money. Money and the Economy," *Leidschrift* 13 (1998): 7–30.

"Economic Growth Before and After the Industrial Revolution. A Modest Proposal," in Maarten Prak, ed., *Early Modern Capitalism* (London: Routledge, 2001), pp. 177–94.

"Connecting Europe and Asia. A Quantitative Analysis of the Cape-route Trade, 1497–1795," in Dennis Flynn, Arturo Giráldez, and Richard von Glahn, eds., *Global Connections and Monetary History, 1470–1800* (Aldershot, Hants.: Ashgate, 2003), pp. 35–106.

"Luxury in the Dutch Golden Age in Theory and Practice," in Berg and Eger, eds., *Luxury in the Eighteenth Century*, pp. 41–56.

de Vries, Jan, and David Freedberg, eds. *Art in History, History in Art* (Santa Monica, Calif.: Getty Center, 1991).

de Vries, Jan, and Ad van der Woude. *The First Modern Economy. Success, Failure, and Perseverance of the Dutch Economy, 1500–1815* (Cambridge: Cambridge University Press, 1997).

Dewald, J. *Pont-St.-Pierre, 1398–1789. Lordship, Community, and Capitalism in Early Modern France* (Berkeley: University of California Press, 1987).

Dibbits, Hester. "Between Society and Family Values. The Linen Cupboard in Early Modern Households," in Anton Schuurman and Pieter Spierenburg, eds., *Private Domain, Public Inquiry. Families and Life-Styles in the Netherlands and Europe, 1550 to the Present* (Hilversum: Verloren, 1996), pp. 125–45.

Vertrouwd bezit. Materiële cultuur in Doesburg en Maassluis, 1650–1800 (Amsterdam: SUN Memoria, 2000).

Diderot, Dennis. "Regrets on Parting with My Old Dressing Gown" [Regrets sur ma vieille robe de chambre ou avis à ceux qui plus de gout que de fortune (1772)], in *Rameau's Nephew and Other Works by Dennis Diderot* (New York: Bobbs-Merrill, 1964; trans. Jacques Barzun), pp. 309–17.

Douglas, Mary, and Baron Isherwood, *The World of Goods. Toward an Anthropology of Consumption* (New York: W. W. Norton, 1979).

Duesenberry, James S. *Income, Savings, and the Theory of Consumer Behavior* (Cambridge, Mass.: Harvard University Press, 1949).

Dyer, Christopher. *Standards of Living in the Later Middle Ages. Social Change in England c. 1200–1520* (Cambridge: Cambridge University Press, 1989).

Dwyer, Daisy, and Judith Bruce, ed., *A Home Divided. Women and Income in the Third World* (Stanford, Calif.: Stanford University Press, 1988).

Earl, Peter E. *Lifestyle Economics* (New York: St. Martin's Press, 1986).

Earle, Peter. *The World of Defoe* (London: Weidenfeld and Nicolson, 1976).

The Making of the English Middle Class. Business, Society, and Family Life in London, 1660–1730 (London: Methuen, 1989).

"The Female Labour Market in London in the Late Seventeenth and Early Eighteenth Centuries," *Economic History Review* 42 (1989): 328–53

Eden, Sir Frederick Morton. *The State of the Poor. A History of the Labouring Classes in England, With Parochial Reports* ([3 vols., London, 1797] abridged ed., A. G. L. Rogers, ed., London: George Routledge and Sons, 1928).

Edlund, Laila Haider, and Rohindi Pande, "Why Have Women Become Left-Wing? The Political Gender Gap and the Decline of Marriage," *Quarterly Journal of Economics* 117 (2002): 917–61.

"Unmarried Parenthood and Redistributive Politics," *Journal of the European Economics Association* 3 (2005): 95–119.

Eisner, Robert. *The Total Incomes System of Accounts* (Chicago: University of Chicago Press, 1989).

Elias, Norbert. *The Civilizing Process* (Oxford: Basil Blackwell, 1978).

The Court Society (Oxford: Basil Blackwell, 1983).

Ellis, Aytoun. *The Penny Universities. A History of the Coffee-Houses* (London: Secker and Warburg, 1956).

Elvin, Mark. *The Pattern of the Chinese Past* (Stanford, Calif.: Stanford University Press, 1973).

Estabrook, Carl B. *Urbane and Rustic England. Cultural Ties and Social Spheres in the Provinces, 1660–1780* (Manchester: Manchester University Press, 1998).

Evans, Richard J. "Politics and the Family. Social Democracy and the Working-Class Family in Theory and Practice Before 1914," in Richard J. Evans and W. Robert Lee, eds., *The German Family. Essays on the Social History of the Family in Nineteenth- and Twentieth-Century Germany* (London: Croom Helm, 1981).

Eversley, D. E. C. "The Home Market and Economic Growth in England, 1750–1780," in Eric L. Jones and G. E. Mingay, eds., *Land, Labour and Population in the Industrial Revolution* (London: Edward Arnold, 1967), pp. 206–59.

Fairchild, Cissie. "The Production and Marketing of Populuxe Goods in Eighteenth-Century Paris," in Brewer and Porter, eds., *Consumption and the World of Goods*, pp. 228–48.

"Consumption in Early Modern Europe. A Review Article," *Comparative Studies in Society and History* 35 (1993): 850–8.

"Determinants of Consumption Patterns in Eighteenth-Century France," in Schuurman and Walsh, eds. *Material Culture. Consumption, Life-Style, Standard of Living, 1500–1900*, pp. 55–70.

Feinstein, Charles. "Pessimism Perpetuated. Real Wages and the Standard of Living in Britain During and After the Industrial Revolution," *Journal of Economic History* 58 (1998): 625–58.

Fildes, Valarie, ed. *Women as Mothers in Pre-Industrial England. Essays in Memory of Dorothy McLaren* (New York: Routledge, 1990)

Fine, Ben, and Ellen Leopold, "Consumerism and the Industrial Revolution," *Social History* 15 (1990): 151–79.

Finlay, Robert. "The Pilgrim Art. The Culture of Porcelain in World History," *Journal of World History* 9 (1998): 141–87.

Finn, Margot. *The Character of Credit. Personal Debt in English Culture, 1740–1914* (Cambridge: Cambridge University Press, 2003).

Fisher, F. J. "The Development of London as a Centre for Conspicuous Consumption," *Transactions of the Royal Historical Society*, fourth series, 30 (1948): 37–50.

Fletcher, Ron. *The Shaking of the Foundations. Family and Society* (London: Routledge, 1988).

Floud, Roderick, Kenneth Wachter, and A. Gregory. *Height, Health and History. Nutritional Status in the United Kingdom, 1750–1890* (Cambridge: Cambridge University Press, 1990).

Fock, C. W. "Wonen aan het Leidse Rapenburg door de eeuwen heen," in P. M. M. Klep, et al., *Wonen in het verleden* (Amsterdam: NEHA, 1987), pp. 189–205.

Fogel, Robert W. "Nutrition and the Decline in Mortality Since 1700. Some Preliminary Findings," in Stanley Engerman and Robert Gallman, eds., *Long-Term Factors in American Economic Growth* (Chicago: University of Chicago Press, 1986), pp. 439–527.

"The Conquest of High Mortality and Hunger in Europe and America. Timing and Mechanisms," in Patrice Higonnet, David S. Landes, and Henry Rosovsky, eds., *Favorites of Fortune. Technology, Growth, and Economic Development Since the Industrial Revolution* (Cambridge, Mass.: Harvard University Press, 1991), pp. 33–71.

"New Sources and New Techniques for the Study of Secular Trends in Nutritional Status, Health, Mortality, and the Process of Aging," *Historical Methods* 26 (1993): 5–44.

The Escape from Hunger and Premature Death 1700–2100. Europe, America, and the Third World (Cambridge: Cambridge University Press, 2004).

Folbre, Nancy. "Hearts and Spades. Paradigms of Household Economics," *World Development* 14 (1986): 245–55.

Who Pays for the Kids? Gender and the Structures of Constraint (London: Routledge, 1994).

Fontaine, Laurence. "The Circulation of Luxury Goods in Eighteenth-Century Paris. Social Redistribution and an Alternative Currency," in Berg and Eger, eds., *Luxury in the Eighteenth Century*, pp. 89–102.

Fox, Richard Wightman, and T. J. Jackson Lears, eds. *The Culture of Consumption. Critical Essays in American History, 1880–1980* (New York: Pantheon Books, 1983).

Freudenberger, Herman. "Das Arbeitjahr," in Ingomar Bog, et al., eds., *Wirtschaftliche und soziale Strukturen im säkularen Wandel, Vol. 2, Die vorindustrielle Zeit. Ausseragrarische Probleme* (Hanover: M. & H. Schaper, 1974), pp. 307–20.

Freudenberger, Herman, and Gaylord Cummins, "Health, Work, and Leisure Before the Industrial Revolution," *Explorations in Economic History* 13 (1976): 1–12.

Fridlizius, G. "Sex-Differential Mortality and Socio-Economic Change. Sweden, 1759–1910," in Anders Brändström and Lars-Göran Tedebrand, eds., *Society, Health and Population During the Demographic Transition* (Stockholm: Almqvist and Wiksell International, 1988), pp. 237–72.

Fuchs, Victor R. *Women's Quest for Economic Equality* (Cambridge, Mass.: Harvard University Press, 1988).

Furniss, Edgar S. *The Position of Labor in a System of Nationalism* (New York: Houghton Mifflin, 1920).

Galbraith, John Kenneth. *The Affluent Society* (Boston: Houghton Mifflin, 1958).

Gallman, Robert and John Wallis, eds., *American Economic Growth and Standards of Living Before the Civil War* (Chicago: University of Chicago Press, 1992).

Garnot, Benoît. *Un déclin. Chartres au XVIIIe siècle* (Paris: Editions de L.T.H.S., 1991).

La culture matérielle en France aux XVIIe, XVIIe et XVIIIe siècles (Paris: Ophrys, 1995).

Garrioch, David. *Neighbourhood and Community in Paris, 1740–1790* (Cambridge: Cambridge University Press, 1986).

Gershuny, Jonathan. *Social Innovation and the Division of Labour* (Oxford: Oxford University Press, 1983).

Gershuny, Jonathan, and John P. Robinson. "Historical Changes in the Household Division of Labor," *Demography* 25 (1988): 537–52.

Gershuny, Jonathan, M. Godwin, and S. Jones, "The Domestic Labour Revolution. A Process of Lagged Adaptation," in Anderson, Bechhofer, and Gershuny, eds., *The Social and Political Economy of the Household*, pp. 151–97.

Gilboy, Elizabeth Waterman. "Demand as a Factor in the Industrial Revolution," in A. H. Cole, ed., *Facts and Factors in Economic History* (Cambridge, Mass.: Harvard University Press, 1932). Reprinted in Robert M. Hartwell, ed., *The Causes of the Industrial Revolution* (London: Methuen, 1967), pp. 121–38.

Gillis, John R. *For Better, For Worse. British Marriages, 1600 to the Present* (Oxford: Oxford University Press, 1985).

Glass, David. *Social Mobility in Britain* (London: Routledge & Kegan Paul, 1966).

Glennie, Paul. "Consumption within Historical Studies," in Miller, ed., *Acknowledging Consumption*, pp. 164–203.

Glennie, Paul, and Nigel Thrift. "The Spaces of Time" (University of Bristol, unpublished ms, 1999).

Golden, Lonnie, and Deborah M. Figart, eds. *Working Time, International Trends, Theory and Policy Perspectives* (London: Routledge, 2000).

Goldin, Claudia. "Household and Market Production of Families in a Late Nineteenth Century American City," *Explorations in Economic History* 16 (1979): 111–31.

Understanding the Gender Gap. An Economic History of American Women (Oxford: Oxford University Press, 1990).

"The U-Shaped Female Labor Force Function in Economic Development and Economic History," in T. Paul Shultz, ed., *Investment in Women's Human Capital* (Chicago: University of Chicago Press, 1995), pp. 61–90.

"The Quiet Revolution That Transformed Women's Employment, Education, and Family," *American Economic Review* 96 (2006): 1–21.

Goldstone, Jack A. "Gender, Work and Culture. Why the Industrial Revolution Came Early to England but Late to China," *Sociological Perspectives* 39 (1996): 1–22.

Goodman, Dena. "Furnishing Discourses. Reading of a Writing Desk in Eighteenth-Century France," in Berg and Eger, eds., *Luxury in the Eighteenth Century*, pp. 71–88.

Goodman, Jordan. *Tobacco in History. The Cultures of Dependency* (London: Routledge, 1994).

Gorski, Philip S. "The Protestant Ethic Revisited. Disciplinary Revolution and State Formation in Holland and Prussia," *American Journal of Sociology* 99 (1993): 265–316.

The Disciplinary Revolution. Calvinism and the Rise of the State in Early Modern Europe (Chicago: University of Chicago Press, 2003).

Grantham, George. "Agricultural Supply During the Industrial Revolution. French Evidence and European Implications," *Journal of Economic History* 49 (1989): 43–72.

"Division of Labour. Agricultural Productivity and Occupational Specialization in Pre-Industrial France," *Economic History Review* 46 (1993): 478–502.

Gray, Jane. "The Irish and Flemish Linen Industries During the Long Eighteenth Century," in Collins and Ollerenshaw, eds., *The European Linen Industry*, pp. 159–86.

Gray, Jeffrey S. "The Fall in Men's Return to Marriage. Declining Productivity Effects or Changing Selection?," *Journal of Human Resources* 32 (1997): 481–504.

Grossbard-Shechtman, Shoshana. "Marriage Market Models," in Ierulli and Tommasi, eds., *The New Economics of Human Behavior*, pp. 92–112.

Gualerzi, Davide. "Economic Change, Choice and Innovation in Consumption," in Marina Bianchi, ed., *The Active Consumer*, pp. 46–63.

Gullickson, Gay L. "Womanhood and Motherhood. The Rouen Manufacturing Community, Women Workers, and the French Factory Acts," in Rudoph, ed., *European Peasant Family and Society*, pp. 206–32.

Guoto, Zhuang. "The Impact of the Tea Trade in the Social Economy of Northwestern Fujian in the Eighteenth Century," in Leonard Blussè and Femme Gaastra, eds., *On the Eighteenth Century as a Category of Asian History. Van Leur in Retrospect* (Aldershot, Hants.: Ashgate, 1998), pp. 193–216.

Gustafsson, Siv. "Public Policies and Women's Labor Force Participation. A Comparison of Sweden, West Germany, and the Netherlands," in T. Paul Shultz, ed., *Investment in Women's Human Capital* (Chicago: University of Chicago Press, 1995), pp. 91–112.

Habermas, Jurgen. "Konsumkritik," *Frankfurter Hefte* 12 (1957): 641–5.

Hajnal, John. "European Marriage Patterns in Perspective," in D. V. Glass and D. E. C. Eversley, eds., *Population in History. Essays in Historical Demography* (London: Edward Arnold, 1965), pp. 101–43.

"Two Kinds of Preindustrial Household Formation System," *Population and Development Review* 8 (1982): 449–94.

Haines, Michael R. *Fertility and Occupation. Population Patterns in Industrialization* (New York: Academic Press, 1979).

"Industrial Work and the Family Life Cycle," *Research in Economic History* 4 (1979): 289–356.

Hair, P. E. H. "Bridal Pregnancy in Rural England in Earlier Centuries," *Population Studies* 20 (1966): 233–43.

Hall, Catherine. *White, Male, and Middle-Class. Explorations in Feminism and History* (Cambridge: Polity Press, 1992).

Hann, Andrew. *Production and Consumption in English Households, 1600–1750* (London: Routledge, 2004).

Hardy, A. *The Epidemic Streets. Infectious Disease and the Rise of Preventive Medicine, 1856–1900* (Oxford: Oxford University Press, 1993).

Hareven, Tamara K. *Family and Kin in Urban Communities, 1700–1930* (New York: New Viewpoints, 1977).

Family and Kin in Urban Communities, 1700–1930 (New York: Franklin Watts, 1983).

Harte, N. B. "State Control of Dress," in D. C. Coleman and A. H. John, eds., *Trade, Government and Economy in Pre-Industrial England. Essays Presented to F. J. Fisher* (London: Weidenfeld and Nicolson, 1976), pp. 132–65.

"The Economics of Clothing in the Late Seventeenth Century," *Textile History* 22 (1991): 277–96.

Hartman, Mary S. *The Household and the Making of History. A Subversive View of the Western Past* (Cambridge: Cambridge University Press, 2004).

Hartmann, Heidi. "Capitalism, Patriarchy and Job Segregation by Sex," *Signs* 1 (1976): 137–69.

"The Family as the Locus of Gender, Class and Political Struggle. The Example of Housework," *Signs* 6 (1981): 366–94.

Hartwell, Robert M. "The Rising Standard of Living in England, 1800–1850," *Economic History Review* 13 (1961): 397–416.

"The Standard of Living. An Answer to the Pessimists," *Economic History Review* 16 (1963): 135–46.

Hatcher, John. "England in the Aftermath of the Black Death," *Past and Present* 144 (1994): 3–35.

Haupt, H.-G. *Konsum und Handel. Europa im 19. und 20. Jahrhundert* (Göttingen, 2002).

Hausen, Karen. "The German Mother's Day, 1923–33," in David Sabean and Hans Medick, eds., *Interest and Emotion* (Cambridge: Cambridge University Press, 1984), pp. 371–414.

Hayami, Akira. "A Great Transformation. Social and Economic Change in Sixteenth and Seventeenth Century Japan," *Bonner Zeitschrift für Japanologie* 8 (1986): 3–13.

"The Industrious Revolution," *Look Japan* 38 (1992): 38–43.

Hewitt, Patricia. *About Time. The Revolution in Work and Family Life* (London: Rivers Oram Press, 1993).

Higgs, Edward. "Domestic Service and Household Production," in Angela V. John, ed., *Unequal Opportunities. Women's Employment in England 1800–1918* (Oxford: Basil Blackwell, 1986), pp. 125–50.

Higgs, Henry. "Workmen's Budgets," *Journal of the Royal Statistical Society* 56 (1893): 255–85.

Hill, Bridget. *Women, Work and Sexual Politics in Eighteenth-Century England* (Montreal and Kingston: McGill–Queen's University Press, 1989).

Hirsch, Fred. *Social Limits to Growth* (Cambridge, Mass.: Harvard University Press, 1976).

Hirschman, Albert. *The Passions and the Interests. Political Arguments for Capitalism Before its Triumph* (Princeton, N.J.: Princeton University Press, 1977).

Rival Views of Market Society and Other Recent Essays (New York: Viking, 1986).

Hobsbawm, Eric J. "The British Standard of Living, 1790–1850," *Economic History Review* 10 (1957): 46–68.

"The Standard of Living During the Industrial Revolution. A Discussion," *Economic History Review* 16 (1963): 119–34.

Hochshild, Arlie. *The Time Bind* (New York: Metropolitan Books, 1997).

Hodne, Fritz. "New Evidence on the History of Tobacco Consumption in Norway, 1655–1970," *Economy and History* 21 (1978): 114–25.

Holdsworth, Clare. "Women's Work and Family Health. Evidence from the Staffordshire Potteries, 1890–1920," *Continuity and Change* 12 (1997): 103–28.

Honeyman, Katrina, and Jordan Goodman. "Women's Work, Gender Conflict, and Labour Markets in Europe, 1500–1900," *Economic History Review* 44 (1991): 608–28.

Hopkins, Keith. "Work and Leisure in Pre-Industrial Society," *Past and Present* 29 (1964): 50–62.

Hoppe, G., and J. Langton. *Peasantry to Capitalism. Western Ostergotland in the Nineteenth Century* (Cambridge: Cambridge University Press, 1994).

Horkheimer, Max, and Theodor Adorno. *Dialectic of Enlightenment* ([1944] London: Allen Lane, 1973).

Horowitz, David. *The Morality of Spending. Attitudes Toward the Consumer Society in America, 1875–1940* (Baltimore: Johns Hopkins University Press, 1985).

Horrell, Sara. "Home Demand and British Industrialization," *Journal of Economic History* 56 (1996): 561–604.

Horrell, Sara, and Jane Humphries. "Old Questions, New Data and Alternative Perspectives. Families' Living Standards in the Industrial Revolution," *Journal of Economic History* 52 (1992): 849–80.

"Women's Labour Force Participation and the Transition to the Male-Breadwinner Family, 1790–1865," *Economic History Review* 48 (1995): 89–117.

"The Origins and Expansion of the Male Breadwinner Family. The Case of Nineteenth-Century Britain," in Janssens, ed., *The Rise and Decline of the Male Breadwinner Family?*, pp. 25–65.

Horrell, Sara, Jane Humphries, and Has-Joachim Voth. "Stature and Relative Deprivation. Fatherless Children in Early Industrial Britain," *Continuity and Change* 13 (1998): 73–115.

Hout, Michael, and Caroline Hanley. "The Overworked American Family. Trends and Nontrends in Working Hours, 1968–2001" (Survey Research Center Working Paper, University of California at Berkeley, 2002).

Howell, Martha. *Women, Production and Patriarchy in Late Medieval Cities* (Chicago: University of Chicago Press, 1986).

Hudson, Pat, and W. R. Lee, eds. *Women's Work and the Family Economy in Historical Perspective* (Manchester: Manchester University Press, 1990).

Hudson, Pat, and W. R. Lee. "Women's Work and the Family Economy in Historical Perspective," in Hudson and Lee, eds., *Women's Work and the Family Economy*, pp. 2–47.

Hufton, Olwen. "Women and the Family Economy in Eighteenth Century France," *French Historical Studies* 9 (1975): 1–22.

"Women in History. Early Modern Europe," *Past and Present* 101 (1983): 125–41.

Huizinga, Johan. *Dutch Civilization in the Seventeenth Century* ([Original Dutch ed., 1941] London: Collins, 1968).

Hume, David. *Essays Moral, Political and Literary* [1752], T. H. Green and T. H. Grose, eds. (London: Longmans, 1989), Vol. 1: "Of Commerce," pp. 287–99; "Of Refinement in the Arts," pp. 299–309.

A Treatise of Human Nature [1739–40], L. A. Selby-Bigge, ed.; second edition (Oxford: Oxford University Press, 1978).

Humphries, Jane. "Class Struggle and the Persistence of the Working-Class Family," *Cambridge Journal of Economics* 1 (1977): 241–58.

"'The Most Free from Objection...' The Sexual Division of Labor and Women's Work in Nineteenth-Century England," *Journal of Economic History* 47 (1987): 929–50.

"Enclosures, Common Rights and Women. The Proletarianization of Families in the Late Eighteenth and Early Nineteenth Centuries," *Journal of Economic History* 50 (1990): 17–42.

"'Lurking in the wings...' Women in the Historiography of the Industrial Revolution," *Business and Economic History* 20 (1991): 32–44.

Hundert, Edward. *The Enlightenment's Fable. Bernard Mandeville and the Discovery of Society* (Cambridge: Cambridge University Press, 1994).

"Mandeville, Rousseau and the Political Economy of Fantasy," in Berg and Eger, eds., *Luxury in the Eighteenth Century*, pp. 28–40.

Hunt, Alan. *Governance of the Consuming Passions. A History of Sumptuary Law* (New York: St. Martin's Press, 1996).

Hunt, Margaret. *The Middling Sort. Commerce, Gender and the Family in England* (Berkeley: University of California Press, 1996).

Ierulli, Kathryn, Edward L. Glaeser, and Mariano Tommasi. "Introduction," in Tommasi and Ierulli, eds., *The New Economics of Human Behavior*, pp. 1–12.

Imhof, Arthur. *Lebenserwartungen in Deutschland vom 17. bis 19. Jahrhundert* (Weinheim: VCH Verlagsanstalt, 1990).

James, Jeffrey. *Consumption and Development* (New York: St. Martin's Press, 1993).

Jansen, Arne C. "Twee Nederlandstalige gedichten van Bernard Mandeville," *Nieuw letterkundig magazijn* 23 (2005): 2–8.

Jansen, J. C. G. M. "Wilt U koffie of thee? Consumentengedrag in Maastricht in de achttiende eeuw," *NEHA-Jaarboek* 60 (1997): 36–68.

Janssens, Angélique. *Family and Social Change. The Household as a Process in an Industrializing Community* (Cambridge: Cambridge University Press, 1993).

Janssens, Angélique, ed. *The Rise and Decline of the Male Breadwinner Family? International Review of Social History*, Supplement 5 (1997).

Jardine, Lisa. *Worldly Goods. A New History of the Renaissance* (London: Macmillan, 1996).

Jay, Martin. *The Dialectical Imagination. A History of the Frankfurt School and the Institute of Social Research, 1923–1950* (Boston: Little, Brown and Co., 1973).

Jobse-van Putten, Jozien. *Eenvoudig maar voedzaam. Cultuurgeschiedenis van de dagelijkse maaltijd in Nederland* (Nijmegen: SUN Memoria, 1995).

Jörg, C. J. A. "Porcelain for the Dutch in the Seventeenth Century," in Rosemary E. Scott, ed., *The Porcelain of Jingdezhen* (London: Percival David Foundation of Chinese Art, 1993), pp. 183–205.

Johansen, Hans Christian. "How to Pay for Baltic Products?," in Wolfram Fischer, Marvin McInnis, and Jurgen Schneider, eds., *The Emergence of a World Economy 1500–1914*, 2 vols. (Wiesbaden: F. Steiner, 1986) I: 123–42.

John, A. V. ed. *Unequal Opportunities. Women's Employment in England, 1800–1918* (Oxford: Basil Blackwell, 1986).

Johnson, Paul. *Saving and Spending. The Working-class Economy in Britain, 1870–1939* (Oxford: Oxford University Press, 1985).

Johnson, Paul, and Stephen Nicholas. "Male and Female Living Standards in England and Wales, 1812–1857. Evidence from Criminal Height Records," *Economic History Review* 48 (1995): 470–81.

Jones, Colin. "Bourgeois Revolution Revivified. 1789 and Social Change," in Colin Lucas, ed., *Rewriting the French Revolution* (Oxford: Oxford University Press, 1991), pp. 69–118.

"The Great Chain of Buying. Medical Advertisement, the Bourgeois Public Sphere, and the Origins of the French Revolution," *American Historical Review* 101 (1996): 13–40.

Jones, Eric L. *Agriculture and Economic Growth in England, 1650–1815* (London: Methuen, 1967).

Agriculture and the Industrial Revolution (Oxford: Blackwell, 1974).

The European Miracle. Environments, Economies and Geopolitics in the History of Europe and Asia (Cambridge: Cambridge University Press, 1981).

Jones, Eric L., and M. E. Falkus. "Urban Improvement and the English Economy in the Seventeenth and Eighteenth Centuries," *Research in Economic History* 4 (1979): 193–233.

Jones, Jennifer M. "Coquettes and Grisettes. Women Buying and Selling in [the Old Regime] Ancien Regime Paris," in de Grazia and Furlough, eds., *The Sex of Things*, pp. 25–48.

"Repackaging Rousseau. Femininity and Fashion in Old Regime France, *French Historical Studies* 18 (1994): 939–67.

Juhn, Chinhui, and Simon Potter. "Changes in Labor Force Participation in the United States," *Journal of Economic Perspectives* 20 (2006): 27–46.

Juster, F. Thomas. "The Validity and Quality of Time Use Estimates Obtained from Recall Diaries," in Juster and Stafford, eds., *Time, Goods, and Well-Being*, pp. 63–92.

"A Note on Recent Changes in Time Use," in Juster and Stafford, eds., *Time, Goods, and Well-Being*, pp. 313–32.

Juster, F. Thomas, and Frank Stafford, eds. *Time, Goods, and Well-Being* (Ann Arbor: Institute of Social Research, University of Michigan, 1985).

Juster, F. Thomas, and Frank Stafford. "The Allocation of Time. Empirical Findings, Behavioral Models, and Problems of Measurement," *Journal of Economic Literature* 29 (1991): 471–522.

Kaelble, Hartmut. *Industrialisation and Social Inequality in Nineteenth Century Europe* (Leamington Spa: Berg Publishers, 1986).

Kamermans, Johan A. *Materiële cultuur in de Krimpenerwaard in de zeventiende en achttiende eeuw* (Wageningen: A.A.G. Bijdragen 39, 1999).

Kaplan, Steven L. *The Bakers of Paris and the Bread Question, 1700–1775* (Durham, N.C.: Duke University Press, 1996).

Kennedy, R. E. *The Irish. Emigration, Marriage and Fertility* (Berkeley: University of California Press, 1973).

Kermit, Daniel. "The Marriage Premium," in Tommasi and Ierulli, eds., *The New Economics of Human Behavior*, pp. 113–25.

Keynes, John Maynard. "Economic Possibilities for Our Grandchildren," in Keynes, *Essays in Persuasion* ([1931] New York: W. W. Norton, 1961), pp. 358–73.

King, Peter. "Pauper Inventories and the Material Lives of the Poor in the Eighteenth and Early Nineteenth Centuries," in T. Hitchcock, P. King, and P. Sharpe, eds., *Chronicling Poverty. The Voices and Strategies of the English Poor, 1640–1840* (New York: St. Martin's Press, 1997), pp. 155–91.

Kistemaker, Renee, et al., eds. *Peter de Grote en Holland* (Bussem: Amsterdam Historisch Museum, 1996).

Klasen, Stephan. "Marriage, Bargaining, and Intra-Household Resource Allocation. Excess Female Mortality Among Adults During Early German Development" (Harvard University, Ph.D. dissertation, 1994).

Kleinberg, S. J. "Children's and Mothers' Wage Labor in Three Eastern U.S. Cities, 1880–1920," *Social Science History* 29 (2005): 45–76.

Klep, P. M. M. "Female Labour in the Netherlands and Belgium, 1846–1910," (unpublished, Katholieke Universiteit Nijmegen, 1978).

Knotter, Ad. "Problemen van de family economy. Gezinsarbeid en arbeidsmarkt in pre-industrieël Europa," in Baud and Engelen, eds., *Samen wonen, Samen werken?*, pp. 35–71.

Kok, Jan. "Collectieve strategie en individuele levensloop," in Baud and Engelen, eds., *Samen wonen, samen werken?*, pp. 97–121.

Komlos, John. "Shrinking in a Growing Economy? The Mystery of Physical Stature During the Industrial Revolution," *Journal of Economic History* 58 (1998): 779–802.

Komlos, John, and Albert Ritschl. "Holy Days, Work Days and the Standard of Living in the Habsburg Monarchy," *Journal of Interdisciplinary History* 26 (1995): 57–66.

Kotlikoff, Laurence J., and A. Spivak. "The Family as an Incomplete Annuities Market," *Journal of Political Economy* 89 (1981): 942–63.

Kowaleski-Wallace, Elizabeth. *Consuming Subjects. Women, Shopping and Business in the Eighteenth Century* (New York: Columbia University Press, 1993).

Kozub, Robert M. "Evolution of Taxation in England, 1700–1815. A Period of War and Industrialization," *Journal of European Economic History* 32 (2003): 363–88.

Kriedte, Peter, Hans Medick, and Jürgen Schlumbohm, *Industrialization Before Industrialization* (Cambridge: Cambridge University Press, 1981).

Krugman, Paul. "The Myth of Asia's Miracle," *Foreign Affairs* 73 (1994): 62–78.

Kumar, Krishan. "Pre-capitalist and Non-capitalist Factors in the Development of Capitalism. Fred Kirsch and Joseph Schumpeter," in Adrian Ellis and Krishan Kumar, eds., *Dilemmas of Liberal Democracies* (London: Tavistock Publications, 1983), pp. 148–73.

Lancaster, Kelvin. *Modern Consumer Theory* (Aldershot, Hants.: Edward Elgar, 1991).

Landes, David. *The Unbound Prometheus. Technological Change and Industrial Development in Western Europe from 1750 to the Present* (Cambridge: Cambridge University Press, 1969).

The Revolution in Time. Clocks and the Making of the Modern World (Cambridge, Mass.: Harvard University Press, 1983).

Lane, Robert. "Friendship or Commodities? The Road Not Taken. Friendship, Consumerism, and Happiness," *Critical Review* 8 (1994): 521–54.

The Loss of Happiness in Market Democracies (New Haven, Conn.: Yale University Press, 2001).

Laslett, Peter. *The World We Have Lost* (London: Methuen, 1965).

"Long-Term Trends in Bastardy in England," in Peter Laslett, *Family Life and Illicit Love in Earlier Generations* (Cambridge: Cambridge University Press, 1977), pp. 102–59.

"Family and Household as Work Group and Kin Group. Areas of Traditional Europe Compared," in Richard Wall, Jean Robin, and Peter Laslett, eds., *Family Forms in Historic Europe* (Cambridge: Cambridge University Press, 1983), pp. 513–63.

"Introduction," in Peter Laslett, Karla Oosterveen and Richard M. Smith, eds., *Bastardy and Its Comparative History* (Cambridge, Mass.: Harvard University Press, 1980), pp. 1–65.

"Family, Kinship, and Collectivity as Systems of Support in Pre-Industrial Europe. A Consideration of the 'Nuclear Hardship' Hypothesis," *Continuity and Change* 3 (1988): 153–75.

Laslett, Peter, and Richard Wall, eds. *Household and Family in Past Time* (Cambridge: Cambridge University Press, 1972).

Lavoisier, A.-L. *De la richesse territoriale du royaume de France* (Jean Claude Perrot, ed., Paris: Editions du C.T.H.S., 1988).

Lazear, Edward P., and Robert T. Michael, *Allocation of Income within the Household* (Chicago: University of Chicago Press, 1988).

Leboutte, René, ed., *Proto-industrialisation. Recherches recentes et novelles perspectives. Mélanges en souvenir de Franklin Mendels* (Geneva: Librairie Droz, 1996).

Lee, James Z., and Wang Feng. *One Quarter of Humanity. Mathusian Mythology and Chinese Realities* (Cambridge, Mass.: Harvard University Press, 1999).

Lee, W. R. "Women's Work and the Family. Some Demographic Implications of Gender-Specific Rural Work Patterns in Nineteenth-Century Germany," in Hudson and Lee, eds., *Women's Work and the Family Economy*, pp. 50–75.

Lees, Lynn Hollen. "Getting and Spending. The Family Budgets of English Industrial Workers in 1890," in J. M. Merriman, ed., *Consciousness and Class Experience in Nineteenth-Century Europe* (New York: Holmes and Meier, 1979), pp. 169–86.

Lehndorff, Steffen. "Working Time Reduction in the European Union. A Diversity of Trends and Approaches," in Golden and Figart, eds., *Working Time*, pp. 38–56.

Lemire, Beverly. *Fashion's Favourite. The Cotton Trade and the Consumer in Britain, 1660–1800* (Oxford: Oxford University Press, 1991).

  Dress, Culture, and Commerce. The English Clothing Trade Before the Factory, 1660–1800 (New York: St. Martin's Press, 1997).

  "Second-hand Beaux and 'Red-armed Belles'. Conflict and the Creation of Fashions in England, c. 1660–1800," *Continuity and Change* 15 (2000): 391–417.

Lenman, Bruce P. "The English and Dutch East India Companies and the Birth of Consumerism in the Augustan World," *Eighteenth Century Life* 14 (1990): 47–65.

Le Play, Frederic. *Les ouvriers Européens* (Paris: Imprimerie impériale, 1855; 2nd ed. (Tours: Alfred Mame et fils, 1877–9).

Le Roy Ladurie, Emmanuel. "L'histoire immobile," *Annales: Economies, Sociètès. Civilisations.* 29 (1974): 673–92 (English trans. "Motionless History," *Social Science History* 1 (1977): 115–36).

Lesger, Clé. *Huur en conjunctuur. De woningmarkt in Amsterdam, 1550–1850* (Amsterdam: Amsterdamse Historische Reeks No. 10, 1986).

Lesthaeghe, Ronald. "On the Social Control of Human Reproduction," *Population and Development Review* 6 (1980): 527–48.

Leuillot, P. "Influence du commerice oriental sur l'économie occidentale," in Michel Mollat, *Sociètès et compagnies de commerce en orient et dans l'ocean Indien* (Paris, SEVPEN, 1970), pp. 611–29.

Levine, David. *Family Formation in an Age of Nascent Capitalism* (New York: Academic Press, 1977).

  "Consumer Goods and Capitalist Modernisation," *Journal of Interdisciplinary History* 22 (1991): 67–77.

Levy, Frank. *The New Dollars and Dreams. American Incomes and Economic Change* (New York: Russell Sage Foundation, 1998)

Lillywhite, Bryant. *London Coffee Houses* (London: George Allen and Unwin, 1963).

Linder, Staffan B. *The Harried Leisure Class* (New York: Columbia University Press, 1970).

Lindert, Peter. "Probates, Prices and Preindustrial Living Standards," in Baulant, Schuurman, and Servais, eds., *Inventaire après-deces*, pp. 171–80.

Loane, Margery. *The Queen's Poor. Life as They Found It* (London: Edward Arnold, 1910).

Lugar, C. "The Portuguese Tobacco Trade and Tobacco Growers of Bahia in the Late Colonial Period," in D. Alden and W. Dean, eds., *Essays Concerning the Socio-Economic History of Brazil and Portuguese India* (Gainesville, Fla.: University Presses of Florida, 1977).

Lundberg, Shelly J., Robert A. Pollak, and Terence J. Wales, "Do Husbands and Wives Pool Their Resources? Evidence from the United Kingdom Child Benefit," *Journal of Human Resources* 32 (1997): 463–80.

Lundberg, Shelly J., and Robert A. Pollak. "Bargaining and Distribution in Marriage," *Journal of Economic Perspectives* 10 (1996): 139–58.

"The American Family and Family Economics," *Journal of Economic Perspectives* 21 (2007): 3–26.

Lynch, Katherine A. *Family, Class, and Ideology in Early Industrial France. Social Policy and the Working-Class Family, 1825–1848* (Madison: University of Wisconsin Press, 1988).

"The Family and the History of Public Life," *Journal of Interdisciplinary History* 24 (1994): 665–84.

Individuals, Families, and Communities in Europe, 1200–1800. The Urban Foundations of Western Society (Cambridge: Cambridge University Press, 2003).

Lyons, John. "Family Response to Economic Decline. Handloom Weavers in Early Nineteenth Century Lancashire," *Research in Economic History* 12 (1989): 45–91.

McBride, Theresa M. *Domestic Revolution. The Modernisation of Household Service in England and France, 1820–1920* (London: Croom Helm, 1976).

McCants, Anne. "The Not-So-Merry Widows of Amsterdam, 1740–1782," *Journal of Family History* 24 (1999): 441–67.

"Petty Debts and Family Networks. The Credit Markets of Widows and Wives in Eighteenth-Century Amsterdam," in Beverly Lemire, et al., eds., *Women and Credit. Researching the Past, Refiguring the Future* (Oxford: Berg Publishers, 2001), pp. 33–50.

"Poor Consumers as Global Consumers. The Diffusion of Tea and Coffee Drinking in the Eighteenth Century," *Economic History Review* (2007, forthcoming).

"Inequality Among the Poor of Eighteenth-Century Amsterdam," *Explorations in Economic History* 44 (2005): 1–21.

"Goods at Pawn. The Overlapping Worlds of Material Possessions and Family Finance in Early Modern Amsterdam," *Social Science History* 31 (2007): 213–38.

McCusker, John J. "The Business of Distilling in the Old World and the New World During the Seventeenth and Eighteenth Centuries. The Rise of a New Enterprise and Its Connection with Colonial America," in John J. McCusker and Kenneth Morgan, eds., *The Early Modern Atlantic Economy* (Cambridge: Cambridge University Press, 2000), pp. 186–224.

McCusker, John, and Russell Menard. *Economy of British North America, 1607–1789* (Chapel Hill: University of North Carolina Press, 1985).

Macfarlane, Alan. *The Origins of English Individualism. The Family, Property, and Social Transition* (Cambridge: Cambridge University Press, 1978).

Marriage and Love in England. Modes of Reproduction, 1300–1840 (Oxford: Basil Blackwell, 1986).

The Culture of Capitalism (Oxford: Blackwell, 1987).

McKendrick, Neil. "Home Demand and Economic Growth. A New View of the Role of Women and Children in the Industrial Revolution," in Neil McKendrick, ed., *Historical Perspectives. Studies in English Thought and Society in Honour of J. H. Plumb* (London: Europa Publications, 1974), pp. 152–210.

"The Consumer Revolution in Eighteenth-Century England," in McKendrick, Brewer, and Plumb, eds., *The Birth of a Consumer Society*, pp. 9–33.

McKendrick, Neil, John Brewer, and J. H. Plumb, eds. *The Birth of a Consumer Society. The Commercialization of Eighteenth-Century England* (Bloomington: Indiana University Press, 1982).

McKeown, Thomas. *The Modern Rise of Population* (New York: Academic Press, 1976).

Madisson, Angus. *Monitoring the World Economy, 1820–1992* (Paris: OECD, 1995).

The World Economy. A Millennnial Perspective (Paris: OECD, 2001).

Main, Gloria. "Gender, Work and Wages in Colonial New England," *William and Mary Quarterly* 51 (1994): 36–66.

Main, Gloria, and Jackson T. Main. "Economic Growth and the Standard of Living in Southern New England, 1640–1774," *Journal of Economic History* 48 (1988): 27–46.

Malcolmson, R. W. *Life and Labour in England, 1700–1780* (New York: St. Martin's Press, 1981).

Mandeville, Bernard. *The Fable of the Bees, or Private Vices, Public Benefits* [1714, 1723, 1733], Douglas Garmen, ed. (London: Wishart, 1934).

The Fable of the Bees and Other Writings. Abridged and edited by E. J. Hundert ([1732 ed.] Indianapolis and Cambridge: Hackett Publishing, 1997).

De wereld gaat aan deugd ten onder. Collected work, Vol. 1. Translation and commentary by Arne C. Jansen (Zwolle: Lemniscaat, 2006).

Marchand, Roland. *Advertising the American Dream. Making Way for Modernity, 1920–1940* (Berkeley: University of California Press, 1985).

Marcuse, Herbert. *Eros and Civilization. A Philosophical Inquiry into Freud* ([1955] New York: Vintage Books, 1962).

One-Dimensional Man (Boston: Beacon Press, 1964).

Marczewski, Jan. "Some Aspects of the Economic Growth of France, 1660–1958," *Economic Development and Cultural Change* 9 (1961): 369–86.

Mare, Robert D. "Five Decades of Educational Assortative Mating," *American Sociological Review* 56 (1991): 15–32.

Markovitch, T. J. *L'industrie Française de 1789 a 1964* (Paris: Droz, 1964).

Martin, John Levi. "The Myth of the Consumption-oriented Economy and the Rise of the Desiring Subject," *Theory and Society* 28 (1999): 425–53.

Marshall, Alfred. *The Principles of Economics* (London: Macmillan, 1890).

Marx, Karl. *Capital*, 3 vols. (Moscow: International Publishers, 1961).

Mathias, Peter. *The Brewing Industry in England, 1700–1830* (Cambridge: Cambridge University Press, 1959).

"Leisure and Wages in Theory and Practice," in Peter Mathias, *The Transformation of England* (London: Methuen, 1979), pp. 148–67.

Mazumdar, Sucheta. *Sugar and Society in China. Peasants, Technology and the World Market* (Cambridge, Mass.: Harvard University Press, 1998).

Medick, Hans. "The Proto-Industrial Family Economy. The Structural Function of Household and Family During the Transition from Peasant Society to Industrial Capitalism, *"Social History* 3 (1976): 291–315.

"The Proto-Industrial Family Economy" [extended version of article in *Social History*] in Kriede, Medick, and Schlumbohm, eds., *Industrialization Before Industrialization*, pp. 38–73.

"The Structure and Function of Population Development Under the Protoindustrial System," in Kriedte, Medick, and Schlumbohm, eds. *Industrialization Before Industrialization*, pp. 74–93.

Meillassoux, C. *Maidens, Meal and Money. Capitalism and the Domestic Community* (Cambridge: Cambridge University Press, 1981).

Mendels, Franklin. "Proto-Industrialization, the First Phase of the Industrialization Process," *Journal of Economic History* 32 (1972): 241–61.

"Niveau des salaries et âge au marriage en Flandre, XVIIe–XVIIIe siècle," *Annales, Economies, Sociétés, Civilisations* 39 (1984): 939–56.

"Des industries rurales à la proto-industrialisation. Historique d'un changement de perspective," *Annales, Economies, Sociétés, Civilisations* 39 (1984): 997–1008.

Michel, Lawrence, Jared Bernstein, and John Schmitt. *The State of Working America, 2000/2001* (Ithaca, N.Y.: Cornell University Press, 2001).

Michel, Lawrence, Jared Bernstein, and Heather Boushey. *The State of Working America, 2002/2003* (Ithaca, N.Y.: Cornell University Press, 2003).

Michel, Lawrence, Jared Bernstein, and Sylvia Allegretto. *The State of Working America, 2004/2005* (Ithaca, N.Y.: Cornell University Press, 2005).

Miles, Steven. *Consumerism as a Way of Life* (London: Sage, 1998).

Miller, Daniel. "Consumption as the Vanguard of History. A Polemic by Way of an Introduction," in Miller, ed., *Acknowledging Consumption*, pp. 1–57.

"Consumption Studies as the Transformation of Anthropology," in Miller, ed., *Acknowledging Consumption*, pp. 264–95.

Miller, Daniel, ed., *Acknowledging Consumption. A Review of New Studies* (London: Routledge, 1995).

Miller, Michael. *The Bon Marché. Bourgeois Culture and the Department Store, 1869–1920* (Princeton, N.J.: Princeton University Press, 1981).

Mincer, Jacob. "Labor Force Participation of Married Women," in National Bureau for Economic Research, *Aspects of Labor Force Economics* (Princeton, N.J.: Princeton University Press, 1962).

Mintz, Sidney W. *Sweetness and Power. The Place of Sugar in Modern History* (New York: Viking Press, 1985).

Mitch, David. "The Role of Education and Skill in the British Industrial Revolution," in Joel Mokyr, ed., *The British Industrial Revolution. An Economic Perspective* (Boulder, Colo.: Westview Press, 1993), pp. 241–79.

Mitchell, B. R., and Phyllis Deane, *Abstract of British Historical Statistics* (Cambridge: Cambridge University Press, 1969).

Michael Mitterauer, Michael. "Geschlechtsspezifischische Arbeitsteilung und Geschecterrollen in ländlichen Gesellschaften Mitteleuropas," in *Familie und Arbeitsteilung. Historischvergleichende Studien* (Wien/Koln: Böhlau, 1992), pp. 58–148.

Modell, John. "Patterns of Consumption, Acculturation, and Family Income Strategies in Late Nineteenth-Century America," in Tamara Hareven and Maris Vinovskis, eds., *Family and Population in Nineteenth Century America* (Princeton, N.J.: Princeton University Press, 1978), pp. 206–40.

Mohrmann, Ruth-E. *Alltagswelt in Braunschweig. Städtische und ländliche Wohnkultur vom 16. bis zum frühen 20. Jahrhundert*, 2 vols. (Münster: Waxmann, 1990).

Mokyr, Joel. "Demand vs. Supply in the Industrial Revolution," *Journal of Economic History* 37 (1977): 981–1008.

"Is There Still Life in the Pessimist Case. Consumption in the Industrial Revolution, 1790–1850," *Journal of Economic History* 48 (1988): 69–92.

"Editor's Introduction," in Joel Mokyr, ed., *The British Industrial Revolution. An Economic Perspective* (Boulder, Colo.: Westview Press, 1998), pp. 1–127.

The Lever of Riches. Technological Creativity and Economic Progress (Oxford: Oxford University Press, 1990).

"More Work for Mother? Knowledge and Household Behavior, 1870–1945," *Journal of Economic History* 60 (2000): 1–41.

"Accounting for the Industrial Revolution," in Roderick Floud and Paul Johnson, eds., *The Cambridge Economic History of Modern Britain, Vol I., Industrialisation, 1700–1860* (Cambridge: Cambridge University Press, 2004), pp. 1–27.

Montesquieu, Charles Louis de Secondat. Baron du. *The Spirit of the Laws* ([1748] New York: Hafner Publishers, 1949).

Morineau, Michel. *Incroyables gazettes et fabuleux métaux* (London and Paris: Cambridge University Press, 1985).

Muchembled, Robert. *Société et mentalités dans la France moderne, XVIIe–XVIIIe siècle* (Paris: A. Colin, 1990).

Mui, Hoh-Cheung, and Lorna H. Mui. *Shops and Shopkeeping in Eighteenth-Century England* (Kingston and Montreal" McGill–Queen's University Press, 1989).

Mukerji, Chandra. *From Graven Images. Patterns of Modern Materialism* (New York: Columbia University Press, 1983).

Muldrew, Craig. *The Economy of Obligation. The Culture of Credit and Social Relations in Early Modern England* (Basingstoke: Macmillan, 1998).

"'Hard Food for Midas'. Cash and Its Social Value in Early Modern England," *Past and Present* 170 (2001): 78–120.

Mun, Thomas, *England's Treasure by Forraign Trade or the Balance of our Forraign Trade in the Rule of Our Treasure* (London, 1664).

Muzumdar, Sucheta. *Sugar and Society in China. Peasants, Technology, and the World Market* (Cambridge, Mass.: Harvard University Press, 1998).

Nardinelli, Clark. *Child Labor and the Industrial Revolution* (Bloomington: Indiana University Press, 1990).

Nash, Robert C. "The English and Scottish Tobacco Trades in the Seventeenth and Eighteenth Centuries. Legal and Illegal Trade," *Economic History Review* 25 (1982): 354–72.

Nef, John U. *Cultural Foundations of Industrial Civilization* (Cambridge: Cambridge University Press, 1958).

Nenadic, Stana. "Middle-Rank Consumers and Domestic Culture in Edinburgh and Glasgow, 1720–1840," *Past and Present* 145 (1994): 122–56.

"Household Possessions and the Modernizing City. Scotland, c. 1720–1840," in Schuurman and Walsh, eds., *Material Culture*, pp. 147–60.

Nicholas, Stephen, and Deborah Oxley. "The Industrial Revolution and the Genesis of the Male Breadwinner," in Graeme D. Snooks, ed., *Was the Industrial Revolution Necessary?* (London: Routledge, 1994), pp. 96–111.

Noordegraaf, Leo. *Hollands welvaren? Levensstandaard in Holland, 1450–1650* (Bergen: Octavo, 1985).

Nordhaus, William. "Do Real Output and Real Wage Measures Capture Reality? The History of Lighting Suggests Not," in Tim Breshnahan and Robert Gordon, eds., *The Economics of New Goods* (Chicago: University of Chicago Press, 1997), pp. 29–66.

Nordhaus, William, and James Tobin. "Is Growth Obsolete?," in James Tobin, *Essays in Economics, Vol. III, Theory and Policy* (Cambridge, Mass.: MIT University Press, 1982), pp. 360–450.

North, Douglass. *Structure and Change in Economic History* (New York: W. W. Norton, 1981).

North, Dudley. *Discourse upon Trade* (London, 1691).

North, Michael. "Kultur und Konsum – Luxus und Geschmack um 1800," in Rolf Walter, ed., *Geschichte des Konsums* (Stuttgart: F. Steiner Verlag, 2004), pp. 17–33.

Norwich, Julius. *A History of Venice* (New York: Knopf, 1982).

Nye, John V. "The Myth of Free Trade. Britain and Fortress France," *Journal of Economic History* 51 (1991): 23–46.

O'Brien, Patrick. "The Political Economy of British Taxation, 1660–1815," *Economic History Review* 41 (1988), 1–32.

O'Brien, Patrick, and P. Hunt. "The Emergence and Consolidation of the Excise in the English Fiscal System Before the Glorious Revolution," *British Tax Review* 1 (1997): 35–58.

Oddy, Derek J. "Working-Class Diets in Late Nineteenth-Century Britain," *Economic History Review* 23 (1970): 314–23.

"Food, Drink, and Nutrition," in F. M. L. Thompson, ed., *The Cambridge Social History of Britain, 1750–1950*, Vol. 2 (Cambridge: Cambridge University Press, 1990), pp. 251–78.

Oddy, Derek J., and John Burnett. "British Diet Since Industrialization. A Bibliographical Study," in Teuteberg, ed., *European Food History*, pp. 19–44.

OECD. *Employment Outlook* (June 1998).

Offer, Avner. *The Challenge of Affluence. Self-Control and Well-Being in the United States and Britain Since 1950* (Oxford: Oxford University Press, 2006).

Ogilvie, Sheilagh C. "Women and Proto-industrialisation in a Corporate Society. Württemberg Woollen Weaving, 1590–1760," in Hudson and Lee, eds., *Women's Work and the Family Economy*, pp. 76–103.

A Bitter Living. Women, Markets, and Social Capital in Early Modern Germany (Oxford: Oxford University Press, 2003).

"Women and Labour Markets in Early Modern Germany," *Jahrbuch für Wirtschaftsgeschichte* 2004/2 (2004): 25–60.

Ogilvie, Sheilagh C., and Markus Cerman, eds., *European Proto-industrialization* (Cambridge: Cambridge University Press, 1996).

Orem, L. "The Welfare of Women in Laboring Families. England, 1860–1950," in Mary S. Hartman and Lois Banner, eds., *Clio's Consciousness Raised. New Perspectives on the History of Women* (New York: Harper & Row, 1974), pp. 226–44.

Overton, Mark. "Prices from Probate Inventories," in Tom Arkell, Nester Evans, and Nigel Goose, eds., *When Death Do Us Part. Understanding and Interpreting the Probate Records of Early Modern England* (Oxford: Leopard's Head Press, 2000), pp. 120–43.

"Household Wealth, Indebtedness, and Economic Growth in Early Modern England," *Economic History Review* (forthcoming).

Overton, Mark, Jane Whittle, Darron Dean, and Andrew Hann. *Production and Consumption in English Households, 1600–1750* (London: Routledge, 2004).

Pahl, Jan. *Money and Marriage* (London: Macmillan, 1989).

Panhuysen, Bibi. *Maatwerk. kleermakers, naaisters, oudkleerkopers en de gilden (1500–1800)* (Amsterdam: IISG, 2000).

Pardailhé-Galabrun, Annik. *The Birth of Intimacy. Private and Domestic Life in Early Modern Paris* (Cambridge: Polity Press, 1991).

Pareto, Vilfredo. *Manuel d' économie politique*, second ed. (Paris: Giard, 1927).

Parsons, Talcot. "The American Family. Its Relations to Personality and the Social Structure," in Talcot Parsons and Robert F. Bales, eds., *Family, Socialization and Interaction Process* (Glencoe, Ill.: The Free Press, 1955), pp. 3–33.

Pedersen, Susan. *Family, Dependence, and the Origins of the Welfare State. Britain and France, 1914–1945* (Cambridge: Cambridge University Press, 1994).

Perkins, Harold. *Origins of Modern English Society, 1780–1880* (London: Routledge & Kegan Paul, 1969).

Persson, K. G. "Consumption, Labour and Leisure in the Late Middle Ages," in D. Menjot, ed., *Manger et boire au Moyen Age* (Nice: Centre d' Études Médiéveles de Nice, 1984), pp. 211–23.

Petersen, Christian. *Bread and the British Economy, c. 1770–1870* (Aldershot, Hants.: Scolar Press, 1995).

Peterson, Mark A. "Puritanism and Refinement in Early New England. Reflections on Communion Silver," *William and Mary Quarterly* 58 (2001): 307–46.

Pfister, Ulrich. "The Protoindustrial Household Economy. Toward a Formal Analysis," *Journal of Family History* 17 (1992): 201–32.

Die Züricher Fariques. Protoindustrielles Wachstum vom 16. zum 18. Jahrhundert (Zürich: Chronos, 1992).

Phelps Brown, E. H., and Sheila V. Hopkins. "Seven Centuries of Builders' Wage-Rates," *Economics* 22 (1955): 195–206.

"Seven Centuries of Prices of Consumables Compared with Builders' Wage-Rates," *Economics* 23 (1956): 296–314.

Pierenkemper, Toni. *Haushalt und Verbrauch in historischer Perspective* (St. Katharinen: Scripta Mercaturae, 1987).

"Das Rechnungsbuch der Hausfrau – und was wir daraus lernen können," *Geschichte und Gesellshaft* 14 (1988): 38–63.

Zür Ökonomik des Privaten Haushalts (Frankfurt: Campus Verlag, 1991).

Pinchbeck, Ida. *Women Workers and the Industrial Revolution, 1750–1850* (London: Frank Cass, 1969).

Pitkin, Hanna. *Fortune Is a Woman. Gender and Politics in the Thought of Niccolo Machiavelli* (Berkeley: University of California Press, 1984).

Plantenga, Janneke. *Een afwijkend patroon. Honderd jaar vrouwenarbeid in Nederland en (West-) Duitsland* (Amsterdam: SUA, 1993).

Pocock, J. G. A. *The Machiavellian Moment. Florentine Political Thought and the Atlantic Republican Tradition* (Princeton, N.J.: Princeton University Press, 1975).

"The Mobility of Property and the Rise of Eighteenth-Century Sociology," in J. G. A. Pocock, *Virtue, Commerce and Society* (Cambridge: Cambridge University Press, 1985), pp. 103–25.

Pollard, Sidney. *The Genesis of Modern Management* ([1965] Harmondsworth: Penguin, 1969).

"Labour in Great Britain," in Peter Mathias and M. M. Poston, eds., *Cambridge Economic History of Europe* Vol. 7 (Cambridge: Cambridge University Press, 1978), pp. 97–179.

Pollexfen, John. *A Discourse on Trade, Coyne, and Paper Credit* (London, 1697).

Pomeranz, Kenneth. *The Great Divergence. China, Europe, and the Making of the Modern World* (Princeton, N.J.: Princeton University Press, 2000).

"Political Economy and Ecology on the Eve of Industrialization. Europe, China and the Global Conjucture," *American Historical Review* 107 (2002): 425–46.

Popenoe, David. *Disturbing the Nest. Family Change and Decline in Modern Societies* (New York: A. de Gruyter, 1988).

"The Family Condition of America. Cultural Change and Public Policy," in H. J. Aaron, T. E. Mann, and T. Taylor, eds., *Values and Public Policy* (Washington: The Brookings Institution, 1994), pp. 81–112.

Porter, G. R. "On the Self-Imposed Taxation of the Working-Classes in the United Kingdom," *Journal of the Royal Statistical Society* 13 (1850): 358–64.

Postlethwayt, Malachy. *Britain's Commercial Interest Explained and Improved,* 2 vols. ([London, 1757] Reprinted, New York: Augustus M. Kelly, 1968).

Pott-Buter, Hettie A. *Facts and Fairy Tales about Female Labor, Family and Fertility. A Seven-Country Comparison, 1850–1990* (Amsterdam: Amsterdam University Press, 1993).

Prescott, Edward C. "Why Do Americans Work So Much More Than Europeans?," *Federal Reserve Bank of Minneapolis Quarterly Review* 28 (2004): 2–15.

Preston, Samuel. "Children and the Elderly. Divergent Paths for America's Dependents," *Demography* 21 (1984): 435–57.

Price, Jacob M. *France and the Chesapeake. A History of the French Tobacco Monopoly, 1674–1775, and Its Relationship to the British and American Tobacco Trades,* 2 vols. (Ann Arbor: University of Michigan Press, 1973).

Putnam, Robert D. *Bowling Alone. The Collapse and Revival of American Community* (New York: Simon and Schuster, 2000).

Ranchetti, Fabio. "Choice without Utility? Some Reflections on the Loose Foundations of Standard Consumer Theory," in Bianchi, ed., *The Active Consumer* pp. 21–45.

Ransom, Roger L., and Richard Sutch. "Did Rising Out-Migration Cause Fertility to Decline in Antebellum New England? A Life-Cycle Perspective on Old-Age Security Motives, Child Default, and Farm Family Fertility," California Institute of Technology Social Science Working Papers no. 610 (April 1986).

Reher, David Sven. "Family Ties in Western Europe. Persistent Contrasts," *Population and Development Review* 24 (2) (1998): 203–34.

Richards, Eric. "Women in the British Economy Since about 1700. An Interpretation," *History* 59 (1974): 337–57.

Ringen, Stein. *Citizens, Families, and Reform* (Oxford: Oxford University Press, 1997).

Rive, Alfred. "Consumption of Tobacco Since 1600," *Economic Journal* (Economic History Supplement, Vol. 1, 1926–9), January 1926, pp. 57–75.

Roberts, Elizabeth. "Working-Class Standard of Living in Barrow and Lancaster, 1890–1914," *Economic History Review* 30 (1977): 306–21.

Robertson, John. *The Case for the Enlightenment. Scotland and Naples 1680–1760* (Cambridge: Cambridge University Press, 2005).

Robinson, John P. "Changes in Time Use. An Historical Overview," in F. T. Juster and Frank P. Stafford, eds., *Time Goods and Well-Being*, pp. 33–62.

Roche, Daniel. *Le Peuple de Paris. Essai sur la culture populaire au XVIIIe siècle* (Paris: Aubier Montaigne, 1981).

The Culture of Clothing. Dress and Fashion in the Ancien Regime (Cambridge: Cambridge University Press, 1994).

Histoire des choses banales. Naissance de la consommation dans les sociétés traditionnelles (xviie-xixe siècles) (Paris: Fayard, 1997).

"Between a 'Moral Economy' and a 'Consumer Economy'. Clothes and Their Function in the 17th and 18th Centuries," in Robert Fox and Anthony Turner, eds., *Luxury Trades and Consumerism in Ancien Règime Paris. Studies in the History of the Skilled Workforce* (Aldershot, Hants.: Ashgate, 1998), pp. 219–29.

Roessingh, H. K. *Inlandse tabak. Expansie en contrtactie van een handelsgewas in de 17e en 18e eeuw in Nederland* (Zutphen: De Walburg Pers, 1976).

Rorabaugh, William J. *The Alcoholic Republic. An American Tradition* (Oxford: Oxford University Press, 1979).

Rose, Sonya. "Gender Antagonism and Class Conflict. Exclusionary Strategies of Male Trade Unionists in Nineteenth Century Britain," *Social History* 13 (1988): 191–208.

Rowntree, B. Seebohm. *Poverty. A Study of Town Life* (London: Macmillan, 1902).

Rozman, Gilbert. *Urban Networks in Ch'ing China and Tokugawa Japan* (Princeton, N.J.: Princeton University Press, 1973).

Rubin, Rose M., and Bobye J. Riney. *Working Wives and Dual-Earner Families* (Westport, Conn.: Praeger, 1994).

Rudolph, Richard L. "The European Peasant Family and Economy. Central Themes and Issues," *Journal of Family History* 17 (1992): 119–38.

Rudolph, Richard L., ed. *The European Peasant Family and Society. Historical Studies* (Liverpool: Liverpool University Press, 1995).

Ruggin, F.-J. *Les elites et les villes moyennes en France et en Angleterre (xvii-xviiie siècle)* (Paris: L'Harmattan, 1997).

Rule, John. *The Experience of Labour in Eighteenth-Century Industry* (London: Croom Helm, 1981).

The Labouring Classes in Early Industrial England, 1750–1850 (London: Longman, 1986).

Rybczynski, Witwold. *Home. A Short History of an Idea* (New York: Viking Press, 1986).

Sabean, David. *Property, Production, and Family in Neckerhausen, 1700–1850* (Cambridge: Cambridge University Press, 1990).

Sahlins, Marshall. *Stone Age Economics* (Chicago: University of Chicago Press, 1972).

Saito, Osamu. "Labour Supply Behavior of the Poor in the English Industrial Revolution," *Journal of European Economic History* 10 (1981): 633–52.

"Population and the Peasant Family Economy in Proto-Industrial Japan," *Journal of Family History* 8 (1983): 30–54.

"The Rural Economy. Commercial Agriculture, By-employment and Wage Work," in M. Jansen and G. Rozman, eds., *Japan in Transition. From Tokugawa to Meiji* (Princeton, N.J.: Princeton University Press, 1986), pp. 400–20.

"Work, Leisure and the Concpet of Planning in the Japanese Past," (unpublished, Institute of Economic Research, Hitotsubashi University, 1996).

"Gender, Workload and Agricultural Progress. Japan's Historical Experience in Perspective," in Laboutte, ed., *Proto-industrialization* (1996), pp. 129–51.

Samuelson, Paul. "A Note on the Pure Theory of Consumers' Behavior," *Economica* 5 (1938): 61–71.

"Consumption Theory in Terms of Revealed Preference," *Economica* 15 (1948): 243–53.

"Social Indifference Curves," *Quarterly Journal of Economics* 70 (1956): 1–22.

Sandgruber, Roman. *Die Anfänge der Konsumgesellschaft. Konsumgüterverbrauch, Lebensstandard und Alltagskultur in Österreich im 18. und 19. Jahrhundert* (Vienna: Verlag für Geschichte und Politik, 1982).

"Nutrition in Austria in the Industrial Age," in Teuteberg, ed., *European Food History*, pp. 146–67.

"Leben und Lebensstandard im Zeitalter des Barock – Quellen und Ergebnisse," in Othmar Pickl and Helmuth Feigl, eds., *Methoden und Probleme der Alltagsforschung im Zeitalter des Barock* (Vienna: Verlag der Österreichischen Akademie der Wissenschaften, 1992), pp. 171–190.

Sarti, Raffaella. *Europe at Home. Family and Material Culture, 1500–1800* (New Haven, Conn.: Yale University Press, 2002).

Savage, Mike, and Andrew Miles. *The Remaking of the British Working Class, 1840–1940* (London: Routledge, 1994).

Schama, Simon. *The Embarrassment of Riches* (New York: Knopf, 1985).

Schelstraete, C., H. Kintaert, and D. de Ruyck. *Het einde van de onveranderlijkheid. Arbeid, beszit en woonomstandigheden in het land van Nevel tijdens de 17e en 18e eeuw* (Nevele: Heemkundig Kring 'Het Land van Nevele', 1986).

Schilling, Heinz. "Confessionalization in the Empire," in Heinz Schilling, ed., *Religion, Political Culture, and the Emergence of Early Modern Society* (Leiden: E. J. Brill, 1992), pp. 205–46.

Schneider, Jürgen. "Produktion, handel und konsum von Kaffee (15. bus ende 18. jh.)," in Hans Pohl, ed., *The European Discovery of the World and Its Economic Effects on Pre-Industrial Society, 1500–1800* (Stuttgart: F. Steiner Verlag, 1990), pp. 122–40.

"The Effects on European Markets of Imported Overseas Agriculture. The Production, Trade, and Consumption of Coffee (15th to Late 18th Centuries)," in Josè Casus Pardo, ed., *Economic Effects of the European Expansion* (Stuttgart: Franz Steiner Verlag, 1992), pp. 283–306.

Scholliers, Peter. "Family Income, Needs and Mothers' Wages. A Critical Survey of Working-Class Budget Inquiries in Belgium 1853–1929," in T. Pierenkemper, ed., *Zur Okonomik des privaten Haushalts. Haushaltsrechnungen als Quellen historischer Witschafts- und Socialforschung* (Frankfurt: Campus Verlag, 1991), pp. 145–81.

"Historical Food Research in Belgium. Development, Problems and Results in the 19th and 20th Centuries," in Teuteberg, ed., *European Food History*, pp. 71–89.

Schor, Juliet. *The Overworked American. The Unexpected Decline in Leisure* (New York: Basic Books, 1992).

The Overspent American. Upscaling, Downshifting, and the New Consumer (New York: Basic Books, 1998).

Schultz, T. Paul. "Economic Demography and Development. New Directions in an Old Field," in Gustav Ranis and T. P. Schultz, eds., *The State of Development Economics* (Oxford: Basil Blackwell, 1988), pp. 416–58.

Schumpeter, Joseph. *Capitalism, Socialism, and Democracy* (New York: Harper and Brothers, 1941).

Schuurman, Anton. *Materiële cultuur en levensstijl. een onderzoek naar de taal der dingen op her Nederlandse platteland in de 19e eeuw. De Zaanstreek, Oost-Groningen, Oost-Brabant* (Wageningen: AAG Bijdragen 30, 1989).

Schuurman, Anton, and Lorena S. Walsh, eds. *Material Culture. Consumption, Life-Style, Standard of Living, 1500–1900* (Milan: Eleventh International Economic History Congress, 1994).

Scitovsky, Tibor. *The Joyless Economy* (Oxford: Oxford University Press, 1976; rev. ed., 1992).

Seccombe, Wally. "Patriarchy Stabilized. The Construction of the Male Breadwinner Wage Norm in Nineteenth-Century Britain," *Social History* 11 (1986): 53–76.

A Millennium of Family Change. Feudalism to Capitalism in Northwestern Europe (London: Verso, 1992).

Weathering the Storm. Working-class Families from the Industrial Revolution to the Fertility Decline (London: Verso, 1993).

Segalen, Martine. *Love and Power in the Peasant Family. Rural France in the Nineteenth Century* (Chicago: University of Chicago Press, 1983).

Segers, Yves. "Oysters and Rye Bread. Polarizing Living Standards in Flanders, 1800–1860," *European Review of Economic History* 5 (2001): 301–36.

Segers, Yves, et al., eds. *Op weg naar een consumptiemaatschappij. Over het verbruik van voeding, kleding en luxegoederen in België en Nederland (19e-20e eeuw)* (Amsterdam: Aksent, 2002).

Sekora, John. *Luxury. The Concept in Western Thought, Eden to Smollett* (Baltimore: Johns Hopkins University Press, 1977).

Sella, Domenico. "Peasants as Consumers of Manufactured Goods in Italy around 1600," in Richard Rudolph, ed., *The European Peasant Family and Society*, pp. 154–64.

Sellers, Charles. *The Market Revolution. Jacksonian America: 1815–1846* (Oxford: Oxford University Press, 1991).

Selten, Robert, and Pieter Al. "Nederlanders zijn minder gaan werken," *Sociaal-economische trends* (2005–1): 14–21.

Sen, Amartya. "Economics and the Family," *Asian Development Review* 1 (1983): 14–26.

Shammas, Carole. "How Self-Sufficient Was Early America?," *Journal of Interdisciplinary History* 13 (1982): 247–72.

"The Eighteenth-Century English Diet and Economic Change," *Explorations in Economic History* 21 (1984): 254–69.

"Explaining Past Changes in Consumption and Consumer Behavior," *Historical Methods* 22 (1989): 61–7.

The Pre-Industrial Consumer in England and America (Oxford: Oxford University Press, 1990).

"The Decline of Textile Prices in England and British America Prior to the Industrial Revolution," *Economic History Review* 47 (1994): 483–507.

Sharpe, Pamela. *Adapting to Capitalism. Working Women in the English Economy, 1700–1850* (New York: St. Martin's Press, 1996).

"Literally Spinsters. A New Interpretation of Local Economy and Demography in Colyton in the Seventeenth and Eighteenth Centuries," *Economic History Review* 44 (1991): 46–65.

Shi, David E. *The Simple Life. Plain Living and High Thinking in American Culture* (Oxford: Oxford University Press, 1985).

Shoemaker, Robert. *Gender in English Society, 1650–1850. The Emergence of Separate Spheres?* (London: Longman, 1998).

Shorter, Edward. *The Making of the Modern Family* (New York: Basic Books, 1975).

Simmel, Georg. "Fashion," *International Quarterly* 10 (1904): 130–55.

The Philosophy of Money ([1900] London: Routledge, 1978).

Slicher van Bath, B. H. *The Agrarian History of Western Europe, 500–1850* (London: Edward Arnold, 1963).

Smelser, Niel. *Social Change in the Industrial Revolution. An Application of Theory to the Lancashire Cotton Industry, 1740–1840* (London: Routledge & Kegan Paul, 1959).

Smith, Adam. *Lectures on Jurisprudence* [1762–3, 1766] R. L. Meek, D. D. Raphael, and P. G. Stein, eds. (Oxford: Oxford University Press, 1978).

The Theory of Moral Sentiments ([1760, rev. 1790] D. D. Raphael and A. L. Macfie, eds. Oxford: Oxford University Press, 1976).

An Inquiry into the Nature and Causes of The Wealth of Nations ([1776] Cannon edition, London: Methuen, 1904; reprinted, Chicago: University of Chicago Press, 1976).

Smith, S. D. "Accounting for Taste. British Coffee Consumption in Historical Perspective," *Journal of Interdisciplinary History* 27 (1996): 183–214.

Smith, Woodruff D. *Consumption and the Making of Respectability, 1600–1800* (London: Routledge, 2002).

Snell, K. D. M. *Annals of the Labouring Poor. Social Change and Agrarian England, 1660–1900* (Cambridge: Cambridge University Press, 1985).

Söderberg, Johan, Ulf Jonsson, and Christer Persson. *A Stagnating Metropolis. The Economy and Demography of Stockholm, 1750–1850* (Cambridge: Cambridge University Press, 1991).

Sokoll, Thomas. "Early Attempts at Accounting the Unaccountable. Davies and Eden's Budgets of Agricultural Labouring Families in Late Eighteenth-Century England," in Pierenkemper, ed., *Zür Ökonomik des Privaten Haushalts*, pp. 34–60.

Sombart, Werner. *Luxury and Capitalism* ([1913] Ann Arbor: University of Michigan Press, 1967).

Sonenscher, Michael. "Fashion's Empire. Trade and Power in Early 18th Century France," in Robert Fox and Anthony Turner, eds., *Luxury Trades and Consumerism in Ancien Régime Paris. Studies in the History of the Skilled Workforce* (Aldershot, Hants.: Ashgate, 1998), pp. 231–54.

Spufford, Margaret. *The Great Reclothing of Rural England. Petty Chapmen and Their Wares in the Seventeenth Century* (London: Hambleton Press, 1984).

"The Cost of Apparel in Seventeenth-Century England, and the Accuracy of Gregory King," *Economic History Review* 53 (2000): 677–705.

Stallybrass, Peter. "Marx's Coat," in Patricia Spyer, ed., *Border Fetishisms. Material Objects in Unstable Spaces* (New York: Routledge, 1998), pp. 183–207.

Stedman Jones, Gareth. "Working-class Culture and Working-class Politics in London, 1870–1900. Notes on the Remaking of the Working Class," *Journal of Social History* 7 (1974): 460–508.

Stearns, Peter N. "Stages in Consumerism. Recent Work on the Issues of Periodization," *Journal of Modern History* 69 (1997): 102–17.

Consumerism in World History. The Global Transformation of Desire (London: Routledge, 2001).

Steckel, Richard H. "Stature and Living Standards in the United States," in Gallmanand Wallis, eds., *American Economic Growth and Standards of Living Before the Civil War*, pp. 265–310.

"Stature and Living Standards," *Journal of Economic Literature* 33 (1995): 1903–40.

Steedman, Ian. *Consumption Takes Time. Implications for Economic Theory* (London: Routledge, 2001).

Steegen, Erwin. "Kleinhandel en kramers. De verkoop van genotsmiddelen in Maastricht in de achttiende eeuw," *NEHA-Jaarboek* 61 (1998): 163–95.

Stein, Robert. "The French Sugar Business in the Eighteenth Century. A Quantitative Study," *Business History* 22 (1980): 3–17.

Steuart, Sir James. *An Inquiry into the Principles of Political Economy* (London: Printed for A. Miller and T. Cadell, 1767).

Stigler, George. "Domestic Servants in the United States, 1900–1940" (NBER occasional paper no. 24, 1946).

Stone, Lawrence. *The Family, Sex and Marriage in England, 1500–1800* (New York: Harper & Row, 1977).

Strasser, S., C. McGovern, and M. Judt, eds. *Getting and Spending. European and American Consumer Societies in the Twentieth Century* (Cambridge: Cambridge University Press, 1998).

Styles, John. "Manufacturing, Consumption and Design in Eighteenth-Century England," in Brewer and Porter, eds., *Consumption and the World of Goods*, pp. 527–54.

"Clothing the North. The Supply of Non-Elite Clothing in the Eighteenth-Century North of England," *Textile History* 25 (1994): 139–66.

"Product Innovation in Early Modern London," *Past and Present* 168 (2000): 124–69.

"Custom or Consumption? Plebian Fashion in Eighteenth-Century England," in Berg and Eger, eds., *Luxury in the Eighteenth Century*, pp. 103–18.

Subramanian, Shankar, and Angus Deaton. "The Demand for Food and Calories," *Journal of Political Economy* 104 (1996): 133–62.

Sugihara, Kaoru. "Labour-Intensive Industrialisation in Global History," presented at the 13th International Economic History Congress, Buenos Aires, 2001.

"The East Asian Path of Economic Development. A Long-Term Perspective," in Giovanni Arrighi, Takeshi Hamashita, and Amark Selden, eds., *The Resurgence of East Asia. 500, 150, and 50 Year Perspectives* (London: Routledge, 2003), pp. 78–123.

"The State and the Industrious Revolution in Tokugawa Japan," London School of Economics, Working paper No. 02/04 (February 2004).

Sweeney, Kevin M. "Furniture and Domestic Environment in Wethersfield, Connecticut, 1639–1800," *The Connecticut Antiquarian* 36 (1984): 10–39.

Szreter, Simon. "Mortality and Public Health, 1815–1914," in Anne Digby and Charles Feinstein, eds., *New Directions in Economic History*, Vol. 2 (London: Macmillan, 1992), pp. 136–48.

Tabutin, Dominique. "La Surmortalité feminine en Europe avant 1940," *Population* 33 (1978): 121–48.

Takemura, Eiji. *The Perception of Work in Tokugawa Japan* (New York: University Press of America, 1997).

Temple, R. C., ed. *The Travels of Peter Mundy in Europe and Asia, 1608–1667*, Vol. IV (1639–47) (Cambridge: Hakluyt Society, 1925).

Tentler, Leslie. *Wage-Earning Women* (Oxford: Oxford University Press, 1982).

Teuteberg, Hans J. "Food Consumption in Germany Since the Beginning of Industrialisation. A Quantitative Longitudinal Approach," in Baudet and Van der Meulen, eds., *Consumer Behavior and Economic Growth in the Modern Economy*, pp. 233–77.

Teuteberg, Hans J., ed. *European Food History. A Research Review* (Leicester: Leicester University Press, 1992).

Thirsk, Joan. *Economic Policies and Projects. The Development of a Consumer Society in Early Modern England* (Oxford: Oxford University Press, 1978).

Thomas, Janet. "Women and Capitalism. Oppression or Emancipation?" *Comparative Studies in Society and History* 30 (1988): 534–49.

Thompson, E. P. "Time, Work-discipline, and Industrial Capitalism," *Past and Present* 38 (1967): 56–97.

"The Moral Economy Reviewed," in E. P Thompson, *Custom in Common* (New York: New Press, 1993), pp. 239–351.

Thornton, Peter. *Seventeenth-Century Interior Decoration in England, France and Holland* (New Haven, Conn.: Yale University Press, 1978).

Tilly, Lousie A. "Women, Women's History, and the Industrial Revolution," *Social Research* 61 (1994): 115–37.

Tilly, Louise A., and Miriam Cohen. "Does the Family Have a History? A Review of Theory and Practice in Family History," *Social Science History* 6 (1982): 131–79.

Tilly, Louise A., and Joan A. Scott. *Women, Work, and Family* (New York: Holt, Rinehart and Winston, 1978; revised ed., London: Routledge, 1987).

Tobey, Ronald. *Technology as Freedom. The New Deal and the Electrical Modernization of the American Home* (Berkeley: University of California Press, 1994).

Tommasi, Mariano, and Kathryn Ierulli, eds. *The New Economics of Human Behavior* (Cambridge: Cambridge University Press, 1995).

Topalov, Christian. *Le Logement en France* (Paris: Presses de la Fondation nationale des sciences politiques, 1987).

Toutain, Jean-Claude. "La consommation alimentaire en France de 1789 à 1962," *Economie et societé* 5 (1971): 1909–2049.

Townsend, Joseph. *Dissertation on the Poor Laws* (London, 1786).

Tranter, Nick. "The Labour Supply, 1780–1860," in Roderick Floud and Donald McCloskey, eds., *The Economic History of Britain Since 1700*, First Edition (Cambridge: Cambridge University Press, 1981), pp. 204–26.

Trentman, Frank. "Beyond Consumerism. New Historical Perspectives on Consumption," *Journal of Contemporary History* 39 (2004): 373–401.

Tuttle, Carolyn. *Hard at Work in Factories and Mines. The Economics of Child Labor During the British Industrial Revolution* (Boulder, Colo.: Westview Press, 1999).

Unger, Richard. *A History of Brewing in Holland 900–1900* (Leiden: Brill, 2001).

Uusitalo, Liisa. "Consumption in Postmodernity. Social Structuration and the Construction of Self," in Marina Bianchi, ed., *The Active Consumer* (London: Routledge, 1998), pp. 215–35.

Valenze, Deborah. *The First Industrial Woman* (Oxford: Oxford University Press, 1995).

van Aert, Laaura. "To Thrive or Survive? Retailers in Antwerp (ca. 1648–ca. 1748)" (unpublished, University of Antwerpen, 2005).

van Ark, Bart, and Robert H. McGucklin. "Perspectives on the Global Economy. The Euro's Impact on European Labor Markets," The Conference Board Europe, Report Number 1236–99-RR (1999).

van Bavel, B. J. P. "Arable yields and total arable output in the Netherlands from the late Middle Ages to the end of the Ancien Regime," in van Bavel and Thoen, *Land Productivity and Agro-Systems in the North Sea Area* (Turnhout: Brepols, 1999), pp. 85–113.

van Bavel, B. J. P., and E. Thoen, eds. *Land Productivity and Agro-Systems in the North Sea Area* (Turnhout: Brepols, 1999).

Vandenbroeke, Chris. *Agriculture et alimentation dans les Pays-Bas autrichiens* (Gent-Leuven: Centre Belge d' Histoire Rurale, 1975).

"Le problème de la durée du travail aux Temps Modernes," in Leboutte, ed., *Proto-industrialization* (1996), pp. 237–42.

van den Eeckhout, Patricia. "Family Income in Ghent Working-Class Families, c. 1900," *Journal of Family History* 18 (1993): 87–110.

Vanderlint, Jacob. *Money Answers All Things* [1734] Jacob H. Hollander, ed., (Baltimore: Johns Hopkins University Press, 1914)

van der Valk, Johan. "Arbeidsdeelname van paren," *Sociaal-economische trends* (2005–3): 27–31.

van der Valk, Johan, and Annemarie Boelens. "Vrouwen op de arbeidsmarkt," *Sociaal-economische trends* (2004–3): 19–25.

van der Veen, D. J., and J. L. van Zanden. "Real-Wage Trends and Consumption Patterns in the Netherlands, c. 1870–1940," in Peter Scholliers, ed., *Real Wages in 19th and 20th Century Europe. Historical and Comparative Perspectives* (Munich: Berg Publishers, 1989), pp. 205–28.

van der Woud, Auke. *Het lege land. De ruimtelijke ordre van Nederland, 1798–1848* (Amsterdam: Meulenhoff, 1987).

van der Woude, Ad. "The Volume and Value of Paintings in Holland at the Time of the Dutch Republic," in de Vries and Freedberg, eds., *Art in History, History in Art*, pp. 285–330.

"Alfabetisering als gezinsgeschiedenis," in Ad van der Woude, *Leven met geschiedenis. Theorie, praktijk en toepassing van historische kennis* (Amsterdam: Balans, 2000), pp. 225–94.

Vanhaute, Eric. "Breadwinner Models and Historical Models. Transitions in Labour Relations and Labour Markets in Belgium, 19th–20th Centuries," in Henrik Jensen, ed., *The Welfare State. Past, Present, Future* (Pisa: Edizioni Plus-Università di Pisa, 2002), pp. 59–76.

van Koolbergen, H. "De materiële cultuur van Weesp en Weesperkarspel in de zeventiende en achttiende eeuw," *Volkskundig Bulletin* 9 (1983): 3–52.

Vardi, Liana. *The Land and the Loom. Peasants and Profit in Northern France, 1680–1800* (Durham, N.C.: Duke University Press, 1993).

Varian, Hal. *Intermediate Microeconomics. A Modern Approach*, sixth edition (New York: W. W. Norton, 2003).

Veblen, Thorstein. *The Theory of the Leisure Class. An Economic Study of Institutions* ([1899] New York: New American Library, 1953).

Velgema, Wyger, R. E. "Ancient and Modern Virtue Compared. De Beaufort and Van Effen on Republican Citizenship," *Eighteenth-Century Studies* 30 (1997): 437–48.

Verdon, Michael. *Rethinking Households. An Atomistic Perspective on European Living Arrangements* (London: Routledge, 1998).

Vickery, Amanda. "Golden Age to Separate Spheres? A Review of the Categories and Chronology of English Women's History," *Historical Journal* 36 (1993): 383–414.

Vincent, David. *Bread, Knowledge and Freedom. A Study of Nineteenth-Century Working-Class Autobiography* (London: Methuen, 1981).

Vlasblom, Jan Dirk, and Joop J. Schippers. "Increases in Female Labour Force Participation in Europe. Similarities and Differences," Tjalling C. Koopmans Research Institute Discussion Paper Series nr. 04-12 (Utrecht University, 2004).

Vögele, Jörg. *Urban Mortality Change in England and Germany, 1870–1913* (Liverpool: Liverpool University Press, 1998).

Vogler, Carolyn. "Money in the Household," in Anderson, Bechhofer, and Gershuny, eds., *The Social and Political Economy of the Household*, pp. 225–66.

Voskuil, J. J. "De weg naar Luilekkerland," *Bijdragen en mededelingen van de geschiedenis der Nederlanden* 98 (1983): 460–84.

"De verspreiding van koffie en thee in Nederland," *Volkskundig Bulletin* 14 (1988): 77–83.

Voth, Hans-Joachim. "Seasonality of Baptisms as a Source for Historical Time-Budget Analysis. Tracing the Disappearance of Holy Days in Early Modern England," *Historical Methods* 27 (1994): 127–32.

"Height, Nutrition, and Labor. Recasting the 'Austrian Model'," *Journal of Interdisciplinary History* 25 (1995): 627–36.

"Physical Exertion and Stature in the Habsburg Monarachy, 1730–1800," *Journal of Interdisciplinary History* 27 (1996): 263–75.

"Time and Work in Eighteenth-Century London," *Journal of Economic History* 58 (1998): 29–58.

Time and Work in England, 1760–1830 (Oxford: Oxford University Press, 2001).

Waite, Linda J. "U.S. Women at Work," *Population Bulletin* 36 (1981): entire.

Walcha, Otto. *Meissen Porcelain* (New York: Putnam, 1981).

Wall, Richard. "The Age at Leaving Home," *Journal of Family History* 3 (1978): 181–202.

"Some Implications of the Earnings, Income and Expenditure Patterns of Married Women in Populations in the Past," in John Henderson and Richard Wall, eds., *Poor Women and Children in the European Past* (London: Routledge, 1994), pp. 312–35.

Wall, Richard, Jean Robin, and Peter Laslett, eds. *Family Forms in Historic Europe* (Cambridge: Cambridge University Press, 1983).

Walsh, Lorena. "Consumer Behavior, Diet, and the Standard of Living in Late Colonial and Early Antebellum America, 1770–1840," in Gallman and Wallis, eds., *American Economic Growth and Standards of Living Before the Civil War*, pp. 217–61.

Warren, Elizabeth, and Amelia Warren Tyagi. *The Two-Income Trap. Why Middle-Class Mothers and Fathers Are Going Broke* (New York: Basic Books, 2003).

Watkins, Susan Cotts, Jane A. Menken, and John Bongaarts. "The Demographic Foundations of Family Change," *American Sociological Review* 52 (1993): 47–84.

Weatherill, Lorna. *The Pottery Trade and North Staffordshire, 1660–1760* (Manchester: Manchester University Press, 1971).

"The Growth of the Pottery Industry in England, 1660–1815," *Post-Medieval Archaeology* 17 (1983): 15–46.

"A Possession of One's Own. Women and Consumer Behavior in England, 1660–1749," *Journal of British Studies* 25 (1986): 131–56.

Consumer Behavior and Material Culture in Britain, 1660–1760 (London: Routledge, 1988).

"Consumer Behavior, Textiles, and Dress in the Late Seventeenth and Early Eighteenth Centuries," *Textile History* 22 (1991): 297–310.

"The Meaning of Consumer Behavior in Late Seventeenth- and Early Eighteenth-Century England," in Brewer and Porter, eds., *Consumption and the World of Goods*, pp. 206–27.

Weber, Max. *The Protestant Ethic and the Spirit of Capitalism* ([1903/04] New York: Harper & Row, 1930).

Weiner, Lynn. *From Working Girl to Working Mother. The Female Labor Force in the U.S.* (Chapel Hill: University of North Carolina Press, 1985).

Weir, David. "Parental Consumption Decisions and Child Health During the Early French Fertility Decline, 1790–1914," *Journal of Economic History* 53 (1993): 259–74.

Wells, Roger A. E. *Wretched Faces. Famine in Wartime England, 1793–1801* (New York: St. Martin's Press, 1988).

Welsh, Evelyn. *Shopping in the Renaissance* (New Haven, Conn.: Yale University Press, 2005).

White, Jonathan. "The 'Slow but Sure Poyson'. The Representation of Gin and Its Drinkers, 1736–1751," *Journal of British Studies* 42 (2003): 35–64.

Wijsenbeek-Olthuis, Thera. *Achter de gevels van Delft. Bezit en bestaan wan rijk en arm in een periode van achteruitgang (1700–1800)* (Hilversum: Verloren, 1987).

"The Social History of the Curtain," in Baulant, Schuurman, and Servais, eds., *Inventaires Après-Deces*, pp. 381–7.

"A Matter of Taste. Lifestyle in Holland in the 17th and 18th Centuries," in Schuurman and Walsh, eds., *Material Culture*, pp. 43–54.

Wilk, Richard R. "Decision Making and Resource Flows within the Household. Beyond the Black Box," in Richard R. Wilk, ed., *The Household Economy*, pp. 23–52.

Wilk, Richard R. ed., *The Household Economy. Reconsidering the Domestic Mode of Production* (Boulder, Colo.: Westview Press, 1989).

Williams, Rosalind. *Dream Worlds. Mass Consumption in Late Nineteenth-Century France* (Berkeley: University of California Press, 1982).

Wilson, Adrian. "Illegitimacy and Its Implications in Mid-Eighteenth Century London," *Continuity and Change* 4 (1989): 103–64.

Wilson, James Q. *The Marriage Problem. How Our Culture Has Weakened Families* (New York: HarperCollins, 2002).

Winch, Donald. *Riches and Poverty. An Intellectual History of Political Economy in Britain, 1750–1834* (Cambridge: Cambridge University Press, 1996).

Wolf, Eric. *Peasants* (Englewood Cliffs, N.J., Prentice-Hall, 1966).

Woods, Robert I., P. A. Watterson, and J. H. Woodward. "The Causes of Rapid Infant Mortality Decline in England and Wales, 1861–1921," *Population Studies* 42 (1988): 343–66; 43 (1989): 113–32.

Wrigley, E. A. "Urban Growth and Agricultural Change. England and the Continent in the Early Modern Period," *Journal of Interdisciplinary History* 15 (1985): 683–728.

"Men on the Land and Men in the Countryside," in L. Bonfield, et al., eds., *The World We Have Gained* (Oxford: Basil Blackwell, 1986), pp. 295–336.

Continuity, Chance and Change. The Character of the Industrial Revolution in England (Cambridge: Cambridge University Press, 1988).

Wrigley, E. A., and R. S. Schofield. *The Population History of England, 1541–1871. A Reconstruction* (London: Edward Arnold, 1981).

Yang, Xiaokai, and Jeff Borland, "A Microeconomic Mechanism for Economic Growth," *Journal of Political Economy* 99 (1991): 460–82.

Young, Allyn. "Increasing Returns and Economic Progress," *The Economic Journal* 38 (1928): 527–42.

Young, Michael. "Distribution of Income within the Family," *British Journal of Sociology* 3 (1952): 305–21.

Zahedieh, Nuala. "London and the Colonial Consumer in the Late Seventeenth Century," *Economic History Review* 47 (1994): 239–61.

Zelizer, Viviana. *The Social Meaning of Money* (New York: Basic Books, 1994).

Zweig, F. *The Worker in an Affluent Society* (London: Heinemann Educational Books, 1961).

Zwingli, Huldreich. "Von Erkeisen und Freiheit der Speisen. 16 April 1522," in Emil Egli and Georg Finsler, eds., *Huldrich Zwinglis sämtliche Werke*, Vol 1: *Corups reformatorum* (Berlin, 1904), pp. 74–136.

Index